# Collins

# AQA GCSE
## Maths

### Foundation Teacher Pack

Rob Ellis
Kath Hipkiss
Brian Speed
Colin Stobart

William Collins' dream of knowledge for all began with the publication of his first book in 1819. A self-educated mill worker, he not only enriched millions of lives, but also founded a flourishing publishing house. Today, staying true to this spirit, Collins books are packed with inspiration, innovation and practical expertise. They place you at the centre of a world of possibility and give you exactly what you need to explore it.

Collins. Freedom to teach

Published by Collins
An imprint of HarperCollins*Publishers*
The News Building
1 London Bridge Street
London SE1 9GF

Browse the complete Collins catalogue at
www.collins.co.uk

© HarperCollins*Publishers* Limited 2015

10 9 8 7 6 5 4 3 2 1

ISBN 978-0-00-811392-6

A Catalogue record for this publication is available from the British Library

Rob Ellis, Kath Hipkiss, Brian Speed and Colin Stobart assert their moral rights to be identified as the authors of this work.

Commissioned by Lucy Rowland and Katie Sergeant
Project managed by Elektra Media
Project edited by Caroline Green and Jennifer Yong
Development edited by Gudrun Kaiser
CD-ROM additional content authored by Kath Hipkiss
With thanks to Jo-Anne Lees and Christine Watson
Copyedited by Sue Gardner, Joan Miller and Jim Newall
Proofread by Helen Atkinson and Joanna Shock
Illustrations by Ann Paganuzzi
Typeset by Jouve India Private Limited
Designed by Ken Vail Graphic Design
Cover design by We Are Laura
Cover photographs by Godruma/Shutterstock (top) and Georgios Kollidas/Shutterstock (bottom)
Production by Rachel Weaver
Printed and bound by RR Donnelley at Glasgow, UK

**Acknowledgements**

The publishers gratefully acknowledge the permissions granted to reproduce copyright material in this book. Every effort has been made to contact the holders of copyright material, but if any have been inadvertently overlooked, the publisher will be pleased to make the necessary arrangements at the first opportunity.

# Contents

# Introduction

Welcome to Collins *AQA GCSE Maths Foundation Teacher Pack*, which has been written for the 2015 AQA GCSE Mathematics Specification (8300). This Teacher Pack accompanies Collins *AQA GCSE Maths Foundation Student Book 4th edition*, which contains the material needed to complete the AQA course.

The new GCSE contains some types of question that have not appeared in GCSE Mathematics exams before. This guide and its lesson plans will help you prepare students to tackle the new aspects with confidence.

## Aims and learning outcomes

In mathematics, topics are taught in progressively greater depth over the secondary phase. GCSE outcomes may reflect or build on subject content knowledge that is typically taught at KS3. There is no expectation that such content will be repeated during the GCSE course, when it has already been taught effectively at an earlier stage. This allows for some increase in content, with the Government recommendation that mathematics is taught for a minimum of seven hours per fortnight.

This GCSE course is designed to provide a broad and coherent course of study that encourages students to develop confidence in, and a positive attitude towards, mathematics. It enables students to recognise the importance of mathematics in their own lives and to society.

The aims and objectives of this GCSE Mathematics course are to enable students to:
* develop fluent knowledge, skills and understanding of mathematical methods and concepts
* acquire, select and apply mathematical techniques to solve problems
* reason mathematically, make deductions and inferences, and draw conclusions
* comprehend, interpret and communicate mathematical information in a variety of forms, appropriate to the information and context.

The new GCSE will have more focus on making sure that every student masters the fundamentals of mathematics. These have been defined by the Department for Education as areas such as calculation, ratio and proportion.

## Key changes to GCSE Mathematics:
* new content in both Foundation and Higher tiers
* longer assessment time (four hours)
* additional content in the Foundation tier
* more formulae need to be known (only cone, sphere and kinematics are given)
* seven hours of study per fortnight is recommended.

## Modified content

Some content:
* is a result of more knowledge assumed from earlier key stages, for example, knowledge of up to the 12 times table from Key Stage 2
* is more explicitly stated but may or may not have been implied previously, for example, 'expansion of more than two binomials' and 'unique factorisation theorem'.

**Content added to Foundation and Higher**
Some content is completely new to both tiers, for example:
- systematic listing strategies
- Fibonacci-type sequences
- quadratic sequences
- simple geometrical progression
- pressure
- functions
- frequency trees
- Venn diagrams.

**Examples of content added to Foundation, previously only in the Higher Tier:**
- calculate exactly using multiples of $\pi$
- standard form
- apply and interpret limits of accuracy
- expand the product of two binomials
- solve quadratic equations by factorisation
- solve linear simultaneous equations
- trigonometric ratios in 2D right-angled triangles
- fractional scale enlargements in transformations
- lengths of arcs and areas of sectors of circles
- vectors (but not proofs)
- density
- tree diagrams.

**Examples of content no longer in the Foundation specification:**
- Trial and improvement
- Tessellations
- Questionnaires and surveys

**New Assessment Objectives**
Assessment Objectives (AOs) are related to those skills that are linked to subject content, but not specifically. In mathematics there were, and still are, three AOs. There are significant changes in the focus of the AOs to bring a new challenge to the examination papers.

The DfE summarises these changes as follows:

*'The assessment objectives place more emphasis on reasoning and problem solving.'*

First, the language of the AOs has changed:

- AO1 *'Recall and use their knowledge'* has become *'Use and apply'*
- AO2 *'Select, apply methods ...'* is now *'Reason, interpret and communicate'*.

Both changes suggest a stronger emphasis on application rather than on recall.

Secondly, the revised version provides more guidance as to what they mean in practice. For example, the old AO3 stated that students needed to *'interpret and analyse problems'*; the new AO3 states that they need to *'solve problems within mathematics and other contexts'*. This includes making connections between different areas of mathematics.

Finally, the weighting has changed, with more marks for AO3 than before, and a new separation of Foundation and Higher weighting.

- AO1 still includes recall and standard procedures, but has been extended to include multi-step solutions and questions set in context.
- AO2 is all about interpreting information and communicating solutions and arguments, giving these areas much more emphasis than previously.
- AO3 is still about solving problems, but the emphasis is on translating problems into mathematical processes, linking different areas of mathematics and evaluating solutions.

| | Assessment Objectives | Weightings | |
|---|---|---|---|
| | | Higher | Foundation |
| AO1 | **Use and apply standard techniques**<br>Students should be able to:<br>• Accurately recall facts, terminology and definitions.<br>• Use and interpret notation correctly.<br>• Accurately carry out routine procedures of set tasks requiring multi-step solutions. | 40% | 50% |
| AO2 | **Reason, interpret and communicate mathematically**<br>Student should be able to:<br>• Make deductions, inferences and draw conclusion from mathematical information.<br>• Construct chains of reasoning to achieve a given result.<br>• Interpret and communicate information accurately.<br>• Present arguments and proofs.<br>• Assess the validity of an argument and critically evaluate a given way of presenting information.<br>Where problems require candidates to 'use and apply standard techniques' or to independently 'solve problems', attribute a proportion of those marks to the corresponding Assessment Objective. | 30% | 25% |
| AO3 | **Solve problems within mathematics and in other contexts**<br>Students should be able to:<br>• Translate problems in mathematical or non-mathematical contexts into a process or a series of mathematical processes.<br>• Make and use connections between different parts of mathematics.<br>• Interpret results in the context of a given problem.<br>• Evaluate methods used and results obtained.<br>• Evaluate solutions to identify how they may have been affected by assumptions made.<br>Where problems require candidates to 'use and apply standard techniques' or to 'reason, interpret and communicate mathematically', attribute a proportion of those marks to the corresponding Assessment Objective. | 30% | 25% |

The new GCSE is now split across five content areas:

| Number | Algebra | Ratio and proportion | Geometry and measure | Probability and statistics |
|---|---|---|---|---|
| 15% | 30% | 20% | 20% | 15% |

*There is ±3% flexibility with these weightings.*

## Grading[1]

| New grading structure | | | | | | | | | |
|---|---|---|---|---|---|---|---|---|---|
| 9 | 8 | 7 | 6 | 5 | 4 | 3 | 2 | 1 | U |
| Broadly the same proportion of students will achieve a Grade 7 and above as will achieve an A and above. | | | | C ≈ 4 | | Broadly the same proportion of students will achieve a Grade 4 and above as currently achieve a Grade C and above.<br><br>The bottom of Grade 1 will be aligned with the bottom of grade G. | | | |
| A* | | A | B | C | | D | E | F | G | U |
| Current grading structure | | | | | | | | | |

**Foundation Tier: grades 1–5**
**Higher Tier: grades 4–9**

## The structure of the AQA Mathematics papers

| Paper 1 : non- calculator | Paper 2 : calculator | Paper 3 : calculator |
|---|---|---|
| **Content** from any part of the specification may be assessed | **Content** from any part of the specification may be assessed | **Content** from any part of the specification may be assessed |
| **Assessment**<br>• 1 hour 30 minutes<br>• Written exam<br>• 80 marks<br>• 33% of GCSE<br>• Four multiple-choice questions at the start<br>• First 50% of questions to focus on grades 1, 2, lower 3<br>• Second 50% of questions to focus on grades upper 3, 4, 5<br>• 'Allowed' formulae integrated into question<br>• No formula sheet | **Assessment**<br>• 1 hour 30 minutes<br>• Written exam<br>• 80 marks<br>• 33% of GCSE<br>• Four multiple-choice questions at the start<br>• First 50% of questions to focus on grades 1, 2, lower 3<br>• Second 50% of questions to focus on grades upper 3, 4, 5<br>• 'Allowed' formulae integrated into question<br>• No formula sheet | **Assessment**<br>• 1 hour 30 minutes<br>• Written exam<br>• 80 marks<br>• 33% of GCSE<br>• Four multiple-choice questions at the start<br>• First 50% of questions to focus on grades 1, 2, lower 3<br>• Second 50% of questions to focus on grades upper 3, 4, 5<br>• 'Allowed' formulae integrated into question<br>• No formula sheet |

---

[1] Note that this is based on the information from the Department of Education publicly available at the time of going to print.

# How to use this book

## Chapter overview

Each chapter starts with an outline of the content covered in the entire chapter, to help you plan ahead with ease.

- **Overview** shows the topic in each lesson at a glance.
- **Prior learning** indicates the mathematical ideas with which students will need to be secure, to enable them to access the topic content.
- **Learning objectives** list what students will learn.
- **Extension** suggests ways to broaden and deepen mathematical understanding with appropriate challenge for higher-attaining students.
- **Curriculum references** show how the material meets the requirements of the new GCSE curriculum with references to the KS3 and KS4 Programmes of Study.
- **Route mapping chart** for all exercises indicates, at a glance, the level of work students will meet. Key questions are referenced. These require a step-up in understanding or application and/or provide opportunities for students to demonstrate mastery of a concept.
- **About this chapter** explains how the content in the chapter links mathematical ideas and **makes connections**. The **relevance** to everyday life is highlighted, with references to core skills and possible career foci. Some ideas for probing questions are included to encourage students to **work mathematically** and suggestions are made for **assessment**. In addition, there are suggestions on how to use the **worked exemplars from the Student Book**.

## Lesson plans

Every section in the Student Book is supported by a sequence of lesson plans. Each lesson plan follows the same format, making them easy to use as an aid in preparing lessons.

- **Resources and homework** provide the corresponding **Student Book page numbers** and **Practice Book references.**
- **Learning objectives** indicate clearly what the lesson is about and the level of the content, providing a useful tool for measuring the success of a lesson.
- **Making mathematical connections** identifies areas of mathematics that require similar skills.
- **Making cross-curricular connections** identifies how the skills and knowledge are used in other areas of the curriculum.
- **Prior learning** identifies the skills and knowledge that students will need in order to access the lesson.
- **Working mathematically** highlights and develops core skills that enable students to work independently and explain and apply their mathematics.
- **Common misconceptions and remediation** explores common errors that students may make, with suggested approaches for identifying or avoiding the errors. It also highlights possible areas of misunderstanding.
- **Probing questions** offer some possible questions for teachers to ask of students to encourage mathematical thinking and explanations, and to broaden and deepen their understanding of the core ideas.
- **Literacy focus** identifies the key terms and vocabulary. It also suggests written or spoken activities, where appropriate.

- **A three-part lesson plan for each section of the chapter**
  **Part 1, Part 2** and **Part 3** structure the route through the lesson, with references to Student Book exercises. This enables teachers to identify the core ideas to be taught before students attempt the relevant exercises and activities. Part 1 is intended to be an introductory activity, Part 2 is the main, application, part of the lesson and Part 3 is the plenary or assessment opportunity.

## Answers to questions

- Answers to the exercises and questions that appear in the **Student Book** are available online at **www.collins.co.uk/gcsemaths4eanswers** or on the CD-ROM that accompanies this Teacher Pack.
- Answers to the **Practice Book** questions can be found online at **www.collins.co.uk/gcsemaths4eanswers**

## Schemes of Work

Flexible 2-, 3- and 5-year Schemes of Work are available at the front of this Teacher Pack and also on the CD-ROM. These are based on the Collins *Maths Frameworking 3rd edition Pupil Books* 1.1, 1.2, 2.1, 2.2, 3.1 and 3.2 plus the *AQA GCSE Maths Foundation Student Book, 4th edition*.

## CD-ROM

The CD-ROM contains the entire Teacher Pack material in Word, to enable you to customise lessons.

It also includes:

- Activities (quick starter activities and extension activities)
- Literacy activities
- 2-, 3- and 5-year Schemes of Work
- Answers to the Student Book questions.

# 2-year AQA Foundation tier Route Map — Year 10

| SEPTEMBER | | OCTOBER | | NOVEMBER |
|---|---|---|---|---|
| **Weeks 1–3** Number: Basic Number | **Weeks 4–6** Geometry and measures: Measures and scale drawings | **Week 7** Statistics: Charts, tables and averages | **Week 8** *Holiday* | **Week 9** Statistics: Charts, tables and averages |

| NOVEMBER | DECEMBER | | |
|---|---|---|---|
| **Weeks 10–12** Geometry and measures: Angles | **Weeks 13–15** Number: Number properties | **Week 16** *Holiday* | **Week 17** *Holiday* |

| JANUARY | | FEBRUARY | | |
|---|---|---|---|---|
| **Weeks 18–19** Number: Approximations | **Weeks 20–21** Number: Decimals and fractions | **Weeks 22–23** Algebra: Linear graphs | **Week 24** *Holiday* | **Week 25** Algebra: Linear graphs |

| MARCH | | APRIL | | |
|---|---|---|---|---|
| **Weeks 26–28** Algebra: Expressions and formulae | **Weeks 29–30** Ratio and proportion and rates of change: Ratio, speed and proportion | **Week 31** *Holiday* | **Week 32** *Holiday* | **Weeks 33–34** Geometry and measures: Perimeter and area |

| APRIL | MAY | | JUNE |
|---|---|---|---|
| **Weeks 35–36** Geometry and measures: Transformations | **Week 37** Probability: Probability and events | **Week 38** *Holiday* | **Week 39** Probability: Probability and events |

| JUNE | | | | JULY |
|---|---|---|---|---|
| **Week 40** Geometry and measures: Volumes and surface areas of prisms | **Week 41** *Summer examinations and revision* | **Week 42** *Summer examinations and revision* | **Week 43** Geometry and measures: Volumes and surface areas of prisms | **Weeks 44–45** Algebra: Linear equations |

# 2-year AQA Foundation tier Route Map — Year 11

| SEPTEMBER | | OCTOBER | | NOVEMBER |
|---|---|---|---|---|
| **Weeks 1–3** Ratio and proportion and rates of change: Percentages and compound measures | **Weeks 4–6** Ratio and proportion and rates of change: Percentages and variation | **Weeks 5–7** Statistics: Representation and interpretation | **Week 8** *Holiday* | **Weeks 9–10** Geometry and measures: Constructions and loci |

| NOVEMBER | DECEMBER | | | |
|---|---|---|---|---|
| **Weeks 11–12** Geometry and measures: Curved shapes and pyramids | **Week 13** *Revision and review* | **Weeks 14–15** *Mock examinations and revision* | **Week 16** *Holiday* | **Week 17** *Holiday* |

| JANUARY | | FEBRUARY | | MARCH |
|---|---|---|---|---|
| **Weeks 18–19** Algebra: Number and sequences | **Weeks 20–21** Geometry and measures: Right-angled triangles | **Week 22** Geometry and measures: Right-angled triangles | **Week 23** *Holiday* | **Weeks 24–25** Geometry and measures: Congruency and similarity |

| MARCH | APRIL | | | |
|---|---|---|---|---|
| **Weeks 26–27** Probability: Combined events | **Weeks 28–29** Number: Powers and standard form | **Week 30** *Holiday* | **Week 31** *Holiday* | **Week 32** Number: Powers and standard form |

| APRIL | MAY | | JUNE |
|---|---|---|---|
| **Weeks 33–35** Algebra: Simultaneous equations and linear inequalities | **Weeks 36–37** Algebra: Non-linear graphs | **Week 38** *Holiday* | **Weeks 39–40** *Revision* |

| JUNE | | | JULY | |
|---|---|---|---|---|
| **Week 41** *June examinations* | **Week 42** *June examinations* | **Week 43** | **Week 44** | **Week 45** |

# 2-year Scheme of Work

| | | Week | Hours | Chapter: Topic | Topic break-down (sub-topics) | Learning Objectives: Students will be able to: |
|---|---|---|---|---|---|---|
| Year 10 | Term 1 | 1–3 | 10 | 1: Number: Basic Number | 1.1 Place value and ordering numbers | • use a number line to represent negative numbers<br>• use inequalities with negative numbers compare and order positive and negative numbers. |
| | | | | | 1.3 The four rules | • use the four rules of arithmetic with integers and decimals. |
| | | | | | 1.2 Order of operations and BIDMAS | • work out the answers to problems with more than one mathematical operation. |
| | | 4–6 | 10 | 2: Geometry and measures: Measures and scale drawings | 2.1 Systems of measurement | • convert from one metric unit to another<br>• convert from one imperial unit to another. |
| | | | | | 2.2 Conversion factors | • use approximate conversion factors to change between imperial units and metric units. |
| | | | | | 2.3 Scale drawings | • read and draw scale drawings<br>• use a scale drawing to make estimates. |
| | | | | | 2.4 Nets | • draw nets of some 3D shapes<br>• identify a 3D shape from its net. |
| | | | | | 2.5 Using an isometric grid | • read from and draw on isometric grids<br>• interpret diagrams to draw plans and elevations. |
| | | 7 | 3 | 3: Statistics: Charts, tables and averages | 3.1 Frequency tables | • use tally charts and frequency tables to collect and represent data<br>• use grouped frequency tables to collect and represent data. |
| | | | | | 3.2 Statistical diagrams | • draw pictograms to represent statistical data<br>• draw bar charts and vertical line charts to represent statistical data. |
| | | 8 | | HALF TERM | | |
| | | 9 | 4 | 3: Statistics: Charts, tables and averages | 3.3 Line graphs | • draw a line graph to show trends in data. |
| | | | | | 3.4 Statistical averages | • work out the mode, median, mean and range of small sets of data<br>• decide which is the best average to use to represent a data set. |
| | | 10–12 | 10 | 4: Geometry and measures: Angles | 4.1 Angles facts | • calculate angles on a straight line<br>• calculate angles around a point<br>• use vertically opposite angles. |
| | | | | | 4.2 Triangles | • recognise and calculate the angles in different sorts of triangle. |
| | | | | | 4.3 Angles in a polygon | • calculate the sum of the interior angles in a polygon. |
| | | | | | 4.4 Regular polygons | • calculate the exterior angles and the interior angles of a regular polygon. |
| | | | | | 4.5 Angles in parallel lines | • calculate angles in parallel lines. |
| | | | | | 4.6 Special quadrilaterals | • use angle properties in quadrilaterals. |
| | | | | | 4.7 Bearings | • use a bearing to specify a direction. |
| | | 13–15 | 10 | 5: Number: Number properties | 5.1 Multiples of whole numbers | • find multiples of whole numbers.<br>• recognise multiples of numbers. |
| | | | | | 5.2 Factors of whole numbers | • identify the factors of a number. |
| | | | | | 5.3 Prime numbers | • identify prime numbers. |
| | | | | | 5.4 Prime factors, | • identify prime factors |

| | | | | | LCM and HCF | • identify the lowest common multiple (LCM) of two numbers<br>• identify the highest common factor (HCF) of two numbers. |
|---|---|---|---|---|---|---|
| | | | | | 5.5 Square numbers | • identify square numbers<br>• use a calculator to find the square of a number. |
| | | | | | 5.6 Square roots | • recognise the square roots of square numbers up to 225<br>• use a calculator to find the square roots of any number. |
| | | | | | 5.7 Basic calculations on a calculator | • use some of the important keys when working on a calculator. |
| | | 16–17 | | | CHRISTMAS HOLIDAY | |
| | | 18–19 | 7 | 6: Number: Approximations | 6.1 Rounding whole numbers | • round a whole number. |
| | | | | | 6.2 Rounding decimals | • round decimal numbers to a given accuracy. |
| | | | | | 6.3 Approximating calculations | • identify significant figures<br>• round numbers to a given number of significant figures<br>• use approximation to estimate answers and check calculations<br>• round a calculation at the end of a problem, to give what is considered to be a sensible answer. |
| | | 20–21 | 7 | 7: Number: Decimals and fractions | 7.1 Calculating with decimals | • multiply and divide with decimals. |
| | Term 2 | | | | 7.2 Fractions and reciprocals | • recognise different types of fraction, reciprocal, terminating decimal and recurring decimal<br>• convert terminating decimals to fractions<br>• convert fractions to decimals<br>• find reciprocals of numbers or fractions. |
| | | | | | 7.3 Writing one quantity as a fraction of another | • work out a fraction of a quantity<br>• find one quantity as a fraction of another. |
| | | | | | 7.4 Adding and subtracting fractions | • add and subtract fractions with different denominators. |
| | | | | | 7.5 Multiplying and dividing fractions | • multiply proper fractions<br>• multiply mixed numbers<br>• divide by fractions. |
| | | | | | 7.6 Fractions on a calculator | • use a calculator to add and subtract fractions<br>• use a calculator to multiply and divide fractions. |
| | | 22–23 | 7 | 8: Algebra: Linear graphs | 8.1 Graphs and equations | • use flow diagrams to draw graphs<br>• work out the equations of horizontal and vertical lines. |
| | | | | | 8.2 Drawing linear graphs by finding points | • draw linear graphs without using flow diagrams. |
| | | | | | 8.3 Gradient of a line | • work out the gradient of a straight line<br>• draw a line with a certain gradient. |
| | | | | | 8.4 $y=mx+c$ | • draw graphs using the gradient-intercept method<br>• draw graphs using the cover-up method. |
| | | | | | 8.5 Finding the equation of a line from its graph | • work out the equation of a line, using its gradient and y-intercept<br>• work out the equation of a line given two points on the line. |

| | | | | 8.6 The equation of a parallel line | • work out the equation of a linear graph that is parallel to another line and passes through a specific point. |
|---|---|---|---|---|---|
| | **24** | | | | **HALF TERM** |
| | 25 | 4 | 8: Algebra: Linear graphs | 8.7 Real-life uses of graphs | • convert from one unit to another unit by using a conversion graph<br>• use straight-line graphs to work out formulae. |
| | | | | 8.8 Solving simultaneous equations using graphs | • solve simultaneous linear equations using graphs. |
| | 26–28 | 10 | 9: Algebra: Expressions and formulae | 9.1 Basic algebra | • write an algebraic expression<br>• recognise expressions, equations, formulae and identities. |
| | | | | 9.2 Substitution | • substitute into, simplify and use algebraic expressions. |
| | | | | 9.3 Expanding brackets | • expand brackets such as $2(x - 3)$expand and simplify brackets. |
| | | | | 9.4 Factorisation | • factorise an algebraic expression. |
| | | | | 9.5 Quadratic expansion | • expand two linear brackets to obtain a quadratic expression. |
| | | | | 9.6 Quadratic factorisation | • factorise a quadratic expression of the form $x^2 + ax + b$ into two linear brackets. |
| | | | | 9.7 Changing the subject of a formula | • change the subject of a formula. |
| | 29–30 | 7 | 10: Ratio and proportion and rates of change: Ratio, speed and proportion | 10.1 Ratio | • simplify a ratio<br>• express a ratio as a fraction<br>• divide amounts into given ratios<br>• complete calculations from a given ratio and partial information. |
| | | | | 10.2 Speed, distance and time | • recognise the relationship between speed, distance and time<br>• calculate average speed from distance and time<br>• calculate distance travelled from the speed and the time taken<br>• calculate the time taken on a journey from the speed and the distance. |
| | | | | 10.3 Direct proportion problems | • recognise and solve problems that involve direct proportion. |
| | | | | 10.4 Best buys | • find the cost per unit mass<br>• find the mass per unit cost<br>• use the above to find which product is better value. |
| | **31–32** | | | | **EASTER HOLIDAY** |
| Term 3 | 33–34 | 7 | 11: Geometry and measures: Perimeter and area | 11.1 Rectangles | • calculate the perimeter and area of a rectangle. |
| | | | | 11.2 Compound shapes | • calculate the perimeter and area of a compound shape made from rectangles. |
| | | | | 11.3 Area of a triangle | • calculate the area of a triangle<br>• use the formula for the area of a triangle. |
| | | | | 11.4 Area of a parallelogram | • calculate the area of a parallelogram<br>• use the formula for the area of a parallelogram. |
| | | | | 11.5 Area of a trapezium | • calculate the area of a trapezium<br>• use the formula for the area of a trapezium. |
| | | | | 11.6 Circles | • recognise terms used for circle work<br>• calculate the circumference of a circle. |

| | | | | 11.7 The area of a circle | • calculate the area of a circle |
|---|---|---|---|---|---|
| | | | | 11.8 Answers in terms of π | • give answers for circle calculations in terms of ð. |
| 35–36 | 7 | 12: Geometry and measures: Transformations | 12.1 Rotational symmetry | • work out the order of rotational symmetry for a 2D shape<br>• recognise shapes with rotational symmetry. |
| | | | | 12.2 Translation | • translate a 2D shape |
| | | | | 12.3 Reflections | • reflect a 2D shape in a mirror line. |
| | | | | 12.4 Rotations | • rotate a 2D shape about a point |
| | | | | 12.5 Enlargements | • enlarge a 2D shape by a scale factor |
| | | | | 12.6 Using more than one transformation | • use more than one transformation. |
| | | | | 12.7 Vectors | • represent vectors<br>• add and subtract vectors. |
| 37 | 3 | 13: Probability: Probability and events | 13.1 Calculating probabilities | • use the probability scale and the language of probability<br>• calculate the probability of an outcome of an event. |
| | | | | 13.2 Probability that an outcome will not happen | • calculate the probability of an outcome not happening when you know the probability of that outcome happening. |
| | | | | 13.3 Mutually exclusive and exhaustive outcomes | • recognise mutually exclusive and exhaustive outcomes. |
| 38 | | | HALF TERM | | |
| 39 | 4 | 13: Probability: Probability and events | 13.4 Experimental probability | • calculate experimental probabilities and relative frequencies from experiments<br>• recognise different methods for estimating probabilities. |
| | | | | 13.5 Expectation | • predict the likely number of successful outcomes, given the number of trials and the probability of any one outcome. |
| | | | | 13.6 Choices and outcomes | • apply systematic listing and counting strategies to identify all outcomes for a variety of problems. |
| 40 | 3 | 14: Geometry and measures: Volumes and surface areas of prisms | 14.1 3D shapes | • use the correct terms when working with 3D shapes. |
| | | | | 14.2 Volume and surface area of a cuboid | • calculate the surface area and volume of a cuboid. |
| 41–42 | 7 | | Summer examinations and revision | | |
| 43 | 4 | 14: Geometry and measures: Volumes and surface areas of prisms | 14.3 Volume and surface area of a prism | • calculate the volume and surface area of a prism. |
| | | | | 14.4 Volume and surface area of cylinders | • calculate the volume and surface area of a cylinder. |
| 44–45 | 7 | 15: Algebra: Linear equations | 15.1 Solving linear equations | • solve linear equations such as<br>• $3x - 1 = 11$ where the variable only appears on one side<br>• use inverse operations and inverse flow diagrams<br>• solve equations by balancing<br>• solve equations in which the variable (the letter) appears in the numerator of a fraction |
| | | | | 15.2 Solving equations with brackets | • solve equations where you have to first expand brackets. |
| | | | | 15.3 Solving | • solve equations where the variable |

| | | | | | equations with the variable on both sides | appears on both sides of the equals sign. |
|---|---|---|---|---|---|---|
| | | | | | END OF YEAR 10 / SUMMER HOLIDAY | |
| Year 11 | Term 1 | 1–2 | 7 | 16: Ratio and proportion and rates of change: Percentages and compound measures | 16.1 Equivalent percentages, fractions and decimals | • convert percentages to fractions and decimals and vice versa. |
| | | | | | 16.2 Calculating a percentage of a quantity | • calculate a percentage of a quantity |
| | | | | | 16.3 Increasing and decreasing quantities by a percentage | • increase and decrease quantities by a percentage. |
| | | | | | 16.4 Expressing one quantity as a percentage of another | • express one quantity as a percentage of another<br>• work out percentage change. |
| | | | | | 16.5 Compound measures | • recognise and solve problems involving the compound measures of rates of pay, density and pressure |
| | | 3–4 | 7 | 17: Ratio and proportion and rates of change: Percentages and variation | 17.1 Compound interest and repeated percentage change | • calculate simple interest<br>• calculate compound interest<br>• solve problems involving repeated percentage change |
| | | | | | 17.2 Reverse percentage (working out the original value) | • calculate the original amount, given the final amount, after a known percentage increase or decrease |
| | | | | | 17.3 Direct proportion | • solve problems in which two variables have a directly proportional relationship (direct variation)<br>• work out the constant of proportionality<br>• recognise graphs that show direct variation |
| | | | | | 17.4 Inverse proportion | • solve problems in which two variables have an inversely proportional relationship (inverse variation)<br>• work out the constant of proportionality |
| | | 5–7 | 10 | 18: Statistics: Representation and interpretation | 18.1 Sampling | • obtain a random sample from a population<br>• collect unbiased and reliable data for a sample |
| | | | | | 18.2 Pie charts | • draw and interpret pie charts |
| | | | | | 18.3 Scatter diagrams | • draw, interpret and use scatter diagrams<br>• draw and use a line of best fit |
| | | | | | 18.4 Grouped data and averages | • identify the modal group<br>• calculate an estimate of the mean from a grouped table |
| | | 8 | | | HALF TERM | |
| | | 9–10 | 7 | 19: Geometry and measures: Constructions and loci | 19.1 Constructing triangles | • construct accurate drawings of triangles, using a pair of compasses, a protractor and a straight edge |
| | | | | | 19.2 Bisectors | • construct bisectors of lines and angles<br>• construct angles of 60° and 90° |
| | | | | | 19.3 Defining a locus | • draw a locus for a given rule |
| | | | | | 19.4 Loci problems | • solve practical problems using loci |
| | | 11–12 | 7 | 20: Geometry and measures: Curved shapes and pyramids | 20.1 Sectors | • calculate the length of an arc<br>• calculate the area and angle of a sector. |
| | | | | | 20.2 Pyramids | • calculate the volume and surface area of a pyramid |
| | | | | | 20.3 Cones | • calculate the volume and surface area of a cone |

| | | | | | 20.4 Spheres | • calculate the volume and surface area of a sphere |
|---|---|---|---|---|---|---|---|
| | | 13 | 3 | | | Revision and review | |
| | | 14–15 | 7 | | | Mock Exams and Revision | |
| | | 16–17 | | | | CHRISTMAS HOLIDAY | |
| | Term 2 | 18–19 | 7 | 21: Algebra: Number and sequences | 21.1 Patterns in number | • recognise patterns in number sequences | |
| | | | | | 21.2 Number sequences | • recognise how number sequences are built up<br>• generate sequences, given the $n$th term. | |
| | | | | | 21.3 Finding the $n$th term of a linear sequence | • find the $n$th term of a linear sequence. | |
| | | | | | 21.4 Special sequences | • recognise and continue some special number sequences<br>• understand how prime, odd and even numbers interact in addition, subtraction and multiplication problems. | |
| | | | | | 2.5 General rules from given patterns | • find the $n$th term from practical problems involving sequences. | |
| | | 20–22 | 10 | 22: Geometry and measures: Right-angled triangles | 22.1 Pythagoras' theorem | • Know what Pythagoras' theorem is<br>• calculate the length of the hypotenuse in a right-angled triangle. | |
| | | | | | 22.2 Calculating the length of a shorter side | • calculate the length of a shorter side in a right-angled triangle. | |
| | | | | | 22.3 Applying Pythagoras' theorem in real-life situations | • solve problems using Pythagoras' theorem. | |
| | | | | | 22.4 Pythagoras' theorem and isosceles triangles | • use Pythagoras' theorem in isosceles triangles. | |
| | | | | | 22.5 Trigonometric ratios | • define, understand and use the three trigonometric ratios | |
| | | | | | 22.6 Calculating lengths using trigonometry | • use trigonometric ratios to calculate a length in a right-angled triangle. | |
| | | | | | 22.7 Calculating angles using trigonometry | • use the trigonometric ratios to calculate an angle. | |
| | | | | | 22.8 Trigonometry without a calculator | • work out and remember trigonometric values for angles of 30°, 45°, 60° and 90°. | |
| | | | | | 22.9 Solving problems using trigonometry | • solve practical problems using trigonometry<br>• solve problems using an angle of elevation or an angle of depression. | |
| | | | | | 22.10 Trigonometry and bearings | • solve bearing problems using trigonometry. | |
| | | | | | 22.11 Trigonometry and isosceles triangles | • use trigonometry to solve problems involving isosceles triangles. | |
| | | 23 | | | | HALF TERM | |
| | | 24–25 | 7 | 23: Geometry and measures: Congruency and similarity | 23.1 Congruent triangles | • demonstrate that two triangles are congruent. | |
| | | | | | 23.2 Similarity | • recognise similarity in any two shapes<br>• show that two shapes are similar<br>• work out the scale factor between similar shapes. | |
| | | 26–27 | 7 | 24: Probability: | 24.1 Combined events | • work out the probabilities when two or more events occur at the same time. | |

| | | | | Combined events | 24.2 Two-way tables | • read two-way tables and use them to work out probabilities. |
| | | | | | 24.3 Probability and Venn diagrams | • use Venn diagrams to solve probability questions. |
| | | | | | 24.4 Tree diagrams | • understand frequency tree diagrams and probability tree diagrams<br>• use probability tree diagrams to work out the probabilities involved in combined events. |
| | | 28–29 | 7 | 25: Number: Powers and standard form | 25.1 Powers (indices) | • write a number as a power of another number<br>• use powers (also known as indices)<br>• multiply and divide by powers of 10. |
| | | | | | 25.2 Rules for multiplying and dividing powers | • use rules for multiplying and dividing powers<br>• multiply and divide numbers by powers of 10. |
| | | 30–31 | | EASTER HOLIDAY | | |
| | Term 3 | 32 | 4 | 25: Number: Powers and standard form | 25.3 Standard form | • write a number in standard form<br>• calculate with numbers in standard form. |
| | | 33–35 | 11 | 26: Algebra: Simultaneous equations and linear inequalities | 26.1 Elimination method for simultaneous equations | • solve simultaneous linear equations in two variables using the elimination method. |
| | | | | | 26.2 Substitution method for simultaneous equations | • solve simultaneous linear equations in two variables using the substitution method. |
| | | | | | 26.3 Balancing coefficients to solve simultaneous equations | • solve simultaneous linear equations by balancing coefficients. |
| | | | | | 26.4 Using simultaneous equations to solve problems | • solve problems using simultaneous linear equations. |
| | | | | | 26.5 Linear inequalities | • solve a simple linear inequality and represent it on a number line. |
| | | 36–37 | 7 | 27: Algebra: Non-linear graphs | 27.1 Distance-time graphs | • interpret distance–time graphs<br>• draw a graph of the depth of liquid as a container is filled. |
| | | | | | 27.2 Plotting quadratic graphs | • draw and read values from quadratic graphs. |
| | | | | | 27.3 Solving quadratic equations by factorisation | • solve a quadratic equation by factorisation. |
| | | | | | 27.4 The significant points of a quadratic curve | • identify the significant points of a quadratic function graphically<br>• identify the roots of a quadratic function by solving a quadratic equation<br>• identify the turning point of a quadratic function. |
| | | | | | 27.5 Cubic and reciprocal graphs | • recognise and plot cubic and reciprocal graphs. |
| | | 38 | | HALF TERM | | |
| | | 39–40 | | Revision | | |
| | | 41–42 | | June Examinations | | |

# 3-year AQA Foundation tier Route Map — Year 9

| SEPTEMBER | | OCTOBER | | NOVEMBER |
|---|---|---|---|---|
| **Weeks 1–3** **Number:** Basic Number | **Weeks 4–6** **Geometry and measures:** Measures and scale drawings | **Week 7** *Review and revision 1* | **Week 8** *Holiday* | **Weeks 9–10** **Statistics:** Charts, tables and averages |

| NOVEMBER | | DECEMBER | | |
|---|---|---|---|---|
| **Weeks 11–12** **Geometry and measures:** Angles | **Weeks 13–14** **Number:** Number properties | **Week 15** *Year 9 examinations and revision* | **Week 16** *Holiday* | **Week 17** *Holiday* |

| JANUARY | | | FEBRUARY | | MARCH |
|---|---|---|---|---|---|
| **Weeks 18–19** **Number:** Number properties | **Weeks 20–21** **Number:** Approximations | **Week 22** **Number:** Decimals and fractions | **Week 23** *Review and Revision 2* | **Week 24** *Holiday* | **Weeks 25–26** **Number:** Decimals and fractions |

| MARCH | | APRIL | | | MAY | |
|---|---|---|---|---|---|---|
| **Weeks 27–29** **Algebra:** Linear graphs | **Week 30** *Review and revision 3* | **Week 31** *Holiday* | **Week 32** *Holiday* | **Week 33** **Algebra:** Linear graphs | **Weeks 34–35** **Algebra:** Expressions and formulae | **Week 36** *Review and revision 4* |

| MAY | | JUNE | | | JULY |
|---|---|---|---|---|---|
| **Week 37** *Review and revision 4* | **Week 38** *Holiday* | **Weeks 39–40** **Algebra:** Expressions and formulae | **Week 41** *Summer examinations and revision* | **Week 42** *Summer examinations and revision* | **Weeks 43–45** **Ratio and proportion and rates of change:** Ratio, speed and proportion |

# 3-year AQA Foundation tier Route Map — Year 10

| SEPTEMBER | | OCTOBER | | | NOVEMBER | |
|---|---|---|---|---|---|---|
| **Week 1** *Review and revision 5* | **Week 2–4** **Geometry and measures:** Perimeter and area | **Weeks 5–6** **Geometry and measures:** Transformations | **Week 7** *Review and revision 6* | **Week 8** *Holiday* | **Week 9** **Geometry and measures:** Transformations | **Week 10** **Probability:** Probability and events |

| NOVEMBER | | DECEMBER | | |
|---|---|---|---|---|
| **Weeks 11–12** **Probability:** Probability and events | **Week 13** **Geometry and measures:** Volumes and surface areas of prisms | **Week 15** *Year 9 examinations and revision* | **Week 16** *Holiday* | **Week 17** *Holiday* |

| JANUARY | | | FEBRUARY | | MARCH |
|---|---|---|---|---|---|
| **Weeks 18–19** **Geometry and measures:** Volumes and surface areas of prisms properties | **Week 20** **Number:** Recap and review | **Weeks 21–22** **Algebra:** Linear equations fractions | **Week 23** *Review and Revision 7* | **Week 24** *Holiday* | **Weeks 25–26** **Algebra:** Linear equations |

| MARCH | | APRIL | | | MAY | |
|---|---|---|---|---|---|---|
| **Week 27** **Statistics:** Recap and review | **Weeks 28–29** **Ratio and proportion and rates of change:** Percentages and compound measures | **Week 31** *Holiday* | **Week 32** *Holiday* | **Weeks 33–35** **Ratio and proportion and rates of change:** Percentages and variation | **Week 36** *Review and revision 9* | **Week 37** *Review and revision 9* |

| MAY | JUNE | | | JULY | |
|---|---|---|---|---|---|
| **Week 38** *Holiday* | **Weeks 39–40** **Statistics:** Representation and interpretation | **Week 41** *Summer examinations and revision* | **Week 42** *Summer examinations and revision* | **Week 43** **Statistics:** Representation and interpretation | **Weeks 44–45** **Geometry and measures:** Constructions and loci |

# 3-year AQA Foundation tier Route Map — Year 11

| SEPTEMBER | | | OCTOBER | | |
|---|---|---|---|---|---|
| **Week 1**<br>*Review and revision 10* | **Weeks 2–4**<br>**Geometry and measures:**<br>Curved shapes and pyramids | **Weeks 5–6**<br>**Algebra:**<br>Number and sequences | **Week 7**<br>*Review and revision 11* | **Week 8**<br>*Holiday* | **Week 9**<br>**Algebra:** Recap and review |

| NOVEMBER | | | DECEMBER | | |
|---|---|---|---|---|---|
| **Weeks 10–11**<br>**Geometry and measures:**<br>Right-angled triangles | **Weeks 12–13**<br>**Geometry and measures:**<br>Right-angled triangles | **Week 14**<br>*Mock examinations and revision* | **Week 15**<br>*Mock examinations and revision* | **Week 16**<br>*Holiday* | **Week 17**<br>*Holiday* |

| JANUARY | | | FEBRUARY | | MARCH |
|---|---|---|---|---|---|
| **Weeks 18–19**<br>**Geometry and measures:**<br>Congruency and similarity | **Weeks 20–21**<br>**Probability:**<br>Combined events | **Week 22**<br>*Review and revision 12* | **Week 23**<br>*Holiday* | **Weeks 24–26**<br>**Number:**<br>Powers and standard form | **Weeks 27–28**<br>**Algebra:**<br>Simultaneous equations and linear inequalities |

| MARCH | APRIL | | | | MAY | |
|---|---|---|---|---|---|---|
| **Week 29**<br>*Review and revision 13* | **Week 30**<br>*Holiday* | **Week 31**<br>*Holiday* | **Week 32**<br>**Algebra:**<br>Simultaneous equations and linear inequalities | **Weeks 33–35**<br>**Algebra:**<br>Non-linear graphs | **Weeks 36–37**<br>*Revision* | **Week 38**<br>*Holiday* |

| JUNE | | | JULY | | |
|---|---|---|---|---|---|
| **Weeks 39–40**<br>*Revision* | **Week 41**<br>*June examinations* | **Week 42**<br>*June examinations* | **Week 43** | **Week 44** | **Week 45** |

# 3-year Scheme of Work

| | | Week | Hours | Chapter: Topic | Topic break-down (sub-topics) | Learning Objectives: Students will be able to: |
|---|---|---|---|---|---|---|
| Year 9 | Term 1 | 1–3 | 10 | 1: Number: Basic number | 1.1 Place value and ordering numbers | • use a number line to represent negative numbers<br>• use inequalities with negative numbers<br>• compare and order positive and negative numbers. |
| | | | | | 1.3 The four rules | • use the four rules of arithmetic with integers and decimals. |
| | | | | | 1.2 Order of operations and BIDMAS | • work out the answers to problems with more than one mathematical operation. |
| | | 4–6 | 11 | 2: Geometry and measures: Measures and scale drawings | 2.1 Systems of measurement | • convert from one metric unit to another<br>• convert from one imperial unit to another. |
| | | | | | 2.2 Conversion factors | • use approximate conversion factors to change between imperial units and metric units. |
| | | | | | 2.3 Scale drawings | • read and draw scale drawings<br>• use a scale drawing to make estimates. |
| | | | | | 2.4 Nets | • draw nets of some 3D shapes<br>• identify a 3D shape from its net. |
| | | | | | 2.5 Using an isometric grid | • read from and draw on isometric grids<br>• interpret diagrams to draw plans and elevations. |
| | | 7 | 3 | Review and revision 1 | Number | |
| | | 8 | | HALF TERM | | |
| | | 9–10 | 7 | 3: Statistics: Charts, tables and averages | 3.1 Frequency tables | • use tally charts and frequency tables to collect and represent data<br>• use grouped frequency tables to collect and represent data. |
| | | | | | 3.2 Statistical diagrams | • draw pictograms to represent statistical data<br>• draw bar charts and vertical line charts to represent statistical data. |
| | | | | | 3.3 Line graphs | • draw a line graph to show trends in data. |
| | | | | | 3.4 Statistical averages | • work out the mode, median, mean and range of small sets of data<br>• decide which is the best average to use to represent a data set. |
| | | 11–12 | 7 | 4: Geometry and measures: Angles | 4.1 Angles facts | • calculate angles on a straight line calculate angles around a point<br>• use vertically opposite angles. |
| | | | | | 4.2 Triangles | • recognise and calculate the angles in different sorts of triangle. |
| | | | | | 4.3 Angles in a polygon | • calculate the sum of the interior angles in a polygon. |
| | | | | | 4.4 Regular polygons | • calculate the exterior angles and the interior angles of a regular polygon. |
| | | | | | 4.5 Angles in parallel lines | • calculate angles in parallel lines. |
| | | | | | 4.6 Special quadrilaterals | • use angle properties in quadrilaterals. |
| | | | | | 4.7 Bearings | • use a bearing to specify a direction. |
| | | 13–14 | 7 | 5: Number: Number properties | 5.1 Multiples of whole numbers | • find multiples of whole numbers<br>• recognise multiples of numbers. |
| | | | | | 5.2 Factors of whole numbers | • identify the factors of a number. |
| | | | | | 5.3 Prime numbers | • identify prime numbers. |
| | | 15 | 4 | Y9 examinations and revision | | |
| | | 16–17 | | CHRISTMAS HOLIDAY | | |

| | | 18–19 | 7 | 5: Number: Number properties | 5.4 Prime factors, LCM and HCF | • identify prime factors<br>• identify the lowest common multiple (LCM) of two numbers<br>• identify the highest common factor (HCF) of two numbers. |
|---|---|---|---|---|---|---|
| | | | | | 5.5 Square numbers | • identify square numbers use a calculator to find the square of a number. |
| | | | | | 5.6 Square roots | • recognise the square roots of square numbers up to 225<br>• use a calculator to find the square roots of any number. |
| | | | | | 5.7 Basic calculations on a calculator | • use some of the important keys when working on a calculator. |
| | | 20–21 | 7 | 6: Number: Approximations | 6.1 Rounding whole numbers | • round a whole number. |
| | | | | | 6.2 Rounding decimals | • round decimal numbers to a given accuracy. |
| | | | | | 6.3 Approximating calculations | • identify significant figures<br>• round numbers to a given number of significant figures<br>• use approximation to estimate answers and check calculations<br>• round a calculation at the end of a problem, to give what is considered to be a sensible answer. |
| | | 22 | 3 | 7: Number: Decimals and fractions | 7.1 Calculating with decimals | • multiply and divide with decimals. |
| | | 23 | 4 | Review and revision 2 | | |
| | | 24 | | HALF TERM | | |
| | Term 2 | 25–26 | 7 | 7: Number: Decimals and fractions | 7.2 Fractions and reciprocals | • recognise different types of fraction, reciprocal, terminating decimal and recurring decimal<br>• convert terminating decimals to fractions<br>• convert fractions to decimals<br>• find reciprocals of numbers or fractions. |
| | | | | | 7.3 Writing one quantity as a fraction of another | • work out a fraction of a quantity<br>• find one quantity as a fraction of another. |
| | | | | | 7.4 Adding and subtracting fractions | • add and subtract fractions with different denominators. |
| | | | | | 7.5 Multiplying and dividing fractions | • multiply proper fractions<br>• multiply mixed numbers<br>• divide by fractions. |
| | | | | | 7.6 Fractions on a calculator | • use a calculator to add and subtract fractions<br>• use a calculator to multiply and divide fractions. |
| | | 27–29 | 10 | 8: Algebra: Linear graphs | 8.1 Graphs and equations | • use flow diagrams to draw graphs<br>• work out the equations of horizontal and vertical lines. |
| | | | | | 8.2 Drawing linear graphs by finding points | • draw linear graphs without using flow diagrams. |
| | | | | | 8.3 Gradient of a line | • work out the gradient of a straight line<br>• draw a line with a certain gradient. |
| | | | | | 8.4 $y = mx + c$ | • draw graphs using the gradient-intercept method<br>• draw graphs using the cover-up method. |
| | | | | | 8.5 Finding the equation of a line from its graph | • work out the equation of a line, using its gradient and y-intercept<br>• work out the equation of a line given two points on the line. |
| | | | | | 8.6 The equation of a parallel line | • work out the equation of a linear graph that is parallel to another line and |

| | | | | | | | |
|---|---|---|---|---|---|---|---|
| | | | | | 8.7 Real-life uses of graphs | • convert from one unit to another unit by using a conversion graph<br>• use straight-line graphs to work out formulae. | |
| | | 30 | 4 | | Review and revision 3 | | |
| | | 31–32 | | EASTER HOLIDAY | | | |
| | | 33 | 4 | 8: Algebra: Linear graphs | 8.8 Solving simultaneous equations using graphs | • solve simultaneous linear equations using graphs. | |
| | | 34–35 | 7 | 9: Algebra: Expressions and formulae | 9.1 Basic algebra | • write an algebraic expression<br>• recognise expressions, equations, formulae and identities. | |
| | | | | | 9.2 Substitution | • substitute into, simplify and use algebraic expressions. | |
| | | | | | 9.3 Expanding brackets | • expand brackets such as $2(x - 3)$<br>• expand and simplify brackets. | |
| | | | | | 9.4 Factorisation | • factorise an algebraic expression. | |
| | | 36 | 3 | | Review and revision 4 | | |
| | | 37 | 4 | | Review and revision 4 | | |
| | | 38 | | HALF TERM | | | |
| | Term 3 | 39–40 | 7 | 9: Algebra: Expressions and formulae | 9.5 Quadratic expansion | • expand two linear brackets to obtain a quadratic expression. | |
| | | | | | 9.6 Quadratic factorisation | • factorise a quadratic expression of the form $x^2 + ax + b$ into two linear brackets. | |
| | | | | | 9.7 Changing the subject of a formula | • change the subject of a formula. | |
| | | 41 | 3 | | Summer examinations and revision | | |
| | | 42 | 4 | | Summer examinations and revision | | |
| | | 43–45 | 10 | 10: Ratio and proportion and rates of change: Ratio, speed and proportion | 10.1 Ratio | • simplify a ratio<br>• express a ratio as a fraction<br>• divide amounts into given ratios<br>• complete calculations from a given ratio and partial information. | |
| | | | | | 10.2 Speed, distance and time | • recognise the relationship between speed, distance and time<br>• calculate average speed from distance and time<br>• calculate distance travelled from the speed and the time taken<br>• calculate the time taken on a journey from the speed and the distance. | |
| | | | | | 10.3 Direct proportion problems | • recognise and solve problems that involve direct proportion. | |
| | | | | | 10.4 Best buys | • find the cost per unit mass<br>• find the mass per unit cost<br>• use the above to find which product is better value. | |
| | | END OF YEAR 9 / SUMMER HOLIDAY | | | | | |
| | | 1 | 3 | | Review and revision 5 | | |
| Year 10 | Term 1 | 2–4 | 10 | 11: Geometry and measures: Perimeter and area | 11.1 Rectangles | • calculate the perimeter and area of a rectangle. | |
| | | | | | 11.2 Compound shapes | • calculate the perimeter and area of a compound shape made from rectangles. | |
| | | | | | 11.3 Area of a triangle | • calculate the area of a triangle<br>• use the formula for the area of a triangle. | |
| | | | | | 11.4 Area of a parallelogram | • calculate the area of a parallelogram<br>• use the formula for the area of a parallelogram. | |
| | | | | | 11.5 Area of a trapezium | • calculate the area of a trapezium<br>• use the formula for the area of a trapezium. | |
| | | | | | 11.6 Circles | • recognise terms used for circle work<br>• calculate the circumference of a circle. | |

| | | | | 11.7 The area of a circle | • calculate the area of a circle. |
|---|---|---|---|---|---|
| | | | | 11.8 Answers in terms of π | • give answers for circle calculations in terms of ð. |
| | 5–6 | 7 | 12: Geometry and measures: Transformations | 12.1 Rotational symmetry | • work out the order of rotational symmetry for a 2D shape<br>• recognise shapes with rotational symmetry. |
| | | | | 12.2 Translation | • translate a 2D shape. |
| | | | | 12.3 Reflections | • reflect a 2D shape in a mirror line. |
| | | | | 12.4 Rotations | • rotate a 2D shape about a point |
| | | | | 12.5 Enlargements | • enlarge a 2D shape by a scale factor. |
| | | | | 12.6 Using more than one transformation | • use more than one transformation. |
| | 7 | 3 | Review and revision 6 | | |
| | 8 | | HALF TERM | | |
| | 9 | 3 | 12: Geometry and measures: Transformations | 12.7 Vectors | • represent vectors<br>• add and subtract vectors. |
| | 10–12 | 11 | 13: Probability: Probability and events | 13.1 Calculating probabilities | • use the probability scale and the language of probability<br>• calculate the probability of an outcome of an event. |
| | | | | 13.2 Probability that an outcome will not happen | • calculate the probability of an outcome not happening when you know the probability of that outcome happening. |
| | | | | 13.3 Mutually exclusive and exhaustive outcomes | • recognise mutually exclusive and exhaustive outcomes. |
| | | | | 13.4 Experimental probability | • calculate experimental probabilities and relative frequencies from experiments<br>• recognise different methods for estimating probabilities. |
| | | | | 13.5 Expectation | • predict the likely number of successful outcomes, given the number of trials and the probability of any one outcome. |
| | | | | 13.6 Choices and outcomes | • apply systematic listing and counting strategies to identify all outcomes for a variety of problems. |
| | 13 | 3 | 14: Geometry and measures: Volumes and surface areas of prisms | 14.1 3D shapes | • use the correct terms when working with 3D shapes. |
| | | | | 14.2 Volume and surface area of a cuboid | • calculate the surface area and volume of a cuboid. |
| | 14 | 3 | Examinations and revision | | |
| | 15 | 4 | Examinations and revision | | |
| | 16–17 | | CHRISTMAS HOLIDAY | | |
| Term 2 | 18–19 | 7 | 14: Geometry and measures: Volumes and surface areas of prisms | 14.3 Volume and surface area of a prism | • calculate the volume and surface area of a prism. |
| | | | | 14.4 Volume and surface area of cylinders | • calculate the volume and surface area of a cylinder. |
| | 20 | 3 | Number: Recap and review | | |
| | 21–22 | 7 | 15: Algebra: Linear equations | 15.1 Solving linear equations | • solve linear equations such as<br>• $3x - 1 = 11$ where the variable only appears on one side<br>• use inverse operations and inverse flow diagrams<br>• solve equations by balancing<br>• solve equations in which the variable (the letter) appears in the numerator of a fraction |
| | 23 | 4 | Review and revision 7 | | |
| | 24 | | HALF TERM | | |
| | 25–26 | 7 | 15: Algebra: | 15.2 Solving equations | • solve equations where you have to first |

| | | | | Linear equations | with brackets | • expand brackets. |
|---|---|---|---|---|---|---|
| | | | | | 15.3 Solving equations with the variable on both sides | • solve equations where the variable appears on both sides of the equals sign. |
| | | 27 | 3 | Statistics: Recap and review | | |
| | | 28–29 | 7 | 16: Ratio and proportion and rates of change: Percentages and compound measures | 16.1 Equivalent percentages, fractions and decimals | • convert percentages to fractions and decimals and vice versa. |
| | | | | | 16.2 Calculating a percentage of a quantity | • calculate a percentage of a quantity. |
| | | | | | 16.3 Increasing and decreasing quantities by a percentage | • increase and decrease quantities by a percentage. |
| | | | | | 16.4 Expressing one quantity as a percentage of another | • express one quantity as a percentage of another<br>• work out percentage change. |
| | | | | | 16.5 Compound measures | • recognise and solve problems involving the compound measures of rates of pay, density and pressure. |
| | | 30 | 4 | Review and revision 8 | | |
| | | 31–32 | | EASTER HOLIDAY | | |
| | Term 3 | 33–35 | 10 | 17: Ratio and proportion and rates of change: Percentages and variation | 17.1 Compound interest and repeated percentage change | • calculate simple interest<br>• calculate compound interest<br>• solve problems involving repeated percentage change. |
| | | | | | 17.2 Reverse percentage (working out the original value) | • calculate the original amount, given the final amount, after a known percentage increase or decrease. |
| | | | | | 17.3 Direct proportion | • solve problems in which two variables have a directly proportional relationship (direct variation) work out the constant of proportionality<br>• recognise graphs that show direct variation. |
| | | | | | 17.4 Inverse proportion | • solve problems in which two variables have an inversely proportional relationship (inverse variation)<br>• work out the constant of proportionality. |
| | | 36 | 3 | Review and revision 9 | | |
| | | 37 | 4 | Review and revision 9 | | |
| | | 38 | | HALF TERM | | |
| | | 39–40 | 7 | 18: Statistics: Representation and interpretation | 18.1 Sampling | • obtain a random sample from a population<br>• collect unbiased and reliable data for a sample. |
| | | | | | 18.2 Pie charts | • draw and interpret pie charts. |
| | | | | | 18.3 Scatter diagrams | • draw, interpret and use scatter diagrams<br>• draw and use a line of best fit. |
| | | 41 | 3 | Summer examinations and revision | | |
| | | 42 | 4 | Summer examinations and revision | | |
| | | 43 | 3 | 18: Statistics: Representation and interpretation | 18.4 Grouped data and averages | • identify the modal group<br>• calculate an estimate of the mean from a grouped table. |
| | | 44–45 | 7 | 19: Geometry and measures: Constructions and loci | 19.1 Constructing triangles | • construct accurate drawings of triangles, using a pair of compasses, a protractor and a straight edge. |
| | | | | | 19.2 Bisectors | • construct the bisectors of lines and angles<br>• construct angles of 60° and 90° |
| | | | | | 19.3 Defining a locus | • draw a locus for a given rule. |
| | | | | | 19.4 Loci problems | • solve practical problems using loci. |
| | | | | END OF YEAR 10 / SUMMER HOLIDAY | | |
| Year 11 | Ter m 1 | 1 | 4 | Review and revision 10 | | |
| | | 2–4 | 10 | 20: Geometry and | 20.1 Sectors | • calculate the length of an arc<br>• calculate the area and angle of a |

| | | | | | sector. |
|---|---|---|---|---|---|
| | | | | 20.2 Pyramids | • calculate the volume and surface area of a pyramid. |
| | | | | 20.3 Cones | • calculate the volume and surface area of a cone. |
| | | | | 20.4 Spheres | • calculate the volume and surface area of a sphere. |
| | 5–6 | 7 | 21: Algebra: Number and sequences | 21.1 Patterns in number | • recognise patterns in number sequences. |
| | | | | 21.2 Number sequences | • recognise how number sequences are built up<br>• generate sequences, given the nth term. |
| | | | | 21.3 Finding the nth term of a linear sequence | • find the nth term of a linear sequence. |
| | | | | 21.4 Special sequences | • recognise and continue some special number sequences<br>• understand how prime, odd and even numbers interact in addition, subtraction and multiplication problems. |
| | | | | 2.5 General rules from given patterns | • find the nth term from practical problems involving sequences. |
| | 7 | 3 | Review and revision 11 ||| 
| | 8 | | HALF TERM ||||
| | 9 | 4 | Algebra: Recap and review | | |
| | 10–13 | 14 | 22: Geometry and measures: Right-angled triangles | 22.1 Pythagoras' theorem | • Know what Pythagoras' theorem is<br>• calculate the length of the hypotenuse in a right-angled triangle. |
| | | | | 22.2 Calculating the length of a shorter side | • calculate the length of a shorter side in a right-angled triangle. |
| | | | | 22.3 Applying Pythagoras' theorem in real-life situations | • Solve problems using Pythagoras' theorem |
| | | | | 22.4 Pythagoras' theorem and isosceles triangles | • use Pythagoras' theorem in isosceles triangles. |
| | | | | 22.5 Trigonometric ratios | • define, understand and use the three trigonometric ratios. |
| | | | | 22.6 Calculating lengths using trigonometry | • use trigonometric ratios to calculate a length in a right-angled triangle. |
| | | | | 22.7 Calculating angles using trigonometry | • use the trigonometric ratios to calculate an angle. |
| | | | | 22.8 Trigonometry without a calculator | • work out and remember trigonometric values for angles of 30°, 45°, 60° and 90°. |
| | | | | 22.9 Solving problems using trigonometry | • solve practical problems using trigonometry<br>• solve problems using an angle of elevation or an angle of depression. |
| | | | | 22.10 Trigonometry and bearings | • solve bearing problems using trigonometry. |
| | | | | 22.11 Trigonometry and isosceles triangles. | • use trigonometry to solve problems involving isosceles triangles. |
| | 14 | 3 | Mock examinations and revision ||| 
| | 15 | 4 | Mock examinations and revision ||| 
| | 16–17 | | CHRISTMAS HOLIDAY ||||
| Term 2 | 18–19 | 7 | 23: Geometry and measures: Congruency and similarity | 23.1 Congruent triangles | • demonstrate that two triangles are congruent. |
| | | | | 23.2 Similarity | • recognise similarity in any two shapes<br>• show that two shapes are similar<br>• work out the scale factor between similar shapes. |
| | 20–21 | 7 | 24: Probability: | 24.1 Combined events | • work out the probabilities when two or more events occur at the same time. |

| | | | | 24.2 Two-way tables | • read two-way tables and use them to work out probabilities. |
|---|---|---|---|---|---|
| | | | Combined events | 24.3 Probability and Venn diagrams | • use Venn diagrams to solve probability questions. |
| | | | | 24.4 Tree diagrams | • understand frequency tree diagrams and probability tree diagrams use probability tree diagrams to work out the probabilities involved in combined events. |
| | 22 | 3 | | Review and revision 12 | |
| | 23 | | | HALF TERM | |
| | 24–26 | 11 | 25: Number: Powers and standard form | 25.1 Powers (indices) | • write a number as a power of another number<br>• use powers (also known as indices)<br>• multiply and divide by powers of 10. |
| | | | | 25.2 Rules for multiplying and dividing powers | • use rules for multiplying and dividing powers<br>• multiply and divide numbers by powers of 10. |
| | | | | 25.3 Standard form | • write a number in standard form<br>• calculate with numbers in standard form. |
| | 27–28 | 7 | 26: Algebra: Simultaneous equations and linear inequalities | 26.1 Elimination method for simultaneous equations | • solve simultaneous linear equations in two variables using the elimination method. |
| | | | | 26.2 Substitution method for simultaneous equations | • solve simultaneous linear equations in two variables using the substitution method. |
| | | | | 26.3 Balancing coefficients to solve simultaneous equations | • solve simultaneous linear equations by balancing coefficients. |
| | 29 | 4 | | Review and revision 13 | |
| | 30–31 | | | EASTER HOLIDAY | |
| Term 3 | 32 | 4 | 26: Algebra: Simultaneous equations and linear inequalities | 26.4 Using simultaneous equations to solve problems | • solve problems using simultaneous linear equations. |
| | | | | 26.5 Linear inequalities | • solve a simple linear inequality and represent it on a number line. |
| | 33–35 | 10 | 27: Algebra: Non-linear graphs | 27.1 Distance-time graphs | • interpret distance-time graphs<br>• draw a graph of the depth of liquid as a container is filled. |
| | | | | 27.2 Plotting quadratic graphs | • draw and read values from quadratic graphs. |
| | | | | 27.3 Solving quadratic equations by factorisation | • solve a quadratic equation by factorisation. |
| | | | | 27.4 The significant points of a quadratic curve | • identify the significant points of a quadratic function graphically<br>• identify the roots of a quadratic function by solving a quadratic equation.<br>• identify the turning point of a quadratic function. |
| | | | | 27.5 Cubic and reciprocal graphs | • recognise and plot cubic and reciprocal graphs. |
| | 36–37 | 7 | | Revision | |
| | 38 | | | HALF-TERM | |
| | 39–40 | 7 | | Revision | |
| | 41 | 3 | | June examinations | |
| | 42 | 4 | | June examinations | |

*AQA GCSE Maths*
Foundation Teacher Pack – 3-year Scheme of Work

xxix

© HarperCollins*Publishers* Ltd 2015

# 5-year AQA Foundation tier Route Map — Year 7

| SEPTEMBER | | | OCTOBER | | | NOVEMBER | |
|---|---|---|---|---|---|---|---|
| Weeks 1–2 Using Numbers | Weeks 3–4 Sequences | Weeks 5–6 Perimeter and area | Week 7 *Extended project Revision and assessment* | | Week 8 *Holiday* | Week 9 Decimal numbers | Week 10 Decimal numbers |

| NOVEMBER | | DECEMBER | | | JANUARY | |
|---|---|---|---|---|---|---|
| Weeks 11–12 Working with numbers | Weeks 13–14 Statistics | Week 15 *Assessment and review* | Week 16 *Holiday* | Week 17 *Holiday* | Weeks 18–19 Algebra | Weeks 20 - 21 Fractions |

| JANUARY | FEBRUARY | | | MARCH | APRIL | |
|---|---|---|---|---|---|---|
| Weeks 22–23 Angles | Week 23 Assessment | Week 24 *Holiday* | Weeks 25–26 Coordinates and graphs | Weeks 27–28 Percentages | Weeks 29–30 Probability | Week 31 *Holiday* |

| APRIL | | | MAY | | | JUNE | |
|---|---|---|---|---|---|---|---|
| Week 32 *Holiday* | Weeks 33–34 Symmetry | Weeks 35–36 Equations | Weeks 36–37 Interpreting data | Week 37 Assessment | Week 38 *Holiday* | Weeks 39–40 3D shapes | Weeks 41–42 Ratio |

| JUNE | JULY |
|---|---|
| Weeks 43 - 44 Extended project | Week 45 *Assessment* |

# 5-year AQA Foundation tier Route Map — Year 8

| SEPTEMBER | | OCTOBER | | NOVEMBER | |
|---|---|---|---|---|---|
| Weeks 1–2 Working with numbers | Weeks 3 - 4 Geometry | Weeks 5–6 Probability | Week 7 *Extended project* Revision and assessment | Week 8 *Holiday* | Week 9 Percentages |

| NOVEMBER | | DECEMBER | | | |
|---|---|---|---|---|---|
| Week 10 Percentages | Weeks 11–12 Sequences | Weeks 13–14 Area | Week 15 *Assessment and review* | Week 16 *Holiday* | Week 17 *Holiday* |

| JANUARY | | FEBRUARY | | | MARCH |
|---|---|---|---|---|---|
| Weeks 18–19 Graphs | Weeks 20–21 Simplifying numbers | Weeks 22–23 Interpreting data | Week 23 *Assessment* | Week 24 *Holiday* | Weeks 25–27 Algebra |

| MARCH | APRIL | | | | MAY |
|---|---|---|---|---|---|
| Weeks 28–29 Congruence and scaling | Week 30 Revision and assessment | Week 31 *Holiday* | Week 32 *Holiday* | Weeks 33–35 Fractions and decimals | Weeks 35–36 Proportion |
| | | | | | Week 37 Circles |

| MAY | | JUNE | | JULY | |
|---|---|---|---|---|---|
| Week 37 Assessment | Week 38 *Holiday* | Weeks 39–40 Equations and formulae | Weeks 41–42 Comparing data | Weeks 43–44 *Extended project* | Week 45 *Assessment* |

# 5-year AQA Foundation tier Route Map — Year 9

| SEPTEMBER | | | OCTOBER | | |
|---|---|---|---|---|---|
| Weeks 1–2 Percentages | Weeks 3–4 Equations and formulae | Weeks 5–6 Polygons | Weeks 6–7 Using data | Week 7 *Assessment* | Week 8 *Holiday* |

| NOVEMBER | | | DECEMBER | | |
|---|---|---|---|---|---|
| Week 9 Circles | Week 10 Circles | Weeks 10–11 Applications of graphs | Weeks 12–13 Pythagoras' theorem | Week 14 Enlargements | Week 15 *Assessment and review* |

| DECEMBER | | JANUARY | | | FEBRUARY | |
|---|---|---|---|---|---|---|
| Week 16 *Holiday* | Week 17 *Holiday* | Weeks 18–19 Fractions | Week 20–21 Algebra | Weeks 22–23 Decimal numbers | Week 23 *Assessment* | Week 24 *Holiday* |

| FEBRUARY | MARCH | | | APRIL | |
|---|---|---|---|---|---|
| Weeks 25–26 Surface area and volume of 3D shapes | Weeks 27–28 Prisms and cylinders | Weeks 28–30 Solving equations graphically | Week 30 *Revision and assessment* | Week 31 *Holiday* | Week 32 *Holiday* |

| APRIL | | MAY | | | JUNE |
|---|---|---|---|---|---|
| Weeks 33–34 Distance, speed and time | Week 35–36 Compound units | Week 36–37 Similar triangles | Week 37 *Assessment* | Week 38 *Holiday* | Weeks 39–40 Right-angled triangles |

| JUNE | JULY | |
|---|---|---|
| Weeks 41–42 *Revision and GCSE preparation* | Weeks 43–44 *Extended project* | Week 45 *Assessment* |

# 5-year AQA Foundation tier Route Map — Year 10

| SEPTEMBER | OCTOBER | | | NOVEMBER |
|---|---|---|---|---|
| Weeks 1–3 **Number:** Basic Number | Weeks 4–6 **Geometry and measures:** Measures and scale drawings | Week 7 **Statistics:** Charts, tables and averages | Week 8 *Holiday* | Week 9 **Statistics:** Charts, tables and averages |

| NOVEMBER | | DECEMBER | | JANUARY | |
|---|---|---|---|---|---|
| Weeks 10–12 **Geometry and measures:** Angles | Weeks 13–15 **Number:** Number properties | Week 16 *Holiday* | Week 17 *Holiday* | Weeks 18–19 **Number:** Approximations | Weeks 20–21 **Number:** Decimals and fractions |

| JANUARY | FEBRUARY | | MARCH | APRIL |
|---|---|---|---|---|
| Weeks 22–23 **Algebra:** Linear Graphs | Week 24 *Holiday* | Week 25 **Algebra:** Linear Graphs | Weeks 26–28 **Algebra:** Expressions and formulae | Weeks 29–30 **Ratio and proportion and rates of change:** Ratio, speed and proportion |

| APRIL | | | | MAY | |
|---|---|---|---|---|---|
| Week 31 *Holiday* | Week 32 *Holiday* | Weeks 33–34 **Geometry and measures:** Perimeter and area | Weeks 35–36 **Geometry and measures:** Transformations | Week 37 **Probability:** Probability and events | Week 38 *Holiday* |

| MAY | JUNE | | | JULY |
|---|---|---|---|---|
| Week 39 **Probability:** Probability and events | Week 40 **Geometry and measures:** Volumes and surface areas of prisms | Week 41 *Summer examinations and revision* | Week 43 **Geometry and measures:** Volume and surface areas of prisms | Weeks 44–45 **Algebra:** Linear equations |

# 5-year AQA Foundation tier Route Map  Year 11

| SEPTEMBER | | OCTOBER | | NOVEMBER |
|---|---|---|---|---|
| **Weeks 1–2**<br>**Ratio and proportion and rates of change:**<br>Percentages and compound measures | **Weeks 3–4**<br>**Ratio and proportion and rates of change:**<br>Percentages and variation | **Weeks 5–7**<br>**Statistics:**<br>Representation and interpretation | **Week 8**<br>*Holiday* | **Weeks 9–10**<br>**Geometry and measures:**<br>Constructions and loci |

| NOVEMBER | DECEMBER | | | | JANUARY | |
|---|---|---|---|---|---|---|
| **Weeks 11–12**<br>**Geometry and measures:**<br>Curved shapes and pyramids | **Week 13**<br>*Revision and review* | **Weeks 14–15**<br>*Mock examinations and revision* | **Week 16**<br>*Holiday* | **Week 17**<br>*Holiday* | **Weeks 18–19**<br>**Algebra:**<br>Number and sequences | **Weeks 20–21**<br>**Geometry and measures:**<br>Right-angled triangles |

| JANUARY | FEBRUARY | | | MARCH | APRIL |
|---|---|---|---|---|---|
| **Week 22**<br>**Geometry and measures:**<br>Right-angled triangles | **Week 23**<br>*Holiday* | **Weeks 24–25**<br>**Geometry and measures:**<br>Congruency and similarity | **Weeks 26–27**<br>**Probability:**<br>Combined events | **Weeks 28–29**<br>**Number:**<br>Powers and standard form | **Week 30**<br>**Number:**<br>Powers and standard form |

| APRIL | | | MAY | | JUNE |
|---|---|---|---|---|---|
| **Week 31**<br>*Holiday* | **Week 32**<br>*Holiday* | **Weeks 33–35**<br>**Algebra:**<br>Simultaneous equations and linear inequalities | **Weeks 36–37**<br>**Algebra**<br>Non-linear graphs | **Week 38**<br>*Holiday* | **Weeks 39–40**<br>*Revision* |

| JUNE | | JULY | | |
|---|---|---|---|---|
| **Week 41**<br>*June examinations* | **Week 42**<br>*June examinations* | **Week 43** | **Week 44** | **Week 45** |

# 5-year Scheme of Work

This 5-year Foundation Scheme of Work offers a flexible approach for Year 7 to Year 11. It is based on a minimum of seven one hour Maths lessons per fortnight (assuming a two week timetable of three lessons in one week and four in the second). This accounts for an average of 140 teaching hours per academic year, with the exception of Year 11, which has 115 due to GCSE examinations in summer (2). In addition to this, there are assessment and review sessions built in.

Core texts are Maths Frameworking (3rd edition) Pupil Books 1.1, 1.2, 2.1, 2.2, 3.1, 3.2 and AQA GCSE Maths (4th Edition) Foundation Student Book.

Mathematical reasoning, problem solving activities and applications are an integral part of each topic.

Students should progress at their own rate with book 2 not being appropriate for all.

There are opportunities for extended projects throughout, which are intended to span a sequence of lessons and give students the opportunity to use, apply and experience the mathematics they have learned in practical real-life situations or in a problem solving and reasoning context.

| | | Week | Hours | Book: Chapter: Topic | Topic break-down (sub-topics) | Learning Objectives: Students will be able to: |
|---|---|---|---|---|---|---|
| Year 7 | Term 1 | 1–2 | 7 | 1.1:1:Using numbers 1.2:1: Using numbers | 1.1 The Calendar | • read and use calendars |
| | | | | | 1.2 The 12-hour and 24-hour clocks | • read and use 12-hour and 24-hour clocks<br>• convert between 12-hour and 24-hour systems |
| | | | | | 1.3 Managing money | • work out everyday money problems |
| | | | | | 1.1 Timetables, charts and money | • carry out calculations from information given in tables and charts |
| | | | | | 1.4 Positive and negative numbers | • use a number line to order positive and negative whole numbers<br>• solve problems involving negative temperatures |
| | | | | | 1.5 Adding negative numbers | • carry out additions and subtractions involving negative numbers<br>• use a number line to calculate with negative numbers |
| | | | | | 1.6 Subtracting negative numbers | • carry out subtractions involving negative numbers |
| | | 3–4 | 7 | 1.1:2: Sequences 1.2:2: Sequences | 2.1 Function machines | • use function machines to generate inputs and outputs |
| | | | | | 2.2 Sequences and rules | • recognise, describe and write down sequences that are based on a simple rule |
| | | | | | 2.3 Finding terms in patterns | • find missing terms in a sequence |
| | | | | | 2.4 The square numbers | • introduce the sequence of square numbers |
| | | | | | 2.5 The triangular numbers | • introduce the sequence of triangular numbers |
| | | | | | 2.4 Other sequences | • know and understand square and triangular number sequences |
| | | 5–6 | 7 | 1.1:3: Perimeter and area 1.2:3: Perimeter, | 3.1 Length and perimeter | • measure and draw lines accurately<br>• work out the perimeter of a shape |

| | | | | | 3.2 Area | • work out the area of a shape by counting squares |
|---|---|---|---|---|---|---|---|
| | | | | | 3.1 Perimeter and area | • work out the perimeter and area of 2D shapes |
| | | | | | 3.3 Perimeter and area of rectangles 3.2 Perimeter and area of rectangles | • work out the perimeter of a rectangle<br>• work out the area of a rectangle<br>• use a simple formula to calculate the area and perimeter of a rectangle |
| | | | | | 3.3 Perimeter and area of compound shapes | • work out the perimeter and area of compound shapes |
| | | | | | 3.4 Volume of cubes and cuboids | • work out the volume of a cube or cuboid using a simple formula<br>• work out the capacity of a cube or cuboid |
| | 7 | 3 | | | Extended project opportunity / revision | |
| | 7 | 1 | | | Assessment | |
| | 8 | | | | HALF TERM | |
| | 9–10 | 7 | 1.1:4: Decimal numbers 1.2:4: Decimal numbers | | 4.1 Multiplying and dividing by 10, 100 and 1000 | • multiply and divide decimal numbers by10, 100 and 1000 |
| | | | | | 4.2 Ordering decimals | • order decimal numbers according to size |
| | | | | | 4.3 Estimates | • estimate calculations in order to spot possible errors |
| | | | | | 4.4 Adding and subtracting decimals | • add and subtract decimal numbers |
| | | | | | 4.5 Multiplying and dividing decimals | • be able to multiply and divide decimal numbers by any whole number |
| | 11–12 | 7 | 1.1:5: Working with numbers 1.2:5: Working with numbers | | 5.1 Square numbers | • recognise and use square numbers up to 225 ($15^2$) |
| | | | | | 5.1 Square numbers and square roots | • recognise and use square roots up to $\sqrt{225}$ |
| | | | | | 5.2 Rounding | • round numbers to the nearest whole number 10, 100 or 1000 |
| | | | | | 5.3 Order of operations | • use the conventions of BIDMAS to carry out calculations |
| | | | | | 5.4 Long and short multiplication | • choose a written method for multiplying two numbers together<br>• use written methods to carry out multiplications accurately |
| | | | | | 5.5 Long and short division | • choose a written method for dividing one number by another<br>• use written methods to carry out divisions accurately |
| | | | | | 5.6 Calculations with measurements | • convert between common metric units<br>• use measurements in calculations<br>• recognise and use appropriate metric units |
| | 13 - 14 | 7 | 1.1:6: Statistics 1.2:6: Statistics | | 6.1 Mode, median and range | • understand the meaning of mode, median and range |
| | | | | | 6.2 The Mean | • understand and calculate the mean average of data |
| | | | | | 6.2 Reading data from tables and charts | • read data from tables and charts |
| | | | | | 6.3 Using a tally chart | • create and use a tally chart |
| | | | | | 6.3 Statistical diagrams | • be able to read and interpret different statistical diagrams |

| | | | | 6.4 Using data<br>6.4 Collecting and using data | • understand how to use (and collect) data |
| | | | | 6..5 Grouped frequency | • understand and use grouped frequency |
| | | | | 6.6 Data collection | • gain a greater understanding of data collection |
| | 15 | 3 | Assessment and review ||
| | 16–17 | | CHRISTMAS HOLIDAY |||
| | 18–19 | 7 | 1.1:7: Algebra<br>1.2:7: Algebra | 7.1 Expressions and substitution | • use algebra to write simple expressions<br>• substitute numbers into expressions to work out their value |
| | | | | 7.2 Simplifying expressions | • learn the rules for simplifying expressions |
| | | | | 7.3 Using formulae | • use formulae |
| | | | | 7.4 Writing formulae | • write formulae |
| | 20–21 | 7 | 1.1:8: Fractions<br>1.2:8: Fractions | 8.1 Equivalent fractions | • find simple equivalent fractions<br>• write fractions in their simplest form |
| | | | | 8.2 Comparing fractions | • compare and order two fractions |
| | | | | 8.3 Adding and subtracting fractions | • add and subtract fractions with the same denominator<br>• The add and subtract fractions with different denominators |
| | | | | 8.4 Mixed numbers and improper fractions | • convert between mixed numbers and improper fractions |
| | | | | 8.5 Calculations with mixed numbers | • add and subtract simple mixed numbers with the same denominator<br>• add and subtract simple mixed numbers with different denominators |
| Term 2 | 22–23 | 6 | 1.1:9: Angles<br>1.2:9: Angles | 9.1 Using the compass to give directions | • use a compass to give directions |
| | | | | 9.2 Measuring angles | • know the different types of angles<br>• use a protractor to measure an angle |
| | | | | 9.3 Drawing angles | • use a protractor to draw an angle |
| | | | | 9.4 Calculating angles | • calculate angles at a point<br>• calculate angles on a straight line<br>• calculate opposite angles |
| | | | | 9.3 Angles in a triangle | • know that the sum of the angles in a triangle is 180° |
| | | | | 9.4 Angles in a quadrilateral | • know that the sum of the angles in a quadrilateral is 360° |
| | | | | 9.5 Properties of triangles and quadrilaterals | • understand the properties of parallel, intersecting and perpendicular lines<br>• understand and use the properties of a triangle<br>• understand and use the properties of quadrilaterals |
| | 23 | 1 | Assessment ||
| | 24 | | HALF TERM |||
| | 25–26 | 7 | 1.1:10: Coordinates and graphs<br>1.2:10: Coordinates and graphs | 10.1 Coordinates | • understand and use coordinates to locate points. |
| | | | | 10.2 From mappings to graphs | • work out coordinates from a rule<br>• draw a graph for a simple rule |
| | | | | 10.3 Naming graphs | • recognise and draw line graphs of fixed values |
| | | | | 10.2 Graphs from relationships | • draw a graph for a simple relationship |

| | | | | | 10.3 Graphs for fixed values of $x$ and $y$ | • recognise and draw line graphs with fixed values of $x$ and $y$ |
|---|---|---|---|---|---|---|
| | | | | | 10.4 Graphs of the form $y = ax$ | • recognise and draw lines of the form $y = ax$ |
| | | | | | 10.5 Graphs of the form $x + y = a$ | • recognise and draw graphs of the form $x + y = a$ |
| | | | | | 10.4 Graphs from the real world | • learn how graphs can be used to represent real-life situations<br>• draw and use real-life graphs |
| | | 27–28 | 7 | 1.1:11: Percentages<br>1.2:11: Percentages | 11.1 Fractions and percentages | • understand what a percentage is<br>• understand the equivalence between some simple fractions and percentages |
| | | | | | 11.2 Fractions of a quantity | • find a fraction of a quantity |
| | | | | | 11.3 Percentages of a quantity | • find a percentage of a quantity |
| | | | | | 11.4 Percentages with a calculator | • write a percentage as a decimal<br>• use a calculator to find a percentage of a quantity |
| | | | | | 11.5 Percentage increases and decreases | • work out the result of a simple percentage change |
| | | 29–30 | 5 | 1.1:12: Probability<br>1.2:12: Probability | 12.1 Probability words | • learn and use words about probability |
| | | | | | 12.2 Probability scales | • know and use the 0 – 1 probability scale<br>• work out probabilities based on equally likely outcomes |
| | | | | | 12.3 Experimental probability | • learn about and understand experimental probability<br>• understand the difference between theoretical and experimental probability |
| | | 30 | 2 | Assessment and review | | |
| | | 31–32 | | EASTER HOLIDAY | | |
| Term 3 | | 33–34 | 7 | 1.1:13: Symmetry<br>1.2:13: Symmetry | 13.1 Line symmetry | • recognise shapes that have reflective symmetry<br>• draw lines of symmetry on a shape |
| | | | | | 13.2 Rotational symmetry | • recognise shapes that have rotational symmetry<br>• find the order of rotational symmetry for a shape |
| | | | | | 13.3 Reflections | • understand how to reflect a shape<br>• use a coordinate grid to reflect shapes |
| | | | | | 13.4 Tessellations | • understand how to tessellate shapes |
| | | 35–36 | 5 | 1.1:14: Equations<br>1.2:14: Equations | 14.1 Finding unknown numbers | • find missing numbers in simple calculations |
| | | | | | 14.2 Solving equations | • understand what an equation is<br>• solve equations involving one operation |
| | | | | | 14.3 Solving more complex equations | • solve equations involving two operations |
| | | | | | 14.4 Setting up and solving equations | • use algebra to set up and solve equations |
| | | 36–37 | 5 | 1.1:15 Interpreting data<br>1.2:15 interpreting data | 15.1 Pie charts | • read data from pie charts, where the data is given in simple sectors<br>• use a scaling method to draw a pie chart |
| | | | | | 15.2 Comparing data by median and the range | • use the median and range to compare data<br>• make sensible decisions by comparing the median and range of two sets of data |

| | | | | | 15.2 Comparing mean and range | • use the mean and range to compare data<br>• make sensible decisions by comparing the mean and range of two sets of data |
|---|---|---|---|---|---|---|
| | | | | | 15.3 Statistical surveys | • use charts and diagrams to interpret data. |
| | | 37 | 1 | | Assessment | |
| | | 38 | | | HALF TERM | |
| | | 39–40 | 7 | 1.1:16 3D Shapes<br>1.2:16 3D Shapes | 16.1 3D shapes and nets | • know how to count the faces, edges and vertices on a 2D shape<br>• draw nets for 3D shapes |
| | | | | | 16.1 Naming and drawing 3D shapes | • be familiar with the names of 3D shapes and their properties<br>• use isometric paper to draw shapes made from cubes |
| | | | | | 16.2 Using nets to construct 3D shapes | • construct 3D shapes from nets. |
| | | | | | 16.3 3D investigations | • work out the rule connecting faces, edges and vertices in 3D shapes (Euler) |
| | | 41–42 | 7 | 1.1:17 Ratio<br>1.2:17 Ratio | 17.1 Introduction to ratios | • introduce ratio notation<br>• use ratios to compare quantities |
| | | | | | 17.2 Simplifying ratios | • write a ratio as simply as possible |
| | | | | | 17.3 Ratios and sharing | • use ratios to find missing quantities |
| | | | | | 17.4 Ratios and fractions | • understand the connection between ratios and fractions |
| | | 43–44 | 7 | | Extended project opportunity / revision | |
| | | 45 | 4 | | Assessment, revision and review | |
| | | | | | END OF YEAR 7 / SUMMER HOLIDAY | |
| Year 8 | Term 1 | 1–2 | 7 | 2.1:1: Working with numbers<br>2.2:1: Working with numbers | 1.1 Adding and subtracting with negative numbers | • carry out additions and subtractions involving negative numbers |
| | | | | | 1.2 Multiplying and dividing negative numbers | • carry out multiplications and divisions involving negative numbers |
| | | | | | 1.3 Factors and highest common factors (HCF) | • understand and use highest common factors |
| | | | | | 1.4 Multiples and lowest common multiple (LCM) | • understand and use lowest common multiples |
| | | | | | 1.5 Squares, cubes and roots | • understand and use squares and square roots<br>• understand and use cubes and cube roots |
| | | | | | 1.4 Powers and roots | • understand and use powers and roots |
| | | | | | 1.6 Prime factors | • know what prime numbers are<br>• identify the prime factors of a number |
| | | 3–4 | 7 | 2.1:2: Geometry<br>2.2:2: Geometry | 2.1 Parallel and perpendicular lines | • identify parallel lines<br>• identify perpendicular lines |
| | | | | | 2.1 Angles in parallel lines | • calculate angles in parallel lines |
| | | | | | 2.2 Angles in triangles and quadrilaterals | • know that the sum of the angles in a triangle is 180°<br>• know that the sum of the angles in a quadrilateral is 360° |
| | | | | | 2.2 The geometric properties of quadrilaterals | • know the geometric properties of quadrilaterals |

| | | | 2.3 Translations | • know how translate a point or shape |
|---|---|---|---|---|
| | | | 2.4 Rotations | • know how rotate a shape |
| | | | 2.5 Constructions | • construct the mid-point and perpendicular bisector of a line<br>• construct an angle bisector |
| 5–6 | 7 | 2.1:3: Probability<br>2.2:3: Probability | 3.1 Probability scales | • use a probability scale represent a chance |
| | | | 3.2 Collecting data on a frequency table | • collect data and use it find probabilities<br>• decide if an event is fair or biased |
| | | | 3.2 Mutually exclusive events | • recognise mutually exclusive events |
| | | | 3.3 Mixed events | • recognise mixed events where you can distinguish different probabilities |
| | | | 3.3 Using a sample space calculate probabilities | • use a sample space calculate probabilities |
| | | | 3.4 Experimental probability<br>3.5 Experimental probability | • calculate probabilities from experiments |
| 7 | 3 | | Extended project opportunity / revision | |
| 7 | 1 | | Assessment | |
| 8 | | | HALF TERM | |
| 9–10 | 7 | 2.1:4: Percentages<br>2.2:4: Percentages | 4.1 Calculating percentages | • write one percentage as a percentage of another |
| | | | 4.2 Calculating the result of a percentage change<br>4.2 Calculating percentage increases and decreases | • calculate the result of a percentage increase or decrease<br>• use a multiplier calculate a percentage change |
| | | | 4.3 Calculating a percentage change | • work out a change in value as a percentage increase or decrease. |
| 11–12 | 7 | 2.1:5: Sequences<br>2.2:5: Sequences | 5.1 The Fibonacci sequence<br>5.4 The Fibonacci sequence | • know and understand the Fibonacci sequence |
| | | | 5.2 Algebra and function machines | • use algebra with function machines |
| | | | 5.3 The $n$th term of a sequence | • use the $n$th term of a sequence |
| | | | 5.3 Working out the $n$th term of a sequence | • work out the $n$th term of a sequence |
| 13–14 | 7 | 2.1:6: Area<br>2.2:6: Area of 2D and 3D shapes | 6.1 Area of a rectangle | • use a formula work out the area of a rectangle |
| | | | 6.2 Areas of compound shapes | • work out the area of a compound shape |
| | | | 6.3 Area of a triangle | • use a formula work out the area of a triangle |
| | | | 6.4 Area of a parallelogram | • work out the area of a parallelogram |
| | | | 6.3 Area of a trapezium | • work out the area of a trapezium |
| | | | 6.4 Surface areas of cubes and cuboids | • find the surface areas of cubes and cuboids |
| 15 | 3 | | Assessment and review | |
| 16–17 | | | CHRISTMAS HOLIDAY | |

| | | 18–19 | 7 | 2.1:7: Graphs<br>2.2:7: Graphs | 7.1 Rules from coordinates | • recognise patterns with coordinates |
|---|---|---|---|---|---|---|
| | | | | | 7.2 Graphs from rules | • draw graphs of linear rules |
| | | | | | 7.1 Graphs from linear equations | • recognise and draw the graph of a linear equations |
| | | | | | 7.2 Gradient (steepness) of a straight line | • work out the gradient in a graph from a linear equation<br>• work out an equation of the form $y = mx + c$ from the graph |
| | | | | | 7.3 Graphs from simple quadratic equations<br>7.3 Graphs from simple quadratic equations | • recognise and draw the graph from a simple quadratic equation |
| | | | | | 7.4 Distance-time graphs | • read and draw distance-time graphs |
| | | | | | 7.4 Real-life graphs | • draw graphs from real-life situations illustrate the relationship between two variables |
| | Term 2 | 20–21 | 7 | 2.1:8: Simplifying numbers<br>2.2:8: Simplifying numbers | 8.1 Powers of 10 | • multiply and divide by 100 and 1000 |
| | | | | | 8.2 Large numbers and rounding | • round large numbers |
| | | | | | 8.3 Significant figures | • round one significant figure |
| | | | | | 8.4 Estimating answers | • use rounding estimate rough answers calculations |
| | | | | | 8.5 Problem solving with decimals | • solve problems involving decimals |
| | | | | | 8.4 Standard form with large numbers | • write a large number in standard form |
| | | | | | 8.5 Multiplying with numbers in standard form | • multiply with numbers in standard form |
| | | 22–23 | 6 | 2.1:9: Interpreting data<br>2.2:9: Interpreting data | 9.1 Information from charts | • revise reading from charts and tables |
| | | | | | 9.2 Reading pie charts | • interpret a pie chart |
| | | | | | 9.3 Creating pie charts | • use a scaling method draw pie charts |
| | | | | | 9.3 Scatter graphs and correlation | • read scatter graphs<br>◦ understand correlations |
| | | | | | 9.4 Creating scatter graphs | • create scatter graphs |
| | | 23 | 1 | Assessment | | |
| | | 24 | | HALF TERM | | |
| | | 25–27 | 10 | 2.1:10: Algebra<br>2.2:10: Algebra | 10.1 Algebraic notation | • simplify algebraic expressions involving the four basic operations |
| | | | | | 10.2 Like terms | • simplify algebraic expression by combining like terms |
| | | | | | 10.3 Expanding brackets | • remove brackets from an expression |
| | | | | | 10.4 Using algebra<br>10.4 Using algebraic expressions | • use algebraic expressions in different contexts<br>• manipulate algebraic expressions<br>• identify equivalent expressions |
| | | | | | 10.5 Using powers<br>10.5 Using index notation | • write algebraic expressions involving powers |
| | | 28–29 | 7 | 2.1:11: Congruence and | 11.1 Congruent shapes | • recognise congruent shapes |

| | | | | | 11.2 Shape and ratio | • use ratio compare lengths and areas of 2D shapes |
|---|---|---|---|---|---|---|---|
| | | | | | 11.2 Enlargements | • enlarge a 2D shape by a scale factor |
| | | | | | 11.3 Scale diagrams 11.4 Scales | • understand and use scale diagrams • know how use map ratios |
| | | 30 | 3 | | Revision | |
| | | 30 | 1 | | Assessment and review | |
| | | 31–32 | | | EASTER HOLIDAY | |
| | | 33–35 | 9 | 2.1:12: Fractions and decimals 2.2:12: Fractions and decimals | 12.1 Adding and subtracting fractions | • add and subtract fractions and mixed numbers |
| | | | | | 12.2 Multiplying fractions and integers | • multiply by a fraction or a mixed number by an integer |
| | | | | | 12.3 Dividing with integers and fractions | • divide a unit fraction by an integer • divide an integer by a unit fraction |
| | | | | | 12.4 Multiplication with powers of ten 12.4 Multiplication with large and small numbers | • multiply by a power of ten • multiply with combinations of large and small numbers mentally |
| | | | | | 12.5 Division with powers of ten 12.5 Division with large and small numbers | • mentally divide by a power of ten • divide combinations of large and small numbers mentally |
| Term 3 | | 35–36 | 4 | 2.1:13: Proportion 2.2:13: Proportion | 13.1 Direct proportion | • understand the meaning of direct proportion • find missing values in problems involving proportion |
| | | | | | 13.2 Graphs and direct proportion | • represent direct proportion graphically and algebraically |
| | | | | | 13.3 Inverse proportion | • understand what is meant by inverse proportion • solve problems using inverse proportion |
| | | | | | 13.4 Comparing direct proportion and inverse proportion | • recognise direct and inverse proportion and work out missing values |
| | | 37 | 4 | 2.1:14: Circles 2.2:14: Circles | 14.1 The circle and its parts | • know the definition of a circle and the names of its parts |
| | | | | | 14.2 Circumference of a circle | • work out the relationship between the circumference and the diameter of a circle |
| | | | | | 14.3 A formula work out the approximate circumference of a circle 14.3 Formula for the circumference of a circle | • use a formula calculate the circumference of a circle |
| | | | | | 14.4 Formula for the area of a circle | • use a formula calculate the area of a circle |
| | | 37 | 1 | | Assessment | |
| | | 38 | | | HALF TERM | |
| | | 39–40 | 7 | 2.1:15: Equations and formulae 2.2:15: Equations and formulae | 15.1 Equations | • solve simple equations |
| | | | | | 15.2 Equations with brackets | • solve equations that include brackets |
| | | | | | 15.2 Equations with the variable on both sides | • solve equations with the variable on both sides |

| | | Week | Hrs | Spec reference | Section | Learning objectives |
|---|---|---|---|---|---|---|
| | | | | | 15.3 More complex equations | • solve equations involving two operations |
| | | | | | 15.4 Substituting informulae | • substitute values ina variety of formulae |
| | | | | | 15.4 Rearranging formulae | • change the subject of a formula |
| | | 41–42 | 7 | 2.1: 16: Comparing data 2.2:16: Comparing data | 16.1 Frequency tables | • create a frequency table from raw data |
| | | | | | 16.2 The mean | • understand and use the mean average of data |
| | | | | | 16.1 Grouped frequency tables | • create a grouped frequency table from raw data |
| | | | | | 16.3 Drawing frequency diagrams | • be able draw a diagram from a frequency table |
| | | | | | 16.4 Comparing data | • use the mean and range compare data from two sources |
| | | | | | 16.5 Which average use? | • understand when each different type of average is most useful |
| | | 43–44 | 7 | Extended project opportunity / revision | | |
| | | 45 | 4 | Assessment, revision and review | | |
| | | END OF YEAR 8 / SUMMER HOLIDAY | | | | |
| Year 9 | Term 1 | 1–2 | 7 | 3.1:1: Percentages 3.2:1: Percentages | 1.1 Simple interest | • understand what simple interest is<br>• solve problems involving simple interest |
| | | | | | 1.2 Percentage increases and decreases | • calculate the result of a percentage increase or decrease<br>• choose the most appropriate method calculate percentage change |
| | | | | | 1.3 Calculating the original value | • Given the result of a percentage change, calculate the original value |
| | | | | | 1.4 Using percentages | • make links between fractions, decimals and percentages<br>• choose the correct calculation work out a percentage |
| | | 3–4 | 7 | 3.1:2: Equations and formulae 3.2:2: Equations and formulae | 2.1 Multiplying out brackets | • multiply out brackets |
| | | | | | 2.2 Factorising algebraic expressions | • factorise expressions |
| | | | | | 2.3 Equations with brackets | • solve equations with one or more sets of brackets |
| | | | | | 2.4 Equations with fractions | • solve equations with fractions |
| | | | | | 2.5 Rearranging formulae | • change the subject of a formula |
| | | 5–6 | 5 | 3.1:3: Polygons 3.2:3: Polygons | 3.1 Polygons | • know the names of polygons<br>• know the difference between an irregular and a regular polygon |
| | | | | | 3.2 Angles in polygons | • work out the sizes of the interior angles of regular polygons |
| | | | | | 3.2 Constructions | • make accurate geometric constructions |
| | | | | | 3.3 Angles in regular polygons | • work out the exterior and interior angles of a regular polygon |
| | | | | | 3.4 Regular polygons and tessellations | • work out which regular polygons tessellate |
| | | 6–7 | 5 | 3.1:4: Using data 3.2:4: Using data | 4.1 Scatter graphs and correlation | • infer a correlation from two related scatter graphs |
| | | | | | 4.2 Interpreting graphs and diagrams | • use and interpret a variety of graphs and diagrams |
| | | | | | 4.2 Time-series graphs | • use and interpret a variety of time-series graphs |

| | | | | | 4.3 Two-way tables | • interpret a variety of two-way tables |
|---|---|---|---|---|---|---|
| | | | | | 4.4 Comparing two or more sets of data | • compare two sets of data from statistical diagrams |
| | | | | | 4.5 Statistical investigations | • plan a statistical investigation |
| | | 7 | 1 | | Assessment | |
| | | 8 | | | HALF TERM | |
| | | 9–10 | 6 | 3.1:5: Circles | 5.1 The formula for the circumference of a circle | • calculate the circumference of a circle |
| | | | | | 5.2 The formula for the area of a circle | • calculate the area of a circle |
| | | | | | 5.3 Mixed problems | • solve problems involving the circumference and area of a circle |
| | | 10–11 | 5 | 3.2:5: Applications of graphs | 5.1 Step graphs | • interpret step graphs |
| | | | | | 5.2 Time graphs | • interpret and draw time graphs |
| | | | | | 5.3 Exponential growth graphs | • interpret and draw exponential growth graphs |
| | | 12–13 | 7 | 3.2:6: Pythagoras' theorem | 6.1 Introducing Pythagoras' theorem | • understand Pythagoras' theorem |
| | | | | | 6.2 Calculating the length of the hypotenuse | • calculate the length of the hypotenuse in a right-angled triangle |
| | | | | | 6.3 Calculating the length of a shorter side | • calculate the length of a shorter side in a right-angled triangle<br>• show that a triangle is right-angled |
| | | | | | 6.4 Using Pythagoras' theorem solve problems | • use Pythagoras' theorem solve problems |
| | | 14 | 3 | 3.1: 6: Enlargements | 6.1 Scale factors and enlargements | • use a scale factor show an enlargement |
| | | | | | 6.2 The centre of enlargement | • enlarge a shape around a centre of enlargement |
| | | | | | 6.3 Enlargements on grids | • enlarge a shape on a coordinate grid |
| | | 15 | 3 | | Assessment and review | |
| | | 16–17 | | | CHRISTMAS HOLIDAY | |
| | Term 2 | 18–19 | 7 | 3.1:7 Fractions<br>3.2:7 Fractions | 7.1 Adding and subtracting fractions | • add or subtract any two fractions |
| | | | | | 7.2 Multiplying fractions | • multiply two fractions |
| | | | | | 7.3 Multiplying mixed numbers | • multiply one mixed number by another |
| | | | | | 7.3 Dividing fractions<br>7.4 Dividing fractions and mixed numbers | • divide one fraction or mixed number by another |
| | | 20–21 | 7 | 3.1:8 Algebra<br>3.2:8: Algebra | 8.1 Expanding brackets<br>8.1 More about brackets | • multiply out brackets with a variable or constant outside them |
| | | | | | 8.2 Factorising algebraic expressions<br>8.2 Factorising expressions containing powers | • factorise expressions<br>• take out a variable as a factor |
| | | | | | 8.3 Expand and simplify<br>8.3 Expanding the product of two brackets | • expand expressions with two brackets and simplify them |
| | | 22–23 | 6 | 3.1:9: Decimal numbers | 9.1 Multiplication of decimals | • multiply decimal numbers |

| | | | | 9.2 Powers of ten | • understand and work with both positive and negative powers of ten |
|---|---|---|---|---|---|
| | | | | 9.2 Standard form | • understand and work with standard form, using both positive and negative powers of ten |
| | | | | 9.3 Rounding suitably<br>9.3 Rounding appropriately | • round numbers a suitable or appropriate degree of accuracy |
| | | | | 9.4 Dividing decimals | • divide with decimals |
| | | | | 9.4 Mental calculations | • learn and understand some routines that can be used when calculating mentally |
| | | | | 9.5 Solving problems | • solve real-life problems involving multiplication or division |
| 23 | 1 | | Assessment | | |
| 24 | | | HALF TERM | | |
| 25–26 | 7 | 3.1:10: Surface area and volume of 3D shapes | 10.1 Surface areas of cubes and cuboids | • work out the surface areas of cubes or cuboids | |
| | | | 10.2 Volume formulae for cubes and cuboids | • use a simple formula work out the volume of a cube or cuboid | |
| | | | 10.3 Volumes of triangular prisms | • work out the volume of a triangular prism | |
| 27–28 | 6 | 3.2:10: Prisms and cylinders | 10.1 Metric units for area and volume | • convert from one metric unit another | |
| | | | 10.2 Volume of a prism | • calculate the volume of a prism | |
| | | | 10.3 Surface area of a prism | • calculate the surface area of a prism | |
| | | | 10.4 Volume of a cylinder | • calculate the volume of a cylinder | |
| | | | 10.5 Surface area of a cylinder | • calculate the curved surface area of a cylinder<br>• calculate the total surface area of a cylinder | |
| 28–30 | 6 | 3.1:11: Solving equations graphically<br>3.2:11: Solving equations graphically | 11.1 Graphs from equations in the form $y = mx + c$ | • draw a linear graph from any linear equation<br>• solve a linear equation from a graph | |
| | | | 11.2 Problems involving straight-line graphs | • draw graphs solve some problems | |
| | | | 11.1 Graphs from equations in the form $ay \pm bx = c$ | • draw any linear graph from any linear equation<br>• solve a linear equation from a graph | |
| | | | 11.2 Graphs from quadratic equations | • draw graphs from quadratic equations | |
| | | | 11.3 Solving simple quadratic equations by drawing graphs<br>11.3 Solving quadratic equations by drawing graphs | • solve a quadratic equation by drawing a graph | |
| | | | 11.4 Problems involving quadratic graphs | • solve problems that use quadratic graphs | |
| | | | 11.4 Solving simultaneous equations by graphs | • solve a pair of simultaneous equations graphically | |
| 30 | 2 | | Assessment and review | | |
| 31–32 | | | EASTER HOLIDAY | | |

| | | 33–34 | 7 | 3.1:12 Distance, speed and time | 12.1 Distance | • work out the distance travelled in a certain time at a given speed<br>• use and interpret distance-time graphs |
|---|---|---|---|---|---|---|
| | | | | | 12.2 Speed | • work out the speed of an object, given the distance travelled and the time taken |
| | | | | | 12.3 Time | • work out the time an object will take on its journey, given its speed and the distance travelled |
| | | 35–36 | 5 | 3.2:12: Compound units | 12.1 Speed | • understand and use measures of speed |
| | | | | | 12.2 More about proportion | • understand and use density and other compound measures |
| | | | | | 12.3 Unit costs | • understand and use unit pricing |
| | | 36–37 | 5 | 3.1:13: Similar triangles | 13.1 Similar triangles | • understand what similar triangles are |
| | | | | | 13.2 A summary of similar triangles | • use and recall facts about similar triangles |
| | | | | | 13.3 Using triangles solve problems | • know that triangles can be used solve some real-life problems |
| | Term 3 | 37 | 1 | Assessment | | |
| | | 38 | | HALF TERM | | |
| | | 39–40 | 7 | 3.2:13 Right-angled triangles | 13.1 Introducing trigonometric ratios | • understand what trigonometric ratios are |
| | | | | | 13.2 How find trigonometric ratios of angles | • understand what the trigonometric ratios sine, cosine and tangent are |
| | | | | | 13.3 Using trigonometric ratios find angles | • find the angle identified from a trigonometric ratio |
| | | | | | 13.4 Using trigonometric ratios find lengths | • find an unknown length of a right-angled triangle, give one side and another angle |
| | | 41–42 | 7 | 3.1:14: Revision and GCSE preparation<br>3.2:14: Revision and GCSE preparation | Practice | • practise topics covered in this course |
| | | | | | Revision | • revise topics covered in this course |
| | | | | | GCSE-type questions | • be introduced the GCSE course |
| | | 43–44 | 7 | Extended project | | |
| | | 45 | 4 | Assessment, revision and review | | |
| | | END OF YEAR 9 / SUMMER HOLIDAY | | | | |
| Year 10 | Term 1 | 1–3 | 10 | F:1: Number: Basic Number | 1.1 Place value and ordering numbers | • use a number line represent negative numbers<br>• use inequalities with negative numbers<br>• compare and order positive and negative numbers |
| | | | | | 1.2 Order of operations and BIDMAS | • work out the answers problems with more than one mathematical operation |
| | | | | | 1.3 The four rules | • use the four rules of arithmetic with integers and decimals |
| | | 4–6 | 10 | F:2: Geometry and measures: Measures and scale drawings | 2.1 Systems of measurement | • convert from one metric unit another<br>• convert from one imperial unit another |
| | | | | | 2.2 Conversion factors | • use approximate conversion factors change between imperial units and |

| | | | | 2.3 Scale drawings | • read and draw scale drawings<br>• use a scale drawing make estimates |
|---|---|---|---|---|---|
| | | | | 2.4 Nets | • draw nets of some 3D shapes<br>• identify a 3D shape from its net |
| | | | | 2.5 Using an isometric grid | • read from and draw on isometric grids<br>• interpret diagrams draw plans and elevations |
| | 7 | 3 | F:3: Statistics: Charts, tables and averages | 3.1 Frequency tables | • use tally charts and frequency tables collect and represent data<br>• use grouped frequency tables collect and represent data |
| | | | | 3.2 Statistical diagrams | • draw pictograms represent statistical data<br>• draw bar charts and vertical line charts represent statistical data |
| | 8 | | HALF TERM | | |
| | 9 | 4 | F:3: Statistics: Charts, tables and averages | 3.3 Line graphs | • draw a line graph show trends in data |
| | | | | 3.4 Statistical averages | • work out the mode, median, mean and range of small sets of data<br>• decide which is the best average use represent a data set |
| | 10–12 | 10 | F:4:Geometry and measures: Angles | 4.1 Angles facts | • calculate angles on a straight line<br>• calculate angles around a point<br>• use vertically opposite angles |
| | | | | 4.2 Triangles | • recognise and calculate the angles in different sorts of triangle |
| | | | | 4.3 Angles in a polygon | • calculate the sum of the interior angles in a polygon |
| | | | | 4.4 Regular polygons | • calculate the exterior angles and the interior angles of a regular polygon |
| | | | | 4.5 Angles in parallel lines | • calculate angles in parallel lines |
| | | | | 4.6 Special quadrilaterals | • use angle properties in quadrilaterals |
| | | | | 4.7 Bearings | • use a bearing specify a direction |
| | 13–15 | 10 | F:5: Number: Number properties | 5.1 Multiples of whole numbers | • find multiples of whole numbers<br>• recognise multiples of numbers |
| | | | | 5.2 Factors of whole numbers | • identify the factors of a number |
| | | | | 5.3 Prime numbers | • identify prime numbers |
| | | | | 5.4 Prime factors, LCM and HCF | • identify prime factors<br>• identify the lowest common multiple (LCM) of two numbers<br>• identify the highest common factor (HCF) of two numbers |
| | | | | 5.5 Square numbers | • identify square numbers<br>• use a calculator find the square of a number |
| | | | | 5.6 Square roots | • recognise the square roots of square numbers up 225<br>• use a calculator find the square roots of any number |
| | | | | 5.7 Basic calculations on a calculator | • use some of the important keys when working on a calculator |
| | 16–17 | | CHRISTMAS HOLIDAY | | |
| | 18–19 | 7 | F:6: Number: Approximations | 6.1 Rounding whole numbers | • round a whole number |

| | | | | | 6.2 Rounding decimals | • round decimal numbers a given accuracy |
|---|---|---|---|---|---|---|---|
| | | | | | 6.3 Approximating calculations | • identify significant figures<br>• round numbers a given number of significant figures<br>• use approximation estimate answers and check calculations<br>• round a calculation at the end of a problem, give what is considered be a sensible answer |
| | | | 20–21 | 7 | F:7: Number: Decimals and fractions | 7.1 Calculating with decimals | • multiply and divide with decimals |
| | | | | | | 7.2 Fractions and reciprocals | • recognise different types of fraction, reciprocal, terminating decimal and recurring decimal<br>• convert terminating decimals fractions<br>• convert fractions decimals<br>• find reciprocals of numbers or fractions |
| | | | | | | 7.3 Writing one quantity as a fraction of another | • work out a fraction of a quantity<br>• find one quantity as a fraction of another |
| | | | | | | 7.4 Adding and subtracting fractions | • add and subtract fractions with different denominators |
| | | | | | | 7.5 Multiplying and dividing fractions | • multiply proper fractions<br>• multiply mixed numbers<br>• divide by fractions |
| | | | | | | 7.6 Fractions on a calculator | • use a calculator add and subtract fractions<br>• use a calculator multiply and divide fractions |
| | | | 22–23 | 7 | F:8: Algebra: Linear graphs | 8.1 Graphs and equations | • use flow diagrams draw graphs<br>• work out the equations of horizontal and vertical lines |
| | | | | | | 8.2 Drawing linear graphs by finding points | • draw linear graphs without using flow diagrams |
| | | | | | | 8.3 Gradient of a line | • work out the gradient of a straight line<br>• draw a line with a certain gradient |
| | | | | | | 8.4 $y = mx + c$ | • draw graphs using the gradient-intercept method<br>• draw graphs using the cover-up method |
| | | | | | | 8.5 Finding the equation of a line from its graph | • work out the equation of a line, using its gradient and y-intercept<br>• work out the equation of a line given two points on the line |
| | | | | | | 8.6 The equation of a parallel line | • work out the equation of a linear graph that is parallel another line and passes through a specific point |
| | | | 24 | | | HALF TERM | |
| | | | 25 | 4 | F:8: Algebra: Linear graphs | 8.7 Real-life uses of graphs | • convert from one unit another unit by using a conversion graph<br>• use straight-line graphs work out formulae |
| | | | | | | 8.8 Solving simultaneous equations using graphs | • solve simultaneous linear equations using graphs |
| | | | 26–28 | 10 | F:9: Algebra: Expressions and formulae | 9.1 Basic algebra | • write an algebraic expression<br>• recognise expressions, equations, formulae and identities |

| | | | | 9.2 Substitution | • substitute into, simplify and use algebraic expressions |
|---|---|---|---|---|---|
| | | | | 9.3 Expanding brackets | • expand brackets such as $2(x-3)$<br>• expand and simplify brackets |
| | | | | 9.4 Factorisation | • factorise an algebraic expression |
| | | | | 9.5 Quadratic expansion | • expand two linear brackets obtain a quadratic expression |
| | | | | 9.6 Quadratic factorisation | • factorise a quadratic expression of the form $x^2 + ax + b$ intwo linear brackets |
| | | | | 9.7 Changing the subject of a formula | • change the subject of a formula |
| | 29–30 | 7 | F:10: Ratio and proportion and rates of change: Ratio, speed and proportion | 10.1 Ratio | • simplify a ratio<br>• express a ratio as a fraction<br>• divide amounts ingiven ratios<br>• complete calculations from a given ratio and partial information |
| | | | | 10.2 Speed, distance and time | • recognise the relationship between speed, distance and time<br>• calculate average speed from distance and time<br>• calculate distance travelled from the speed and the time taken<br>• calculate the time taken on a journey from the speed and the distance |
| | | | | 10.3 Direct proportion problems | • recognise and solve problems that involve direct proportion |
| | | | | 10.4 Best buys | • find the cost per unit mass<br>• find the mass per unit cost<br>• use the above find which product is better value. |
| | 31–32 | | | EASTER HOLIDAY | |
| Term 3 | 33–34 | 7 | F:11: Geometry and measures: Perimeter and area | 11.1 Rectangles | • calculate the perimeter and area of a rectangle |
| | | | | 11.2 Compound shapes | • calculate the perimeter and area of a compound shape made from rectangles |
| | | | | 11.3 Area of a triangle | • calculate the area of a triangle<br>• use the formula for the area of a triangle |
| | | | | 11.4 Area of a parallelogram | • calculate the area of a parallelogram<br>• use the formula for the area of a parallelogram |
| | | | | 11.5 Area of a trapezium | • calculate the area of a trapezium<br>• use the formula for the area of a trapezium |
| | | | | 11.6 Circles | • recognise terms used for circle work calculate the circumference of a circle |
| | | | | 11.7 The area of a circle | • calculate the area of a circle |
| | | | | 11.8 Answers in terms of π | • give answers for circle calculations in terms of ð |
| | 35–36 | 7 | F:12:Geometry and measures: Transformations | 12.1 Rotational symmetry | • work out the order of rotational symmetry for a 2D shape<br>• recognise shapes with rotational symmetry |
| | | | | 12.2 Translation | • translate a 2D shape |
| | | | | 12.3 Reflections | • reflect a 2D shape in a mirror line |
| | | | | 12.4 Rotations | • rotate a 2D shape about a point |
| | | | | 12.5 Enlargements | • enlarge a 2D shape by a scale |

| | | | | | | | |
|---|---|---|---|---|---|---|---|
| | | | | | | | factor |
| | | | | | 12.6 Using more than one transformation | • | use more than one transformation |
| | | | | | 12.7 Vectors | •<br>• | represent vectors<br>add and subtract vectors |
| | | 37 | 3 | F:13: Probability: Probability and events | 13.1 Calculating probabilities | •<br><br>• | use the probability scale and the language of probability<br>calculate the probability of an outcome of an event |
| | | | | | 13.2 Probability that an outcome will not happen | • | calculate the probability of an outcome not happening when you know the probability of that outcome happening |
| | | | | | 13.3 Mutually exclusive and exhaustive outcomes | • | recognise mutually exclusive and exhaustive outcomes |
| | | 38 | | | HALF TERM | | |
| | | 39 | 4 | F:13: Probability: Probability and events | 13.4 Experimental probability | •<br><br><br>• | calculate experimental probabilities and relative frequencies from experiments<br>recognise different methods for estimating probabilities |
| | | | | | 13.5 Expectation | • | predict the likely number of successful outcomes, given the number of trials and the probability of any one outcome |
| | | | | | 13.6 Choices and outcomes | • | apply systematic listing and counting strategies identify all outcomes for a variety of problems |
| | | 40 | 3 | F:14:Geometry and measures: Volumes and surface areas of prisms | 14.1 3D shapes | • | use the correct terms when working with 3D shapes |
| | | | | | 14.2 Volume and surface area of a cuboid | • | calculate the surface area and volume of a cuboid |
| | | 41–42 | 7 | | Summer examinations and revision | | |
| | | 43 | 4 | F:14:Geometry and measures: Volumes and surface areas of prisms | 14.3 Volume and surface area of a prism | • | calculate the volume and surface area of a prism |
| | | | | | 14.4 Volume and surface area of cylinders | • | calculate the volume and surface area of a cylinder |
| | | 44–45 | 7 | F:15: Algebra: Linear equations | 15.1 Solving linear equations | •<br>•<br>•<br>•<br><br>•<br>• | solve linear equations such as<br>$3x - 1 = 11$ where the variable only<br>appears on one side<br>use inverse operations and inverse flow diagrams<br>solve equations by balancing<br>solve equations in which the variable (the letter) appears in the numerator of a fraction |
| | | | | | 15.2 Solving equations with brackets | • | solve equations where you have first expand brackets |
| | | | | | 15.3 Solving equations with the variable on both sides | • | solve equations where the variable appears on both sides of the equals sign. |
| | | | | | END OF YEAR 10 / SUMMER HOLIDAY | | |
| Year 11 | Term 1 | 1–2 | 7 | F:16: Ratio and proportion and rates of change: Percentages and | 16.1 Equivalent percentages, fractions and decimals | • | convert percentages fractions and decimals and vice versa |

| | | | | 16.2 Calculating a percentage of a quantity | • calculate a percentage of a quantity |
|---|---|---|---|---|---|
| | | | | 16.3 Increasing and decreasing quantities by a percentage | • increase and decrease quantities by a percentage |
| | | | | 16.4 Expressing one quantity as a percentage of another | • express one quantity as a percentage of another<br>• work out percentage change |
| | | | | 16.5 Compound measures | • recognise and solve problems involving the compound measures of rates of pay, density and pressure |
| 3–4 | 7 | F:17: Ratio and proportion and rates of change: Percentages and variation | 17.1 Compound interest and repeated percentage change | • calculate simple interest<br>• calculate compound interest<br>• solve problems involving repeated percentage change |
| | | | 17.2 Reverse percentage (working out the original value) | • calculate the original amount, given the final amount, after a known percentage increase or decrease |
| | | | 17.3 Direct proportion | • solve problems in which two variables have a directly proportional relationship (direct variation)<br>• work out the constant of proportionality<br>• recognise graphs that show direct variation |
| | | | 17.4 Inverse proportion | • solve problems in which two variables have an inversely proportional relationship (inverse variation)<br>• work out the constant of proportionality |
| 5–7 | 10 | F:18: Statistics: Representation and interpretation | 18.1 Sampling | • obtain a random sample from a population<br>• collect unbiased and reliable data for a sample |
| | | | 18.2 Pie charts | • draw and interpret pie charts. |
| | | | 18.3 Scatter diagrams | • draw, interpret and use scatter diagrams<br>• draw and use a line of best fit |
| | | | 18.4 grouped data and averages | • identify the modal group<br>• calculate an estimate of the mean from a grouped table |
| 8 | | HALF TERM | | | |
| 9–10 | 7 | F:19: Geometry and measures : Constructions and loci | 19.1 Constructing triangles | • construct accurate drawings of triangles, using a pair of compasses, a protractor and a straight edge |
| | | | 19.2 Bisectors | • construct the bisectors of lines and angles<br>• construct angles of 60° and 90° |
| | | | 19.3 Defining a locus | • draw a locus for a given rule |
| | | | 19.4 Loci problems | • solve practical problems using loci |
| 11–12 | 7 | F:20: Geometry and measures: Curved shapes and pyramids | 20.1 Sectors | • calculate the length of an arc<br>• calculate the area and angle of a sector |
| | | | 20.2 Pyramids | • calculate the volume and surface |

| | | | | | area of a pyramid |
|---|---|---|---|---|---|
| | | | | 20.3 Cones | • calculate the volume and surface area of a cone |
| | | | | 20.4 Spheres | • calculate the volume and surface area of a sphere |
| | | 13 | 3 | Revision and review | |
| | | 14–15 | 7 | Mock Exams and Revision | |
| | | 16–17 | | CHRISTMAS HOLIDAY | |
| | Term 2 | 18–19 | 7 | F:21: Algebra: Number and Sequences | 21.1 Patterns in number | • recognise patterns in number sequences |
| | | | | | 21.2 Number sequences | • recognise how number sequences are built up<br>• generate sequences, given the nth term |
| | | | | | 21.3 Finding the *n*th term of a linear sequence | • find the nth term of a linear sequence |
| | | | | | 21.4 Special sequences | • recognise and continue some special number sequences<br>• understand how prime, odd and even numbers interact in addition, subtraction and multiplication problems |
| | | | | | 2.5 General rules from given patterns | • find the nth term from practical problems involving sequences. |
| | | 20–22 | 10 | F:22: Geometry and measures: Right-angled triangles | 22.1 Pythagoras' theorem | • know what Pythagoras' theorem is<br>• calculate the length of the hypotenuse in a right-angled triangle |
| | | | | | 22.2 Calculating the length of the shorter side | • calculate the length of a shorter side in a right-angled triangle |
| | | | | | 22.3 Applying Pythagoras' theorem in real-life situations | • solve problems using Pythagoras' theorem |
| | | | | | 22.4 Pythagoras' theorem and isosceles triangles | • use Pythagoras' theorem in isosceles triangles |
| | | | | | 22.5 Trigonometric ratios | • define, understand and use the three trigonometric ratios |
| | | | | | 22.6 Calculating lengths using trigonometry | • use trigonometric ratios calculate a length in a right-angled triangle |
| | | | | | 22.7 Calculating angles using trigonometry | • use the trigonometric ratios calculate an angle |
| | | | | | 22.8 Trigonometry without a calculator | • work out and remember trigonometric values for angles of 30°, 45°, 60° and 90° |
| | | | | | 22.9 Solving problems using trigonometry | • solve practical problems using trigonometry<br>• solve problems using an angle of elevation or an angle of depression |
| | | | | | 22.10 Trigonometry and bearings | • solve bearing problems using trigonometry |
| | | | | | 22.11 Trigonometry and isosceles triangles | • use trigonometry solve problems involving isosceles triangles |
| | | 23 | | HALF TERM | |
| | | 24–25 | 7 | F:23: Geometry and measures: Congruency and similarity | 23.1 Congruent triangles | • demonstrate that two triangles are congruent |
| | | | | | 23.2 Similarity | • recognise similarity in any two shapes<br>• show that two shapes are similar |

| | | | | | • | work out the scale factor between similar shapes |
|---|---|---|---|---|---|---|
| | 26–27 | 7 | F:24: Probability: Combined events | 24.1 Combined events | • | work out the probabilities when two or more events occur at the same time |
| | | | | 24.2 Two-way tables | • | read two-way tables and use them work out probabilities |
| | | | | 24.3 Probability and Venn diagrams | • | use Venn diagrams solve probability questions |
| | | | | 24.2 Tree diagrams | • • | understand frequency tree diagrams and probability tree diagrams <br> use probability tree diagrams work out the probabilities involved in combined events |
| | 28–29 | 7 | F:25: Number: Powers and standard form | 25.1 Powers (indices) | • • • | write a number as a power of another number <br> use powers (also known as indices) <br> multiply and divide by powers of 10. |
| | | | | 25.2 Rules for multiplying and dividing powers | • • | use rules for multiplying and dividing powers <br> multiply and divide numbers by powers of 10. |
| | 30–31 | | EASTER HOLIDAY | | | |
| Term 3 | 32 | 4 | F:25: Number: Powers and standard form | 25.3 Standard form | • • | write a number in standard form <br> calculate with numbers in standard form |
| | 33–35 | 11 | F:26: Algebra: Simultaneous equations and linear inequalities | 26.1 Elimination method for simultaneous equations | • | solve simultaneous linear equations in two variables using the elimination method |
| | | | | 26.2 Substitution method for simultaneous equations | • | solve simultaneous linear equations in two variables using the substitution method |
| | | | | 26.3 Balancing coefficients solve simultaneous equations | • | solve simultaneous linear equations by balancing coefficients |
| | | | | 26.4 Using simultaneous equations solve problems | • | solve problems using simultaneous linear equations |
| | | | | 26.5 Linear inequalities | • | solve a simple linear inequality and represent it on a number line |
| | 36–37 | 7 | F:27: Algebra: Non-linear graphs | 27.1 Distance-time graphs | • • | interpret distance–time graphs <br> draw a graph of the depth of liquid as a container is filled |
| | | | | 27.2 Plotting quadratic graphs | • | draw and read values from quadratic graphs |
| | | | | 27.3 Solving quadratic equations by factorisation | • | solve a quadratic equation by factorisation |
| | | | | 27.4 The significant points of a quadratic curve | • • • | identify the significant points of a quadratic function graphically <br> identify the roots of a quadratic function by solving a quadratic equation <br> identify the turning point of a quadratic function |
| | | | | 27.5 Cubic and reciprocal graphs | • | recognise and plot cubic and reciprocal graphs |
| | 38 | | HALF-TERM HOLIDAY | | | |
| | 39–40 | | Revision | | | |
| | 41–42 | | June Examinations | | | |
| | | | SUMMER HOLIDAY / END OF COURSE | | | |

# Chapter 1 Number: Basic number

## Overview

| | |
|---|---|
| **1.1** Place value and order numbers | **1.3** The four rules |
| **1.2** Order of operations and BIDMAS | |

---

**Prior learning**

Know the multiplication tables up to 12 × 12 and associated division facts.
Know squares of numbers, up to 15 × 15 = 225 and the square roots of the square numbers up to 225.
Know the addition and subtraction of numbers less than 20.
Know how to multiply numbers by 10 and 100.
Know what a fraction and a negative number represent.

**Learning objectives**

**By the end of this chapter, ensure that students can: compare and order positive and negative numbers; use the order of operations when calculating; add, subtract, multiply and divide positive and negative integers and positive decimals without a calculator.**

In the examination, students will be expected to:
- use a number line to represent negative numbers
- use inequalities with negative numbers
- compare and order positive and negative numbers
- work out to rules of arithmetic with integers and decimals.

**Extension**

Ask students to write problem-solving questions based on real-life situations.

## Curriculum references

| Section | GCSE specification |
|---|---|
| 1.1 | N1 |
| 1.2 | N2, 3 |
| 1.3 | N2, 3 |

## Route mapping

| Exercise | Accessible | Intermediate | Challenging | AO1 | AO2 MR CM | AO3 PS EV | Key questions |
|---|---|---|---|---|---|---|---|
| 1A | 1–13 | 14 | | 1–3, 8, 10 | 7, 9, 11–13 | 4–6, 14 | 4, 6, 12, 14 |
| 1B | 1–16 | | | 1–6, 9, 14 | 7, 8, 10, 13, 16 | 11, 12, 15 | 1, 2, 4, 11, 12 |
| 1C | 1–16 | | | 1–5, 9–11, 14, 15 | 16 | 6–8, 12, 13 | 3, 9, 10, 11 |
| 1D | 1–7 | | | 1–3, 5 | 4 | 6, 7 | 2, 3, 5 |
| 1E | 1–16 | 17 | | 1–10 | 11–13 | 14–17 | 2, 10, 13 |
| 1F | 1–12 | 13 | | 1, 2, 5–7, 10, 11a, b, 13 | 3, 4, 11c, 12 | 8, 9 | 2, 10, 12 |
| 1G | 1–7 | | | 1, 2, 4 | 3, 7 | 5, 6 | 1, 5, 6 |
| 1H | 1–8 | 9 | | 1–3, 7 | 6, 9 | 4, 5, 8 | 1, 4, 5 |
| 1I | 1–5 | | | 1, 2, 4 | | 3, 5 | 1, 2 |

*Key questions are those that demonstrate mastery of the concept, or which require a step-up in understanding or application. Key questions could be used to identify the questions that students must tackle, to support differentiation, or to identify the questions that should be teacher-marked rather than student-marked.*

## About this chapter

**Making connections**: This chapter teaches students how to explain an easy way to do multiplications and divisions mentally, and why the knowledge of factors will help them with this. It also teaches students why we use brackets in some calculations, and the advantages of using inequality signs.

**Relevance**: Linking questions into real-life problems involving the four rules, including negative numbers.

**Working mathematically**: Students question what to look for when deciding if they can do a calculation mentally. Students explain the steps of the calculation, and write the steps in order. Students think about what happens when they subtract a negative number from another negative number.

**Assessment**: In each section of this chapter, ensure that students have a good grasp of the key questions in each exercise before moving on. (Refer to the 'Route mapping' table.) Encourage students to read and think about the 'Ready to progress?' statements on page 32 of the Student Book. Check students' understanding at the end of the chapter, formatively, using peer assessment. Students could do a mini test in the form of the 'Review questions' on pages 32–33 of the Student Book. Follow up the test with an individual target-getting session, based on any areas for development that a student may have.

### Worked exemplars from the Student Book (page 31) – suggestions for use
- Present students with the same question but different numbers. They should use the exemplar to mirror the working, in full or just refer to the notes.
- Copy and cut the exemplars into cards. Students match the working with the notes.
- Alternatively, copy and cut the working into cards but split the label/description from the working.

**Answers to the Student Book questions are available on the CD-ROM provided.**

# Section 1.1 Place value and ordering numbers

## Learning objectives

- Use a number line to represent negative numbers
- Use inequalities with negative numbers
- Compare and order positive and negative numbers

## Resources and homework

- Student Book 1.1: pages 9–11
- Practice Book 1.1

## Making mathematical connections

- Multiplying and dividing by powers of 10
- Multiplying and dividing decimals

## Making cross-curricular connections

- **Science** – place value in calculations; ordering a set of results from an experiment
- **Relevance** – students must be able to understand these basic concepts

## Prior learning

- **Students should know the size order of the words units, tens, hundreds, thousands, ten thousands, hundred thousands and million, and understand the relative values of the terms.**
- **Students could sort number cards into order as a test of this knowledge.**

## Working mathematically

- Structure tasks so students can work out the methods for themselves, either by increasing the difficulty incrementally or through one straightforward and one complex example.
- Ask students to describe a set of numbers using inequalities.

## Common misconceptions and remediation

- **Students may find it difficult to identify and say very large numbers, particularly those that include zeros, for example: 70 403. (Seventy thousand, four hundred and three)**
- **Students will sometimes confuse inequality signs. Encourage them to remember: The crocodile eats the largest number. Or, students may prefer to remember that the arrow points to the smaller number.**

## Probing questions

- How would you order this set of numbers?
- Is –9 bigger or smaller than –2?
- How do you know that one number is bigger than another?

## Literacy focus

- Key terms: digit, positive, inequality, place value, negative
- Ask students to write some of the larger numbers in Exercise 1A in words.

## Part 1

- Remind students that numbers can carry on to infinity – however large a number they think of, they can always add one more.
- It is the number and order of digits in a number, not the value of the individual digits, which determines the size of a number. Hold up some digit cards. Shuffle them and place them

face down. Ask students to draw four empty boxes next to each other. Say that you will pick four numbers at random, and they should write them down, one at a time, deciding where to place each digit in the boxes to make the biggest four-digit number possible.

- Play this several times, giving a point to each student who makes the biggest number each time.
- Extend this by asking students to find the biggest odd number or the biggest even number.

## Part 2

### The number line

- Remind students of place values – units, tens, hundreds, thousands, millions, and so on. **Less able** students may wish to continue using the place-value cards.
- Show students a four-digit number and ask for the value of each digit; for example, display the number 3657 and ask for the value of the 6 (600). Repeat for larger numbers.
- Point out that when writing numbers with more than four digits, the convention is to leave narrow spaces between groups of three digits, starting from the right. (Commas are not used as separators, to avoid confusion, because they are used as the decimal marker in many countries.) These spaces help to identify the number. For example, 2 678 000 is two million, six hundred and seventy-eight thousand.
- Write the number 3 001 002 on the board and ask students to read it aloud. Demonstrate the importance of zeros – in this example, the number would become 312 (three hundred and twelve) if the zeros were left out.
- Ask students to use the numbers 1, 2 and 3 (once each) to make as many three-digit numbers as possible. They should then sort them into order, from the smallest to the largest (123, 132, 213, 231, 312, 321).
- Take students through Example 1 to consolidate their understanding of place values.
- Now go through inequality signs with students explaining their uses.
- A **more able** class may finish Exercise 1A quite quickly. If this is the case, ask students to work in pairs to make up their own questions on place values and ordering, taking turns to create a question and answer it.
- **Students can now do Exercise 1A from the Student Book.**

| N 1–3, 8, 10 | Calculator n/a | CM 12, 13 | MR 7, 9, 11 | PS 4–6, 14 | EV n/a |

## Part 3

- Read out some numbers such as 109, 7043 or 4508, and ask students to write them down in figures.
- If there is time, ask students to make up a number with a zero in one of the places and read it out for the rest of the class to write down.

### Learning objectives

- Work out the answers to problems with more than one mathematical operation

### Resources and homework

- Student Book 1.2: pages 12–14
- Practice Book 1.2

### Making mathematical connections

- Expanding quadratic expressions
- Rearranging formulae
  Substituting into expressions with brackets

### Making cross-curricular connections

- **Science** – uses in various scientific formulae

## Prior learning

- Students should know the number bonds to 20 and the multiplication tables up to 10 × 10.

## Working mathematically

- By the end of this section, make sure that students can confidently apply BIDMAS/BODMAS to calculations.

## Common misconceptions and remediation

- Some students ignore the conventions in the order of operations and work from left to right; for example, they may work out the answer to $4 \lessgtr 5 \times 6$ as 54 rather than 34.
- Encourage students to recognise questions on this topic and to work in the correct order. As a reminder before doing the calculation they should write down the mnemonic BIDMAS/ BODMAS (Brackets; Indices/Powers; Division; Multiplication; Addition; Subtraction).

## Probing questions

- Where would you place brackets in order to make this calculation correct?
- What is the answer to this calculation: $4 + 3 \times 6$? Why?

## Literacy focus

- Key terms: None in this section
- From memory, ask students to write down the words for the mnemonic BIDMAS as quickly as they can.

## Part 1

- Ask students to work out:
  $4 \div 4 + 4 - 4 \ (= 1)$      $(4 + 4) \div (4 + 4) \ (= 1)$      $(4 \div 4) \times (4 \div 4) \ (= 1)$
- Make sure that students understand that the parts in brackets must be done first.
- Ask students to make any number other than 1, using only four 4s. For example:
  $(4 \div 4) + (4 \div 4) = 2$      $(4 + 4 + 4) \div 4 = 3$
  $(4 - 4) \div 4 + 4 = 4$      $(4 \times 4 + 4) \div 4) = 5$
- Ask students to feed back their calculations to the class and take time to explain any calculations that need adjusting in order to use brackets correctly.
- Give students four different numbers (e.g. 1, 2, 3, 4) and ask them to use these numbers to make 21, e.g.: $(1 + 2) \times (3 + 4)$. Tell students that all these calculations require them to use the operations in the correct order.

## Part 2

- Write $2 + 3 \times 4$ on the board. Ask students to work out their answers on a blank sheet of paper. Write the numbers 14 and 20 on the board and collect students' answer sheets.
- Write a tally under the numbers 14 and 20 to show how many students got each answer.
- Explain that 14 is the correct answer because the convention is that multiplication is worked out before addition, so $2 + 3 \times 4 = 2 + 12$. Say that there is a convention for the order of carrying out operations in calculations and they must follow it. Refer students to the BIDMAS/BODMAS list in the Student Book. Explain that all calculators are programmed to use BIDMAS/BODMAS.
- Explain that, if a calculation has brackets in it, that part must be worked out first, and so on.
- Write $2 + 3 \times 4$ and $(2 + 3) \times 4$ on the board. Remind students that the answer to the first calculation is 14. Ask students for the answer to the second calculation (20).
- Write $(1 + 2 + 3) \times 4$ and ask students to give the answer (24).
- Explain that sometimes brackets are not needed; for example, $3 \times 4 + 2$ is just as mathematically correct as $(3 \times 4) + 2$ because $3 \times 4$ will be the first calculation in both cases.
- Ask students to work in pairs, using the numbers 1, 2, 3 and 4 and a combination of brackets, division, multiplication, addition and subtraction, to create as many different answers as possible. Allow them to combine numbers, e.g. 1 and 2 to be used as 12.
- For **less able** students, limit the number of numbers they use. If the class is **more able**, give them extra rules that they must take into account when making their calculations, e.g. using four numbers from 1 to 20 only once to create as many answers as possible.
- Now go through Example 2 in the Student Book with the class.
- **Students can now do Exercise 1B from the Student Book.**

| N 1–6, 9, 14 | Calculator n/a | CM 8, 10 | MR 7, 13, 16 | PS 11, 12, 15 | EV n/a |

## Part 3

- Play a game of 'Countdown', choosing a set of numbers such as: 25, 6, 3, 10, 4, 1.
- Give students 30 seconds to make, for example, 254 (e.g. $25 \times 10 + 4$) or 60 seconds to make, for example, 287 ($25 \times 10 + (6 + 3) \times 4 + 1$).
- Pick other target numbers of varying difficulty, depending on the ability of the class.

# Section 1.3 The four rules

## Learning objectives

- Use the four rules of arithmetic with integers and decimals

## Making mathematical connections

- Statistical calculations

## Resources and homework

- Student Book 1.2: pages 15–30
- Practice Book 1.2

## Making cross-curricular connections

- **Science** – calculating experimental results
- **Food technology** – calculating the cost of ingredients
- **Relevance** – essential for daily use

## Prior learning

- **Students should know the number bonds to 10.**
- **Students should know the multiplication tables up to 10 ×10, including calculations with zero.**

## Working mathematically

- **Students may find it helpful when copying out questions for addition and subtraction to set the digits into columns (as in Example 3 of the Student Book).**
- Encourage students to use their preferred method for calculations.

## Common misconceptions and remediation

- When subtracting, students may take the smaller digit from the larger in a column rather than 'bottom from top'. This revisits earlier teaching methods of subtracting by taking smaller from larger. Emphasise the correct method and explain how to 'borrow' numbers.
- When multiplying and dividing, students may ignore zeros, or forget to add any carried digits.
- **Make students aware of these errors and encourage them to check their work carefully.**
- Make sure that pupils overcome the confusion about 'two negatives make a positive', for example: $6 - -9 = 6 + 9$ or $-6 \times -9 = 54$.

## Probing questions

- Before starting each exercise, give students questions with errors and say: Spot the errors.

## Literacy focus

- Key terms: column method, grid method, partition method
- Ask students to write a step-by-step guide for each of their preferred calculation methods.

## Part 1

- Give students a two-digit number. Say: What number must we add to make 100? Repeat, making the numbers more difficult. Next, ask students questions such as: If $7 \times 10$ is 70, what is $70 \times 10$? Extend this by giving answers to multiplications; ask for possible questions.

## Part 2

**Addition with positive numbers; Subtraction with positive numbers**

- Work through Example 3 with the class. Say: the answer will always be larger than the larger number; add the units column first; when the digits total in a column is more than 9, write the carried digit under the next column on the left so that you do not forget to add it in.

- Work through Example 4. Say: the answer will be smaller than the larger number; subtract the units column first; 'decompose' a number from the next column to the left, if necessary.

**Multiplication with positive numbers; Division with positive numbers**

- Work through Example 5. Say: 'When multiplying, write the bigger number first: multiply the units. When working with positive numbers larger than 1, expect a bigger answer than the numbers you began with'.
- Students may prefer to use a grid method. Say that this is acceptable but show students that these methods do the same thing, e.g. 14 × 4 = 10 × 4 + 4 × 4 (10 fours and 4 fours).
- Work through Example 6. Point out that in division (when working with numbers that are larger than 1) the answer will be smaller.
- **Students can now do Exercise 1C from the Student Book.**

| N 1–5, 9–11, 14, 15 | Calculator n/a | CM n/a | MR 16 | PS 8, 12, 13 | EV 6,7 |
|---|---|---|---|---|---|

**Arithmetic with negative numbers**

- Work through the Student Book text and Examples 7 and 8. Provide a variety of addition and subtraction questions involving negative numbers using the thermometer or a number scale.
- **Students can now do Exercise 1D from the Student Book.**

| N 1 –3, 5 | Calculator n/a | CM n/a | MR 4 | PS 6, 7 | EV n/a |
|---|---|---|---|---|---|

**Adding and subtracting negative numbers**

- Work through Examples 9 and 10 in the Student Book with the class.
- **Students can now do Exercise 1E from the Student Book.**

| N 1–10, 12, 13 | Calculator 10 | CM 11 | MR n/a | PS 14–17 | EV n/a |
|---|---|---|---|---|---|

**Multiplying and dividing with negative numbers**

- Work through the text and Example 11 in the Student Book with the class.
- **Students can now do Exercise 1F from the Student Book.**

| N 1, 2, 5–7, 10, 11a, b, 13 | Calculator n/a | CM 11c | MR 3, 4 | PS 8, 9 | EV 12 |
|---|---|---|---|---|---|

**Long multiplication with integers**

- Work through the text and Examples 12, 13 and 14 with the class. If there is a preferred method that your class likes to use, do a few more examples using this method.
- **Students can now do Exercise 1G from the Student Book.**

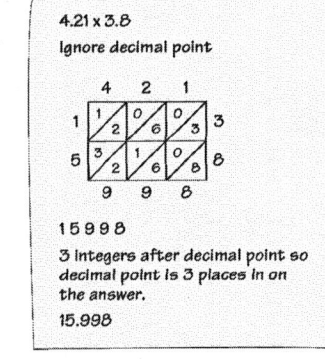

4.21 x 3.8
Ignore decimal point

15998

3 integers after decimal point so decimal point is 3 places in on the answer.

15.998

| N 1, 2, 4 | Calculator n/a | CM 7 | MR 3 | PS 5, 6 | EV n/a |
|---|---|---|---|---|---|

**Long division**

- Work through the text and Examples 15, 16 and 17 with the class. Some students will still use a short division method, which you should allow if their answers are accurate.
- **Students can now do Exercise 1H from the Student Book.**

| N 1–3, 7 | Calculator n/a | CM n/a | MR 6, 9 | PS 4, 5, 8 | EV n/a |
|---|---|---|---|---|---|

**Long multiplication with decimals**

- Work through Example 18 with the class. Another method is to ignore all decimal places and multiply using students' preferred method. Then students simply count how many digits there are after the decimal points and use place value to insert the decimal point.
- **Students can now do Exercise 1I from the Student Book.**

| N 1, 2, 4 | Calculator n/a | CM n/a | MR n/a | PS 3, 5 | EV n/a |
|---|---|---|---|---|---|

# Part 3

- Check students' understanding of the rules, concentrating on subtraction.
- Ask some questions involving mental skills such as: How many negative fours make negative 16?
- Encourage pupils to say the problem to themselves in their head.

# Chapter 2 Geometry and measures: Measures and scale drawings

## Overview

| | |
|---|---|
| **2.1** Systems of measurement | **2.4** Nets |
| **2.2** Conversion factors | **2.5** Using an isometric grid |
| **2.3** Scale drawings | |

**Prior learning – what students should already know**

The basic units used for measuring length, mass and capacity.
How to multiply or divide numbers by 10, 100 or 100.
The names of common 3D shapes.
How to measure lines accurately.

**Learning objectives – what students will learn**

**By the end of this chapter, ensure that students can: convert from one metric unit to another; convert from one imperial unit to another; convert from imperial units to metric units; read and draw scale drawings; read map scales; draw nets of 3D shapes and identify 3D shapes from their nets; draw plans and elevations.**

In the examination, students will be expected to:
- convert from one metric unit to another
- convert from one imperial unit to another
- use approximate conversion factors to change between imperial units and metric units
- read and draw scale drawings
- use a scale drawing to make estimates
- draw nets of some 3D shapes
- identify a 3D shape from its net
- read from and draw on isometric grids
- interpret diagrams to draw plans and elevations.

**Extension**

Ask students to create 3D shapes on an isometric grid and then draw the corresponding net.

## Curriculum references

| Section | GCSE specification |
|---|---|
| 2.1 | N13, R1, G14 |
| 2.2 | N13 |
| 2.3 | R2 |
| 2.4 | G13 |
| 2.5 | G13 |

## Route mapping

| Exercise | Accessible | Intermediate | Challenging | AO1 | AO2 MR CM | AO3 PS EV | Key questions |
|----------|-----------|--------------|-------------|-----|-----------|-----------|---------------|
| 2A | 1–8 | | | 1, 4, 5 | 2, 6, 7 | 3, 8 | 4, 5 |
| 2B | 1–5 | | | 1, 2 | 3, 5 | 4 | 1, 2 |
| 2C | 1 | 2–7 | | 1, 4 | 2, 3 | 5–7 | 1, 4 |
| 2D | 1–9 | | | 2, 3 | 6 | 1, 4, 5, 7–9 | 3, 4, 6 |
| 2E | 1–5 | | | 1–3 | 4 | 5 | 1, 3, 4 |
| 2F | 1–8 | | | 1, 2, 4, 5 | 7, 8 | 3, 6 | 2, 5 |
| 2G | 1 | 2–8 | | 1–4, 8 | 7 | 5, 6 | 1, 3, 7 |

*Key questions are those that demonstrate mastery of the concept, or which require a step-up in understanding or application. Key questions could be used to identify the questions that students must tackle, to support differentiation, or to identify the questions that should be teacher-marked rather than student-marked.*

## About this chapter

**Making connections**: This chapter will show students how to convert between standard units of measure. They will also learn how to interpret scale drawings, including map scales. Finally, students will learn how to draw and interpret plans and elevations of 3D shapes.

**Relevance**: The ability to convert between standard measures and to interpret scale drawings, plans and elevations of 3D shapes are important skills that have relevance in a range of areas including engineering, architecture, planning and navigation.

**Working mathematically**: Students describe how to convert between two units of measure. They work out the distance, in real life, represented by 3 cm on a map drawn to the scale scale of 1 : 25 000. Students talk through how to draw the net of a given 3D shape and explain what is meant by an 'elevation'.

**Assessment**: In each section of this chapter, ensure that students have a good grasp of the key questions in each exercise before moving on. (Refer to the 'Route mapping' table.) Encourage students to read and think about the 'Ready to progress?' statements on page 54 of the Student Book. Check students' understanding at the end of the chapter, formatively, using peer assessment. Students could do a mini test in the form of the 'Review questions' on pages 54–55 of the Student Book. Follow up the test with an individual target-getting session, based on any areas for development that a student may have.

### Worked exemplars from the Student Book (page 52) – suggestions for use
- Present students with the same question but different numbers. They should use the exemplar to mirror the working, in full, or just refer to the notes.
- Copy and cut the exemplars into cards. Students should match the working with the notes.
- Alternatively, copy and cut the working into cards but split the label/description from the working.

### Answers to the Student Book questions are available on the CD-ROM provided.

# Section 2.1 Systems of measurement

## Learning objectives
- Convert from one metric unit to another
- Convert from one imperial unit to another

## Resources and homework
- Student Book 2.1: pages 35–39
- Practice Book 2.1

## Making mathematical connections
- Map scales and ratio
- Areas and volumes
- Compound measures

## Making cross-curricular connections
- **Geography** – working with different measures
- **Technology** – converting between measures
- **Relevance** – essential use in daily life

## Prior learning
- Students should be familiar with the basic metric units: millimetre, centimetre, metre, kilometre, tonne, millilitre, litre.
- Students should be familiar with the basic imperial units: inch, foot, yard, mile, ounce, pound, stone, ton, pint, gallon.
- More importantly, students should have a rough idea, at least, of the size of each unit.

## Working mathematically
- Students will learn how to solve problems such as: How many 50 g bags of crisps will there be in a 2.5 kg box of crisps? (To work this out, convert 2.5 kg into grams and divide by 50.)

## Common misconceptions and remediation
- Students often assume that 1 'm' means one mile, whatever the context. This problem is made worse by the fact that students see signs on motorways that use 'm' for miles. Remind students to think logically about whether the 'm' unit of measurement should be for 'miles' or for 'metres'.
- There may also be confusion about which units relate to what measures, e.g. whether centimetres measure length, volume or mass.

## Probing questions
- Is 300 cm longer than 30 000 mm? How do you know?
- Talk me through how you would convert millimetres into metres.
- Talk me through how you would convert centimetres into inches or inches into centimetres.

## Literacy focus
- Key terms: centilitre (cl), ounce (oz), foot (ft), pound (lb), gallon (gal), stone (st), imperial, ton (T), inch (in), tonne (t), metric, yard (yd)
- Students should learn the correct spellings for the different units of measure.

## Part 1
- Give students practice in using the numbers they will need to manipulate imperial measures.
- Multiply and divide various numbers by 10, 100, 1000.
- Multiply and divide numbers by 8 (pints and gallons).
- Multiply and divide numbers by 12 (inches and feet).
- Multiply and divide numbers by 3 (feet and yards).

# Part 2

Work through the text and the table in the Student Book with the class.

### Metric units

* Explain that metric units are based on the decimal system, which uses powers of ten, such as 10s, 100s and 1000s.
* Ask for an estimate of the thickness of a pen or pencil. Make it clear that millimetres are used for small measurements.
* Now discuss the height of the room, which is probably 3 or 4 metres. Explain that they should estimate bigger heights such as a room, in metres rather than centimetres.
* Talk through the other metric measures with students.
* Go through the Student Book text on units, using the table to summarise the conversions and which to use when. Ask students to copy the metric unit conversions into their books.
* Now go through examples 1 and 2 from the Student Book.
* **Less able** students will need a lot of practice with each type of unit. Stay with length until they are confident, then move on to mass and finally, cover capacity.
* **Students can now do Exercise 2A from the Student Book.**

| G&M 1, 4, 5 | Calculator n/a | CM 7 | MR 2, 6 | PS 8 | EV 3 |
|---|---|---|---|---|---|

### Imperial units

* Ask the class how tall they think you are. You are not interested so much in an accurate estimate, as in the units they use. Some may give an answer in feet and inches, some may give an answer in centimetres. Use this as a discussion on the fact that we use different units. The UK has used imperial units for centuries but, over the last 30 years, the UK has been gradually decimalised. It is a slow process – hence the different units used for height.
* Ask how far it is from school to a place that students will know. Talk about using miles or kilometres. Tell the class that, although we still measure distances in miles in the UK they will sometimes need to convert such distances to kilometres.
* Talk through the different imperial measures with students.
* Go through the Student Book text about units, using the table to summarise the conversions and which to use when. Ask students to copy the imperial unit conversions into their books.
* Go through Example 3 from the Student Book with the class.
* **Students can now do Exercise 2B from the Student Book.**

| G&M 1, 2 | Calculator all | CM n/a | MR 3, 5 | PS 4 | EV n/a |
|---|---|---|---|---|---|

# Part 3

* Go over the links between millimetre, centimetre, metre, kilometre, millilitre, litre, milligram, gram, kilogram and tonne.
* Ask students to link these meausures to everyday objects, e.g. A bag of sugar weighs 1 kg.
* Go through the links between different imperial measures and ask students to convert between them.

## Section 2.2 Conversion factors

### Learning objectives

- Use use approximate conversion factors to change between imperial units and metric units

### Making mathematical connections

- Areas and volumes
- Map scales

### Resources and homework

- Student Book 2.2: pages 39–40
- Practice Book 2.2

### Making cross-curricular connections

- **Food Technology** – converting the mass of ingredients
- **Relevance** – uses in manufacturing, architecture, quantity surveying

## Prior learning

- Students should have developed some idea of the relative sizes of the various units and be able to decide which metric units relate to which imperial units. For example, students should know that they would convert a measurement that is in inches to centimetres.

## Working mathematically

- Students will learn metric equivalents of imperial measures that we still use, for example, feet, miles, pounds, stone, pints and gallons and how to make the appropriate conversions.

## Common misconceptions and remediation

- Students may not remember the conversion factors, or they might divide when they should multiply, and vice versa. Point out these errors as they occur.

## Probing questions

- How would you change, for example, metres to feet, centimetres to inches, kilometres to miles, pints to litres? What information do you need in order to do these conversions?

## Literacy focus

- Key terms: None in this section
- It is important for students to know the correct spelling for all the units they have met. A short spelling test would be useful here. Or, students can test one another, in groups.

## Part 1

- Ask students to recall as many imperial units as they can.
- Ask them to give conversion factors such as, for example: 12 inches = 1 foot.
- If students researched imperial units in the previous section, ask them to describe some of the units they discovered.

## Part 2

- Talk to students about going abroad. Ask about the main differences on the roads.
- Apart from driving on the 'wrong' side, all the road distances are in kilometres and must be converted to miles. How can they do this?
- Start a discussion to bring out the estimate that 5 miles is equivalent to about 8 kilometres.
- Ask how this estimate helps to change 115 kilometres, for example, to miles. The answer is to divide by 8 and multiply by 5. Remind **less able** students that the distance in miles will be

a smaller number (because a mile is bigger than a kilometre) so they need to divide first by the large number.

- **Less able** students can use calculators to find the answer of about 72 miles. **More able** students should try to do this mentally: $115 \div 8 \approx 14$, multiply by 5 to give 70 m.
- Work out a few more conversions with the class until they can remember the routine. When they are confident with changing kilometres to miles, ask them what they think someone from France would do, when the distance is shown as 115 miles. How would they change miles to kilometres? Discuss this and draw out the answer: divide by 5 then multiply by 8.
- Remind **less able** students that the distance in kilometres will be a bigger number (because a kilometre is smaller than a mile) so they need to divide first by the small number.
- Again, **less able** students can use calculators but encourage **more able** students to do this mentally: $115 \div 5 \approx 23$, multiplied by 8 to give approximately 184 km.
- Ask students to look at the table above Example 4 in the Student Book. Say that they do not need to know all these for the GCSE examination, but it is useful to have some idea as a general life skill.
- Ask students to write down and try to learn the key facts they need for GCSE:
2.2 pounds (lb) $\approx$ 1 kilogram (kg) , 5 miles $\approx$ 8 kilometres (km), 1 gallon $\approx$ 4.5 litres, 1 inch (in) $\approx$ 2.5 centimetres (cm).
- Work through Example 4 from the Student Book with the class, reminding them about changing units: large to small, multiply, and vice versa.
- Encourage **less able** students to write down the conversion factors each time, to help them consolidate the information.
- **Students can now do Exercise 2C from the Student Book.**

| G&M 1, 4 | Calculator all | CM 2, 3 | MR n/a | PS 5–7 | EV n/a |
| --- | --- | --- | --- | --- | --- |

## Part 3

- Go over the links between metric and imperial units.
- Ask students to link them to everyday objects, e.g. a bag of sugar or the mass of a car, and ask them to convert them to appropriate imperial units.

# Section 2.3 Scale drawings

## Learning objectives
- Read and draw scale drawings
- Use a scale drawing to make estimates

## Resources and homework
- Student Book 2.3: pages 40–45
- Practice Book 2.3

## Making mathematical connections
- Ratio
- Proportion
- Area and volume

## Making cross-curricular connections
- **Technology (graphics)** – making scale drawings of designs
- **Relevance** – links to manufacturing, architecture and planning

## Prior learning
- Students should be able to measure and draw lines.
- They should know that 100 cm ∇ 1 m and 1000 m ∇ 1 km.
- They should be familiar with multiplying and dividing by powers of 10.

## Working mathematically
- Students will learn how to interpret scale drawings and map scales.
- They will also learn how to estimate lengths from scale drawings. It may be useful to introduce some Ordnance Survey maps into the lesson as an extension exercise.

## Common misconceptions and remediation
- Students may not be able to work out how many kilometres there are in, for example,
- 3 000 000 cm or how many centimetres there are in, for example, 0.5 km.
- For **less able** students, initially use only questions with given units, e.g. 1 cm : 20 km. Some **less able** students will require a great deal of practice with 1 : 20 000 type questions in order to be able to change it to 200 m or 0.2 km. You could use the 'drip feed' method and give one question (e.g. change 1 000 000 cm to metres and kilometres) as each lesson starts.
- Direct **more able** students to question 9 in Exercise 2D. Make sure that you have maps of Britain for students to use.

## Probing questions
- What does the map scale 1 : 50 000 represent?
- Using a scale of 1 cm to 15 m, how high would a drawing of the Eiffel tower (300 m) be?

## Literacy focus
- Key terms: estimate, scale drawing, ratio, scale factor
- Ask students to write a step-by-step guide on how to use map scales to work out distances.

## Part 1
- Students will need a lot of practice with converting between metric units.
- Ask the class how they multiply whole numbers by 10, 100 and 1000. (Place one zero, two zeros and three zeros at the end.)
- Write on the board: 100 cm = 1 m and 1000 m = 1 km.
- Ask individuals how to convert various metric units, e.g. change: five metres to centimetres; seven kilometres to metres; four kilometres to centimetres. (500, 7000, 400 000)
- **Less able** students may need more practice with doing this.

- Give **more able** students examples that involve decimals, e.g. change 3.8 metres to centimetres; change 6.5 kilometres to metres. If time permits, do a few examples involving division, e.g. change 900 centimetres to metres; change 12 000 metres to kilometres.

## Part 2

### Scale drawings

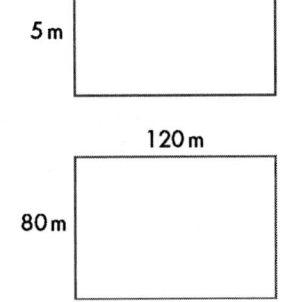

- Ask the class for examples of who uses scale drawings or where they are used (architects, designers, maps, sports). Explain that a scale drawing is a larger or smaller version of an original shape or object.
- Draw the diagram on the right on the board. It represents the dimensions of the floor of a room. Explain that, to make a scale drawing of the room, first you need to choose a scale. A suitable scale would be one centimetre represents one metre. Lead students to make this scale drawing in their books. Point out that the scale should be written to one side of the scale drawing, as in Example 5.
- Draw another rectangle on the board to represent a football pitch. Ask, What scale could be used?
- Possible answers: 1 cm represents 10 m, 1 cm represents 20 m or 1 cm represents 40 m. Ask which one is most suitable. For ease of drawing in their books, students should suggest using 1 cm represents 20 m. Work through Example 5 and the Student Book text to make sure that students are confident with this topic.
- **More able** students will need to be able to write a scale in a ratio format. Show how the two scales for the diagrams above can be given as ratios.
- 1 cm represents 1 m is the same as 1 cm represents 100 cm. As a ratio this is 1 : 100.
- 1 cm represents 20 m is the same as 1 cm represents 2000 cm. As a ratio this is 1 : 2000.
- Now, show **more able** students how to interpret a map scale, e.g. on a map the scale is given as 1 : 500 000 and the direct distance between two towns on the map is 8 cm. What is the actual direct distance between the two towns?
- Students should show the calculation as 1 : 500 000, which in this case is 1 cm represents 500 000 cm, which is 5000 m or 5 km in real life. The scale is 1 cm represents 5 km. Therefore the direct distance between the two towns is 8 × 5 = 40 km.
- It would be helpful to adapt the example and use a map of the local area.
- Use Example 6 and the text in the Student Book to reinforce this work.
- **Students can now do Exercise 2D from the Student Book.**

| G&M 2, 3 | Calculator all | CM n/a | MR 6 | PS 1, 4, 5, 7, 8 | EV 9 |

### Sensible estimates for scales

- Ask the class how tall they think the classroom door is. Now tell them the answer and ask how they could use this information to estimate the height or length of the classroom.
- Give different measurements such as a pencil length or book length and ask students to estimate the length or height of a desk. Work through the text in the Student Book and Example 7 with the class. Introduce the idea of using tracing paper for the questions.
- **Students can now do Exercise 2E from the Student Book.**

| G&M 1–3 | Calculator all | CM n/a | MR 4 | PS n/a | EV 5 |

## Part 3

- Ask: 'How many centimetres are there in: 1 km, 2 km, 10 km, 0.5 km, 1.5 km?'
- Ask: 'How many metres are there in: 2000 cm, 10 000 cm, 15 000 cm, 4 000 000 cm?'
- Ask: 'How many kilometres are there in: 4 000 000 cm, 15 000 cm, 10 000 cm, 2 000 cm?'

## Section 2.4 Nets

### Learning objectives
- Draw nets of some 3D shapes
- Identify a 3D shape from its net

### Resources and homework
- Student Book 2.4: pages 46–47
- Practice Book 2.4

### Making mathematical connections
- Surface areas
- Volumes

### Making cross-curricular connections
- **Technology** – cutting nets of objects using a laser cutter
- **Relevance** – manufacturing, design, engineering

### Prior learning
- Cardboard packaging is almost always based a net, which means that a box is made from one sheet of cardboard.
- Students should know the names of 3D shapes (cube, cuboid, pyramid and prism) as well as the 2D shapes such as square, rectangle and triangle (equilateral, isosceles and right-angled).

### Working mathematically
- Students will learn how to draw and interpret accurate nets of 3D shapes and how to identify a 3D shape from its net.
- These skills have uses in questions on surface areas and volumes in later chapters.

### Common misconceptions and remediation
- A common error that students make is to draw the two sides that should join the 3D shape as different lengths. Remind them of this and point out errors as they make them.
- Students' drawings are often outside the maximum 2 mm error allowed. They need to be aware of this when drawing nets.
- **Less able** students often confuse 'accurate drawing' with 'sketch'. Check that these students understand the difference as they work through the exercise.

### Probing questions
- How do you know these two sides should be the same length (referring to a net)?
- What clues do you look for in a net to decide on what its 3D shape would be?

### Literacy focus
- Key terms: net, 3D shape
- Make sure students are familiar with the meanings of the key terms, that is, the derivation of the term '3D' (three-dimensional).

### Part 1
- Show the class a collection of cardboard boxes such as cereal packets or triangular prism chocolate boxes. Ask students how they would make the shapes from card.
- Most students should be familiar with the word 'net'.
- Remind the class that a net is a flat 2D shape that can be folded into a 3D shape.

- Open out one of the cuboid boxes to show the net and explain that it is made from six rectangles with three pairs the same size. Point out that when a net is drawn, it is not necessary to put on the tabs. The tabs are only drawn if the shape is to be made up.

First draw the base.     Then add the front and back.     Then add the two sides.     Finally add the top to complete the net.

- Open out a different shape, e.g. the triangular prism, to show the class the net.

# Part 2

- It is useful to have a supply of centimetre-squared paper for this lesson.
- For **less able** students, a collection of 3D shapes including cubes, cuboids, square-based pyramids, tetrahedrons and prisms, is also useful.
- Draw this cuboid on the board. Show the class how to draw an accurate net for the cuboid. Make sure they understand that there are three pairs of rectangles that make up the shape. **Less able** students could make sketches of them first. Ask students to draw the net on centimetre-squared paper, using a pencil and ruler.

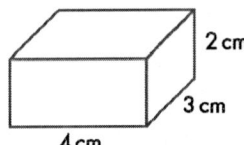
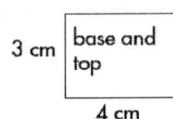
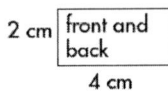
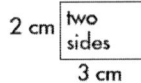

- You could ask **more able** students if they can think of other nets for the same cuboid.
- Explain that sometimes, for some 3D shapes, only a sketch of a net is required. Students will still need to use a pencil and ruler, but the measurements need not be accurate.
- Draw a sketch of a net for the square-based pyramid shown here.
- The net is made from a square and four identical isosceles triangles.
- Therefore, a net will look like the diagram on the right.
- Use Example 8 from the Student Book to summarise this work.
- **Students can now do Exercise 2F from the Student Book.**

| G&M 1, 2, 4, 5 | Calculator n/a | CM 8 | MR 7 | PS 6 | EV 3 |

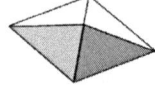
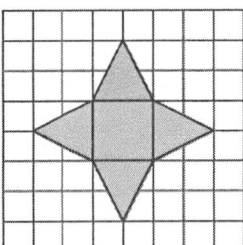

# Part 3

- Show the class a more complex 3D shape such as a hexagonal prism.
- Allow the class to work in pairs or small groups and ask them to draw a sketch of the shape.
- Ask the groups to compare their drawings. You could make a display of students' work.
- You could ask **more able** students why it is difficult to draw nets for cylinders and cones.
- If there is time, have a short class discussion about this.

# Section 2.5 Using an isometric grid

## Learning objectives
- Read from and draw on isometric grids
- Interpret diagrams to draw plans and elevations

## Resources and homework
- Student Book 2.5: pages 48–51
- Practice Book 2.5

## Making mathematical connections
- Areas and volumes
- Scale drawings

## Making cross-curricular connections
- **Technology** – drawing designs in isometric
- **Relevance** – uses in manufacturing, architecture and general design such as kitchen planning

## Prior learning
- Students should recognise 3D shapes made from cubes and cuboids.

## Working mathematically
- Students will learn how to interpret and draw 3D objects accurately, using an isometric grid.
- They will also learn about plans and elevations.
- Both topics have important real-life uses, which you should discuss with students.

## Common misconceptions and remediation
- Remind students that in class, they should use paper in landscape view, not portrait view.
- In examinations the most common errors are: drawing 'see-through' 3D cubes; vertices not being accurately drawn to the dots (or intersection of lines); not using measurements that are given.
- Questions that ask for plans and elevations from an isometric drawing, or the isometric drawing from a plan and elevations, are very challenging for many students, not only the **less able**, so spend extra time on these, as necessary.

## Probing questions
- What angles are in an isometric grid?
- How would you draw a 3D shape without the grid?
- Using a 3D drawing on isometric paper, ask:
  - How many faces, edges and vertices does the shape have?
  - How would you draw the plan and elevation of the shape?
- Using the plan and elevations of a 3D shape ask:
  - Which sides are opposite each other?
  - How many faces does the shape have?
  - How would you draw the shape on isometric paper?

## Literacy focus
- Key terms: elevation, isometric grid, plan
- Make sure students are familiar with the meanings of the key terms in this section.

## Part 1
- Ask students to draw a sketch of a cuboid of any size.
- Invite students to show the class how they drew it.

- Students have different strategies for drawing cubes or cuboids. **Less able** students will probably be unsure of how to draw cuboids, so have a collection of different cuboids available. Cuboids made from multi-link cubes are ideal.

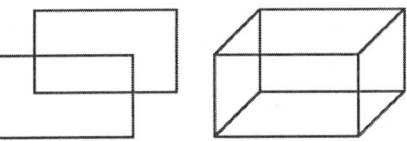

- Show students one or some of the ways of drawing a cuboid. For example: draw the front and back overlapping, then add the remaining edges.
- Explain that, when drawing 3D shapes in this perspective, it is usual to show the hidden edges as dotted lines. This makes them look more like 3D shapes.

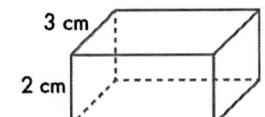

# Part 2

### Isometric grids
- Have a good supply of centimetre-squared paper and isometric grids, both lined and dotted. For **less able** students, also have a collection of cubes, cuboids and multi-link cubes.
- Draw the cuboid on the right on the board. Explain that it is not possible to draw this cuboid exactly because of the perspective.
- If the actual lengths need to be shown, the shape is better drawn on an isometric grid. Go through the Student Book text, which demonstrates this clearly.
- Move on to show students the triangular dot grid, which is also used to make isometric drawings. Point out to students that when they are using an isometric dot grid, the columns of dots must be vertical. Show students how to draw the cuboid on the grid. Point out that it is not necessary to add the hidden edges.

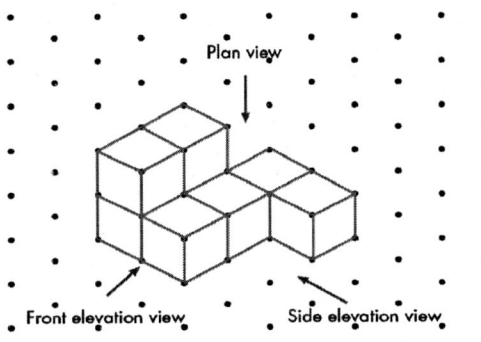

- Explain to students that architects, builders and designers often need to draw plans and elevations, particularly when drawing plans for new houses.

### Plans and elevations
- Draw the 3D shape, as shown, made from eight cubes on an isometric grid.
- Explain to students that the plan is the view from above the shape and the elevations are the views from two different sides. Note that the front and side elevations can be interchanged.
- The three views can now be drawn on centimetre-squared paper, as shown.

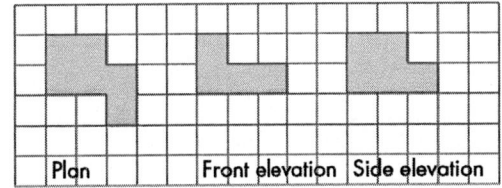

- **Less able** students may find it helpful to construct the solid shown in the diagram and to turn it, viewing it from the different elevations.
- Now work through Example 9 from the Student Book with the class.
- **Students can now do Exercise 2G from the Student Book.**

| G&M 1–4, 8 | Calculator n/a | CM n/a | MR 7 | PS 5 | EV 6 |
|---|---|---|---|---|---|

# Part 3

- Using multi-link cubes, ask how many different shapes can be made with three cubes (2) and four cubes (8). If multi-link cubes are not available, ask for sketches on isometric paper.
- Students could work in pairs or small groups to produce a display of the different shapes, drawn on isometric paper.

# Chapter 3 Statistics: Charts, tables and averages

## Overview

| | |
|---|---|
| **3.1** Frequency tables | **3.3** Line graphs |
| **3.2** Statistical diagrams | **3.4** Statistical averages |

| **Prior learning** |
|---|
| Know how to use a tally for recording data.<br>Know how to read information from charts and tables. |
| **Learning objectives** |
| **Ensure that students can: use tally charts and frequency tables to collect and organise data; represent data on various types of diagram; draw a line graph to show trends in data; work out the mode, median, mean and range of small sets of data; decide which is the best average to use; use an average and the range to compare sets of data.**<br><br>In the examination, students will be expected to:<br>• use tally charts and frequency tables to collect and represent data<br>• use grouped frequency tables to collect and represent data<br>• draw pictograms to represent statistical data<br>• draw bar charts and vertical line charts to represent statistical data<br>• draw a line graph to show trends in data<br>• work out the mode, median, mean and range of small sets of data<br>• decide which is the best average to use to represent a data set. |
| **Extension** |
| Show **more able** students how to calculate averages from frequency tables and the mean from a grouped frequency table. |

### Curriculum references

| Section | GCSE specification |
|---|---|
| 3.1 | S2 |
| 3.2 | S2 |
| 3.3 | S2 |
| 3.4 | S4 |

## Route mapping

| Exercise | Accessible | Intermediate | Challenging | AO1 | AO3 MR CM | AO3 PS EV | Key questions |
|---|---|---|---|---|---|---|---|
| 3A | 1–7 | | | 1, 4 | 2, 3, 5, 7 | 6 | 2–4, 6 |
| 3B | 1–10 | 11 | | 1, 9, 10 | 3–8 | 2, 11 | 3–5, 9, 10 |
| 3C | 1–7 | | | 1, 4, 6 | 3, 5, 7 | 2 | 2, 3, 5 |
| 3D | 1–8 | | | 1, 2 | 3–6, 8 | 7 | 1, 3, 4 |
| 3E | 1–6 | 7, 8 | | 3 | 1, 2, 5 | 4, 6–8 | 1, 4, 8 |
| 3F | 1–7 | 8–10 | | 1–3, 6 | 7, 9 | 4, 5, 8, 10 | 1–3, 7 |
| 3G | 1–3 | 4–9 | | 1 | 2–5, 7, 8 | 6, 9 | 1, 3, 4 |
| 3H | 1–5 | 6–8 | | 1, 2 | 4, 5, 7 | 3, 6, 8 | 1, 5, 6 |

*Key questions are those that demonstrate mastery of the concept, or which require a step-up in understanding or application. Key questions could be used to identify the questions that students must tackle, to support differentiation, or to identify the questions that should be teacher-marked rather than student-marked.*

## About this chapter

**Making connections**: How many people are there in our country? How many people are there in the world? How do these people live? What do they eat and drink? How big are their families? Encourage students to consider how statistics are used to explore questions such as these. For example, a census is a huge survey that is used to find out information about every man, woman and child in a country. Students need to consider how to present information once it has been collected. Students also need to think about how we use statistics to model populations where it is difficult or, in many cases, impossible to gather all the population information.

**Relevance**: Statistical graphs are seen every day. Analysing these graphs is an important skill that is necessary for many jobs. Think about how many times you have seen a television programme in which statistical diagrams are being shown or interpreted.

**Working mathematically**: Students should understand that pie charts are suitable mainly for categorical data. They should be able to draw pie charts by hand or by using computer software. Students should be able to draw compound bar charts with subcategories and use frequency diagrams for continuous data.

**Assessment**: In each section of this chapter, ensure that students have a good grasp of the key questions in each exercise before moving on. (Refer to the 'Route mapping' table.) Encourage students to read and think about the 'Ready to progress?' statements on page 86 of the Student Book. Check students' understanding at the end of the chapter, formatively, using peer assessment. Students could do a mini test in the form of the 'Review questions' on pages 86–87 of the Student Book. Follow up the test with an individual target-getting session, based on any areas for development that a student may have.

## Worked exemplars from the Student Book (page 84) – suggestions for use
- Present students with the same question but different numbers.
- They should use the exemplar to mirror the working, in full or just refer to the notes.
- Copy and cut the exemplars into cards. Students should match the working with the notes.
- Alternatively, copy and cut the working into cards but split the label/description from the working.

## Answers to the Student Book questions are on the CD-ROM provided.

# Section 3.1 Frequency tables

## Learning objectives
- Use tally charts and frequency tables to collect and represent data
- Use grouped frequency tables to collect and represent data

## Resources and homework
- Student Book 3.1: pages 57–61
- Practice Book 3.1

## Making mathematical connections
- Histograms
- Mean from a grouped frequency table

## Making cross-curricular connections
- **Science** – collating experimental data
- **Geography** – comparing climate data
- **Business Studies** – tabulating data from questionnaires
- **Relevance** – uses in business, research marketing

## Prior learning
- Students should know how to use the five-bar gate method to tally.

## Working mathematically
- Students need to appreciate the need to be methodical when recording data in tally charts and tables.
- Provide opportunities for them to work with increasingly complex and unfamiliar situations.

## Common misconceptions and remediation
- A common source of confusion for students when using grouped data is deciding on the boundaries. Give students opportunities to explore deciding the boundaries means, using examples of discrete and continuous data.
- Discuss examples that involve measurements with which students are familiar, for example, age and height. This will encourage students to discuss what particular groupings actually mean. It will also allow them to make links to work they have done on degrees of accuracy and how this affects the grouping.

## Probing questions
- Give an example of when you might use grouped data in real life.
- Give one example using discrete data and one using continuous data.

## Literacy focus
- Key terms: class interval, data collection sheet, experiment, frequency, frequency table, grouped frequency table, observation, sample, tally chart
- Ensure that students know the correct spellings and definitions of all the key terms.

## Part 1
- Ask students to move around the classroom, asking classmates that they know less well how they travel to school.
- Have a class discussion about what students think is the most common form of transport for travelling to school.

# Part 2

- Ask the class: What methods of transport do students use to travel to school?
- Write the question on the board and record their answers. Students can draw on the activity in Part 1 to help them answer this question.
- Tell the class that you require some data from them to answer this question. Ask them how you might record their responses.
- Put the following tally chart on the board, as an example. Then draw another empty chart and complete it by asking each student in turn.

| Transport | Tally | Frequency |
|-----------|-------|-----------|
| Bus | JHT JHT I | 11 |
| Car | IIII | 4 |
| Bike | I | 1 |
| Walk | JHT JHT III | 13 |
| Other | I | 1 |

- Now ask students to make their own record of the class data, writing it in their books.
- Go through the text and examples 1 and 2 from the Student Book with the class.

### Grouped data

- Ask the class: How many times have you walked to school this term?
- As the discussion develops about when and why students walk to school, write down the (approximate) number of times that each student has walked to school this term.
- At some stage, talk about the need to group some of the answers, pointing out that you could have 30 different numbers to graph. This leads to a discussion about class intervals and a grouped frequency table.
- Talk about how to chart the information. The obvious way is to use a bar chart, but show students how to put reasons onto the bars to make it more interesting or informative.
- Work through the text and Example 3 from the Student Book with the class.
- **Students can now do Exercise 3A from the Student Book.**

| S 1, 4 | Calculator n/a | CM 3 | MR 2, 5, 7 | PS 6 | EV n/a |
|--------|----------------|------|------------|------|--------|

# Part 3

- Ask what class size students might use for a survey on pocket money. Bring into the discussion the aspect of 'no amount' as a boundary of a class.
- Ask what class size they might use for car prices, again mentioning boundaries.
- Discuss with students if there is any type of data that does not have the problem of class boundaries. This can lead into a discussion about *discrete data*.
- Illustrate clearly the difference between discrete data and *non-discrete data*.
- You may wish to use the term *continuous*, but students do not need to know this term at this stage.

# Section 3.2 Statistical diagrams

## Learning objectives

- Draw pictograms to represent statistical data
- Draw bar charts and vertical line charts to represent statistical data

## Resources and homework

- Student Book 3.2: pages 61–69
- Practice Book 3.2

## Making mathematical connections

- Scatter graphs
- Histograms
- Frequency polygons

## Making cross-curricular connections

- **History** – comparing population data over time
- **Physical Education** – comparing performance data to support athletic training programmes
- **Relevance** – uses in sales, business, manufacturing, engineering

## Prior learning

- Students must be able to understand data that has been presented in tabular form.
- It will help if students have a good command of the multiplication tables for this section.

## Working mathematically

- The questions in Exercise 3B in the Student Book require students to apply their learning to real-life problems involving graphs. Students are also required to make links to fractions.
- You may want to revisit comparing simple fractions if **less able** students struggle with the required comparisons.

## Common misconceptions and remediation

- **Less able** students often use one symbol to represent one unit of data. Encourage them to think whether it is more sensible to choose another scale.
- A common mistake is to use different symbols, or symbols of different sizes, in the different classes of the pictogram. When this occurs, remind students that the symbols are used to compare the frequencies, therefore they must be the same shape and size throughout.
- With bar charts, students sometimes confuse the two axes and consequently draw the bars the wrong way round, possibly without a correctly spaced frequency axis. This is most likely to happen with numerical data. Work through the examples in the Student Book (and others that you provide) carefully with the class in order to minimise these errors.

## Probing questions

- How do you know what type of chart to use?
- What information do you need to be able to draw a chart?

## Literacy focus

- Key terms: bar chart, composite bar chart, dual bar chart, key, pictogram, vertical line chart
- Make sure students are familiar with the correct spellings and meanings of the key terms.

## Part 1

- Select some newspaper clippings with bar charts and pictograms. Distribute these among the class. This works best if students work in pairs or small groups.

- Ask for a summary of what each chart shows or represents.
- Discuss why the journalists decided to use these charts.

# Part 2

## Pictograms

- On the board, display a very simple pictogram such as: Walk, Bus, Car, with some simple stick people after each one (e.g. four people walk, three people by bus and one person by car).
- Ask the class what this information might represent. From the discussion, a suggestion might be: Ways of getting to school.
- Ask students: How many walked to school? Some students may give the answer as 'four'; others may say that they 'cannot tell', which is correct.
- Go through Example 4 in the Student Book, which shows a basic pictogram with one symbol representing two phone calls.
- Talk about the need for a key to the figures, as the whole point of a pictogram is that one small drawing can represent a number of people (or objects). For the travelling to school example, suggest that each stick person represents six people. Then ask how many people there are in each category. Go through this stage carefully for **less able** students so that they can visualise that one stick man represents six people; it is a concept they find difficult.
- Ask: How could you represent four people travelling by car rather than six? Lead students to grasp that they can divide the symbol – conveniently, the stick man has six parts (head, body, two arms, two legs); in this case, they could draw a person with two parts missing!
- Now go through examples 5 and 6 in the Student Book with the class.

## Bar charts and vertical line charts

- Ask the class to look at Example 7 in the Student Book, or display it on the whiteboard. Talk about the familiar bar chart. Ask students to discuss the special aspects of a bar chart that they must bear in mind when drawing one (same-width bars and labelled axes).
- Talk about the fact that the bars are usually vertical, but they can also be drawn horizontally. Using Example 7, ask questions relating to the data on the bar chart. Now go through Example 8, which deals with groups.
- Ask students to look at Example 9, or display it on the whiteboard. Ask what is so different about this chart (dual bar chart, showing more than one set of data). Say that in this case a key is essential, to identify which data set is which. Remind **less able** students that this is two bar charts on one diagram. In order to use the bar charts, they must keep reminding themselves of the key, as it tells them which bar chart is for which set of data.
- Again, ask questions about the chart, e.g. 'What was the temperature in Turkey in May?' (80° C) 'How much cooler was England than Turkey in August?' (30 degrees)
- Go through Example 10, which is a composite bar chart. Explain to students that this is essentially the same as a dual bar chart but one bar is on top rather than at the side.
- **Students can now do Exercise 3B from the Student Book.**

| S 1, 9, 10 | Calculator n/a | CM n/a | MR 3–8 | PS 11 | EV 2 |

# Part 3

- Recap with small groups of numbers and a symbol unit, and ask for the quantity of symbols to represent each number. For example: 'How many symbols are required for the numbers 18, 21, 36 and 42, with each symbol representing 6?' (3, 3.5, 6, 7) Repeat with variations.

### Learning objectives

- Draw a line graph to show trends in data

### Resources and homework

- Student Book 3.3: pages 69–71
- Practice Book 3.3

### Making mathematical connections

- Linear graphs
- Frequency polygons

### Making cross-curricular connections

- **Geography** – using temperature graphs
- **Business Studies** – working with monthly sales figures
- **Relevance** – uses in business manufacturing, sales

### Prior learning

- Students must be able to understand data that has been presented in tabular form.
- Students need to be able to plan and read scales on axes in a variety of situations.

### Working mathematically

- Explain to students that it is sometimes better to start the vertical axis at a number other than zero, as shown in Example 11 in the Student Book. This allows the use of a scale, which makes it easier to plot points or read them from the graph.

### Common misconceptions and remediation

- The most common mistakes that students make are the poor choice – or incorrect use – of scales to represent times.
- Students also make intermediate or future estimates without giving the data realistic thought.
- Point out these errors and go through examples with students to reduce their occurrence.

### Probing questions

- What are the advantages of drawing a line graph rather than a bar chart?
- When would you choose to use a line graph instead of other graphs?

### Literacy focus

- Key terms: line graph, time series graph, trend
- Explain the meaning of the word 'trend' to the class and ask them to use it in a sentence involving statistical interpretation.

### Part 1

- Present the class with a number of line segments with different numbers of sections along them; two, four and five sections are the most usual.
- Put a number at each end of the line and ask students for the numbers that go at other positions along the line segment.
- Repeat the above with units of time along the line segments (e.g. minutes, years, dates).

## Part 2

- Draw a bar chart on the board, based on the data from Example 11 in the Student Book.
- Say that the bar chart represents outside temperatures at various times.
- Ask the class: Why is this type of bar chart not quite as helpful as it could be? (It does not provide any information about the temperatures between adjacent points.)
- Now put a cross on the middle of the top of each bar and join the crosses.
- Ask: Is this any better? The answer should be 'Yes'.
- For **less able** students, you will need to demonstrate why this is better.
- Point to a position along the line and ask: 'What time is this? What is the temperature?'
- Talk about the fact that we often use line graphs instead of bar charts when we are talking about time.
- Tell **more able** students that 'time series' is the correct term, but that they do not need to use it. Time charts enable us to estimate values, in this case temperatures, between the plotted points.
- Remind students that times are always plotted on the horizontal axis and that it is not always sensible to start numbering the axis at zero.
- Look at Example 12 with the class and talk about the fact that, although the time is in years, it is still a time series, and there is a time interval between adjacent marked points.
- With **more able** students you could discuss the possible time of the year marked. Try to end the discussion with the assumption that this is the end of the year, that is, 31 December, so that the intermediate points may have more relevant meaning. However, this will depend on the company, for which some periods during the year may be more profitable than others.
- **Students can now do Exercise 3C from the Student Book.**

| S 1, 4, 6 | Calculator all | CM n/a | MR 3, 5, 7 | PS n/a | EV 2 |
|-----------|----------------|--------|------------|--------|------|

## Part 3

- Ask students to write a summary of line graphs, e.g. when they can be used and why they can be useful, how to draw them, and so on.

# Section 3.4 Statistical averages

## Learning objectives

- Work out the mode, median, mean and range of small sets of data
- Decide which is the best average to use to represent a data set

## Resources and homework

- Student Book 3.4: pages 72–83
- Practice Book 3.4

## Making mathematical connections

- Mean from grouped data
- Modal groups
- Interquartile range

## Making cross-curricular connections

- **Geography** – calculating averages, e.g. from temperature, population, rainfall data
- **Science** – calculating averages from experiments
- **Relevance** – wide usage in everyday life

## Prior learning

- Students need to be able to draw line graphs and bar charts.
- They should know how to create a tally chart and draw bar charts and pictograms.

## Working mathematically

- Students apply their understanding to real-life problems, decoding the statistical meaning behind familiar and less familiar situations.

## Common misconceptions and remediation

- Students get confused because of the vague and often inaccurate use of the language for central tendency and range in real life. Encourage students to explore and evaluate the use of this language. Say that every average is a measure of central tendency. Also encourage students to think carefully about the statistical measures they use and why they use them.

## Probing questions

- Find five numbers that have the mode as 7 and the range as 9. How did you do it?
- Two sets of data both have the same range but the first one has a median of 6 and the second has a mode of 6. Explain how these two distributions may differ.

## Literacy focus

- Key terms: average, categorical, consistency, modal, outlier, range, representative, spread
- Write a sentence for a real-life situation, using one or more of the key terms.

## Part 1

- Write a list of positive numbers on the board, e.g. 7, 3, 9, 2, 10, 8, 5, 4, 14, 12.
- Ask students to put the numbers in numerical order, with the smallest first.
- Ask students if they have any strategy for doing this.
- Repeat for another list of numbers, e.g. 34, 67, 38, 19, 44, 57, 24, 31, 62, 20.
- What about any strategies now? Identify the 10s column first.
- Write a list of positive and negative numbers on the board, e.g. 2, −3, 1, 4, −4, 0, 5, −2.
- Ask students to put the numbers in numerical order, with the smallest first.
- What about any strategies now? Remind students about number lines.

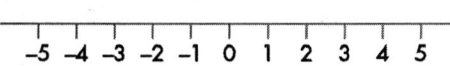

## Part 2

- **The mode:** Explain the term *average*; give common examples of when the word is used, e.g. average rainfall, average examination mark, average height. Ask students for examples.
- An average is a single value that represents a set of data.
- Explain how to find the *mode* for a set of data: the mode is the value that occurs most often in a set of data, e.g. for the data set 5, 6, 8, 2, 4, 5, 3, 5 the mode is 5.
- Explain that some sets of data have no mode because all the values are different, or no single value occurs more often than other values.
- Work through examples 13 and 14 from the Student Book with the class.
- **Students can now do Exercise 3D from the Student Book.**

| S 1, 2 | Calculator n/a | CM n/a | MR 3–6, 8 | PS 7 | EV n/a |
|---|---|---|---|---|---|

- **The median:** Explain how to find the *median* for a set of data: the median is the middle value for a set of data when the values are put in numerical order, e.g. when the data set 6, 8, 3, 7, 5, 2, 4 is written in order: 2, 3, 4, 5, 6, 7, 8, it is easy to see that the median is 5.
- Show that for set with an odd number of values, there is only one middle value.
- Show that for a set with an even number of values, there are two middle values and the median is the value between these two values, e.g. for the data set 5, 7, 7, 8, 10, 12, 14, 15, the middle values are 8 and 10, so the median is 9.
- Work through examples 15 and 16 from the Student Book with the class.
- **Students can now do Exercise 3E from the Student Book.**

| S 3 | Calculator n/a | CM n/a | MR 1, 2, 5 | PS 6–8 | EV 4 |
|---|---|---|---|---|---|

- **The mean:** Go through the text in the Student Book and explain how to find the mean of a data set using: $\text{mean} = \dfrac{\text{sum of all values}}{\text{total number of values}}$
- Now work through examples 17, 18 and 19 from the Student Book with the class.
- **Students can now do Exercise 3F from the Student Book.**

| S 1–3, 6 | Calculator all | CM n/a | MR 7, 9 | PS 4, 8, 10 | EV 5 |
|---|---|---|---|---|---|

- **Which average to use?** Refer to the table in the Student Book; discuss the advantages and disadvantages of each type of average and the reasons for using each average. Remind students that the mean is most commonly used, and the only average that considers every value. This is why people often, sometimes inaccurately, call the mean the average.
- **Students can now do Exercise 3G from the Student Book.**

| S 1 | Calculator all | CM 5 | MR 2–4, 7, 8 | PS n/a | EV 6, 9 |
|---|---|---|---|---|---|

- **The range:** Explain how to find the *range* for a set of data: the range is the largest value minus the smallest value; the range is not an average; it shows how data is spread out.
- A small range shows that the values in a set of data are similar in size.
- A large range shows that the values in a set of data differ considerably.
- Work through Example 20 with students.
- **Students can now do Exercise 3H from the Student Book.**

| S 1, 2 | Calculator all | CM n/a | MR 4, 5, 7 | PS 6, 8 | EV 3 |
|---|---|---|---|---|---|

## Part 3

- On the board, write two short lists of numbers.
- Ask students to explain how to find the mode, median, mean and range for each set of data.

# Chapter 4 Geometry and measures: Angles

### Overview

| | |
|---|---|
| **4.1** Angle facts | **4.5** Angles in parallel lines |
| **4.2** Triangles | **4.6** Special quadrilaterals |
| **4.3** Angles in a polygon | **4.7** Bearings |
| **4.4** Regular polygons | |

### Prior learning

Know how to use a protractor to measure an angle.

Know the meaning of the terms 'acute', 'obtuse', 'reflex', 'right' and how to use these terms to describe angles.

Know the names and angle properties of quadrilaterals.

Know how to use three-letter notation to describe any angle.

Know what a polygon is and the names of polygons with up to ten sides.

Know that a diagonal is a line joining two non-adjacent vertices of a polygon.

Know the meaning of the terms 'parallel' and 'perpendicular' in relation to lines.

### Learning objectives

**Ensure that students can: calculate angles on a line and around a point; calculate angles in a triangle and in any polygon; calculate angles in parallel lines; calculate interior and exterior angles in polygons; use bearings.**

In the examination, students will be expected to:
* calculate angles on a straight line
* calculate angles around a point
* use vertically opposite angles
* recognise and calculate the angles in different sorts of triangle
* calculate the sum of the interior angles in a polygon
* calculate the exterior angles and the interior angles of a regular polygon
* calculate angles in parallel lines
* use angle properties in quadrilaterals
* use a bearing to specify a direction.

### Extension

**More able** students can design their own questions, based on the exercises, and share them with the class. Students could also use actual maps and set bearing questions based on the maps.

### Curriculum references

| Section | GCSE specification |
|---|---|
| 4.1 | G 1, 3 |
| 4.2 | G 1, 3, 4 |
| 4.3 | G 1, 3, 4 |
| 4.4 | G 1, 3, 4 |
| 4.5 | G 1, 3 |
| 4.6 | G 1, 3, 4 |
| 4.7 | G 1, 3, 15 |

## Route mapping

| Exercise | Accessible | Intermediate | Challenging | AO1 | AO2 MR CM | AO3 PS EV | Key questions |
|---|---|---|---|---|---|---|---|
| 4A | 1–8 | | | 1, 2 | 3, 7 | 4–6, 8 | 1, 2, 4–6 |
| 4B | 1–8 | | 9–13 | 1–8 | 10, 11, 13 | 9, 12 | 1, 6, 7 |
| 4C | 1–5 | | | 1–5 | | | 4, 5 |
| 4D | 1–4 | 5, 6 | 7, 8 | 1, 3–5 | 2, 7 | 6, 8 | 1, 5 |
| 4E | | 1–10 | 11, 12 | 1–4 | 5–7, 12 | 8–11 | 1, 2, 10 |
| 4F | | 1–9 | | 1, 3 | 2, 6, 8, 9 | 4, 5, 7 | 1–4 |
| 4G | | 1–9 | 10–12 | 1–5, 7 | 9, 12 | 6, 8, 10, 11 | 1–5 |
| 4H | | 1–9 | 10 | 1, 2, 4, 5, 7 | 3, 6 | 8–10 | 1, 6, 9 |

*Key questions are those that demonstrate mastery of the concept, or which require a step-up in understanding or application. Key questions could be used to identify the questions that students must tackle, to support differentiation, or to identify the questions that should be teacher-marked rather than student-marked.*

## About this chapter

**Making connections**: This chapter will explain how to find connections between various shapes and their angles.

**Relevance**: Explain to students that angles help us construct many things, from tables to skyscrapers. It is essential that they understand them, as they literally shape our world. There are applications in engineering, architecture and many more areas.

**Working mathematically**: What do you look for when calculating an unknown angle in a shape? What is the least information you need to be able to calculate all the angles in the shape? What do you look for when solving a geometrical problem? How do you decide where to start? How would you explain to somebody that the exterior angles of a polygon add up to 360°?

**Assessment**: In each section of this chapter, ensure that students have a good grasp of the key questions in each exercise before moving on. (Refer to the 'Route mapping' table.) Encourage students to read and think about the 'Ready to progress?' statements on page 112 of the Student Book. Check students' understanding at the end of the chapter, formatively, using peer assessment. Students could do a mini test in the form of the 'Review questions' on pages 112–113 of the Student Book. Follow up the test with an individual target-getting session, based on any areas for development that a student may have.

## Worked exemplar from the Student Book (page 111) – suggestions for use

- Present students with the same question but different numbers. They should use the exemplar to mirror the working, in full or just refer to the notes.
- Copy and cut the exemplars into cards. Students match the working with the notes.
- Alternatively, copy and cut the working into cards but split the label/description from the working.

**Answers to the Student Book questions are available on the CD-ROM provided.**

## Section 4.1 Angle facts

### Learning objectives

- Calculate angles on a straight line
- Calculate angles around a point
- Use vertically opposite angles

### Resources and homework

- Student Book 4.1: pages 89–91
- Practice Book 4.1

### Making mathematical connections

- Bearings
- Trigonometry

### Making cross-curricular connections

- **Design and technology** – using angles when designing
- **Art** – using angle facts in symmetrical designs
- **Relevance** – applications in engineering, manufacturing and architecture

### Prior learning

- Students should be able to work out complements to 180° and 360°.

### Working mathematically

- Students should be able to calculate angles on a straight line or at a point, e.g. the angle between the hands of a clock, or intersecting diagonals in a quadrilateral.

### Common misconceptions and remediation

- Students often think that the angle sum on a straight line is 200° or a complete turn is 380°.
- Students sometimes confuse angles at a point with angles on a straight line. Reinforce these concepts in order to avoid errors in calculations.

### Probing questions

- Why do angles on a straight line add up to 180°?
- Why do angles at a point add up to 360°?

### Literacy focus

- Key terms: angles around a point, angles on a straight line, vertically opposite angles
- Ask students to explain what each key term means.

### Part 1

- Ask students to do some mental arithmetic involving complements of 90, 180 and 360, e.g. say a number such as 35 and ask for the complement to 90 (55), 180 (145) and 360 (325).

### Part 2

- Explain to students that they should not attempt to measure angles from a geometric diagram when they are asked to calculate. This is because the diagrams will not be drawn to scale. Angles on diagrams can be calculated from given geometrical information.
- Angles for which the values are not given are often denoted by letters (e.g. $a$, $b$, $c$) and are called *unknown angles*.

**Angles on a line**

- Copy the diagram onto the board and say that: $a + b + c = 180°$.

- Use the examples in the Student Book (and others) to show students how to calculate the sizes of unknown angles on a line.

**Angles around a point**
- Draw this diagram on the board and explain how to calculate the sizes of unknown angles around a point, using various examples.

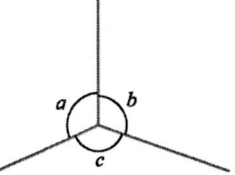

$a + b + c = 360°$

- Work through examples 1 and 2 in the Student Book with the class.

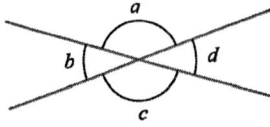

**Vertically opposite angles**
- Draw this diagram on the board and explain how to calculate the sizes of unknown angles, using various examples.

$a = d$ and $b = c$

- Notice that the adjacent angles add up to 180°: $a + b = 180°$.
- Work through Example 3 from the Student Book with the class.
- **Students can now do Exercise 4A from the Student Book.**

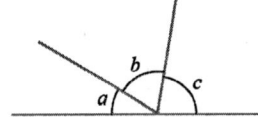

| G&M 1, 2 | Calculator all | CM 3, 7 | MR | PS 4–6, 8 | EV n/a |
|----------|---------------|---------|-----|-----------|--------|

# Part 3

- Given that $a = 70°$ and $b = 110°$, calculate the value of $c$.
- Given that $a = x$, $b = 2x$ and $c = 3x$, calculate the value of $x$.
- Given that $a = b = c$, find the value of $a$.

# Section 4.2 Triangles

## Learning objectives

- Recognise and calculate the angles in different sorts of triangle

## Resources and homework

- Student Book 4.2: pages 92–95
- Practice Book 4.2

## Making mathematical connections

- Pythagoras' theorem
- Trigonometry

## Making cross-curricular connections

- **Design and technology** – using triangles when designing
- **Art** – using triangles in symmetrical designs
- **Science** – using triangles of forces
- **Relevance** – applications in engineering and architecture

## Prior learning

- Students should know the meanings of the terms 'acute', 'obtuse', 'reflex' and 'right angle' and be able to use these terms to describe angles.

## Working mathematically

- Students will learn the skills required in order to calculate unknown angles in triangles, including isosceles triangles or right-angled triangles, when only one other angle is given.

## Common misconceptions and remediation

- Students often think that the sum of the angles in a triangle is 200° or 360°. It is therefore useful to display facts about the different types of triangle.
- Students may be confused by all the different names for types of triangle. Go through the different types in the Student Book and set quick-fire questions after students have learned them all.

## Probing questions

- Can you draw a triangle with:
  - one acute angle
  - two acute angles
  - one obtuse angle
  - two obtuse angles?

## Literacy focus

- Key terms: acute-angled triangle, equilateral triangle, isosceles triangle, obtuse-angled triangle, right-angled triangle, scalene triangle
- Ask students to describe each type of triangle.

## Part 1

- Ask students: What are the different types of triangle? What can you say about the angles in a triangle?
- Many students should recollect most of the information they will require for this topic.

## Part 2

### Special triangles

- Draw the triangle ABC on the board.
- Remind the class that they already know that the sum of the interior angles of a triangle is 180°.
  In the diagram on the right: $a + b + c = 180°$.
- On the board, draw a scalene triangle, an isosceles triangle, an equilateral triangle, a right-angled triangle, an obtuse-angled triangle and an acute-angled triangle – as shown here.

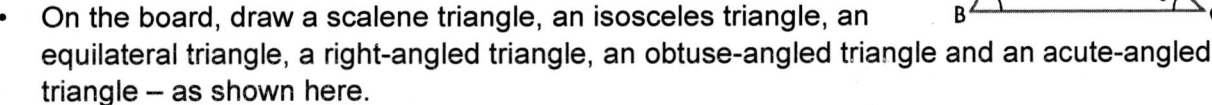

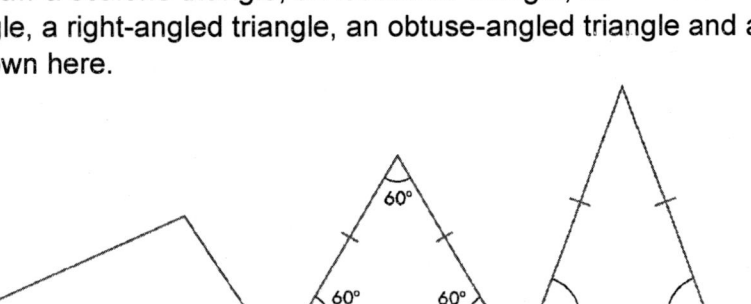

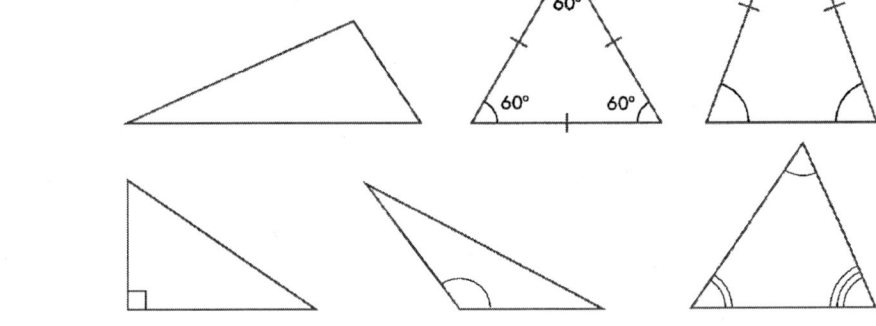

- Ask the class to describe how they can recognise each type of triangle. Make sure students understand that the two base angles of an isosceles triangle are equal and that the three interior angles of an equilateral triangle are equal (each 60°).

- Next, draw an isosceles triangle with an angle of 40° at the apex.
- Ask the class to work out the base angles. Repeat with other values for the angle at the apex.
- The angle marked y on the diagram below is an **exterior angle** of the triangle.
- Show the class how to work out the size of such an angle.
  Angles in a triangle add up to 180°, so:
  $x = 180° - 48° - 110°$
  $x = 22°$
  Angles on a straight line add up to 180°, so:
  $y = 180° - 22°$
  $x = 158°$

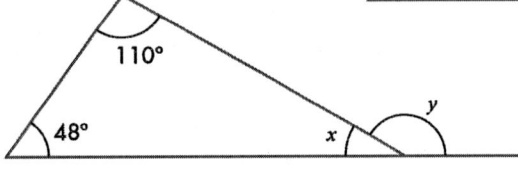

- Now work through Example 4 in the Student Book with the class.
- **Students can now do Exercise 4B from the Student Book.**

| G&M 1–8 | Calculator all | CM 10, 11 | MR 13 | PS 12 | EV 9 |
|---------|----------------|-----------|-------|-------|------|

## Part 3

- Ask the class to explain how to calculate an unknown angle in a triangle.
- Ask a student to explain how to calculate an exterior angle of a triangle.
- Draw several different triangles on the board, including some isosceles triangles.
- After annotating the angles, ask individual students to work out the unknown angles.
- Ask students to learn the different types of triangle and their properties for homework.
- Follow up the homework task by testing them. (Students should use mini whiteboards.)

# Section 4.3 Angles in a polygon

## Learning objectives

- Calculate the sum of the interior angles in a polygon

## Resources and homework

- Student Book 4.3: pages 95–98
- Practice Book 4.3

## Making mathematical connections

- Locus
- 3D shapes

## Making cross-curricular connections

- **Science** – using geometric shapes in chemistry
- **Design and technology** – constructing models of designs
- **Geography** – identifying locations on maps by descriptions of the 2D representation of manufactured objects
- **Relevance** – applications in engineering and architecture

## Prior learning

- Students need to know that the angles in a triangle add up to 180°.
- They need to know that the sum of the interior angles in a quadrilateral is 360°.
- Students should be able to solve simple linear equations.

## Working mathematically

- How could you explain to someone how to find the sum of the interior angles of a polygon?
- Does this work for all polygons? Why?

## Common misconceptions and remediation

- Students may misunderstand or misuse the expression $180°(n - 2)$, e.g. interpreting it as $180n° - 2$. This requires care in the first few examples.

## Probing questions

- What clues do you look for when solving a geometrical problem?
- How do you decide where to start? Is it possible to solve the problem in a different way?
- How would you convince a friend that each of the angles in … is equal to …?

## Literacy focus

- Key terms: interior angle, polygon
- Ask students to make up sentences or questions using these words.

## Part 1

- Draw a triangle and establish the angle sum.
- Draw a quadrilateral and split it into two triangles.
- Establish that the angle sum of each triangle is 180° and therefore the angle sum of the quadrilateral is 360°.

# Part 2

### Angle sums from triangles

- Draw a quadrilateral and a pentagon on the board.
- Show students how to split the two shapes into triangles from one vertex to find the sum of the interior angles.
- Ask students to do the same for a hexagon and a heptagon. They should use convex irregular polygons, not regular polygons.
- Encourage students to draw their own polygons and split them into triangles.
- Ensure that students draw all the diagonals from one vertex of the polygon.
- You could provide **less able** students with a worksheet of ready-drawn polygons.
- **Students can now do Exercise 4C from the Student Book.**

| G&M 1–5 | Calculator all | CM n/a | MR n/a | PS n/a | EV n/a |
|---------|----------------|--------|--------|--------|--------|

### *n*-sided polygon

- Ask students to work out the sum of the interior angles for octagons, nonagons and decagons without drawing the shapes. Ask them to record their results in a table.
- **Less able** students should take note of the formula in words:
  sum of interior angles = 180° × (number of sides – 2)
- **More able** students should write down this algebraic formula:
  $S = 180(n – 2)°$ where $S$ is the sum of the interior angles and $n$ is the number of sides.
- Work through Example 5 from the Student Book with the class
- **Students can now do Exercise 4D from the Student Book.**

| G&M 1, 3–5 | Calculator all | CM 2 | MR 7 | PS 6, 8 | EV n/a |
|------------|----------------|------|------|---------|--------|

# Part 3

- Ask students to give the names of *n*-sided shapes, starting with 'triangle' and going as far as 'decagon' (triangle, quadrilateral, pentagon, hexagon, heptagon, octagon, nonagon, decagon).
- An 11-sided shape is called a hendecagon and a 12-sided shape is a dodecagon.
- Ask students to work out the sum of the interior angles for each polygon.

# Section 4.4 Regular polygons

## Learning objectives

- Calculate the exterior angles and the interior angles of a regular polygon

## Resources and homework

- Student Book 4.4: pages 99–102
- Practice Book 4.4

## Making mathematical connections

- Locus
- 3D shapes

## Making cross-curricular connections

- **Science** – using geometric shapes in chemistry
- **Design and technology** – constructing models of designs
- **Geography** – identifying locations on maps by descriptions of the 2D representation of manufactured objects
- **Relevance** – applications in engineering and architecture

## Prior learning

- Students should know that the sum of the interior angles of a triangle is 180° and that the sum of the interior angles in a quadrilateral is 360°.
- Students should also know how to calculate the sum of interior angles in a polygon.

## Working mathematically

- Students work to understand the logic rather than trying to learn justifications of this type by memory. This way, they will see the transferable nature of the thinking process.
- Discuss the logical process with students and provide opportunities to identify the steps in the process and use similar logic in different contexts.

## Common misconceptions and remediation

- Make sure students are clear in their understanding of regular and irregular polygons and how this translates into calculating angles.

## Probing questions

- What happens to the interior angle of a regular polygon as the number of sides increases?
- Why?

## Literacy focus

- Key term: exterior angle
- Ask students to explain the difference between an exterior angle and an interior angle.

## Part 1

- Play 'Guess the shape'. Tell the class that you are thinking of a 2D shape (e.g. a square, an isosceles triangle, a trapezium, a regular decagon, a circle).
- Tell students that they can ask 10 closed questions to guess exactly what the shape is and that you will answer only 'Yes' or 'No'.
- Repeat this activity regularly, adjusting the questions to suit the ability of your students.

## Part 2

- Define a regular polygon as one in which all the sides are equal and all the angles are equal.
- Display diagrams of a square, a regular pentagon and a regular hexagon.
- Ask students to find the size of each interior angle for the regular polygons and record their results in a table.
  **Interior and exterior angles of regular shapes**
- Remind students what an exterior angle is and that the sum of an interior angle and its exterior angle is 180°. Referring to the Student Book text, ask students to find the size of each exterior angle for the regular polygons in their tables.
- **Less able** students should notice that the formula in words for finding each exterior angle and interior angle in a regular polygon is:
  - exterior angle = 360° ÷ number of sides
  - interior angle = 180° − exterior angle.
- **More able** students should write down the algebraic formulae for any regular polygon:

$$E = \frac{360°}{n} \qquad\qquad I = 180° - E \qquad\qquad = 180° - \frac{360°}{n}$$

  where $E$ is the exterior angle, $I$ is the interior angle, and $n$ is the number of sides.
- Point out that when students need to work out the size of an interior angle of a regular polygon, it is more straightforward to find the size of the exterior angle first.
- Work through Example 6 with students.
- **Students can now do Exercise 4E from the Student Book.**

| G&M 1–4 | Calculator all | CM 5, 6 | MR 7, 12 | PS 8–11 | EV n/a |
|---------|----------------|---------|----------|---------|--------|

# Part 3

- Draw a regular pentagon on the board. Establish the interior and exterior angles.
- Draw lines from each vertex to the centre.
- Establish the angles in each triangle.
- Discuss the connections.
- Repeat with a hexagon to show that the connections are true for all regular polygons.
- Students should be aware that each angle at the centre of a regular polygon is equal to the size of the exterior angle.

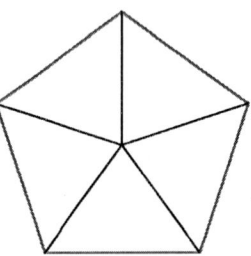

### Learning objectives

- Calculate angles in parallel lines

### Resources and homework

- Student Book 4.5: pages 102–104
- Practice Book 4.5

### Making mathematical connections

- Trigonometry
- Bearings

### Making cross-curricular connections

- **Science** – calculating forces
- **Art** – using designs involving parallel lines and angles
- **Relevance** – applications in engineering and architecture

### Prior learning

- Students should understand the nature of parallel lines and be able to calculate complements of 180 confidently.

### Working mathematically

- Students work to understand the logic rather than trying to learn justifications of this type by memory. This way they will see the transferable nature of the thinking process.
- Discuss the logical process with students and provide opportunities to identify the steps in the process and use similar logic in different contexts.

### Common misconceptions and remediation

- Some students may confuse alternate and corresponding angles. Constant reference to them during the lesson is usually beneficial.
- **Note:** Remind students that referring to alternate angles as 'Z angles', or corresponding angles as 'F angles', will not be acceptable in examinations.

### Probing questions

- Refer to a geometrical diagram with parallel lines and lines that intersect them.
- Explain how you would use the information given to you in this diagram.
- How do you decide where to start, in order to find the unknown angles?

### Literacy focus

- Key terms: allied angles, alternate angles, corresponding angles
- Consistent reference to these key terms during the lesson will help students to remember the correct terms.

### Part 1

- Write this grid of numbers on the board.

| 90 | 70 | 50 | 30 | 60 | 58 | 73 |
|-----|-----|-----|-----|-----|-----|-----|
| 45 | 105 | 32 | 17 | 127 | 15 | 165 |
| 63 | 87 | 25 | 120 | 148 | 20 | 3 |
| 163 | 135 | 75 | 110 | 130 | 65 | 40 |

- Ask students to: choose a number from the board and subtract it from 180; find two numbers that add up to 180; add together two numbers to give a total less than 180 and subtract the result from 180; find two numbers that add up to 90; find three numbers that add up to 180.

# Part 2

- Explain to the class that the lesson is about using alternate, corresponding and allied angles within parallel lines to solve problems.
- Draw the letter 'Z' on a card. Ask students what happens to the letter Z when the card is rotated through 180°. (Students should be specific about what happens to the two angles.)
- Demonstrate, by measuring, that the top and bottom angles are equal.

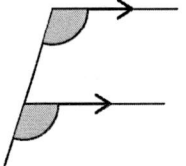

- Now ask the class what happens to the two angles if a letter Z is drawn without the top and bottom lines being *parallel*. (Ensure that students recognise that if the lines are parallel, then the angles are equal, but if they are not parallel, then the angles will be different.)
- Point out that the correct name for angles of this type is *alternate angles*.
- Draw a letter F on the board, as shown, to establish the rules for corresponding angles.
- Point out that the correct name for angles of this type is *corresponding angles*.

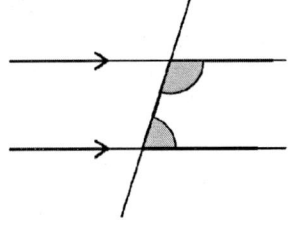

- Now draw the angles as shown below and establish the rules for *allied angles*.
- Students should now add the following text to their notes.

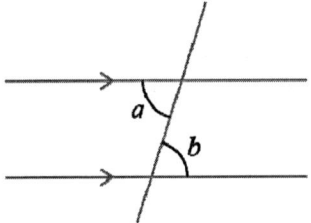
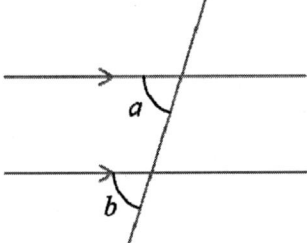
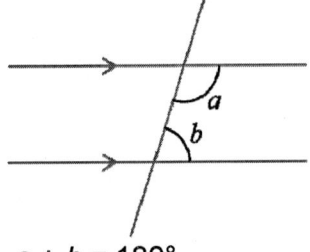

a and b are equal | a and b are equal | a + b = 180°
a and b are alternate angles | a and b are corresponding angles | a and b are allied angles

- Work through Example 7 from the Student Book with the class.
- **Students can now do Exercise 4F from the Student Book.**

| G&M 1, 3 | Calculator all | CM 2, 6, 8, 9 | MR n/a | PS 4, 5 | EV 7 |
|---|---|---|---|---|---|

# Part 3

- Draw this diagram on the board.
- Invite students to name:
  - o a pair of corresponding angles
  - o a pair of alternate angles
  - o a pair of allied angles.

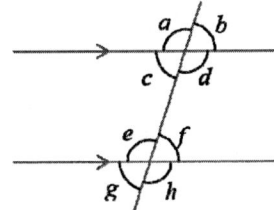

# Section 4.6 Special quadrilaterals

## Learning objectives
- Use angle properties in quadrilaterals

## Resources and homework
- Student Book 4.6: pages 105–107
- Practice Book 4.6

## Making mathematical connections
- Symmetry
- Trigonometry

## Making cross-curricular connections
- **Science** – calculating forces
- **Art** – using designs involving quadrilaterals
- **Relevance** – applications in engineering and architecture

## Prior learning
- Students should know that the sum of the angles in any triangle is 180°, that two of the sides of an isosceles triangle are equal, and that the sum of the angles in a quadrilateral is 360°.
- Students should also know that when a transversal cuts parallel lines, the alternate angles are equal, the corresponding angles are equal and the allied angles are supplementary (have a sum of 180°).

## Working mathematically
- Students should, by the end of the lesson, understand and be able to recall properties of a:
  - parallelogram
  - rectangle
  - rhombus
  - square
  - kite
  - trapezium.

## Common misconceptions and remediation
- Some students may confuse alternate and corresponding angles. Constant reference to them during the lesson is usually beneficial.
- **Note:** Again remind students that, in examinations, it is not acceptable to refer to alternate angles as 'Z angles' or corresponding angles as 'F angles'.

## Probing questions
- What information would you need about a quadrilateral in order to classify it as a: parallelogram, rectangle, rhombus, square, kite, trapezium?
- Can you explain why a rhombus must be a parallelogram, but a parallelogram is not necessarily a rhombus?
- Why can a trapezium not have three acute angles?

## Literacy focus
- Key term: bisect
- Ask students to work in pairs. One student should describe a shape and the partner should try to draw it.

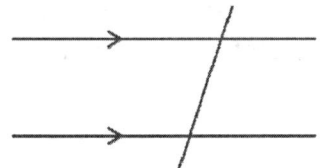

## Part 1

- On the board, draw a pair of parallel lines cut by a transversal.
- Ask a student to mark a pair of alternate angles on the diagram.
- Repeat for a pair of corresponding angles and a pair of allied angles.

## Part 2

- Draw an equilateral triangle and an isosceles triangle on the board. Go through the geometrical properties of both shapes, ensuring that students are familiar with them.

**Parallelogram; rectangle; rhombus; square; kite; trapezium**

- Draw a parallelogram on the board. Go through the geometrical properties of the parallelogram and encourage students to record all the facts for future reference.
- Remind **less able** students about the mathematical conventions for parallel lines, equal sides and naming angles. Talk to **more able** students about the angles created by diagonals in a parallelogram (alternate angles, vertically opposite angles).
- Draw each of these shapes on the board in turn and go through its geometrical properties:
  o a rectangle
  o a rhombus
  o a square
  o a kite
  o a trapezium*.
- Encourage students to record all the facts for future reference.
- *For the trapezium, tell **more able** students that if the sloping sides are equal, the shape is an *isosceles trapezium*.
- Briefly revise the symmetry of the less familiar quadrilaterals, since this is often a problem area for **less able** students.

| Shape | Number of lines of symmetry | Order of rotational symmetry |
|---|---|---|
| Parallelogram | 0 | 2 |
| Rhombus | 2 | 2 |
| Kite | 1 | 0 |
| Trapezium | 0 | 0 |

- **Students can now do Exercise 4G from the Student Book.**

| G&M 1–5, 7 | Calculator all | CM 9, 12 | MR n/a | PS 6, 10, 11 | EV 8 |
|---|---|---|---|---|---|

## Part 3

- On the board, draw an isosceles triangle, a trapezium, a parallelogram, a kite and a rhombus. Do not mark the identical angles and sides.
- Ask students (in turn) to mark pairs of identical angles or sides on the diagrams until all possibilities have been covered.
- Draw the six special quadrilaterals (parallelogram, rectangle, rhombus, square, kite, trapezium) on the board and ask students first to identify, and then to describe, as many properties of each quadrilateral as they can.

## Section 4.7 Bearings

### Learning objectives

- Use a bearing to specify a direction

### Resources and homework

- Student Book 4.7: pages 108–110
- Practice Book 4.7

### Making mathematical connections

- Trigonometry
- Coordinates

### Making cross-curricular connections

- **Geography** – using maps and bearings
- **Relevance** – applications in engineering, navigation and architecture

## Prior learning

- Students should know how to use a protractor to measure and draw angles.
- Students should also be familiar with the directions on a compass.

## Working mathematically

- Once students have established the base point from which to measure the bearing, and they have drawn in the north line through this point, they will place the protractor with its centre over the point and its base line along the line pointing north. They will identify the zero on this line, and read the angle clockwise. For example, in question 1a of Exercise 4H, Totley is on a bearing of 110° from Dore, so students need to draw the north line through Dore.

## Common misconceptions and remediation

- Students may not be clear which of the two points mentioned in a bearing is the base point. Remind students that bearings are always measured from north, so the first thing to do is to add the north line through the point from which the bearing of the other point is to be measured.
- Encourage **less able** students to circle or underline the name of the point from which the bearing is to be taken.

## Probing questions

- Why is it important to write bearings as three figures?
- Talk me through how you would work out a bearing of one point from another.

## Literacy focus

- Key terms: bearing, three-figure bearing
- Discuss the key terms with students to make sure that they understand their meanings.

## Part 1

- Draw a compass rose on the board (shown in the Student Book). Starting from north as 0° and working clockwise, establish that the angles at E, S and W are 90°, 180° and 270°. Mark these on the diagram.
- Angles for NE, SE, SW and NW could also be given (45°, 135°, 225°, 315°).
- Now draw some lines from the centre of the rose and ask **more able** students to estimate the angles measured clockwise from north.

## Part 2

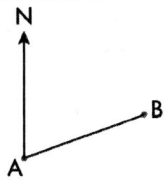

- Draw diagram **i** on the board. Inform the class that A and B represent two towns on a map and you need to know the direction of B from A. The best way is to give the direction as an angle. This angle is known as a bearing. Bearings are always measured in a clockwise direction from the north line, which is normally abbreviated to N.

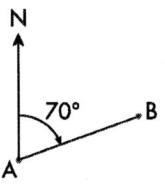

- Now redraw as diagram **ii**. Explain that the bearing of B from A is 70°. Students must be careful to get this the right way round and not confuse it with the bearing of A from B.

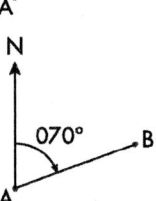

- Explain that a bearing is usually given with three digits and is referred to as a three-figure bearing. A two-digit bearing has a zero put in front of it, so due east is 090°. Now complete diagram **iii**.

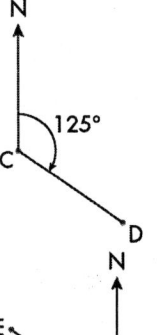

- Bearings may be obtuse or reflex angles, in which case students need to take special care. **Less able** students could use a circular protractor. Emphasise this by going through the following examples: Diagram **iv**: the bearing of D *from* C is 125°. Diagram **v**: the bearing of F *from* E is 305°.
- Ask the class who might use bearings (orienteers, hikers, explorers, yachtsmen, airports, mapmakers).

- Explain that bearings are often used with a scale, e.g. an aircraft flies from X to Y on a bearing of 150° for a distance of 250 km. Draw diagram **vi** to show this journey. Scale: 1 cm represents 50 km (XY should be 5 cm long.)
- Work through Example 8 from the Student Book with the class, referring them to the text above it.
- **Students can now do Exercise 4H from the Student Book.**

| G&M 1, 2, 4, 5, 7 | Calculator n/a | CM 3 | MR 6 | PS 8–10 | EV n/a |
|---|---|---|---|---|---|

## Part 3

- Ask students: If B is on a bearing of 060° from A, what is the bearing of A from B? (240°) Draw a diagram to demonstrate this.
- Repeat for several more bearings such as 045° (225°), 090° (270°), 160° (340°), 290° (110°).
- Tabulate the results so that students can see them clearly.
- **More able** students may notice that there is a connection between the two bearings in each pair. There is always a difference of 180° between them.

# Chapter 5 Number: Number properties

## Overview

| | |
|---|---|
| **5.1** Multiples of whole numbers | **5.5** Square numbers |
| **5.2** Factors of whole numbers | **5.6** Square roots |
| **5.3** Prime numbers | **5.7** Basic calculations on a calculator |
| **5.4** Prime factors, LCM and HCF | |

**Prior learning**

The multiplication tables up to 12 × 12.

**Learning objectives**

**Ensure that students can: find multiples and factors; understand what prime numbers are; break down a number into its prime factors; work out the lowest common multiple of two numbers; work out the highest common factor of two numbers; work out squares and square roots; use a calculator for basic calculations.**

In the examination, students will be expected to:
- find multiples of whole numbers
- recognise multiples of numbers
- identify the factors of a number
- identify prime numbers
- identify prime factors
- identify the lowest common multiple (LCM) of two numbers
- identify the highest common factor (HCF) of two numbers
- identify square numbers
- use a calculator to find the square of a number
- recognise the square roots of square numbers up to 225
- use a calculator to find the square roots of any number
- use some of the important keys when working on a calculator.

**Extension**

Ask students to explore the use of the reciprocal, cube root and mixed number buttons on their calculators.

## Curriculum references

| Section | GCSE specification |
|---|---|
| 5.1 | N4 |
| 5.2 | N4 |
| 5.3 | N4 |
| 5.4 | N4 |

| Section | GCSE specification |
|---|---|
| 5.5 | N6 |
| 5.6 | N6, N7 |
| 5.7 | N2, N3, N6–N9 |
| | |

## Route mapping

| Exercise | Accessible | Intermediate | Challenging | AO5 | AO2 MR CM | AO3 PS EV | Key questions |
|---|---|---|---|---|---|---|---|
| 5A | 1–11 | | | 1–3, 8 | 6, 7, 11 | 4, 5, 9. 10 | 3, 4, 10 |
| 5B | 1–8 | | | 1, 3–5 | 2, 6, 7 | 8 | 4, 6 |
| 5C | 1–6 | 7–9 | | 1, 2 | 3, 5, 6, 8 | 4, 7, 9 | 3, 7 |
| 5D | | 1–8 | | 1–4 | 5, 7 | 6, 8 | 1, 2, 5 |
| 5E | | 1–9 | | 1–3, 5, 7 | 4, 6 | 8, 9 | 5, 7, 8 |
| 5F | 1–10 | | | 1, 4–7a, 8 | 3, 10 | 2, 7b, 9 | 5, 9 |
| 5G | 1–10 | 11–16 | | 1–4, 7, 15 | 5, 6, 8, 10, 16 | 9, 11–14 | 3, 5, 11, 15 |
| 5H | 1–7 | 8–10 | 11–13 | 1–4 | 5, 6, 8–11, 13 | 7, 12 | 3, 7, 12 |
| 5I | 1–3 | 4–13 | | 1–6, 10–12 | 8, 9 | 7, 13 | 3, 8, 11 |

*Key questions are those that demonstrate mastery of the concept, or which require a step-up in understanding or application. Key questions could be used to identify the questions that students must tackle, to support differentiation, or to identify the questions that should be teacher-marked rather than student-marked.*

## About this chapter

**Making connections**: This chapter brings together a group of basic, related concepts – all revolving around factors and multiples. These will be taught separately but then combined to show their connections and relevance to each other.

**Relevance**: This chapter forms the building blocks for many other concepts. In particular, the sections link to topics such as multiplying and dividing, and expansion and factorising, which occur in many other strands of the syllabus. A good grounding in these topics is vital.

**Working mathematically**: Quick recall of the material involved is necessary. Squares and roots as well as basic multiplication table values need to be applied without hesitation, so students will need plenty of drill practice.

**Assessment**: In each section of this chapter, ensure that students have a good grasp of the key questions in each exercise before moving on. (Refer to the 'Route mapping' table.) Encourage students to read and think about the 'Ready to progress?' statements on page 136 of the Student Book. Check students' understanding at the end of the chapter, formatively, using peer assessment. Students could do a mini test in the form of the 'Review questions' on pages 136–137 of the Student Book. Follow up the test with an individual target-getting session, based on any areas for development that a student may have.

### Worked exemplars from the Student Book (page 135) – suggestions for use
- Present students with the same question but different numbers. They should use the exemplar to mirror the working, in full or just refer to the notes.
- Copy and cut the exemplars into cards. Students should match the working with the notes.
- Or, copy and cut the working into cards but split the label/description from the working.

**Answers to the Student Book questions are available on the CD-ROM provided.**

# Section 5.1 Multiples of whole numbers

## Learning objectives
- Find multiples of whole numbers
- Recognise multiples of numbers

## Resources and homework
- Student Book 5.1: pages 115–117
- Practice Book 5.1

## Making mathematical connections
- Finding the lowest common multiple
- Working with factors

## Making cross-curricular connections
- **Business Studies** – collating statistical information; working with data
- **Relevance** – any situation where numbers have to be multiplied together

## Prior learning
- Students will need to know the multiplication tables to 10 × 10.

## Working mathematically
- Students need good recall of multiplication tables; in the examinations, these topics will be on the non-calculator paper, so students will require a lot of drill practice.
- Students also need shortcut strategies to help them – see 'Recognising multiples' in the Student Book text and under Part 2 of this section.

## Common misconceptions and remediation
- Students may fail to interpret the functional aspect of a topic correctly, e.g. if ten people climb into taxis that seat four people, students may give answers of 'two-and-a-half taxis are required' or 'two taxis with two people left behind'. Explain to students that they need to think carefully about their answer. The correct answer here is 'three taxis are required'.

## Probing questions
- List the multiples of negative numbers (e.g. –3, –6, –9, –12 …).
- Are the numbers getting bigger or smaller? Why? (We multiply by a positive number, so students often say, for example, that –4 is greater than –2.)

## Literacy focus
- Key terms: multiple, multiplication table
- Ask students to create a table with nine rows and two columns. List the numbers 2 to 10 in the first column. Fill each row with the multiples of the number in the first column.
- Students could start a dictionary of mathematical terms, with 'multiple' and its definition as the first term.

## Part 1
- Ask individuals, around the class, to take turns to increase an amount by a given number, e.g. the first student may say, '6,' the next, '12,' the next, '18,' and so on. Continue until someone makes a mistake.
- Go beyond the 10 × 10 multiplication tables for **more able** students.
- Move on to counting down, e.g. start at 60 and count down in sixes.

## Part 2

### Recognising multiples

* Remind students that multiples are the answers that appear in multiplication or times tables.
* Encourage students to look at the numbers in various multiplication tables and try to identify patterns or rules.
* For the 10 times table, the answer always ends in 0, numbers in the five times table always end in either 0 or 5, numbers in the two times table are always even. The digits in multiples of three always add up to a multiple of three, the digits in multiples of nine always add up to a multiple of nine. Multiples of six are always even numbers and the digits add up to a multiple of three. Multiples of four are even when divided by 2.
* Make sure that students know how to use a calculator to find multiples; e.g. for multiples of 5 press '5' then '=' then '+5' then repeatedly press '=', and the multiples will be displayed.
* Now display this table and, as students give answers, write the answers on the board.

| 34  | 48  | 55  | 102  |
|-----|-----|-----|------|
| 123 | 470 | 501 | 630  |
| 876 | 991 | 989 | 1000 |

* Which of these numbers are multiples of 2? (34, 48, 102, 470, 630, 876, 1000)
* Which of these numbers are multiples of 3? (48, 102, 123, 501, 630, 876)
* Which of these numbers are multiples of 6? (48, 102, 630, 876)
* Which of these numbers are multiples of 5? (55, 470, 630, 1000)
* Which of these numbers are multiples of 10? (470, 630, 1000).
* Repeat for the multiples of 4 and 9.
* **More able** students could identify the multiple of 18 as multiples of both 2 and 9 (630).
* Remind students that multiples are always whole numbers. The example given in the Student Book, of $341 \div 7 = 48.714\ldots$ demonstrates this. The number 341 is not a multiple of 7 because 341 divided by 7 is a decimal number.
* **Students can now do Exercise 5A from the Student Book.**

| N 1–3, 8 | Calculator 3–9 | CM n/a | MR 6, 7, 11 | PS 4, 5, 9, 10 | EV n/a |
|----------|----------------|--------|-------------|----------------|--------|

## Part 3

* Write the number 392 on the board. Ask students which numbers, from one to ten, this number is a multiple of. Clearly two is one answer. Half of 392 is 146 so four is a multiple. What about other numbers? It is not a multiple of three or nine, as $3 + 9 + 2 \nabla 14$ which is not a multiple of three; it is not a multiple of five or ten as the number does not end in 0 or 5.
* Use calculators to test whether seven is a multiple (it is).
* Repeat with further examples such as 630 or 720.
* Use smaller numbers within the 10 × 10 multiplication table for **less able** students, e.g. 48, 63 and 72.

# Section 5.2 Factors of whole numbers

## Learning objectives
- Identify the factors of a number

## Resources and homework
- Student Book 5.2: pages 117–118
- Practice Book 5.2

## Making mathematical connections
- Finding the highest common factor
- Working with multiples
- Working with prime factor trees

## Making cross-curricular connections
- **Economics; Business Studies; Science** – working with data
- **Relevance** – any situation where numbers have to be divided into each other

## Prior learning
- Students will need to know the multiplication tables to 10 × 10.

## Working mathematically
- Students need good recall of multiplication tables. In the examinations, these topics will be on the non-calculator paper. Provide plenty of drill practice.

## Common misconceptions and remediation
- Students often forget the fact that the number 1 and the number itself are in the list of factors. Remind them always to begin with 1.
- Many students mix up the terms *multiple* and *factor*. Relate 'multiple' to multiplications.

## Probing questions
- Does a complete factor list always have an even number of factors in it? Why? or Why not?
- If the answer is 'No', is there anything special about the number being factorised?

## Literacy focus
- Key terms: factor, factor pair
- Ask students to add 'factor' and 'factor pair' with definitions, to their mathematical dictionary.

## Part 1
- Ask students to draw rectangles, each with an area of 12 cm². Look at the possibilities and list the lengths of the sides. Repeat with other areas.
- Now ask students to find the number between 20 and 30 that has eight factors. (24 → 1, 2, 3, 4, 6, 8, 12 and 24)
- For **more able** students, ask further questions, e.g. 'How many factors does 36 have?' (9 → 1, 2, 3, 4, 6, 9, 12, 18, 36)

## Part 2
- Make sure students realise that factors always come in pairs, so when they have found one factor they can find the other factor.
- There is an exception to this rule – draw out the fact that every number has 1 and itself as a factor pair.
- Introduce the term *factor pair*. Refer to Examples 1 and 2 in the Student Book and introduce the idea of enclosing the 'set' of factors within curly brackets {}.

- Explain that, in order not to miss any factors, it is sensible to start with 1 and work upwards to obtain the factor pairs. Using this method, when students have tried all the numbers up to half the single number itself, students will have found all the factors.
- Work through Examples 1 and 2. Ask students to make a table as shown.

| 1 factor | 2 factors | 3 factors | 4 factors | 5 factors | 6 factors |
|---|---|---|---|---|---|
|  |  |  |  |  |  |

- Under each column, enter numbers from 1 to 20, e.g. 10 has four factors, so is entered in that column.

| 1 factor | 2 factors | 3 factors | 4 factors | 5 factors | 6 factors |
|---|---|---|---|---|---|
| 1 | 2, 3, 5, 7, 11, 13, 17, 19 | 4, 9 | 6, 8, 10, 14, 15 | 16 | 12, 18, 20 |

- **Students can now do Exercise 5B from the Student Book.**
- When using a calculator to find factors, encourage **less able** students, particularly, to work systematically.

| N 1, 3–5 | Calculator 3, 4 | CM 7 | MR 2, 6 | PS 8 | EV n/a |
|---|---|---|---|---|---|

# Part 3

- Give students a number, e.g. 48. Ask them to write it as a multiplication, e.g. 6 × 8.
- Carry on breaking down the separate values as multiplications (do not allow 1 ), e.g. 2 × 3 × 8; then 2 × 3 × 2 × 4, then 2 × 3 × 2 × 2 × 2.
- Ask students how they can use 2 × 3 × 2 × 2 × 2 to obtain factors, e.g. 2 × 2 × 2 × 2 × 16, so the factor pair is 3 and 16.
- Repeat with 20 (2 × 2 × 5), 60 (2 × 3 × 2 × 5), 100 (2 × 2 × 5 × 5), and so on.
- Finally, write the product 1 × 2 × 3 × 5 × 7 ∇ 210 on the board and ask students to give all the factors (1, 2, 3, 5, 6, 7, 10, 14, 15, 21, 30, 35, 42, 70, 105, 210).

# Section 5.3 Prime numbers

## Learning objectives
- Identify prime numbers

## Resources and homework
- Student Book 5.3: page 119
- Practice Book 5.3

## Making mathematical connections
- Factorising
- Prime factor trees
- Finding the highest common factor

## Making cross-curricular connections
- **Business Studies; Science** – working with data
- **Relevance** – any situation where numbers have to be divided into each other

## Prior learning
- Students should know the multiplication tables to 10 × 10.

## Working mathematically
- Students need good recall of multiplication tables, as in the examination, these topics will be on the non-calculator paper. A lot of drill practice will be necessary.

## Common misconceptions and remediation
- Sometimes students confuse prime numbers with odd numbers.
- They frequently include 1 and forget 2.
- Regular practice at reciting the first few prime numbers should help to avoid these errors.

## Probing questions
- Is 0 a prime number? Why? or Why not?
- Can a negative number be a prime number?

## Literacy focus
- Key term: prime number
- Ask students to add 'prime number' with a definition to their mathematical dictionaries.

## Part 1
- Ask students to think of, and list, all the numbers less than 50 that have only two factors.
- Explain that any number with exactly two factors, itself and 1, is called a prime number.
- Tell students that there are 25 prime numbers under 100. Encourage the class to call out the numbers while you list these numbers on the board.

## Part 2
- Give students a 10 by 10 grid with the numbers 1 to 100 on it. The first row should show 1–10, the second row 11–20 and so on. Ask students to shade all the prime numbers that are less than 100.
  (2, 3, 5, 7, 11, 13, 17, 19, 23, 29, 31, 37, 41, 43, 47, 53, 59, 61, 67, 71, 73, 79, 83, 89, 97)
- **More able** students could attempt to list all the prime numbers between 100 and 200.
  (101, 103, 107, 109, 113, 127, 131, 137, 139, 149, 151, 157, 163, 167, 173, 179, 181, 191, 193, 197, 199)

- Explain that to show that a number is not prime, all students need to do is find a factor that is not the number itself (1 is a factor of all numbers). For example, 432 is not a prime number as it is even. The only even prime number is 2.
- You may need to remind **less able** students of the rules for divisibility by 2, 3 and 5.
- **Students can now do Exercise 5C from the Student Book.**

| N 1, 2 | Calculator 4, 5 | CM 5, 8 | MR 3, 6 | PS 4, 7, 9 | EV n/a |
|---|---|---|---|---|---|

## Part 3

- Check students' understanding of prime numbers by playing 'True and false'.
- Say a number and ask students to put their thumbs up if it is a prime number and down if it is not a prime number.
- Ask students to use mini whiteboards to write down a factor of the number if it is not prime that is not the number itself or one; e.g. for 49, the student must display 7.
- Gradually increase the numbers to make this activity more challenging for students.

# Section 5.4 Prime factors, LCM and HCF

## Learning objectives
- Identify prime factors
- Identify the lowest common multiple (LCM) of two numbers
- Identify the highest common factor (HCF) of two numbers

## Resources and homework
- Student Book 5.4: pages 120–126
- Practice Book 5.4

## Making mathematical connections
- Working with multiples
- Working with factors
- Working with primes

## Making cross-curricular connections
- **Business Studies; Science** – working with data
- **Relevance** – classifying or categorising data, finding common values, everyday mental maths

## Prior learning
- Students should recall and understand what factors, multiples and prime numbers are.

## Working mathematically
- Students need to know the multiplication tables to 10 × 10. In the examination, these topics will be on the non-calculator paper, so provide students with plenty of drill practice.

## Common misconceptions and remediation
- A common mistake, when students are using the division method, is to leave out the last factor when rewriting the answer in index notation.
- Encourage students to check their answers by multiplying the factors together and checking that the answer is the original number.

## Probing questions
- If one student starts to create a prime factor tree for 108 with 2 × 54, and another student starts with 3 × 36, will the list of prime factors be different?
- Does this work with any number? Why? or Why not?

## Literacy focus
- Key terms: **factor tree**, **highest common factor**, index notation, **lowest common multiple**, **prime factor**, prime factorisation, product of prime factors, unique factorisation theorem
- Ask students to add the **bold** words with definitions into their mathematical dictionaries.

## Part 1
- Ask students to work in pairs with mini-whiteboards and write 'Prime number' on one board.
- Say a number. Students write the number on the other board and list all its factors below it. If it is a prime number, they should hold up both boards. Otherwise, they hold up the mini-whiteboard with the number and its factors. For example, if the number is 5, students write this on the board, with '1, 5' below it, and hold it up alongside the 'Prime' board. If the number is 6, they write this on the board with '1, 2, 3, 6' below it and just hold up this board.
- Repeat for a variety of numbers.
- When students have realised the importance of recognising prime numbers in this way, explain that prime factors are factors that are also prime numbers.

- Say a number. Students should write the number and its prime factors on the blank board.

## Part 2

- Refer to Examples 3 and 4 in the Student Book and take the class through the methods for finding a list of prime factors starting with continually dividing by a prime number. Make sure students are confident about the convention of writing the answer using index notation.

**Factor trees**
- Often a question will have the phrase, '… as the product of its prime factors.' This method makes use of the correct vocabulary. Examples 5 and 6 in the Student Book illustrate this very well. Work through Example 7 with students using both methods.
- **Students can now do Exercise 5D from the Student Book.**

| N 1–4 | Calculator n/a | CM 7 | MR 5 | PS 6, 8 | EV n/a |
|---|---|---|---|---|---|

**Lowest common multiple**
- Examples 8 and 9 illustrate two very different methods of finding the LCM. Writing out the sets of multiples (Example 8) is a visual method but errors can occur if the list of multiples is not carefully done. Working with prime factors (Example 9) uses more manageable numbers but it is easy to leave one out or include too many. Work through these examples, also using other numbers. In Example 9 it might be better to write the prime factors in columns like this:

| 42 | 2 | 3 | | 7 |
|---|---|---|---|---|
| 63 | | 3 | 3 | 7 |
| LCM | 2 | 3 | 3 | 7 |

- The bottom row use primes that appear in either row (compare to how you would use this grid for HCF, below), so the LCM is, 2 × 3 × 3 × 7 = 126
- Ask students to use either method to find the LCMs of: 14 and 35 (70), 18 and 48 (144)

**Highest common factor**
- Examples 10 and 11 in the Student Book illustrate two ways of finding the HCF.
- Example 10 lists the factors of each number and then identifies the highest factor that appears in each list.
- Students need to take care to ensure they have a full list. Example 10 also uses the products of the prime factors. This can be done using the table method, as used to find the LCM:

| 48 | 2 | 2 | 2 | 2 | 3 | |
|---|---|---|---|---|---|---|
| 120 | 2 | 2 | 2 | | 3 | 5 |
| HCF | 2 | 2 | 2 | | 3 | |

- The bottom row use primes that appear in both rows (compare to how you would use this grid for LCM, above), so the HCF is: 2 × 2 × 2 × 3 = 24.
- Ask students to use either method to find the HCFs of: 30 and 75 (15), 54 and 90 (18)
- **Students can now do Exercise 5E from the Student Book.**

| N 1–3, 5, 7 | Calculator n/a | CM 4 | MR 6 | PS 8, 9 | EV n/a |
|---|---|---|---|---|---|

## Part 3

- The Student Book shows two ways of finding the LCM, which are likely to suit kinaesthetic learners more. A third way is to use Venn diagrams with prime factors.

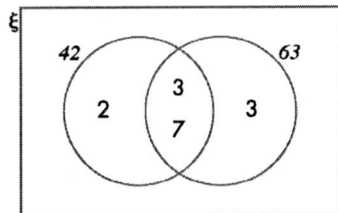

- To find the LCM, multiply all the numbers that appear in the various regions of the diagram: 2 3 3 7 ▽ 126. So the LCM of 42 and 63 is 126. To find the HCF multiply the numbers that appear in the intersection of the sets 3 × 7 = 21. So the HCF of 42 and 63 is 21.
- Finally, let students pick their favourite method to find the LCM and HCF of 28 and 40. (LCM ▽ 280, HCF ▽ 4)

# Section 5.5 Square numbers

## Learning objectives
- Identify square numbers
- Use a calculator to find the square of a number

## Making mathematical connections
- Number patterns
- Square roots

## Resources and homework
- Student Book 5.5: pages 126–129
- Practice Book 5.5

## Making cross-curricular connections
- **Business Studies; Economics; Science; Food Technology** – working with figures
- **Relevance** – everyday mental maths

## Prior learning
- Students will need to know the multiplication tables to 15 × 15.

## Working mathematically
- As with all other sections in this chapter, students need quick and accurate recall of mathematical facts.
- Notation is important, as is knowing how to use the $x^2$ button on a calculator.

## Common misconceptions and remediation
- Students may multiply the number by two instead of squaring it. Encourage students to write out the calculation in full to avoid this error. For example: $3.2^2 = 3.2 \times 3.2 = 10.24$
- When using a calculator **less able** students often enter $-3^2$ and then do not realise that $-9$ is an incorrect answer. Show students that they need to enter $(-3)^2$.

## Probing questions
- The values in the sequence $1^2, 2^2, 3^2, 4^2, 5^2$... increase by 3, 5, 7, 9,...'. What would be connected by an increase of 1?
- What is the connection between $1.5^2, 2.5^2, 3.5^2, 4.5^2$...? (Values increase by 4, 6, 8, 10... .)
- What would be connected by an increase of 2?

## Literacy focus
- Key term: square number
- Continue to add to the mathematical dictionary with a definition for 'square number'.
- When and if there is time during class (or as part of ongoing homework), encourage students to add the key terms from previous sections into their mathematical dictionaries.

## Part 1
- Write the sequence 1, 4, 9, 16, 25 on the board. Ask students if they can give the next two terms (36, 49). Now ask how the pattern is building up. Students may say that it goes up by 3, 5, 7, 9 … but make sure they eventually spot that it is 1 × 1, 2 × 2, 3 × 3 …. Encourage students to carry on the sequence as far as possible without using a calculator.
- Now try the 'Brainwashing' game. This involves asking students a simple multiplication, but when they give the answer they must also say the answer to an agreed square number.
- For example, if the agreed brainwash is '14 squared is equal to 196' ask, 'What is 8 × 8?' The student must reply, '8 × 8 ∇ 64 and 14 squared is equal to 196.'

- Ask the next student, 'What is 6 × 6?'; this student must reply, '6 × 6 = 36 and 14 squared is equal to 196.' Students will soon remember the answer to 14 squared.
- Students are expected to know all square numbers up to 15 × 15 for the GCSE examination.

## Part 2

- When any integer is multiplied by itself, the result is a square number.
- Square numbers can form square patterns when they are drawn as arrays of dots.
- The short way of writing 'squared' is to add a superscript '2' after a number, e.g. 12 squared is written as $12^2$.
- Write on the board: $5^2 = 5 \times 5 = 25$   $50^2 = 50 \times 50 = 2500$   $500^2 = 500 \times 500 = 250\,000$
- Ask students to give the answer to $5000^2$. ($5000 \times 5000 = 25\,000\,000$)
- Ask students to describe the pattern. Then ask for other square numbers and continue the same pattern. For example, ask for $8^2$, $80^2$, $800^2$. Cover all square numbers up to 15  15.
- **Less able** students could start by just looking at the first 10 square numbers, while **more able** students could go beyond 15 × 15.
- Now show students the calculator key for working out square numbers: $x^2$
- **Students can now do Exercise 5F from the Student Book.**

| N 1, 4–6, 7a, 8 | Calculator 1, 4, 6, 7 | CM n/a | MR 3, 10 | PS 2, 9 | EV 7b |
|---|---|---|---|---|---|

- Exercise 5G is a mixed exercise looking at the ideas from the first five sections of this chapter.
- It may be a good idea to revise some of these before starting the exercise.
- **Students can now do Exercise 5G from the Student Book.**

| N 1–4, 7, 15 | Calculator n/a | CM 10 | MR 5, 6, 8, 16 | PS 9, 11–14 | EV n/a |
|---|---|---|---|---|---|

## Part 3

- Write the following on the board: 1 = 1; 1 + 3 = 4; 1 + 3 + 5 = 9
- Ask students if they can continue the pattern, e.g.: 1 + 3 + 5 + 7 = 16
- Ask students to describe what is on each side of the equals sign. (Sum of consecutive odd numbers, square numbers)
- Ask if they can see a connection between the first and last number of the odd numbers and the square number (add them and divide by 2, which gives the number to be squared)
- Can they now find the missing square number for: 1 + 3 + … + 17 + 19 = __
  (100, as the value is $((19 + 1) \div 2)^2$
- Now ask students to give the answers to, e.g. 8 × 8 followed by 7 × 9. (64 and 63)
- Repeat for similar calculations, e.g. 6 × 6; 5 × 7 (36; 35) or 15 × 15; 14 × 16 (225 and 224).
- Ask students if they can see the pattern.

### Learning objectives

- Recognise the square roots of square numbers up to 225
- Use a calculator to find the square roots of any number

### Resources and homework

- Student Book 5.6: pages 130–131
- Practice Book 5.6

### Making mathematical connections

- Number patterns
- Squares

### Making cross-curricular connections

- **Business studies; Economics; Science; Food Technology** – working with figures
- **Relevance** – everyday mental maths

### Prior learning

- Students need to know the multiplication tables to $10 \times 10$ and square numbers to $15 \times 15$.

### Working mathematically

- As with all other sections in this chapter, students need quick and accurate recall of mathematical facts. Notation is important, and students need to know how to use the $\sqrt{x}$ button on their calculators.

### Common misconceptions and remediation

- Students may divide by two instead of finding the square root. Encourage students always to check their answer by squaring it to see if it gives the number in the question.
- The other common mistake is to square a number instead of taking the square root. Students can avoid this by using the symbol when writing down the question, rather than using words.

### Probing questions

- Say to students: $\sqrt{1}$, $\sqrt{4}$, $\sqrt{9}$, $\sqrt{16}$ … give integer (whole number) results. What about $\sqrt{2}$ or $\sqrt{3}$? Did you expect 1.5 or 1.23 or another terminating decimal? (Remind students that multiplication of decimals such as $1.5^2$ or $1.23^2$ will give an answer with more decimal places than the starting number.)
- Does this change your idea of the relationship between a square number and its root?

### Literacy focus

- Key term: square root
- Ask students to add 'square root' with a definition to their mathematical dictionaries.

### Part 1

- Draw a function machine on the board, but leave the operation blank. Give students three inputs and three outputs, e.g. (1, 3), (5, 7), (10, 12); then ask them to give the output for a given input and the input for a given output.

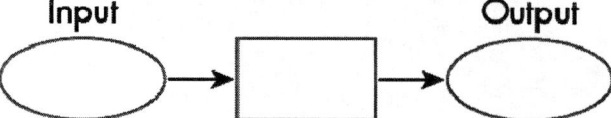

- Once they have spotted the rule (add 2), ask them to describe it and share the inverse rule (subtract 2).

- Repeat with other rules such as 'double', 'divide by 3' and 'double and add 3'.
- Finish with the operation 'square'. Students should have an intuitive idea of what a square root is, with **more able** students being able to describe it.
- Use numbers such as 5 and –5 to show the same output and to demonstrate that a square root has two possible values. Emphasise that finding the square root is the reverse operation of squaring.

## Part 2

- Point out that squaring a number always gives a positive answer, so it is not possible to find a number on a number line that will be the square root of a negative number.
- Ask students to try to work out $\sqrt{-10}$ on their calculators. The display will show an error.
- Now write on the board: $3^2 = 3 \times 3 = 9$, and also: $(-3)^2 = -3 \times -3 = 9$, so $\sqrt{9} = 3$ or $-3$
- Ask students to give the equivalent sentence for the number 4: ($4^2 = 4 \times 4 = 16$, and: $(-4)^2 = -4 \times -4 = 16$, so $\sqrt{16} = 4$ or $-4$)
- Repeat for other numbers up to 15.
- **Less able** students will tend to forget negative square roots so this is worth revisiting during Part 1 for other lessons.
- Check that students realise, for example, that because $5^2 \triangledown 25$ and $6^2 \triangledown 36$, squaring a number between 5 and 6 gives an answer between 25 and 36. Similarly, taking the square root of a number between 25 and 36 gives an answer between 5 and 6.
- **Students can now begin Exercise 5H from the Student Book.**

| N 1–4 | Calculator 3, 4 | CM 10 | MR 5, 6, 8, 9, 11, 13 | PS 7, 12 | EV n/a |
|-------|-----------------|-------|------------------------|----------|--------|

## Part 3

- Allow students to use calculators. Ask them to think of an odd number, say 9. Square the number, add one to the answer and divide by two: $(81 + 1) \div 2 = 41$
- Now square the odd number, subtract one from it and divide by two: $(81 - 1) \div 2 = 40$
- Ask students to square their two results and subtract the second answer from the first answer. Then take the square root of this result.
- If they have done it correctly they will get the number they started with.

## Section 5.7 Basic calculations on a calculator

### Learning objectives

- Use some of the important keys when working on a calculator

### Resources and homework

- Student Book 5.7: pages 131–134
- Practice Book 5.7

### Making mathematical connections

- All areas of the specification

### Making cross-curricular connections

- **Any subject** – where calculation is needed
- **Relevance** – many everyday situations where a calculator is needed

### Prior learning

- Students should be able to estimate answers, giving values correct to one significant figure.
- Students also need to be able to work with formulae or topics with calculations that involve multiplication, division, as well as fractions.
- Students should be familiar with BIDMAS/BODMAS.

### Working mathematically

- Being able to use a calculator correctly is a good skill to have.
- Students need to be confident in keying in the whole calculation in one go rather than a number of smaller ones. If students do break the calculation into smaller steps they need to be able to keep the results of the previous step in the calculator.

### Common misconceptions and remediation

- Students frequently omit the brackets from calculations so it is a good idea to let them see how much this changes the outcome of the calculation.
- The most common error is making mistakes during keying.
- The advantage of working in small groups is that if different answers are obtained any errors will be apparent and students can then redo these questions.

### Probing questions

- If a calculator functions according to the rules of BIDMAS/BODMAS why is it necessary to enter brackets around parts of a calculation?

### Literacy focus

- Key terms: function key, shift key
- Ask students to take one of the calculations in question 5 of Exercise 5I and draw the buttons that need to be pressed for the calculation to be performed correctly – in the same manner as in the examples in this section.

### Part 1

- Ask students to write down their answer to $20 \div 2^2 + 6 \times 5$ (35).
- Now ask them to key it into their calculators. Most scientific calculators will apply correctly the rules of BIDMAS/BODMAS and give the answer 35.
- Discuss why the answer is 35.

- Now ask students to add brackets to the same question so that the answer is 130 [(20 ÷ 2)² + 6 × 5], so the answer is 10 [20 ÷ (2² + 6) × 5].
- Now ask students to key into their calculators 6 ÷ 8. Ask for their answers, which might be $\frac{3}{4}$ or 0.75. Now discuss how to use the calculator to change from one format to the other.
- If necessary, show students how to use the arrow key.

## Part 2

- Work through the text and Examples 19, 20, 21 and 22 in the Student Book with the class.
- Ensure that students are aware of how to enter pi ($\pi$), find the cube of a number ($x^3$), and use the arrow button so that the denominator and numerator of a fraction can be entered after the fraction button has been pressed.
- **Students can now do Exercise 5I from the Student Book.**

| N 1–6, 10–12 | Calculator all | CM n/a | MR 8, 9, 13 | PS 7 | EV n/a |
|---|---|---|---|---|---|

## Part 3

- Ask students to work in pairs. Each student should create a fairly complex question, which their partner must enter into their calculator and produce the correct result.
- Students should then create a second question, but write it out by drawing the buttons that need to be pressed for the calculation to be performed correctly.
- The partner must then rewrite the question in conventional form.

# Chapter 6 Number: Approximations

## Overview

| | |
|---|---|
| **6.1** Rounding whole numbers | **6.3** Approximating calculations |
| **6.2** Rounding decimals | |

---

**Prior learning**

How to multiply and divide whole numbers.

**Learning objectives**

**Ensure that students can: round a number to a given accuracy; estimate the answer to calculations by rounding; find the limits of numbers rounded to a given accuracy; work out the error interval due to rounding or truncation.**

In the examination, students will be expected to:
- round a whole number
- round decimal numbers to a given accuracy
- identify significant figures
- round numbers to a given number of significant figures
- use approximation to estimate answers and check calculations
- round a calculation at the end of a problem, to give what is considered to be a sensible answer.

**Extension**

This is a good opportunity for **more able** students look at lower and upper bounds (limits of accuracy). This is additional Foundation content under N16 of the syllabus, so have ready some worksheets that contain the basic ideas behind this topic.

---

### Curriculum references

| Section | GCSE specification |
|---|---|
| 6.1 | N15 |
| 6.2 | N15 |
| 6.3 | N14, N15 |

### Route mapping

| Exercise | Accessible | Intermediate | Challenging | AO1 | AO2 MR CM | AO3 PS EV | Key questions |
|---|---|---|---|---|---|---|---|
| 6A | 1–11 | | | 1–5, 8, 9 | 6, 7 | 10, 11 | 3, 11 |
| 6B | 1–7 | 8, 9 | 10–13 | 1–4, 9 | 5, 6, 12 | 7, 8, 10, 11, 13 | 3, 13 |
| 6C | | 1–9 | | 1–5 | 6, 7 | 8, 9 | 2, 9 |
| 6D | | 1–14 | 15, 16 | 1–3, 5–8, 13, 14, 16 | 4, 9, 12, 15 | 10, 11 | 1, 8, 11 |

*Key questions are those that demonstrate mastery of the concept, or which require a step-up in understanding or application. Key questions could be used to identify the questions that students must tackle, to support differentiation, or to identify the questions that should be teacher-marked rather than student-marked.*

## About this chapter

**Making connections**: This chapter looks at accuracy when using numbers and making calculations. Working with decimal numbers has a particular connection with questions involving currency, for example.

**Relevance**: The ability to make a good approximation, thinking of the context in which the problem arises and the accuracy required, is a valuable skill. Approximation and estimation can be applied to all areas of the specification, across other subject areas and to everyday life. Students have to be able, for example, to decide whether a worked solution is reasonable, and therefore more likely to be correct.

**Working mathematically**: The sections in this chapter are mostly non-calculator. The idea is that students should be able to simplify the numbers used so that a calculator is not necessary – an exact answer is not required. Calculators can, however, be used to see how close the approximated or estimated answer is to the actual answer. Students need to be confident with mental arithmetic and their times tables.

**Assessment**: In each section of this chapter, ensure that students have a good grasp of the key questions in each exercise before moving on. (Refer to the 'Route mapping' table.) Encourage students to read and think about the 'Ready to progress?' statements on page 150 of the Student Book. Check students' understanding at the end of the chapter, formatively, using peer assessment. Students could do a mini test in the form of the 'Review questions' on pages 150–151 of the Student Book. Follow up the test with an individual target-getting session, based on any areas for development that a student may have.

## Worked exemplars from the Student Book (page 149) – suggestions for use

- Present students with the same question but different numbers. They should use the exemplar to mirror the working, in full or just refer to the notes.
- Copy and cut the exemplars into cards. Students should match the working with the notes.
- Alternatively, copy and cut the working into cards but split the label/description from the working.

**Answers to the Student Book questions are available on the CD-ROM provided.**

# Section 6.1 Rounding whole numbers

## Learning objectives
- Round a whole number

## Resources and homework
- Student Book 6.1: pages 139–142
- Practice Book 6.2

## Making mathematical connections
- Estimation and approximation

## Making cross-curricular connections
- **Science; Geography; History** – using, e.g. mass, land area, population
- **Relevance** – rounding values in everyday life, e.g. to the nearest ten km or metres, hundred tonnes

## Prior learning
- Students should know that numbers are not always given exactly but are sometimes approximated. For example, the attendance at a music festival would probably be reported in the newspapers to the nearest thousand; the numbers in the London marathon would probably be given to the nearest hundred.
- Students will need to have a sound knowledge of place value in order to know the position of the 'decider' digit.

## Working mathematically
- Students will work with place value and the position of the 'decider' digit to round whole numbers.

## Common misconceptions and remediation
- Students often have difficulty when rounding a number involving hundreds to the nearest ten (e.g. rounding 197 to the nearest 10). Students will benefit from extra practice with this type of rounding. Counting in tens may also help.
- It is very important for students to be able to identify the 'decider' digit and to ask 'Has this digit gone *at least half-way?*' If the answer is yes, the digit to the immediate left is rounded up. It might help **less able** students if they draw a line between the 'decider' digit and the digit to the left to give a visual indication of where the number will be rounded.

## Probing questions
- Ask students to copy the table in question 8 of Exercise 6A, but they should place the matches and number of spectators in descending order of the number of spectators.
- Then students should round each number of spectators to the nearest 100 and rewrite the table in descending order with the new rounded figures.
- Does the order of the matches change? Why? or Why not?

## Literacy focus
- Key term: round
- In their notebooks, ask students to write down examples of numbers rounded to the nearest 10 such as: 41 (40), 67 (70), 198 (200), 2396 (2400), and so on. Note that the latter two of these are examples of numbers that sometimes confuse students.

## Part 1

- Write multiples of 10 on the board, e.g. 10, 20, 30, 40, 50, 60, 70, 80, 90.
- Call out numbers randomly (smaller or larger than those you have written on the board).
- Ask students to pick the nearest value from the numbers on the board; e.g. if you call out 43, they should answer 40 and if you call out 65, they should answer 70.
- Use this exercise to reinforce the idea that numbers ending with the digits 5, 6, 7, 8, 9 are rounded up and those ending with the digits 0, 1, 2, 3, 4 are rounded down.
- Write 100, 200, 300, 400, etc. on the board and repeat the exercise.

## Part 2

- Guide students to the idea that rounding gives an approximation and the accuracy of this approximation depends on the number of figures to which it was rounded. Referring to the bulleted points in the Student Book, emphasise that even if the number is rounded, we can still work out what the maximum and minimum values are.
- Work through the text and the values in Example 1 making sure, in each case, that students can identify the 'decider' digit and correctly work out what needs to be done with the number.
- Work through questions 1 and 2 from Exercise 6A as a class, asking each student to answer one question. If a student makes a mistake, start again from 1a until the class has successfully completed them.
- If students are **less able**, allow them to work in pairs to work out the correct answers.
- If the class is **more able**, repeat Part 1, writing multiples of 5 on the board (5, 10, 15, 20, 25, 30, …). Ask for values to the nearest 5. Progress to picking a time (10:32 a.m., 4:17 p.m., 12:21 p.m.) and asking for the time to the nearest 1 hour, 30 minutes or 5 minutes.
- **Students can now do Exercise 6A from the Student Book.**

| N 1–5, 8, 9 | Calculator n/a | CM n/a | MR 6, 7 | PS 10, 11 | EV n/a |
|---|---|---|---|---|---|

## Part 3

- Use real-life examples to practise rounding, for example:
  - The number of sweets in a tube is 30, to the nearest 10 – how many could there be in the tube?
  - There are 25 000 people attending a rugby match to the nearest 1000; what is the least possible attendance? What is the greatest possible attendance?

# Section 6.2 Rounding decimals

## Learning objectives
- Round decimal numbers to a given accuracy

## Resources and homework
- Student Book 6.2: pages 142–144
- Practice Book 6.2

## Making mathematical connections
- Approximation
- Inequalities

## Making cross-curricular connections
- **Science; Business Studies** – working with, e.g. mass, speed, cost price, selling price, profit
- **Relevance** – rounding in everyday life (not just currency and time, but any calculation that does not result in an integer solution)

## Prior learning
- Students need to be able to recognise place value to the right of the decimal point, and recognise that values given are not always exact but may be approximations. For example, the timings (qualifying, lap and race times) in Formula 1 are always given to three decimal places; the scales a shopkeeper uses to price fruit and vegetables will give a cost to the nearest penny (two decimal places).
- Students need a sound knowledge of place value in order to know the position of the 'decider' digit.

## Working mathematically
- Students will work with place value and the position of the 'decider' digit to round decimal numbers.

## Common misconceptions and remediation
- Students often forget that if a value such as 3.698 m is rounded to two decimal places, the 'answer' is not 3.7 m but 3.70 m. The zero must be included so that we know that the value has been rounded to two decimal places – allowing the minimum and maximum values to be worked out correctly.
- It will be useful for students to draw a line between the 'decider' digit and the digit to the left to give a visual indication of where the number is to be rounded. This will ensure that the correct number of digits is provided in the answer.

## Probing questions
- Have the race times for the first five drivers of the most recent Formula 1 Grand Prix available for students to use, together with the number of laps in that race. Convert the race time into seconds.
- Ask students to find, for each driver, the average lap time and then round the answer to three decimal places. Now students should round the race time to the nearest second and again find the average lap time to three decimal places.
- What is the difference in average lap time?
- Over the number of laps in the race what is this difference?
- If you are given the average speed for a race, can you work out the distance (in metres) that this lap time difference represents?

## Literacy focus

- Key terms: decimal fraction, decimal place, decimal point, error interval
- Ask students to write examples of numbers rounded to two decimal places, e.g. 41.6753 (41.68), 67.4948 (67.49), 198.9961 (199.00), 23.496 (23.50). Bear in mind that the latter two sometimes confuse students.
- Encourage students to keep their mathematical dictionaries up to date by writing down the key terms and their meanings.

## Part 1

- Draw a picture of an eight-legged creature (spider, alien, octopus) on the board.
- Write a number such as 163.598346 in the middle of the image.
- Go around the class asking individuals to round the number to five, four, three, two, one, no decimal places, nearest 10, nearest 100. Write the new numbers in the legs as you go.
- Repeat with other numbers.

## Part 2

- Work carefully through the text in the Student Book. Ensure that students understand that writing to the nearest tenth is the same as rounding to one decimal place; writing to the nearest hundredth is the same as rounding to two decimal places, and so on.
- Example 2 in the Student Book should pose no problems if students carried out the activity in Part 1 successfully.
- When illustrating the error interval in Example 3, revise the use of $<$, $\leq$, $>$, $\geq$ which was covered in Section 1.1 of Chapter 1. Ensure the correct use of the symbols, $\leq$ and $<$.
- **Students can now do Exercise 6B from the Student Book.**

| N 1–4, 9 | Calculator n/a | CM n/a | MR 5, 6, 12 | PS 7, 8, 10, 11, 13 | EV n/a |
|---|---|---|---|---|---|

## Part 3

- Have some cards ready that look similar to this and issue one to each student:

| Number | Decimal places | Rounded |
|---|---|---|
| 2.3679029 | | |
| List another 14 or so numbers here, making sure that each number has 7 decimal places. | | |

- Give each student a dice. For each number in the list ask students to roll their dice and write the number that they rolled in the 'Decimal places' column. This is the number of decimal places to which the original number should be rounded.
- Write the rounded number in the 'Rounded' column.
- Ask students to give their completed list to a partner who should mark it.

# Section 6.3 Approximating calculations

## Learning objectives

- Identify significant figures
- Round numbers to a given number of significant figures
- Use approximation to estimate answers and check calculations
- Round a calculation at the end of a problem, to give what is considered to be a sensible answer

## Resources and homework

- Student Book 6.3: pages 145–148
- Practice Book 6.3

## Making mathematical connections

- Error intervals
- Inequalities

## Making cross-curricular connections

- **Science; Business Studies** – working with, e.g. mass, speed, cost price, selling price, profit
- **Relevance** – there are many situations where rounding to significant figures and finding an approximate answer are required.

## Prior learning

- Students should know how to round to the nearest whole number to a given number of decimal places.

## Working mathematically

- Students will identify significant figures (sf) and round numbers to a given number of sf. Rounding a value to one significant figure is a method that is used when working out an approximate answer, and it allows students to find an answer without the use of a calculator.
- Students will round calculations to give sensible answers.

## Common misconceptions and remediation

- Students may leave out the zeros after rounding numbers greater than 9; they may not ignore the zeros in numbers less than 1, and/or they may not round sensibly. Point out these errors, encouraging students to think when rounding and check that answers are sensible.
- It is useful for students to draw a line between the 'decider' digit and the digit to the left to give a visual indication of where the number is to be rounded. This will ensure that the correct number of digits is provided in the 'answer' – not forgetting that zeros might need to be inserted to the right of a number that is greater than 9 to maintain place value.

## Probing questions

- Ask students to look at question 9 of Exercise 6D in the Student Book.
- Say to students: 'What if the number of miles travelled is estimated to the nearest multiple of 5 miles and the number of miles per gallon to 2 sf? What are the minimum and maximum numbers of gallons of petrol used, to 2 sf?' (9.0, 9.4)

## Literacy focus

- Key terms: approximate, significant figure
- Ask students to round (to 2 sf) and write down various numbers, e.g. 41.6753 (42), 7.4948 (7), 198.9961 (200), 0.023496 (0.023). (The latter two sometimes confuse students.)

## Part 1

- Display these numbers: 0.04, 0.4, 4, 40, 400. Ask students what they have in common. Students should answer that they all contain 4. Follow up by asking what else they contain – students might say zeros.
- Now write: 0.065, 0.65, 6.5, 65, 650. Ask students how this set differs from the first set. (These have two non-zero digits.)
- Ask students to give you a set of numbers with three non-zero digits, e.g. 0.0123, 0.123, 1.23, 12.3, 123, 1230). Write a set on the board to use in Part 2.

## Part 2

### Rounding to significant figures

- Discuss the term 'significant figure (sf)'. Explain that in Part 1, the first set of numbers had 1 sf – a figure with value 4; the second set had 2 sf (65); the third set had 3 sf (123).
- Refer to the first table of numbers in the Student Book. Highlight the number 0.003 01, explaining that this is still 3 sf since from 3 to 1 is three places (301).
- Now show students the second table in the Student Book. Ask them to explain why 78 is 80 to 1 sf (only one non-zero digit allowed but place value has to be correct). So 78 to 1 sf is asking for the nearest number to 78 with only one non-zero digit – this is 80.
- Give students lots of quick-fire questions to reinforce the method.
- Now work backwards, saying that if a number is 80 to 1sf, what could the original number have been? (Any number from 75 to 84.999...)
- **Students can now do Exercise 6C from the Student Book.**

| N 1–5 | Calculator n/a | CM n/a | MR 6, 7 | PS 8, 9 | EV n/a |
|---|---|---|---|---|---|

### Approximating calculations

- Explain that approximations or estimations are made easier by rounding numbers to 1 sf.
- Give examples such as 19.8 × 3.01 is approximately 20 × 3 = 60, 491 ÷ 9.6 is approximately 500 ÷ 10 = 50. Ask **more able** students why a better approximation for 432 ÷ 9.1 would be 400 ÷ 10 rather than 400 ÷ 9. (It is easy to work out mentally.)
- **Less able** students are likely to find this subject difficult and may need individual help.
- Work through Example 4, emphasising the idea that this rounding method is intended to make calculation quicker and easier as a mental arithmetic exercise.
- Write 86 ÷ 0.21 on the board. Explain that divisions are often better written as fractions: $\frac{86}{0.21}$. This is then approximated as $\frac{90}{0.2}$. Multiplying top and bottom by 10 will make this easier,

so $\frac{90}{0.2}$ is the same as $\frac{90 \times 10}{0.2 \times 10} = \frac{900}{2} = 450$

**Students can now do Exercise 6D from the Student Book.**

| N 1–3, 5–8, 13, 14, 16 | Calculator 1, 6 | CM 9 | MR 4, 12, 15 | PS 10 | EV 11 |
|---|---|---|---|---|---|

## Part 3

- Check students' understanding of approximating with oral questioning. Talk about the degrees of accuracy that are sensible for different situations.
- Discuss the importance of giving sensible answers. Explain that sensible rounding is used in real-life contexts.

# Chapter 7 Number: Decimals and fractions

**Overview**

| | |
|---|---|
| **7.1** Calculating with decimals | **7.4** Adding and subtracting fractions |
| **7.2** Fractions and reciprocals | **7.5** Multiplying and dividing fractions |
| **7.3** Fractions of quantities | **7.6** Fractions on a calculator |

**Prior learning**

Know how to cancel fractions to their simplest form.
Know how to convert a mixed number to an improper fraction and vice versa.
Know the multiplication tables up to $12 \times 12$.
Know how to multiply and divide whole numbers.

**Learning objectives**

**Ensure that students can: multiply and divide decimals; convert between rational numbers, fractions and decimals; find reciprocals of numbers and fractions; work out one quantity as a fraction of another; add, subtract, multiply and divide fractions, with and without a calculator.**

In the examination, students will be expected to:
*   multiply and divide with decimals
*   recognise different types of fraction, reciprocal, terminating decimal and recurring decimal
*   convert terminating decimals to fractions
*   convert fractions to decimals
*   find reciprocals of numbers or fractions
*   work out a fraction of a quantity
*   find one quantity as a fraction of another
*   add and subtract fractions with different denominators
*   multiply proper fractions
*   multiply mixed numbers
*   divide by fractions
*   use a calculator to add and subtract fractions
*   use a calculator to multiply and divide fractions

**Extension**

Give students questions involving the four operations with three fractions or more complex decimal multiplication and division. **More able** students could design their own questions.

**Curriculum references**

| Section | GCSE specification |
|---|---|
| 7.1 | N2, 14 |
| 7.2 | N2,10 |
| 7.3 | N2, 8; R3 |
| 7.4 | N2, 8 |
| 7.5 | N2, 8 |
| 7.6 | N2, 8 |

## Route mapping

| Exercise | Accessible | Intermediate | Challenging | AO1 | AO2 MR CM | AO3 PS EV | Key questions |
|---|---|---|---|---|---|---|---|
| 7A | 1–6 | 7, 8 | 9 | 1, 2, 6, 9a | 4, 7, 8, 9b, c | 3, 5 | 1, 2, 7 |
| 7B | | 1–15 | | 1, 6–10, 12 | 2–5, 11, 13, 14 | 15 | 1, 2, 6, 7 |
| 7C | | 1–12 | | 1–6 | 7, 8, 12 | 9–11 | 1, 2, 6, 9 |
| 7D | | 1–9 | 10 | 1, 3, 4a, 9 | 2, 6, 7, 10 | 4b, 5, 8 | 1, 3, 8 |
| 7E | | 1–7 | | 1, 2, 5 | 6, 7 | 3, 4 | 1, 2, 5 |
| 7F | 1 | 2–8 | 9 | 1–3, 6, 7 | 4 | 5, 8, 9 | 1, 3, 6, 7 |

*Key questions are those that demonstrate mastery of the concept, or which require a step-up in understanding or application. Key questions could be used to identify the questions that students must tackle, to support differentiation, or to identify the questions that should be teacher-marked rather than student-marked.*

## About this chapter

**Making connections**: Ask students if they have ever wondered why some numbers are written as fractions and some are written as decimals. Explain that sometimes it is easier to use decimals and sometimes it is easier to use fractions. Fractions and decimals are just different ways of writing the same thing. For example, you usually use decimals when writing an amount of money, but fractions when talking about part of an hour.

**Relevance:** The ability to work fluently with fractions and decimals is part of everyday life. Students will need these skills in order to function effectively within the workplace. For example: petrol prices up by 2.2 pence a litre; $\frac{4}{5}$ of parents are happy with the local school.

**Working mathematically:** Give students some examples of the four operations involving fractions with some common errors in them. Ask students to explain the errors and how they would correct them. Ask questions such as: What do you look for when deciding if you can do a calculation mentally? Explain the steps of this calculation. Write the steps in order.

**Assessment:** In each section of this chapter, ensure that students have a good grasp of the key questions in each exercise before moving on. (Refer to the 'Route mapping' table.) Encourage students to read and think about the 'Ready to progress?' statements on page 168 of the Student Book. Check students' understanding at the end of the chapter, formatively, using peer assessment. Students could do a mini test in the form of the 'Review questions' on pages 168–169 of the Student Book. Follow up the test with an individual target-getting session, based on any areas for development that a student may have.

## Worked exemplars from the Student Book (page 167) – suggestions for use
- Present students with the same question but different numbers. They should use the exemplar to mirror the working, in full or just refer to the notes.
- Copy and cut the exemplars into cards. Students should match the working with the notes.
- Alternatively, copy and cut the working into cards but split the label/description from the working.

**Answers to the Student Book questions are available on the CR-ROM provided.**

# Section 7.1 Calculating with decimals

## Learning objectives
- Multiply and divide with decimals

## Resources and homework
- Student Book 7.1: pages 153–154
- Practice Book 7.1

## Making mathematical connections
- Place value manipulation

## Making cross-curricular connections
- **Science** – calculating with decimal numbers
- **Relevance** – essential everyday use

## Prior learning
- Students should know the multiplication tables up to 12 × 12.
- Students also need to know how to multiply and divide whole numbers.

## Working mathematically
- Encourage students to estimate the answer before calculating in order to check how sensible their answer is.
- Structure tasks so students can work out the methods for themselves; either by increasing the difficulty incrementally or through one straightforward and one complex example.

## Common misconceptions and remediation
- Multiplication: students may forget to insert the decimal point or put it in the wrong position.
- Division: students may change both numbers into integers, and then have the decimal point in the wrong place.
- With repeated emphasis on the rules for multiplying and dividing with decimals, students should reduce making these errors.

## Probing questions
- 108.8 ÷ 3.4 = 32.
- Use the calculation above to write down some other questions with the same answer.

## Literacy focus
- Key terms: None in this section
- Remind students to check that their mathematical dictionaries of key terms are up to date.

## Part 1
- Draw a divisibility clock on the board. Put the divisor in the middle and decimal answers around or inside the clock face.
- Point to an answer and ask students to give the number that can be divided by the number in the centre to give this answer.
- Ask questions such as: 'If 26 × 7 = 182, what is 26 × 70? × 700? × 0.7?' Discuss the students' answers.
- Increase the complexity for **more able** students.
- Write on the board: 0.5 × 0.8. Rewrite this as (5 ÷ 10) × (8 ÷ 10).
- This becomes 5 × 8 ÷ 100 = 0.4.
- Discuss this method and investigate it for other numbers.

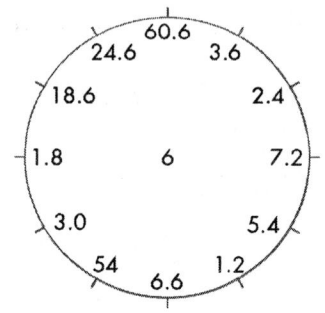

## Part 2

**Multiplying two decimal numbers**

- Ask students to give the answer to 11 × 7 (77). Then ask for the answer to 1.1 × 7 (7.7). Show students the effect of the decimal point by setting out the calculations as shown.

$$\begin{array}{r} 11 \\ \times\ \ 7 \\ \hline 77 \end{array} \qquad \begin{array}{r} 1.1 \\ \times\ \ 7 \\ \hline 7.7 \end{array}$$

- Now show students a more complex multiplication, e.g. 3.56 × 2.7.
- Explain that the calculations now consist of multiplying two decimals together.

$$\begin{array}{r} 3.56 \\ \times\ \ 2.7 \\ \hline 2492 \\ 7120 \\ \hline 9.612 \end{array}$$

- Use the example above again but change 27 to 2.7. Explain that 3.56 × 2.7 is ten times smaller than 3.56 × 27. So 3.56 × 2.7 = 9.612.

$$\begin{array}{r} 3.5\ 6 \\ \times\ \ \ 2.7 \\ \hline 2\ 4\ 9\ 2 \\ 7\ 1\ 2\ 0 \\ \hline 9.6\ 1\ 2 \end{array}$$

- Explain that 3.56 has two decimal places and that 2.7 has one decimal place, so the answer has 2 + 1 = three decimal places.

**Dividing one decimal number by another**

- Write: 36 ÷ 2, 3.6 ÷ 2, 3.6 ÷ 0.2 and 36 ÷ 0.2. Then write the same calculations as fractions:

$$\frac{36}{2}, \frac{3.6}{2}, \frac{3.6}{0.2}, \frac{36}{0.2} \qquad\qquad \frac{3.6}{0.2}\times\frac{10}{10}=\frac{36}{2}=18$$

- Ask for the answers (18, 1.8, 18, 180). Explain that dividing by 2 is easier than dividing by 0.2. Point out that dividing 36 by 2 is the same as dividing 3.6 by 0.2 because:

$$\frac{3.6}{0.2}\times\frac{10}{10}=\frac{36}{2}=18$$

- Multiplying by $\frac{10}{10}$ is multiplying by a whole one and so the answer is unchanged.

- Show an example using division by a two-decimal place number: 3.4 ÷ 0.05. Write it as a fraction: $\frac{3.4}{0.05}$ Explain that to change the format this time it is necessary to multiply by: $\frac{100}{100}$

$$\frac{3.4}{0.05}\times\frac{100}{100}=\frac{340}{5}=68$$

- This can now be done more formally by taking students through Example 2.
- **Students can now do Exercise 7A from the Student Book.**

| N 1, 2, 6, 9a | Calculator n/a | CM 9b | MR 4, 7, 8, 9c | PS 3, 5 | EV n/a |
|---|---|---|---|---|---|

## Part 3

- Given that 56 × 254 = 14 224 find the answers to:
  - 5.6 × 254
  - 56 × 2.54
  - 560 × 25.4
  - 14 224 ÷ 0.56

## Section 7.2 Fractions and reciprocals

### Learning objectives

- Recognise different types of fraction, reciprocal, terminating decimal and recurring decimal
- Convert terminating decimals to fractions
- Convert fractions to decimals
- Find reciprocals of numbers or fractions

### Resources and homework

- Student Book 7.2: pages 155–157
- Practice Book 7.2

### Making mathematical connections

- Probability
- Calculating with fractions
- Irrational numbers
- Graphing reciprocals

### Making cross-curricular connections

- **Science** – converting experimental results between fractions and decimals
- **Relevance** – uses in many jobs including engineering along with essential understanding of basic number for everyday life

### Prior learning

- Students need to know how to round decimals and how to use a calculator to convert fractions into decimals.

### Working mathematically

When converting decimals to fractions, check the number of decimal places is the same as the number of zeros, e.g. $0.107 = \dfrac{107}{1000}$ and $0.12 = \dfrac{12}{100}$.

### Common misconceptions and remediation

- Students often think that $\dfrac{1}{3}$ is equal to 0.3. Regularly reinforce that this is not the case.

### Probing questions

- How do you find the decimal equivalents of any fraction?
- What is a rational number? Explain and give an example.

### Literacy focus

- Key terms: invert, rational number, reciprocal, recurring decimal, terminating decimal
- Make certain students understand the meanings of each of the key terms.

### Part 1

- Ask if twelve-and-a-half lots of eight equal 100. Say: 'This helps us to see that 1 ÷ 8 = 0.125'. Stress what happens to the decimal as the denominator is doubled. Explain that this is a way of working out other decimals when you know that 0.5 is half. Ask: 'What is three-eighths? (0.375) Five-eighths? (0.625) ... How about one-fortieth? (0.025) One-eightieth? (0.0125) One-sixteenth? (0.0625).' Discuss the answers.
- Write fractions on the board and discuss them with students.
- Ask them what one-third is as a decimal (0.333... or $0.\dot{3}$). Make sure students understand the difference between $\dfrac{1}{3}$ and $\dfrac{3}{10}$.

## Part 2

### Fractions

- Make a set of cards, as per the table below. Ask small groups to match pairs of cards. Say that they need to know the conversions of common fractions and how to convert the others.

| $\frac{1}{2}$ | $\frac{1}{3}$ | $\frac{1}{4}$ | $\frac{1}{5}$ | $\frac{1}{8}$ | $\frac{1}{10}$ | $\frac{3}{4}$ | $\frac{2}{3}$ |
|---|---|---|---|---|---|---|---|
| 0.5 | 0.33 | 0.25 | 0.2 | 0.125 | 0.1 | 0.75 | 0.67 |
| 0.13 | 0.37 | 0.23 | 0.09 | 0.01 | 0.003 | 0.007 | 0.919 |
| $\frac{13}{100}$ | $\frac{37}{100}$ | $\frac{23}{100}$ | $\frac{9}{100}$ | $\frac{1}{100}$ | $\frac{3}{1000}$ | $\frac{7}{1000}$ | $\frac{919}{1000}$ |

- Now ask students to look again at $\frac{1}{3}$ = 0.33. Point out that 0.33 is actually $\frac{33}{100}$ but that $\frac{1}{3}$ = 0.333 33... and it is rounded to 0.33. Explain that this is a recurring decimal (one that never ends), and is written as $0.\dot{3}$. Show other recurring decimals, e.g. 0.181818... = $0.\dot{1}\dot{8}$.
- Now go through the text in the Student Book.

### Converting fractions into decimals

- Show students how to convert a fraction into a decimal by dividing the numerator by the denominator.
- Say that this often produces a recurring decimal. Show this using division on a calculator, e.g. with $\frac{2}{11}$ as 2 ÷ 11 or using the fraction buttons. Refer to the Student Book.
- Encourage **less able** students to use a calculator for questions of this type, particularly while they are becoming familiar with the new ideas. **More able** students should attempt at least the easier questions, using mental methods, and use a calculator to check them.

### Converting terminating decimals into fractions

- Show students that terminal decimals can easily be fractions, by taking the decimal number as the numerator, and 10, 100, 1000, and so on (depends on the number of decimal places) as the denominator. Then simplify this fraction if necessary. Refer students to the text.

### Finding reciprocals of numbers or fractions

- Explain that a reciprocal is 1 divided by the number. Write on the board: the reciprocal of $\frac{3}{4}$ is $1 \div \frac{3}{4}$ = 1.33... (or $\frac{4}{3}$, or $1\frac{1}{3}$).
- Explain that dividing 1 by a fraction inverts the fraction, e.g. the reciprocal of $\frac{2}{3}$ is $\frac{3}{2}$.
- Show students the reciprocal button on a calculator (often shown as $x^{-1}$ or $\frac{1}{x}$).
- **Students can now do Exercise 7B from the Student Book.**

| N 1, 6–10, 12 | Calculator all | CM 3–5, 13 | MR 2, 11, 14 | PS 15 | EV n/a |
|---|---|---|---|---|---|

## Part 3

- Students will have found out that $\frac{1}{9}$ = 0.11111... and $\frac{2}{9}$ = 0.2222... . Establish that $\frac{3}{9}$ = 0.3333... and ask students what common fraction this recurring decimal represents.
- Show that $\frac{3}{9}$ cancels to $\frac{1}{3}$. Continue with $\frac{4}{9}, \frac{5}{9}, \frac{6}{9}$ (establish the link to $\frac{2}{3}$), $\frac{7}{9}, \frac{8}{9}$ and $\frac{9}{9}$.
- Students will see that $\frac{9}{9}$ = 0.9999... . Ask them what fraction is represented by $\frac{9}{9}$.

# Section 7.3 Fractions of quantities

## Learning objectives
- Work out a fraction of a quantity
- Find one quantity as a fraction of another

## Resources and homework
- Student Book 7.3: pages 158–159
- Practice Book 7.3

## Making mathematical connections
- Equivalent fractions
- Pie charts

## Making cross-curricular connections
- **Science** – calculating with fractions and decimals in experiments such as mixing chemicals
- **Food Technology** – comparing quantities in different packaging to evaluate different offers
- **Relevance** – everyday use of fractions and fractional quantities

## Prior learning
- Students need to know how to use the fraction button on a calculator. They should also know how to use a calculator to multiply and divide.
- They must know the multiplication tables to 10 × 10.
- Students should be able to simplify fractions. They will need to know basic conversions between units or you could give them to students during the lesson.

## Working mathematically
- Encourage students to check that the units are the same before they write the fraction.
- Point out that, later in the course, students will need to know fractions of 360° for drawing pie charts.
- Structure tasks so that students can work out the methods for themselves, either by increasing the difficulty incrementally or with one straightforward and one complex example.

## Common misconceptions and remediation
- A common mistake is to muddle 'of' and 'off', e.g. $\frac{1}{4}$ of 80 and $\frac{1}{4}$ off 80. Point out that students need to read questions very carefully.
- Students may not match the units before comparing, so, e.g. 25p as a fraction of £2 would be given as $\frac{25}{2}$. Making students aware of this error should help them to avoid it.

## Probing questions
- What clues do you look for when cancelling fractions to their simplest form?
- How do you know when you have the simplest form of a fraction?
- How do you know which part is the numerator and which is the denominator?

## Literacy focus
- Key terms: denominator, numerator
- Make sure students understand the meaning of a quantity and ask them to describe their methods by writing them down or saying them aloud.

## Part 1

- Use a metre rule or draw one on the board.
- Show a length of 20 centimetres on the rule and ask what fraction this is of the whole rule. Ask: 'Can this be simplified?'
- Repeat with other numbers of centimetres and then ask questions such as: 'What fraction is 20 centimetres of two metres?'
- Bring in other measures such as money or time.

## Part 2

- Give students three sets of cards, jumbled up.
- Ask students to organise the cards so that: card from set 1 as a fraction of card from set 2 = card from set 3. For example: 30 cm as a fraction of 1 m = $\frac{3}{10}$.

| Set 1 | Set 2 | Set 3 |
|---|---|---|
| 30 cm | 1 m | $\frac{3}{10}$ |
| 25 p | £1 | $\frac{1}{4}$ |
| 3 hours | 1 day | $\frac{1}{8}$ |
| 2 days | 3 weeks | $\frac{2}{21}$ |
| 4 grams | 1 kg | $\frac{1}{250}$ |

- Students will spot the correct answers but, ultimately, they must know the conversions. **Less able** students may initially need to be given the necessary conversions. **More able** students may guess some of the groupings but encourage students to check them accurately.
- Show students a formal method, e.g. 30 cm as a fraction of 1 m is the same as 30 cm as a fraction of 100 cm.
- 30 as a fraction of 100 is $\frac{30}{100} = \frac{3}{10}$.
- Work through Example 3 from the Student Book with the class.
- Before working through Example 4, it is important to recognise that **less able** students will find it easier to use the word 'of' instead of the symbol '×'. However, to aid their understanding and help their progress with more difficult questions, it is important to plant the idea that 'of' and '×' mean the same thing.
- Work through a few examples, starting with Example 4. If units are given, include them in the answers.
- Check that students are able to do the same calculations on their calculators. Then work through Example 5 with students.
- Depending on the ability of the group, **less able** students can use calculators to complete some of the calculations; **more able** students can use them for checking their answers.
- **Students can now do Exercise 7C from the Student Book.**

| N 1–6 | Calculator n/a | CM 7, 8 | MR 12 | PS 9, 10 | EV 11 |
|---|---|---|---|---|---|

## Part 3

- Check students' understanding by asking quick-fire questions such as:
  - What is three-quarters of eight centimetres?
  - What is two-thirds of 90°?
  - What is three-fifths of 60 minutes?
- Move on to context questions with mixed units. Give the conversions if they are not known.
  - What is $\frac{2}{3}$ of a full turn in degrees?
  - What is one-fifth of an hour, given in minutes?
  - What is $\frac{3}{4}$ of a kilogram, in grams?

## Section 7.4 Adding and subtracting fractions

### Learning objectives
- Work out a fraction of a quantity
- Find one quantity as a fraction of another

### Resources and homework
- Student Book 7.4: pages 159–161
- Practice Book 7.4

### Making mathematical connections
- Rearranging simple formulae including fractions
- Solving equations including fractions

### Making cross-curricular connections
- **Food Technology** – working with fractions of ingredients
- **Economics; Business Studies** – working with VAT, unemployment figures
- **Relevance** – everyday use of fractions and fractional quantities

### Prior learning
- Students should be able to find the lowest common multiple (LCM) of two or three numbers, and be able to convert mixed numbers into improper fractions and vice versa.
- Students should also know how to add and subtract fractions with the same denominator.

### Working mathematically
- How do you find a common denominator when adding or subtracting fractions?
- Is there more than one possible common denominator you could use?
- What would happen if you used a different common denominator?
- Ask students to try to solve a question using different common denominators.

### Common misconceptions and remediation
- Students often fail to convert to equivalent fractions to make the denominators the same; they simply add or subtract the numerators and the denominators.
- Students may change the denominators, but forget to change the numerators.
- Point out these mistakes each time they occur to help to reduce errors.

### Probing questions
- Give students some addition and subtraction of fractions questions with errors in them.
- Ask students to explain the mistakes and how they would correct them.

### Literacy focus
- Key terms: equivalent fraction, lowest common denominator, mixed number
- Ask students to write a bulleted list summarising their method for answering these types of questions.

### Part 1
- Write the numbers 2 to 10 on the board. Ask students for the LCM of 2 and 3 (6), 2 and 4 (4), 2 and 5 (10). For **more able** students use more challenging numbers, e.g. 6 and 8 (24).
- Point out that when fractions with different denominators are added, the lowest common denominator is the LCM of the denominators.

### Part 2
- Write $\frac{2}{3} + \frac{1}{5}$ on the board. Ask students to change each fraction into fifteenths ($\frac{10}{15} + \frac{3}{15}$).

- Now draw a 3 by 5 rectangle.
- Shade 10 squares and then 3 more squares to show that $\dfrac{10}{15} + \dfrac{3}{15} = \dfrac{13}{15}$

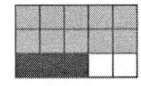

- Work through Example 6. Write $\dfrac{5}{6} - \dfrac{3}{4}$ on the board. Ask students to change the fractions to twelfths. $(\dfrac{10}{12} - \dfrac{9}{12})$
- Now draw a 3 by 4 rectangle. Shade 10 squares and then shade nine of these squares to show that $\dfrac{10}{12} - \dfrac{9}{12} = \dfrac{1}{12}$.

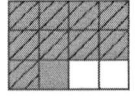

- Now write $2\dfrac{3}{4} - 1\dfrac{5}{6}$ on the board and ask students to change the fractions to twelfths. $(2\dfrac{9}{12} - 1\dfrac{10}{12}$ or $\dfrac{33}{12} - \dfrac{22}{12})$.
- Draw three 4 by 3 rectangles and shade $2\dfrac{3}{4}$ (33 small squares shaded = $\dfrac{33}{12}$) and draw two 4 by 3 rectangles and shade $1\dfrac{5}{6}$ (22 small squares shaded = $\dfrac{22}{12}$).

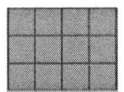 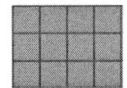 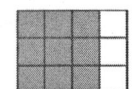 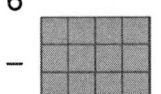 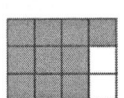 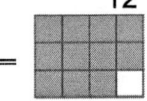

- Taking 22 small squares away from 33 small squares leaves 11 small squares = $\dfrac{11}{12}$, so $2\dfrac{3}{4} - 1\dfrac{5}{6} = \dfrac{11}{12}$.
- Show students how they can do these calculations without using diagrams.

e.g. $2\dfrac{3}{4} - 1\dfrac{5}{6} = 2 + \dfrac{3}{4} - 1 - \dfrac{5}{6}$

$= 1 + \dfrac{3}{4} - \dfrac{5}{6}$

$= 1 + \dfrac{9}{12} - \dfrac{10}{12}$

$= 1 - \dfrac{1}{12}$

$= \dfrac{11}{12}$

- Work through Example 7 in the Student Book with the class.
- **Students can now do Exercise 7D from the Student Book.**

| N 1, 3, 4a, 9 | Calculator n/a | CM 6, 7, 10a | MR 2, 10b | PS 5, 8 | EV 4b |

## Part 3

- Write this calculation on the board: $\dfrac{1}{2} + \dfrac{1}{3} - \dfrac{1}{4} - \dfrac{1}{6}$. Discuss strategies and how to ensure that students find the answers in the most efficient way. $(\dfrac{6}{12} + \dfrac{4}{12} - \dfrac{3}{12} - \dfrac{2}{12} = \dfrac{5}{12})$
- Remind students to use the fraction button on their calculators to check their answers.
- **Less able** students who have not completed the exercise may use a calculator to do so.
- Give students several addition and subtraction questions to complete.
- Show some answers under a visualiser (a mini camera that connects to a computer), if your school has them. Ask students to discuss the method and accuracy.

# Section 7.5 Multiplying and dividing fractions

## Learning objectives

- Multiply proper fractions
- Multiply mixed numbers
- Divide by fractions

## Making mathematical connections

- Rearranging simple formulae containing fractions
- Solving equations containing fractions

## Resources and homework

- Student Book 7.5: pages 161–163
- Practice Book 7.5

## Making cross-curricular connections

- **Food Technology** – calculating the required fractions of ingredients
- **Science** – calculating with fractions in Physics
- **Relevance** – use of fractions in day-to-day calculations

## Prior learning

- Students should know the multiplication tables to 10 × 10 and be able to cancel fractions.
- They should also be familiar with multiplication of fractions.
- Students should be able to convert between mixed numbers and improper fractions.

## Working mathematically

- Students will understand and be able to fluently execute methods involving the four operations with fractions, extending to mixed numbers and questions with more operations.

## Common misconceptions and remediation

- Students work out multiplications incorrectly, e.g. 3 × 3 = 6, and make errors converting mixed numbers to improper fractions. When multiplying mixed numbers, students may multiply the whole numbers and then the fractions, e.g. giving $1\frac{1}{2} \times 2\frac{1}{4} = 2\frac{1}{8}$ instead of $3\frac{3}{8}$. Stress the importance of knowing multiplication tables. Point out errors as they occur.
- When dividing fractions, students may simply divide the numerators and denominators, or they find the reciprocal of the wrong fraction, or of both fractions. Encouraging students to estimate answers should help, e.g. $8\frac{5}{6} \div 1\frac{2}{5} \approx 9 \div 1\frac{1}{2} = 6$ (One-and-a-halves in nine?)

## Probing questions

- Write down two fractions that multiply together to give a bigger answer than either of the fractions you are multiplying. How did you do it?
- What do you know about dividing by a number between 0 and 1?

## Literacy focus

- Key terms: improper fraction, proper fraction
- Ask students to write a bulleted list of their method for answering this type of question.

## Part 1

- Remind students that they learned how to multiply proper fractions in Key Stage 3. They may need further reinforcement of the rule.

- Ask students some quick-fire multiplications of fractions, e.g.
$\frac{1}{2} \times \frac{1}{2} (\frac{1}{4})$, $\frac{1}{2} \times \frac{1}{3} (\frac{1}{6})$, $\frac{1}{5} \times \frac{1}{3} (\frac{1}{15})$, $\frac{1}{8} \times \frac{1}{4} (\frac{1}{32})$.

- Move on to questions involving non-unit fractions, e.g. $\frac{2}{3} \times \frac{1}{2} (\frac{2}{6} = \frac{1}{3})$ and remind students to give all answers in their simplest form.
- Check that students know how to find the reciprocal of fractions and mixed numbers.
- Ask students for the reciprocal of: $\frac{1}{3} (\frac{3}{1} = 3), \frac{2}{7} (\frac{7}{2}), \frac{3}{4} (\frac{4}{3}), \frac{2}{5} (\frac{5}{2}), 1\frac{1}{4} (\frac{4}{5})$ (because $1\frac{1}{4} = \frac{5}{4}$, i.e. first change to a mixed number, then invert the fraction)
- Explain, if necessary, that the reciprocal of a fraction can be found by inverting the fraction.

## Part 2

**Multiplying fractions**
- Draw a 2 by 5 rectangle and shade half of it, as shown.
- Ask students what one-fifth of the half is ($\frac{1}{10}$ or one square), and write $\frac{1}{5} \times \frac{1}{2} = \frac{1}{10}$.
- Ask students how they can work out the answer.
- Prompt **less able** students by writing more fraction calculations on the board. Establish that the rule is to multiply the numerators and multiply the denominators, then cancel if possible.
- Ask students how they will deal with multiplying mixed numbers, prompting them to change to improper fractions, then work through Example 8 from the Student Book.
- Check that students can change mixed numbers into improper fractions, e.g.
$1\frac{7}{18} (\frac{25}{18}), 3\frac{1}{3} (\frac{10}{3})$ and $1\frac{9}{20} (\frac{29}{20})$

**Dividing fractions**
- Write on the board: $3 \div \frac{3}{4} = 4$ and $3 \times \frac{4}{3} = 4$.
- Explain that dividing by a fraction is the same as multiplying by its reciprocal.
- Ask: How many halves in 6? (12). $6 \div \frac{1}{2} = 6 \times 2 = 12$.
- Work through Example 9 from the Student Book with the class. Students often find this a difficult concept so give more examples, as needed. Remind students that, to divide mixed numbers, they must first change the mixed numbers to improper fractions.
- **Students can now do Exercise 7E from the Student Book.**

| N 1, 2, 5 | Calculator n/a | CM 7 | MR 6 | PS 3, 4 | EV n/a |

## Part 3

- On the board, write: $1\frac{2}{5} \times 2\frac{3}{7} = \frac{7}{5} \times \frac{17}{7}$. Tell students that if they simplify the fractions as soon as possible, they will be working with smaller numbers. Show that they should still get the correct answer if they work out $\frac{7 \times 17}{5 \times 7} = \frac{119}{35}$ and then simplify ($\frac{17}{5}$).

- Discuss the following disadvantages: working with large numbers creates more chance of an error; not being able to spot common factors. Result: answer is not reduced to simplest form.
- Give students several multiplication and division questions to complete.
- Ask the class to discuss the method and accuracy.

## Section 7.6 Fractions on a calculator

### Learning objectives

- Use a calculator to add and subtract fractions
- Use a calculator to multiply and divide fractions

### Making mathematical connections

- Efficient use of a calculator

### Resources and homework

- Student Book 7.6: pages 163–166
- Practice Book 7.6

### Making cross-curricular connections

- **Food Technology** – calculating the required fractions of ingredients
- **Science** – calculating with fractions in Physics
- **Relevance** – everyday calculations of fractions with a calculator

### Prior learning

- Students should be able to add and subtract simple fractions without using a calculator.

### Working mathematically

- Using a calculator effectively is a valuable skill that students need to learn.
- Make sure that all students have an appropriate calculator.

### Common misconceptions and remediation

- The most common mistakes are errors made in keying the calculation and then not checking that the answer is sensible.

### Probing questions

- Provide students with some fraction questions and answers with common errors and ask them to identify the mistake in each calculation.
- When would it be appropriate to use a calculator rather than a standard written method?

### Literary focus

- Key term: shift key
- Ask students to write a step-by-step guide for using a calculator to answer calculations with fractions.

### Part 1

- **Note**: Students must have scientific calculators for this lesson.
- Explain to students how to enter fractions on a calculator.
- Give them several fractions including mixed numbers to key in.

### Part 2

**Using a calculator to convert improper fractions to mixed numbers**
- Go through this section in the Student Book. Give students practice with converting improper fractions to mixed numbers. For example, ask students to key in $\frac{16}{7}$ on their calculators and check that they can convert it to a mixed number ($2\frac{2}{7}$).

- Repeat with other improper fractions.
- If students do not get the correct answers, ask them to follow the keying instructions.

**Using a calculator to convert mixed numbers to improper fractions**
- Go through this section with students. Then give them practice in converting mixed numbers to improper fractions. For example, ask students to key in $4\frac{3}{5}$ on their calculators and check that they can convert it to an improper fraction $(\frac{23}{5})$.
- Ask them to convert it back to an improper fraction. Repeat with other mixed numbers.
- If students struggle, ask them to follow the keying instructions in the Student Book.

**Using a calculator to add and subtract fractions**
- Go through Examples 10 and 11 and give students some more questions to try.
- They could display their results on mini-whiteboards.

**Using a calculator to multiply and divide fractions**
- Go through Examples 12 and 13 with students and give them some more questions to try.
- Again, they could display their results on mini-whiteboards.
- **Students can now do Exercise 7F from the Student Book.**

| N 1–3, 6, 7 | Calculator all | CM 4 | MR n/a | PS 5, 9 | EV 8 |
|---|---|---|---|---|---|

# Part 3

- Ask students to key this pattern of multiplications into their calculators.

$$1\frac{1}{2} \times 2\frac{2}{3} \times 3\frac{3}{4} \times 4\frac{4}{5} \times 5\frac{5}{6} \times 6\frac{6}{7}...$$

- Ask students to look at the answers as they are keying in the multiplications and to tell you what they notice. (Every time they multiply a pair of numbers, the answer is a whole number.) With **more able** groups, prove this using algebra.

- $1\frac{1}{2} \times 2\frac{2}{3} = 4$

- $1\frac{1}{2} \times 2\frac{2}{3} \times 3\frac{3}{4} \times 4\frac{4}{5} = 72$

- $1\frac{1}{2} \times 2\frac{2}{3} \times 3\frac{3}{4} \times 4\frac{4}{5} \times 5\frac{5}{6} \times 6\frac{6}{7} = 2880$

- Give students a quick calculator test to check that they can use a calculator efficiently. Read out the following questions or write them on the board.

$$1\frac{1}{2} + 3\frac{2}{3} \left(5\frac{1}{6}\right) \qquad\qquad 1\frac{1}{12} + 2\frac{3}{8} + 1\frac{17}{24} \left(5\frac{1}{6}\right)$$

$$7\frac{5}{12} + 2\frac{3}{8} \left(9\frac{19}{24}\right) \qquad\qquad 5\frac{3}{5} + 2\frac{1}{4} - 2\frac{41}{60} \left(5\frac{1}{6}\right)$$

$$6\frac{3}{4} + 2\frac{1}{6} - 3\frac{2}{3} \left(5\frac{1}{4}\right)$$

- Point out to students the potential for errors if they simply assume that they know an answer rather than working it out.

# Chapter 8 Algebra: Linear graphs

## Overview

| | |
|---|---|
| **8.1** Graphs and equations | **8.5** Finding the equation of a line from its graph |
| **8.2** Drawing linear graphs by finding points | **8.6** The equation of a parallel line |
| **8.3** Gradient of a line | **8.7** Real-life uses of graphs |
| **8.4** $y = mx + c$ | **8.8** Solving simultaneous equations using graphs |

### Prior learning

Know how to substitute numbers into a formula.
Know how to read and estimate from scales.
Know how to plot a graph from a table of values.

### Learning objectives

**Ensure that students can: plot negative coordinates; work out the gradient of a line; draw a straight-line graph from its equation; work out the equation of a linear graph; draw linear graphs parallel to other lines; read information from a conversion graph; use graphs to work out formulae and solve simultaneous linear equations.**

In the examination, students will be expected to:
* use flow diagrams to draw graphs
* work out the equations of horizontal and vertical lines
* work out the coordinates of the midpoint of a straight line
* draw linear graphs without using flow diagrams
* work out the gradient of a straight line
* draw a line with a certain gradient
* draw graphs using the gradient-intercept method
* draw graphs using the cover-up method
* work out the equation of a line, using its gradient and $y$-intercept
* work out the equation of a line given two points on the line
* work out the equation of a linear graph that is parallel to another line and passes through a specific point
* convert from one unit to another unit by using a conversion graph
* use straight-line graphs to work out formulae
* solve simultaneous linear equations using graphs.

### Extension

Ask students to explore solving simultaneous equations graphically, with one quadratic and one linear equation.

### Curriculum references

| Section | GCSE specification |
|---|---|
| 8.1 | A8, 9 |
| 8.2 | A8, 9 |
| 8.3 | A10 |
| 8.4 | A8, 9 |

| Section | GCSE specification |
|---|---|
| 8.5 | A10 |
| 8.6 | A9, 10 |
| 8.7 | A14 |
| 8.8 | A19 |

## Route mapping

| Exercise | Accessible | Intermediate | Challenging | AO1 | AO2 MR CM | AO3 PS EV | Key questions |
|----------|-----------|--------------|-------------|-----|-----------|-----------|---------------|
| 8A | 1–7 | 8–11 | | 1–8 | 9, 10 | 11 | 1 -5 |
| 8B | | 1–10 | | 1–4 | 5, 6 | 7–10 | 1–3 |
| 8C | | 1–9 | | 1, 2, 9 | 5–7 | 3, 4, 8 | 1, 2, 4, 9 |
| 8D | | 1–4 | | 1, 2, 4 | 3 | | 1, 3 |
| 8E | | | 1–6 | 1, 2 | 3, 4 | 5, 6 | 1, 4 |
| 8F | | | 1–10 | 1, 4, 7, 8 | 3, 6, 9, 10 | 2, 5 | 1, 2 |
| 8G | | 1–3 | 4 | 2, 3 | 1 | 4 | 2, 3 |
| 8H | 1–5 | 6 | 7 | 2–4 | 1 | 5, 6 | 1, 2, 3 |
| 8I | | | 1–12 | 1–8 | 11, 12 | 9, 10 | 1–6 |

*Key questions are those that demonstrate mastery of the concept, or which require a step-up in understanding or application. Key questions could be used to identify the questions that students must tackle, to support differentiation, or to identify the questions that should be teacher-marked rather than student-marked.*

## About this chapter

**Making connections**: This chapter starts with students reviewing how to draw a graph using a flow diagram. Students then relate this to finding and drawing the equation of a linear graph; they also find the gradient of a line and use the general equation $y = mx + c$. Students learn how to interpret conversion graphs. Then they learn how to draw linear graphs that are parallel to other graphs. Finally, students learn how to solve simultaneous equations graphically.

**Relevance**: A linear graph (often called a straight-line graph) shows two variables that increase at a constant rate. Students will meet linear graphs and the relationships they represent in various situations in daily life, e.g. exchange rates and the cost of hiring a vehicle along with many other situations.

**Working mathematically**: Students will explain how to plot the graph $y = 3x +2$. They will know and be able to explain the initial steps, e.g. using $x = 2$ to work out the $y$-coordinate of the point (2, 4) on the line $y = x + 2$. Students will write down equations that pass through points and solve two simultaneous equations graphically.

**Assessment**: In each section of this chapter, ensure that students have a good grasp of the key questions in each exercise before moving on. (Refer to the 'Route mapping' table.) Encourage students to read and think about the 'Ready to progress?' statements on page 200 of the Student Book. Check students' understanding at the end of the chapter, formatively, using peer assessment. Students could do a mini test in the form of the 'Review questions' on pages 200–201 of the Student Book. Follow up the test with an individual target-getting session, based on any areas for development that a student may have.

## Worked exemplars from the Student Book (page 198) – suggestions for use
- Present students with the same question but different numbers. They should use the exemplar to mirror the working, in full or just refer to the notes.
- Copy and cut the exemplars into cards. Students match the working with the notes.
- Alternatively, copy and cut the working into cards but split the label/description from the working.

**Answers to the Student Book questions are available on the CD-ROM provided.**

# Section 8.1 Graphs and equations

## Learning objectives
- Use flow diagrams to draw graphs
- Work out the equations of horizontal and vertical lines
- Work out the coordinates of the midpoint of a straight line

## Resources and homework
- Student Book 8.1: pages 171–176
- Practice Book 8.1

## Making mathematical connections
- Quadratic graphs
- Graphs of trigonometric functions
- Statistical graphs

## Making cross-curricular connections
- **Science** – representing experimental results graphically
- **Relevance** – uses in engineering, manufacturing, business

## Prior learning
- Students must be able to read and plot coordinates (even when they are given in table form).

## Working mathematically
- Remind students that they should always use a sharp pencil when drawing linear graphs.
- Mention to students that if a point does not fit on a straight line, then they have calculated or plotted the point incorrectly.

## Common misconceptions and remediation
- Students often work out only two points and draw the line, and do not work out a third point to check that the line is correct. Inadequate algebra skills can also lead to mistakes.

## Probing questions
- Ask students to explain how they would draw the straight line graph of $y = 2x + 1$ using a flow diagram.

## Literacy focus
- Key terms: flow diagram, function, input, intersect, line segment, midpoint, negative coordinates, output, $x$-values, $y$-values
- Make sure students know the meaning of each key term when it is used in algebraic and graphical contexts.

## Part 1
- Write a rule on the board, e.g. × 2 + 1. Ask for the output when the input is 0, 1, 2, 3 and 4. Provide other rules and find the outputs, e.g. × 4 − 5, ÷ 2 − 3.
- Provide negative input numbers for these rules, e.g. −3, −2, −1.

## Part 2
### Flow diagrams
- Talk about the way students have been writing functions and how to write them. For example: $x \rightarrow 3x + 1$. Show this using a flow diagram:

- Explain that we can write functions in different ways, e.g. $y = 3x + 1$, which means the same.
- This is a simpler way of looking at the function if we want to draw a graph of it.
- We can draw a graph of every function; the coordinates come from the combination of inputs and outputs. Tell students that they are going to create some of these graphs.
- On the board, write $x \rightarrow 3x + 1$ and show how we can work with it:

- The $y$ simply tells us the output for different values of $x$.
- We can create a table of values that combines the inputs and outputs. On the board, write:

| $x$ | 0 | 1 | 2 | 3 | 4 | 5 |
|---|---|---|---|---|---|---|
| $y$ | | | | | | |

- Show how we use the flow diagram of $x \rightarrow 3x + 1$ to substitute the different values of $x$ as the inputs to find the outputs ($y$). We can use any values for $x$ that we want, but it is a good idea to use those around 0.
- Now go through the text on flow diagrams in the Student Book.

**Plotting negative coordinates**
- Explain how we use the flow diagram of $x \rightarrow 3x + 1$ to substitute some negative values of $x$ as the inputs to find the outputs ($y$).
- Go through the substitution with the class to give the values in the table, as shown here:

| $x$ | −2 | −1 | 0 | 1 | 2 | 3 |
|---|---|---|---|---|---|---|
| $y$ | −5 | −2 | 1 | 4 | 7 | 10 |

- To draw the graph, we need a pair of axes that includes all the values in the table, that is, $x$ from −2 to 3 and $y$ from −5 to 10.
- Draw the axes on the board.
- Remind students how to plot the coordinates from the table and join them with a straight line.
- Point out that the straight line represents ALL the points that satisfy $y = 3x + 1$.
- Demonstrate this by choosing any non-integer point, e.g. $x = 1.5$; go through the calculations $(1.5 \times 3) + 1 = 5.5$ and show that $(1.5, 5.5)$ is on the line.
- Show that this also works for a few other points, e.g. $x = 2.2$ (7.6) and $x = −0.5$ (−0.5).
- Now go through the text on plotting negative coordinates, including the text on how to find the midpoint of two points; then work through Example 1 in the Student Book.
- **Students can now do Exercise 8A from the Student Book.**

| A 1–8 | Calculator n/a | CM n/a | MR 9, 10 | PS 11 | EV n/a |
|---|---|---|---|---|---|

# Part 3

- Draw a set of axes on the board. Ask a volunteer to draw the line with the equation $y = 2x + 1$ using a flow diagram. If it is correct, ask for the (0, ?) and (?, 0) coordinates (and other points if suitable).
- Repeat with other volunteers and other lines, e.g. $y = 3x - 2$, $y = 6x$, $y = \frac{1}{2}x + 4$.

## Learning objectives

- Draw linear graphs without using flow diagrams

## Resources and homework

- Student Book 8.2: pages 176–179
- Practice Book 8.2

## Making mathematical connections

- Quadratic graphs
- Graphs of trigonometric functions
- Statistical graphs

## Making cross-curricular connections

- **Science** – representing experimental results graphically
- **Relevance** – uses in engineering, manufacturing, business

## Prior learning

- Students must be able to read and plot coordinates (even when they are given in table form).
- Students must also be able to substitute into simple algebraic functions.

## Working mathematically

- Remind students that they should always use a sharp pencil when drawing linear graphs.
- Mention that if a point does not fit on a straight line, then they have calculated or plotted the point incorrectly.

## Common misconceptions and remediation

- Students often work out only two points and draw the line, and do not work out a third point to check that the line is correct. Inadequate algebra skills can also lead to mistakes.

## Probing questions

- How would you draw the straight line graph of $y = 3x + 2$ without using a flow diagram?
- How do you determine the scale on the $x$- and $y$-axes? Does it have to be the same scale?

## Literacy focus

- Key term: linear graphs
- Make sure that students know the meaning of 'linear' when it is used in algebraic contexts.

## Part 1

- Ask students to complete the table using the flow diagram.

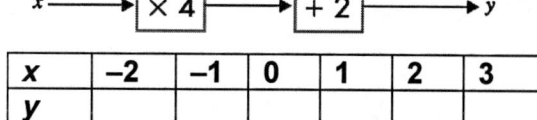

| $x$ | −2 | −1 | 0 | 1 | 2 | 3 |
|-----|----|----|---|---|---|---|
| $y$ |    |    |   |   |   |   |

# Part 2

- Stress these points to students.
  - To draw a straight line requires a minimum of two points, but three is better, as one of the three points can be used as a check.
  - Use a sharp pencil. Drawing thick lines makes it more difficult to read values accurately. Students may be penalised for drawing thick lines in an examination.
  - When drawing points and lines accurately, your eyes should be directly above the paper. One millimetre is the tolerance allowed in an examination.
- Now, with the class, go through Example 2 and the text in the Student Book.
- **Students can now do Exercise 8B from the Student Book.**

| A 1–4 | Calculator n/a | CM 5, 6 | MR n/a | PS 9, 10 | EV 7, 8 |
|-------|----------------|---------|--------|----------|---------|

# Part 3

- On the board, write $y = 5x + 17$ and $y = 5x + 11$.
- Ask what students can tell you about the graphs of these two functions.
- Students should be able to tell you that the lines have the same slope (are parallel), and that the first line intercepts the $y$-axis at a higher number than the second line.

# Section 8.3 Gradient of a line

## Learning objectives

- Work out the gradient of a straight line
- Draw a line with a certain gradient

## Making mathematical connections

- Gradients of quadratic graphs
- Gradients from statistical graphs

## Resources and homework

- Student Book 8.3: pages 180–183
- Practice Book 8.3

## Making cross-curricular connections

- **Science** – analysing experimental results graphically
- **Relevance** – uses in engineering, manufacturing, business

## Prior learning

- Students must have completed Section 8.2 and be able to read and plot coordinates (even when the coordinates are given in table form).
- Students must also be able to substitute into simple algebraic functions.

## Working mathematically

- Students will be able to answer questions, for example:
  o Is the gradient of a linear graph the same at every point on the line?
  o On what types of graphs might the gradient change?
  o Can you draw a graph with gradient 0?
- **More able** students can be shown quadratic graphs and asked how they would find the gradient at a point.

## Common misconceptions and remediation

- Students often ignore the scales on the axes and just count the squares when calculating the gradient, or they divide the change in $x$ over the change in $y$ by mistake. Students may also give the $x$-intercept instead of the $y$-intercept. Make certain that you address these points and that students have a clear understanding of how to do these questions correctly.

## Probing questions

- How do you find the gradient of this line.
- Does it matter if the $x$-axis scale is different to the $y$-axis scale?

## Literacy focus

- Key term: gradient
- Ask students to write a step-by-step guide for finding the gradient from a linear graph.

## Part 1

- Review the previous section by asking students to draw the graphs of:
  $y = 2x + 3$ and $y = x + 2$ from $x = -4$ to 4.
- Ask students about the steepness of the lines.
- Explain that the steepness is called the gradient of the line.

# Part 2

- Go through the introductory text in this section of the Student Book with the class.
- Before referring to Example 3 in the Student Book, stress these points:
  - When drawing a triangle to work out the gradient, always use grid points so that the values are integers.
  - Always divide the distance in the *y*-direction by the distance in the *x*-direction.
  - Lines that slope from top left to bottom right have a negative gradient.

## Drawing a line with a given gradient

- Discuss the text under the heading in the Student Book with the class.
- Then work through Example 4 with students.
- **Students can now do Exercise 8C from the Student Book.**

| A 1, 2, 9 | Calculator n/a | CM 7 | MR 5, 6 | PS 8 | EV 3, 4 |
|-----------|----------------|------|---------|------|---------|

# Part 3

- Ask students to look back at the graphs they drew in Part 1.
- Now ask them to tell you the gradient and the intercept of the line with the *y*-axis.
- Can they see a connection? Discuss this question as a class.

### Learning objectives

- Draw graphs using the gradient-intercept method
- Draw graphs using the cover-up method

### Resources and homework

- Student Book 8.4: pages 184–187
- Practice Book 8.4

### Making mathematical connections

- Quadratic graphs
- Graphs of trig functions
- Statistical graphs

### Making cross-curricular connections

- **Science** – representing experimental results graphically
- **Relevance** – uses in engineering, manufacturing, business

## Prior learning

- Students must have completed sections 8.2 and 8.3 and be able to read and plot coordinates (even when they are given in table form).
- Students must also be able to substitute into simple algebraic functions.

## Working mathematically

- Remind students that drawing a line passing through the intercept will count as a mark in an examination, even if the gradient is wrong.

## Common misconceptions and remediation

- Students often calculate gradients incorrectly, e.g. they calculate $x$-step ÷ $y$-step.
- Students may leave out the minus sign from a negative gradient.
- When using the cover-up method, students may misinterpret the intercept when the constant term is negative, or misunderstand and plot a point on the wrong axis.
- To remediate these problems, provide additional practice and worked examples, plus mnemonic devices such as '$x$ is a cross and goes across'.

## Probing questions

- If you increase or decrease the value of $m$, what effect does this have on the graph?
- What about changes to $c$?
- What have you noticed about the graphs of functions of the form $y = mx + c$?
- What elements are similar? And what elements can be different?

## Literacy focus

- Key terms: coefficient, constant term, cover-up, gradient-intercept, $y$-intercept, $y = mx + c$
- Make sure students link $m$ and $c$ to the gradient and $y$-intercept, as they often forget this.
- Encourage students to make study notes based on this section, in which they include all the key terms.

## Part 1

- Refer to Part 3 in the previous section. Show some graphs or refer to graphs that students have already seen.
- Link the equation to the gradient of the line and the $y$-intercept.
- Students should spot that the number in front of $x$ (the coefficient) is the same as the gradient, and the point where the graph crosses the $y$-axis is given by the constant term.

# Part 2

## Gradient-intercept method

- Part 1 covers the basic principle of the first part of this lesson, so go straight to Example 5 in the Student Book and work through it with the class.
- All students should be able to find the intercept on the y-axis.
- **Less able** students may have trouble drawing the gradients. A printed sheet of the necessary gradients showing the x-step and the y-step may be helpful.
- **Students can now do Exercise 8D from the Student Book.**

| A 1, 2, 4 | Calculator n/a | CM n/a | MR 3 | PS n/a | EV n/a |
|-----------|----------------|--------|------|--------|--------|

## Cover-up method

- Show students a set of axes.
- Ask for a series of points on the y-axis.
- Write these on the board and ask students what they have in common.
- Students should spot that the x-value is 0. Recall that the y-axis has the equation x = 0.
- Repeat with points on the x-axis or ask students what the equation of this line is.
- Recall that the x-axis has the equation y = 0.
- Work through this section and Example 6 from the Student Book with the class.
- **Less able** students may need support. They may have difficulty when the equation involves negative values.
- Remind these students that, when dividing a positive number by a negative number, or a negative number by a positive number, the result is a negative number, and that when dividing a negative number by a negative number, the result is a positive number.
- Challenge **more able** students to find the equation for the line passing through two points in the form $ax + by = c$, e.g. for (5, 0) and (0, −3).
- **Students can now do Exercise 8E from the Student Book.**

| A 1, 2 | Calculator n/a | CM n/a | MR 3, 4 | PS 5 | EV 6 |
|--------|----------------|--------|---------|------|------|

# Part 3

- Write this equation on the board: $4x + 3y = 12$. Use the cover-up rule to plot the graph.
- Work through the following equation. Students may be able to solve this if they have experience of rearranging formulae.

$3y = -4x + 12$

$y = -\dfrac{4}{3}x + 4$

- Link this to the graph. It should have the same gradient and intercept.
- Point out that whatever form the equation is in, if it can be arranged in the form $y = mx + c$, then students can always use the gradient-intercept method to draw it.

# Section 8.5 Finding the equation of a line from its graph

## Learning objectives

- Work out the equation of a line, using its gradient and *y*-intercept
- Work out the equation of a line given two points on the line

## Making mathematical connections

- Quadratic graphs
- Graphs of trigonometric functions
- Statistical graphs

## Resources and homework

- Student Book 8.5: pages 188–191
- Practice Book 8.5

## Making cross-curricular connections

- **Science** – analysing experimental results graphically
- **Relevance** – uses in engineering, manufacturing and business

## Prior learning

- Students should know how to draw a line using the gradient-intercept method.
- Students should also know how to find the gradient of a straight line.

## Working mathematically

- Students will know that they should write the equation as $y = mx + c$, and then substitute the *y*-intercept value as the constant and work from there.

## Common misconceptions and remediation

- Students often fail to recognise a negative gradient. Remind them (if necessary, every time they begin to answer questions about a graph) that lines that slope from top left to bottom right always have a negative gradient: forward slope = positive, backward slope = negative.

## Probing questions

- What effect does changing the value of *m* have on the graph?
- What effect does changing the value of *c* have on the graph?
- What is the same and what is different about the graphs of pairs of functions of the form $y = mx + c$?

## Literacy focus

- Key terms: None in this section
- Recap the meanings of key terms in other sections of this chapter.

## Part 1

- On the board, write:
  - $y = 2x - 1$
  - $4x - 2y = 2$
  - $x = \dfrac{y+1}{2}$
- Ask students which method they would use to plot the graphs of the three equations.
- The gradient-intercept method would be most appropriate for the first equation.
- The cover-up method would be best for the second equation.
- The third equation does not look like anything that students might be familiar with.

- However, choosing *y*-values and calculating *x*-values to get coordinates would be one method, e.g.
  $y = 3$, $x = 2$ and $y = 9$, $x = 5$.
- When students plot these graphs, they will find that they are all the same.

## Part 2

- Show an accurate graph, e.g. $y = 3x + 1$ (unlabelled).
- Ask students if they can say what the equation of the line is.
- By now, students should be able to reverse the gradient-intercept method. If not, prompt them by asking them for the standard form of the equation of a line ($y = mx + c$).
- Eventually, students should link the gradient to $m$ and the intercept to $c$.
- Work them out and write down the equation for this line.
- To consolidate this, work through the text and examples 7 and 8 in the Student Book with the class.
- **Students can now do Exercise 8F from the Student Book.**

| A 1, 4, 7, 8 | Calculator n/a | CM 3, 9 | MR 6, 10 | PS 5 | EV 2 |
|---|---|---|---|---|---|

## Part 3

- Show students several graphs and ask then to describe each one in the form $y = mx + c$.

# Section 8.6 The equation of a parallel line

## Learning objectives

- Work out the equation of a linear graph that is parallel to another line and passes through a specific point

## Resources and homework

- Student Book 8.6: pages 191–192
- Practice Book 8.6

## Making mathematical connections

- Drawing linear graphs
- Quadratic graphs
- Solving simultaneous equations algebraically

## Making cross-curricular connections

- **Science** – finding experimental results using graphs
- **Relevance** – applications to manufacturing, engineering and business

## Prior learning

- Students should be familiar with $y = mx + c$, and measuring gradients.

## Working mathematically

- Students will understand that if two lines are parallel, then their gradients are equal.

## Common misconceptions and remediation

- Students often make sign and arithmetic errors because of poor algebraic skills. Extra practice and worked examples should help to remediate these problems.

## Probing questions

- How can you tell if two lines are parallel just by looking at their equations?

## Literacy focus

- Key term: parallel
- Ask students to write a sentence describing the relationships between the gradients of parallel lines.

## Part 1

- Write the equation $y = 3x - 5$ on the board and ask students to give you the equation of a line parallel to this line.
- They should provide equations such as: $y = 3x + c$.
- Now ask for a line parallel to: $3x + 2y = 6$.
- This may cause some students to pause and attempt to rearrange the equation into the form $y = ...$, but in fact any equation of the form $3x + 2y = c$ is parallel to the example given.

## Part 2

- Students should be familiar with drawing graphs, measuring gradients and $y = mx + c$, and after completing Part 1 students should be aware of the conditions for parallel lines.

### Finding the equation of a parallel line

- Work through the text and Example 9 in the Student Book with the class.
- Explain to students that they now need to be able to find the equations of lines that are parallel to given lines.
- **Less able** students will need support while working on Exercise 8G.

- Students having difficulty with drawing lines and measuring gradients will find this concept difficult and may need support.
- Students are expected to calculate the equations of parallel lines using algebraic methods.
- **More able** students will cope, but you could help **less able** students by drawing the required lines on grids.
- **Students can now begin Exercise 8G from the Student Book.**

| A 2, 3 | Calculator n/a | CM 1 | MR n/a | PS 4 | EV n/a |
|---|---|---|---|---|---|

## Part 3

- This links with the next section ('Real-life uses of graphs').
- Show a sketch of a 'gas bill' graph, which consists of a basic charge and a price per unit.
- Do not put any values on the graph.

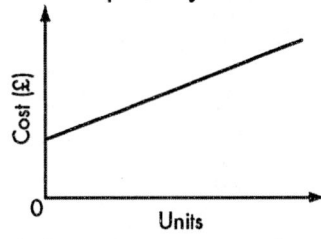

- Ask students to say how they can find the fixed charge from the graph (the intercept).
- Then ask students how they can find the price per unit (the gradient).

# Section 8.7 Real-life uses of graphs

## Learning objectives
- Convert from one unit to another unit by using a conversion graph
- Use straight-line graphs to work out formulae

## Resources and homework
- Student Book 8.7: pages 192–195
- Practice Book 8.7

## Making mathematical connections
- Quadratic graphs
- Graphs of trigonometric functions
- Statistical graphs

## Making cross-curricular connections
- **Science** – finding the formula linked to an experiment graphically
- **Relevance** – uses in engineering, manufacturing, business

## Prior learning
- Students should know how to draw a line using the gradient-intercept or cover-up method.
- They should also know how to find the gradient of a straight line.

## Working mathematically
- Students will know that, when possible, for questions on conversion graphs, they should draw the horizontal and vertical 'tracking' lines on their graphs, for maximum accuracy.

## Common misconceptions and remediation
- Students often plot a point on the wrong axis when using the cover-up method. Providing practice examples should remediate this problem.

## Probing questions
- For everyday problems, explore questions such as:
  o What is the relationship between the gradient and the problem?
  o What is the relationship between the intercept and the problem?

## Literacy focus
- Key term: conversion graph
- Students could write a sentence describing the relationship between variables on a conversion graph.

## Part 1
- Revisit Part 3 from the previous lesson to start this topic.
- Show the sketch of the gas bill graph, which consists of a basic charge and a price per unit.
- Do not put any values on the graph.
- Ask students to produce an equation for the graph using their own units.

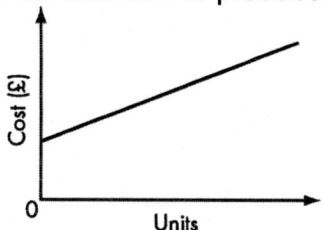

## Part 2

- Explain that this part of the section is about using graphs in practical situations.
- Discuss the text and work through Example 10 from the Student Book with the class.
- Stress these points:
  - The intercept on the vertical axis is the value of the function at zero. This is usually zero on conversion graphs but can be any value on a 'charges for services' graph; it is often called the 'fixed charge' or 'call-out fee'.
  - The gradient of the line is the value per unit. Once again, this may be called something slightly different.
- **Students can now begin Exercise 8H from the Student Book.**

| A 2–4, 7 | Calculator all | CM n/a | MR 1 | PS 5, 6 | EV n/a |

## Part 3

- Explore the following £ to € graph with students.
- Ask questions such as: How many euros is 10 pounds?
  Why does the graph go through the origin?
  What is the equation of the line?
  Can you use the equation of the line to convert the £ to € or € to £?

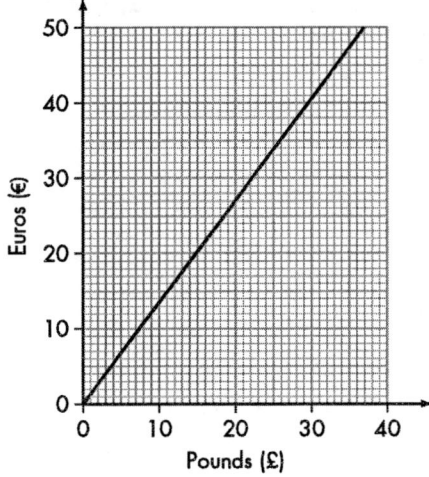

# Section 8.8 Solving simultaneous equations using graphs

## Learning objectives
- Solve simultaneous linear equations using graphs

## Resources and homework
- Student Book 8.8: pages 196–197
- Practice Book 8.8

## Making mathematical connections
- Drawing linear graphs
- Solving simultaneous equations algebraically

## Making cross-curricular connections
- **Science** – finding experimental results using graphs
- **Relevance** – applications to manufacturing, engineering and business

## Prior learning
- Students should be able to find the equation of a line using the gradient and intercept or cover-up method, and they should be able to draw a line given its equation.

## Working mathematically
- Two different straight lines that are not parallel will intersect at one point. This point is the solution of the simultaneous equations of the lines.
- Drawing graphs accurately is the main criterion for solving simultaneous equations.

## Common misconceptions and remediation
- Students often plot a point on the wrong axis when using the cover-up method. Providing practice examples should help students to stop making this mistake.

## Probing questions
- Explain how to solve two simultaneous linear equations graphically.
- Is it possible for two simultaneous linear equations to have more than one pair of solutions or to have no solution? Explain why.

## Literacy focus
- Key term: simultaneous equations
- Ask students to write a step-by-step method for solving simultaneous equations graphically.

## Part 1
- Write the equation $y = 2x + 1$ on the board and ask students to name pairs of $(x, y)$ values that make it true, for example: (1, 3), (0, 1), (3, 7).
- Now write $x + y = 10$ and ask for $(x, y)$ values that make this true, e.g. (0, 10), (1, 9).
- If it has not already been found, ask what pair of values is true for both equations. (3, 7)
- Repeat for the pair of equations: $y = 3x - 1$ and $x - 2y = 5$ (1, −2).

## Part 2

- Refer back to Part 1 and ask students if they can find the $(x, y)$ values that are true for both $y = 3x - 2$ and $2x - 3y = 6$ $(0, -2)$.
- If students have already covered simultaneous equations, solve this algebraically by the substitution method:
  $2x - 3(3x - 2) = 6$, $2x - 9x + 6 = 6$, $-7x = 0$, $x = 0$, $y = -2$.
- Explain that graphs can be used to solve problems like this.
- Now work through Example 11 from the Student Book with the class.
- **Students can now begin Exercise 8I from the Student Book.**

| A 1–8 | Calculator all | CM n/a | MR 11, 12 | PS 9, 10 | EV n/a |
|-------|----------------|--------|-----------|----------|--------|

## Part 3

- On the board, write the equation: $y = \dfrac{3}{4}x - 6$.

- Rearrange this: $4y = 3x - 24$ (multiply through by 4).
  - $4y - 3x = -24$ (subtract $3x$ from both sides)
  - $3x - 4y = 24$ (multiply by $-1$)
- Explain that mathematicians prefer equations without fractions and with as few minus signs as possible.

- Repeat with: $y = 2 - \dfrac{2}{3}x$ $(3y + 2x = 6)$ and $y = \dfrac{3}{5}x + 2$ $(5y - 3x = 10)$.

# Chapter 9 Algebra: Expressions and formulae

## Overview

| | |
|---|---|
| **9.1** Basic algebra | **9.5** Quadratic expansion |
| **9.2** Substitution | **9.6** Quadratic factorisation |
| **9.3** Expanding brackets | **9.7** Changing the subject of a formula |
| **9.4** Factorisation | |

**Prior learning**

Know the BIDMAS/BODMAS rule

**Learning objectives**

**Ensure that students can: use letters to represent numbers; form simple algebraic expressions; simplify expressions by collecting like terms; substitute numbers into expressions and formulae; expand and factorise expressions; expand two pairs of brackets; factorise quadratic expressions; rearrange formulae.**

In the examination, students will be expected to:
- write an algebraic expression
- recognise expressions, equations, formulae and identities
- substitute into, simplify and use algebraic expressions
- expand brackets such as $2(x - 3)$
- expand and simplify brackets
- factorise an algebraic expression
- expand two linear brackets to obtain a quadratic expression
- factorise a quadratic expression of the form $x^2 + ax + b$ into two linear brackets
- change the subject of a formula.

**Extension**

Provide questions for **more able** students to make use of the quadratic formula, to plot quadratics graphically to find solutions, and to find solutions to quadratics.

## Curriculum references

| Section | GCSE specification |
|---|---|
| 9.1 | A1, A3, A6 |
| 9.2 | A6 |
| 9.3 | A4 |
| 9.4 | A4 |

| Section | GCSE specification |
|---|---|
| 9.5 | A4 |
| 9.6 | A18 |
| 9.7 | A5 |

## Route mapping

| Exercise | Accessible | Intermediate | Challenging | AO9 | AO2 MR CM | AO3 PS EV | Key questions |
|---|---|---|---|---|---|---|---|
| 9A | 1–7 | | | 1, 7 | 3, 4 | 2, 5, 6 | 5, 7 |
| 9B | 1–3 | 4–11 | | 1, 2, 4, 5 | 7–9 | 3, 6, 10, 11 | 4, 7, 11 |
| 9C | | 1–4 | | 1 | 4 | 2, 3 | 1, 4 |
| 9D | 1 | 2–6 | 7–9 | 1–6 | 8 | 7, 9 | 5–7, 9 |
| 9E | | 1–7 | | 1, 3 | 4, 5, 7 | 2, 6 | 1, 3, 5, 6 |
| 9F | | 1–3 | | 1, 2 | | 3 | 1–3 |
| 9G | | 1–3 | | 1–3 | | | 1–3 |
| 9H | | 1–4 | 5 | 1–2 | 5 | 3, 4 | 1, 2, 4, 5 |
| 9I | | 1–3 | 4, 5 | 1–3 | 5 | 4 | 1, 3, 5 |
| 9J | | 1 | 2–4 | 1, 2 | | 3, 4 | 2–4 |
| 9K | | | 1–12 | 1–10, 12a, b | 12c | 11 | 9–12 |
| 9L | | | 1–3 | 1 | 3 | 2 | 1–3 |
| 9M | | 1–12 | 13–19 | 1–10, 12–18 | 19 | 11 | 7, 10, 12, 19 |

*Key questions are those that demonstrate mastery of the concept, or which require a step-up in understanding or application. Key questions could be used to identify the questions that students must tackle, to support differentiation, or to identify the questions that should be teacher-marked rather than student-marked.*

## About this chapter

**Making connections**: This chapter brings together students' understanding of an expression and an equation and moves on to describe formulae and identities. Understanding that $2a$ means $2 \times a$, and $a^2$ means $a \times a$, leads students to simplifying expressions, and expanding and factorising linear and quadratic expressions. This chapter also describes how to change the subject of a formula. For much of the chapter, the next step is Higher content such as using the quadratic formula and completing the square.

**Relevance**: The material in this chapter will help students with making judgements, predictions and looking for trends.

**Working mathematically**: Students will identify expressions, equations, formulae and identities; they will collect like terms; expand expressions with single and double brackets and simplify the results, and factorise expressions into single and double brackets. Using all these skills will help students to transpose an equation.

**Assessment**: In each section of this chapter, ensure that students have a good grasp of the key questions in each exercise before moving on. (Refer to the 'Route mapping' table.) Encourage students to read and think about the 'Ready to progress?' statements on page 228 of the Student Book. Check students' understanding at the end of the chapter, formatively, using peer assessment. Students could do a mini test in the form of the 'Review questions' on pages 228–229 of the Student Book. Follow up the test with an individual target-getting session, based on any areas for development that a student may have.

## Worked exemplars from the Student Book (page 226) – suggestions for use

- Present students with the same question but different numbers. They should use the exemplar to mirror the working, in full or just refer to the notes.
- Copy and cut the exemplars into cards. Students match the working with the notes.
- Alternatively, copy and cut the working into cards but split the label/description from the working.

**Answers to the Student Book questions are available on the CD-ROM provided.**

## Learning objectives

- Write an algebraic expression
- Recognise expressions, equations, formulae and identities

## Resources and homework

- Student Book 9.1: pages 203–205
- Practice Book 9.1

## Making mathematical connections

- BIDMAS/BODMAS
- Using negative numbers

## Making cross-curricular connections

- **Science; Engineering** – understanding expressions and formulae
- **Business Studies** – understanding formulae
- **Relevance** – developing logical thinking

## Prior learning

- Students need to know the BIDMAS/BODMAS rule.

## Working mathematically

- Students will write expressions from worded problems, identify expressions, formulae, identities and equations.

## Common misconceptions and remediation

- Students often write '7 less than $x$' as $7 - x$. Students often confuse $x^2$ and $2x$. Emphasise the differences so that students are clear.
- Students multiply or divide indices instead of adding or subtracting, or they multiply the bases together such as $2^a \times 2^b = 4^{a+b}$.
- Students often write $3a + 7b$ as $10ab$. Provide plenty of practice so students are aware of potential errors.

## Probing questions

- What does 'solve' mean? What does 'simplify' mean?
- What is the difference between $2a$ and $a^2$?
- What is the difference between 7 less than $x$ and $x$ less than 7?

## Literacy focus

- Key terms: equation, expression, formula, identity, symbol, term, variable
- Tell students that they should make sure that they write down the expression or equation in the order in which it is written in the question.

## Part 1

- Throw three dice. Tell students the numbers, for example, 6, 3, 5, and ask them to make up five calculations, including using brackets. For example: $6 + 3 + 5 = 14$
  $(6 - 3) \times 5 = 15$ \qquad $6 \times 3 + 5 = 23$ \qquad $6 \times 5 - 3 = 27$ \qquad $6 + 3 - 5 = 4$
- As a class, discuss errors in students' examples, especially those where brackets are used incorrectly. Recall the rules of BIDMAS/BODMAS. Repeat if there is time.

## Part 2

- Tell students that you have a rule in your head such as: 'Add 2'. Ask students to give you the result for a number, for example, if you say 7, students should say 9. (7 add 2 = 9)
- Give students a number; they should give you the result after applying the rule.
- Challenge **more able** students with larger numbers. Do this with numbers for about six students, then give a student $x$. This will probably cause some hesitation.
- It will help **less able** students if you write the operations on the board. For example, if you say 5, the result is 5 + 2 = 7. This will help when you explain that the result for $x$ is $x + 2$.
- Explain that this is a general rule that describes the operation 'add 2' and that $x$ represents any number that they wish to substitute.
- Repeat with a subtraction rule to get the expressions $x - 4$, $3x$ and $x \div 5$ or $\dfrac{x}{5}$, for example.

  You will need to explain the last two; students will probably understand $3 \times x$ but will need to be told that there is an implied multiplication sign between the number (coefficient) and the letter. The notation $\dfrac{x}{5}$ is also a standard way of writing $x \div 5$.
- Go through the introductory text and Examples 1, 2 and 3.
- Examples 1 and 2 go through substituting numbers and then letters into a familiar formula of area and perimeter of a rectangle, to build confidence.
- Example 3 asks students to identify an expression, equation, formula and identity. Students need to be able to identify all of these correctly.
- **Less able** students may need some more reinforcement. Work through some of the questions in the exercise with them to reinforce the key processes that are involved.
- If possible, show students the algebra pyramids (Resource 9.1a). Ask them to complete each pyramid by first adding and then multiplying the expressions in adjacent boxes, writing the answer in the appropriate box in the row above. The answers are: (adding) $6 + 2m$ and $6 + 4u$; (multiplying) $9m^2$ and $12u^3$.
- **Students can now do Exercise 9A from the Student Book.**

| A 1, 7 | Calculator n/a | CM 4 | MR 3 | PS 2, 5, 6 | EV n/a |

## Part 3

- Go through these seven important rules and check that students understand them.
  - 3 more than $x = x + 3$
  - 5 less than (or fewer than) $y = y - 5$ (not $5 - y$) (Make sure students understand the difference.)
  - 4 multiplied by $z = 4z$
  - $b$ divided by $2 = \dfrac{b}{2}$ (not $\dfrac{2}{b}$) (Again, check to make sure students understand the difference.)
  - $7a = 7 \times a$
  - $1 \times c = c$ (not $1c$)
  - $t \times t = t^2$ (Again, discuss the difference between this and $2t$.)
- Check students' understanding by asking them questions such as: 'Give me two expressions that could add to $3x^2$. Give me two expressions that multiply to give $4n^3$.'

## Learning objectives

- Substitute into, simplify and use algebraic expressions

## Resources and homework

- Student Book 9.2: pages 205–208
- Practice Book 9.2

## Making mathematical connections

- BIDMAS/BODMAS
- Negative numbers
- Using a calculator

## Making cross-curricular connections

- **Science; Engineering** – understanding expressions and formulae
- **Business Studies** – understanding expressions and formulae
- **Relevance** – developing logical thinking

## Prior learning

- Students must have a working knowledge of BIDMAS/BODMAS.
- They must also be able to work with negative numbers.
- Students must be familiar with how the calculator they are using works (scientific, non-scientific, DAL).

## Working mathematically

- Students will write expressions from worded problems.
- Students will use both positive and negative numbers.

## Common misconceptions and remediation

- Mistakes occur when students order operations incorrectly and when there is a minus sign before a bracketed expression. When teaching substitution, make sure the examples include and reinforce the correct method of working.
- When working with calculators, the most common mistake is likely to be leaving out brackets where they are needed. Rehearse examples with the class to remedy this.

## Probing questions

- What is $-2^2$? What is $-2^3$? What is $-2 \times 3$?
- What is the order of operations?

## Literacy focus

- Key term: substitute
- Ask students to describe a formula in words, to show that they understand what they are working out and how each formula works.

## Part 1

- Show or give students a copy of the puzzle, supplied on Resource 9.2. Ask them to work out values of A, B, C and D that make the puzzle work. (A = 4, B = 3, C = 1, D = 5)
- Repeat with a puzzle of your own, or ask students to make one up.

# Part 2

- Ask students if they know any examples of a mathematical formula. If they come up with any valid formulae, use these for the introduction. If not, suggest the area of a rectangle.
- Ask students to define their own variables. For example, they may establish a formula such as $A = l \times w$. Write this on the board.
- Ask students what the area would be for a rectangle of length 5 cm and width 3 cm.
- They will probably do this mentally, but make sure they are aware that if they were asked such a question in an examination, they should write the values into the formula before working it out, i.e. $A = 5 \times 3 = 15$ cm$^2$.
- Remind students to use brackets around the numbers, such as $A = (5) \times (3)$. This is particularly useful when dealing with negative numbers.
- Example 4 in the Student Book uses the area of a trapezium formula. Show students how to substitute into the formula and use BIDMAS/BODMAS to find the answer.
- Example 5 uses indices. Show how to use BIDMAS/BODMAS in this equation.
- Example 6 is a real-life model. Review changing to a common unit before substituting into a formula.
- **Students can now do Exercise 9B from the Student Book.**

| A 1, 2, 4, 5 | Calculator n/a | CM n/a | MR 7–9 | PS 3, 6, 10 | EV 11 |
|---|---|---|---|---|---|

# Part 3

- Check students' understanding of substitution, and that they can substitute both positive and negative integers into expressions.
- Make sure students understand BIDMAS/BODMAS and the impact of a minus sign on an expression.

# Section 9.3 Expanding brackets

## Learning objectives

- Expand brackets such as $2(x - 3)$
- Expand and simplify brackets

## Resources and homework

- Student Book 9.3: pages 209–212
- Practice Book 9.3

## Making mathematical connections

- Multiplying terms together
- Simplifying expressions
- Factors

## Making cross-curricular connections

- **Science** – simplifying expressions and formulae
- **Relevance** – developing logical thinking

## Prior learning

- Students need to remember the order in which to carry out operations, following BIDMAS/BODMAS.

## Working mathematically

- Students will use BIDMAS/BODMAS.
- They will expand brackets.
- Students will simplify expressions.

## Common misconceptions and remediation

- The most common error students make is to multiply only the first part of the expression inside the brackets and ignore the rest.
- Students also become confused when there are minus signs.
- Ensure that students are aware of potential errors.

## Probing questions

- What is $a \times b$, $-a \times b$, $a \times -b$ and $-a \times -b$?
- What is $a \times a$, $-a \times a$, $a \times -a$ and $-a \times -a$?
- Can you summarise your findings?

## Literacy focus

- Key terms: expand, like terms, multiply out, simplify
- Ask students to write down the meaning of each key term.

## Part 1

- Tell students that you are thinking of a number. When you multiply by two and add seven, you get the answer 17.
- Ask, 'What number was I thinking of?' (5)
- Repeat, but this time add six, multiply the result by three and give the answer as 30.
- Ask, 'What was the number I started with this time?' (4)
- Discuss the methods students used to get the answers.
- Show students the array of algebraic expressions (Resource 9.1b).
- Ask them to match the expressions, e.g. linking $4x^2$ with $(2x)^2$.
- They can do this individually, in groups or as a class.

## Part 2

- Ask students to write the result of 'multiply a number by 2 and add 3', using algebra. They could write their answer on mini-whiteboards.
- Establish that this is $2x + 3$.
- Now ask students to write the expression 'add 3 and multiply by 2', using algebra.
- Some students may give the same answer as before. However, make sure that everyone understands that the result is $2(x + 3)$. You may need to explain that the 2 is written before the 3; alternatively, write it as $(x + 3) \times 2$.
- Make sure that students grasp the need for the brackets.
- Now ask students to write 'multiply by 2 and add 6', using algebra, to get $2x + 6$.
- Write both expressions, $2(x + 3)$ and $2x + 6$, on the board.
- Divide the class in two and give each half (individually) some simple numbers such 2, 3, 4, 5 and 10 – give both halves of the class the same numbers.
- Ask one half of the class to add 3 to their numbers and then multiply the result by 2.
- Ask the other half to multiply their numbers by 2 and then add 6.
- Ask for answers. Students in both halves with the same starting number will have the same result.
- Now write $2(x + 3) = 2x + 6$ on the board and ask students how these are connected.
- They should see that the number outside the brackets is multiplied by everything inside the brackets. Explain that this is known as expanding the brackets.
- **Students can now do Exercise 9C from the Student Book.**

| A 1 | Calculator n/a | CM n/a | MR 4 | PS 2 | EV 3 |
|-----|----------------|--------|------|------|------|

### Collecting like terms; Expand and simplify

- The second part of the lesson combines collecting like terms and the expansion of two single brackets. Tell students that sometimes they will have to multiply out two or more single brackets and then simplify the answer.
- Example 7 shows how to expand a single bracket followed by another single bracket. The important point here to emphasise is to collect the like terms together at the end once both the single brackets have been expanded.
- Emphasise how important it is not to take any shortcuts and to write the working in full. In particular, explain the need for care with minus signs. In an examination, one error is usually allowed, and provided no further mistakes are made, only one mark is lost; but examiners need to see where the mistake was made.
- **Students can now do Exercise 9D from Student Book.**

| A 1–6 | Calculator 7 | CM n/a | MR 8 | PS 7, 9 | EV n/a |
|-------|--------------|--------|------|---------|--------|

## Part 3

- Write the following on the board: $2(x + 3) + 4(x - 1) = 3(2x + 1) + 2(x - 1)$
- Ask for one difference between this and what students have seen so far. Students will meet these differences later, but challenge them to find the value of $x$ that makes the equation true. Students should suggest expanding the brackets. This has an equals sign and is an equation.
- Expanding and simplifying both sides gives $6x + 2 = 8x + 1$. Students may be able to guess (if given a clue that the answer is a fraction) that the solution is $x = \frac{1}{2}$.

## Learning objectives

- Factorise an algebraic expression

## Resources and homework

- Student Book 9.4: pages 212–214
- Practice Book 9.4

## Making mathematical connections

- Finding factors
- Finding the HCF
- Multiplying terms together

## Making cross-curricular connections

- **Science** – simplifying expressions and formulae
- **Relevance** – developing logical thinking

## Prior learning

- Students need to understand what the term 'factor' means.
- They also need to know the multiplication tables up to $10 \times 10$.

## Working mathematically

- Students will find factors and the highest common factor (HCF).
- They will also factorise an expression.

## Common misconceptions and remediation

- Students may not remove all the common factors; some may not realise that $f$ means $1 \times f$.
- When factorising an expression such as $4a - 12ab$, students may put the $4a$ outside the brackets but not put a 1 inside, or put 0 inside the bracket.
- The best remedy is to provide practice with multiplying out the bracket to see whether or not it is the same as the answer. Students can do this until they are confident with the process.

## Probing questions

- What are the factors of 15, or 21 or 88?
- What are the factors of $2a + 4a$, $4b^2 + 6b$ or $10c^2 - 5cd$?

## Literacy focus

- Key terms: common factor, factorisation
- Ask students to describe how to expand a bracket. Now ask students to reverse the process and explain what they did.

## Part 1

- Ask the class for factors of 12. List them on the board. Ask for factors of 21. List these.
- Make sure students understand that the size of a number is not an indication of how many factors it has.
- Challenge the class to find the number under 100 that has the most factors. (96)

## Part 2

- Write some expansions on the board, for example:
  $2(x + 5) = 2x + 10$        $3(x - 2) = 3x - 6$        $5(x + 3) = 5x + 15$
- Now write: $2x + 14 =$ ....... . Ask students if they can write down the expression that it came from. Most students will realise that the answer is $2(x + 7)$.
- Repeat with other examples such as: $5x - 15$, $6x + 18$.
- Explain that this is called 'factorisation' and is the reverse of expanding.
- Now ask students to factorise $4x + 12$. Many of them may say $2(2x + 6)$.
- Explain that this is only a partial factorisation; the correct answer is $4(x + 3)$.
- Explain that they need to take the HCF out of each term.
- Now ask for the factorisation of $x^2 + 3x$. This may need some more explanation such as:
  $x \times x + 3 \times x = x(x + 3)$
- Work through Example 8. Emphasise that the factorised expression can be multiplied out to check if the answer is the same as the original expression.
- **More able** students can work with a range of values and letters, but you might need to restrict **less able** students to examples with positive values and ones that do not require a letter to be taken out as a factor.
- **Students can now do Exercise 9E from the Student Book.**

| A 1, 3 | Calculator n/a | CM 4, 5 | MR 7 | PS 6 | EV 2 |
|--------|----------------|---------|------|------|------|

## Part 3

- Write the following on the board: $16 \times 18 - 6 \times 18$
- Ask students if they can work this out easily without using a calculator. They will probably find the multiplications difficult and, even if they find these correctly, they may get the subtraction wrong. (Answer: $288 - 108 = 180$)
- Ask students if they can see anything common to each part of the calculation.
- Taking out the common factor of $\times 18$ means they can rewrite the calculation as:
  $(16 - 6) \times 18$.
- They should be able to do this easily. (Answer: 180)
- Repeat with: $17 \times 15 - 7 \times 15$; $23 \times 32 - 3 \times 32$.

# Section 9.5 Quadratic expansion

## Learning objectives

- Expand two linear brackets to obtain a quadratic expression

## Resources and homework

- Student Book 9.5: pages 214–220
- Practice Book 9.5

## Making mathematical connections

- Multiplication
- Multiplying terms together
- Expanding a bracket

## Making cross-curricular connections

- **Science** – simplifying expressions and formulae
- **Relevance** – developing logical thinking

## Prior learning

- Students need to be able to expand a single bracket.
- They should be able to do multiplication using a grid method.
- Students need to know how to multiply terms together and simplify an expression.

## Working mathematically

- Students will multiply terms together, and they will simplify expressions.

## Common misconceptions and remediation

- The most common error students make is to multiply only the first part of the expression inside the brackets and ignore the rest. Students also become confused when there are minus signs. Ensure that students are aware of potential errors.
- Students forget to use FOIL. Multiply the first term in the first bracket by both terms in the second bracket, and also multiply the second term in the first bracket by both terms in the second bracket.

## Probing questions

- Play 'I think of two numbers' with the class, using numbers such as:
  - sum 10, product 25
  - sum 12, product 11
  - sum −1, product −56
  - sum −10, product 21.

## Literacy focus

- Key terms: quadratic expansion, quadratic expression
- Ask students to write down what the key terms mean, and what is meant by 'product', 'coefficient' and 'expanding brackets'.

## Part 1

- Give students the following quadratic expression and its expansion:
  $(x + 4)(x + 2) = x^2 + 6x + 8$.
- Ask students where $x^2$ could have come from.
- Ask where $6x$ could have come from.
- This should promote discussion about simplifying expressions as $4x + 2x = 6x$.
- Ask where 8 could have come from.
- Does anyone notice a link between the numbers in the question and those in the answer?
- Some students may notice that $4 + 2 = 6$ and $4 \times 2 = 8$.

## Part 2

- Example 9 shows expanding a quadratic expression using the expansion method. Discuss with students how every term in the expansion has been worked out. Where does $7x$ come from in the simplified expression? Remind students that they will need to simplify their answers.
- **Students can now do Exercise 9F from the Student Book.**

| A 1, 2 | Calculator n/a | CM n/a | MR n/a | PS n/a | EV 3 |
|---|---|---|---|---|---|

- Example 10 shows the second method used to expand two brackets, FOIL – first, outer, inner and last. Show students how using FOIL ensures that they multiply all terms together. Again remind students that they will still need to simplify their answers.
- **Students can now do Exercise 9G from the Student Book.**

| A 1–3 | Calculator n/a | CM n/a | MR n/a | PS n/a | EV n/a |
|---|---|---|---|---|---|

- Example 11 introduces the box method for expanding two brackets, similar to the grid method for multiplication. Show students how to set up the box method and how to find all the terms. Place emphasis on putting the signs of each term in the box. Remind students that the expression will still need to be simplified in the final steps.
- **Students can now do Exercise 9H from the Student Book.**

| A 1, 2 | Calculator n/a | CM 5 | MR n/a | PS 3, 4 | EV n/a |
|---|---|---|---|---|---|

### Quadratic expansion with non-unit coefficients

- Examples 12 and 13 in the Student Book show how to expand a quadratic where the coefficient of $x^2$ is not 1 or –1.
- Explain to students that although the method is basically the same, they have to remember to multiply the numbers as well as the letters.
- **Students can now do Exercise 9I from the Student Book.**

| A 1–3 | Calculator n/a | CM 5 | MR n/a | PS 4 | EV n/a |
|---|---|---|---|---|---|

### Expanding squares

- Examples 14 and 15 show how to expand squares. Remind students that squared means to multiply by itself. $(x - 1)^2$ is the same as $(x - 1)(x - 1)$. Encourage **less able** students to write down this extra step so that they expand the brackets correctly.
- **Students can now do Exercise 9J from the Student Book.**

| A 1, 2 | Calculator none | CM n/a | MR n/a | PS 4 | EV 3 |
|---|---|---|---|---|---|

## Part 3

- Say to students: 'Four identical rectangles surround the shaded square. Find an expression for the sum of the areas of the four tiles and find the area of the shaded square'.

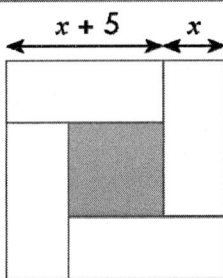

- Students should find it easy to work out the area of one of the rectangles, which is $x(x + 5) = x^2 + 5x$ and thus all four is $4x^2 + 20x$.
- The expression for the total area is $(2x + 5)^2 = 4x^2 + 20x + 25$ and may trip them up.
- Make sure students understand that the area of the shaded square is the total area less the area of the rectangles and is 25.

# Section 9.6 Quadratic factorisation

## Learning objectives

- Factorise a quadratic expression of the form $x^2 + ax + b$ into two linear brackets

## Resources and homework

- Student Book 9.6: pages 220–223
- Practice Book 9.6

## Making mathematical connections

- Finding factors
- Finding the HCF
- Multiplying terms together
- Expanding brackets

## Making cross-curricular connections

- **Science** – simplifying expressions and formulae
- **Relevance** – developing logical thinking

## Prior learning

- Students need to understand what the term 'factor' means.
- They also need to know the multiplication tables up to 10 × 10.
- Students should be able to do quadratic expansion.

## Working mathematically

- Students will find factors and the HCF.
- They will also factorise expressions.

## Common misconceptions and remediation

- Students may not remove all the common factors; some may not realise that $f$ means $1 \times f$.
- When factorising an expression such as $4a - 12ab$, students may put the $4a$ outside the brackets but may not put a 1 inside, or put 0 inside the bracket.
- The best remedy is for students to practise until they are confident with the process.

## Probing questions

- When reading a quadratic expression that you need to factorise, what information is critical for working out the two factors?
- What difference does it make if the constant term is negative?

## Literacy focus

- Key term: difference of two squares
- Ask students to explain and write down the meaning of the key term.

## Part 1

- Ask students to look at the following quadratic expansions and ask them what they notice:
  - $(x + 1)(x + 2) = x^2 + 3x + 2$
  - $(x + 3)(x - 4) = x^2 - x - 12$
  - $(x - 2)(x + 4) = x^2 + 2x - 8$
  - $(x - 3)(x - 5) = x^2 - 8x + 15$
- Try to get students to notice that the sum of the numbers in the brackets is $a$ and the product of the numbers is $b$.
- Say that a quadratic is a polynomial, which has the form $x^2 + ax + b$, where $a$ and $b$ are numbers.

- Add that if $b$ is positive, then the factors they are looking for are either both positive or both negative. If $a$ is positive, then the factors are both positive. If $a$ is negative, then the factors are both negative. In either case, students should look for numbers that have a sum of $a$.
- If $b$ is negative, then the factors students are looking for have different signs; that is, one is negative and one is positive. If $a$ is positive, then the larger factor is positive. If $a$ is negative, then the larger factor is negative. In either case, say to students that they should look for factors that have a sum of $a$.

## Part 2

- Review factorisation with students, giving examples of each, e.g. $x^2 + 5x + 6$ and $x^2 + x - 6$.
- Examples 16 and 17 in the Student Book show factorising with a unitary coefficient of $x^2$.
- Review how we find the factors and when to use the positive or negative sign.
- **Students can now do Exercise 9K from the Student Book.**

| A 1–10, 12a, b | Calculator n/a | CM 12c | MR n/a | PS 11 | EV n/a |
|---|---|---|---|---|---|

### Difference of two squares

- Go through Example 18, which shows a quadratic expression without an $x$ term. Students need to be aware that this is the difference of two squares. Students should be happy with identifying square numbers.
- Go through how to find the number from its square and then how the $x$ term cancels when the brackets are expanded.
- **Students can now do Exercise 9L from the Student Book.**

| A 1 | Calculator n/a | CM 3 | MR n/a | PS 2 | EV n/a |
|---|---|---|---|---|---|

## Part 3

- Encourage students to practise square numbers with a puzzle, many of which are available on the Internet if you have access.
- Into a search engine of your choice, type: 'square number puzzles' or 'square number puzzles practice' and you will find various sites.
- Say to students that many numbers can be expressed as the difference of two perfect squares. For example:
  - $20 = 6^2 - 4^2$
  - $21 = 5^2 - 2^2$
- Challenge students by asking: How many of the numbers from 1 to 20 can you express as the difference of two perfect squares?

# Section 9.7 Changing the subject of a formula

## Learning objectives
- Change the subject of a formula

## Resources and homework
- Student Book 9.7: pages 223–225
- Practice Book 9.7

## Making mathematical connections
- BIDMAS/BODMAS
- Substitution

## Making cross-curricular connections
- **Science; Engineering** – substituting into expressions and formulae
- **Business Studies** – substituting into expressions and formulae
- **Relevance** – developing logical thinking

## Prior learning
- Students must have a working knowledge of BIDMAS/BODMAS. They must also be able to work with negative numbers.
- Make sure that all students have a good working knowledge of their calculator, whether it is scientific, non-scientific or DAL.

## Working mathematically
- Students will substitute values into formulae. They will see formulae they may use in science and rearrange them.
- Students will use positive and negative numbers.
- Students will have a working knowledge of BIDMAS/BODMAS.

## Common misconceptions and remediation
- Students make errors when they do not follow the order of operations correctly and when there is a minus sign before a bracketed expression. When teaching, make sure that the examples you use for substitution include and reinforce the correct method of working.
- Students forget that the inverse operation of $x^2$ is $\sqrt{x}$. Remind students about inverse operations.

## Probing questions
- What is $-2^2$? What is $-2^3$? What is $-2 \times 3$?
- What is the inverse operation of $+3$, $-2$, $\times 8$, $\div 4$, $x^2$, $\sqrt{16}$?

## Literacy focus
- Key terms: inverse operations, rearrange, subject
- Place emphasis on what the inverse operations are; ask students to describe them.

## Part 1
- Explain that sometimes we need to rearrange a formula to find the value of a variable. For example, we may know the area of a circle and need to find the radius. To do this, we rearrange the formula to make the radius the subject.
- The formula for the area of a circle is $A = \pi r^2$.
- We will now rearrange the formula to make $r$ the subject.
$A = \pi r^2$

- Start by dividing both sides by π: $\dfrac{A}{\pi} = r^2$

- Then take the square root of both sides: $\sqrt{\dfrac{A}{\pi}} = r$ or $r = \sqrt{\dfrac{A}{\pi}}$.

- Discuss with students how we use inverse operations to rearrange the formula.

- Use other formulae they might recognise such as: $A = lw$ or $A = \dfrac{1}{2}(a + b)h$.

## Part 2

- Discuss with students that rearranging a formula can help you to find the value of a variable when it is not the subject of the formula.
- Example 20 shows a simple rearrangement with just one step. Discuss the inverse of subtraction, which is addition and we must do this to both sides to rearrange it.
- Example 21 shows a simple rearrangement with just one step. Discuss the inverse of multiplication, which is division and we must do this to both sides to rearrange it.
- Example 22 shows a rearrangement with more than one step. Discuss with students the order in which order to tackle this question.
- Example 23 shows one of the kinematics (associated with movement) formulae. Discuss with students how to rearrange to make a different variable the subject and then how to substitute into the rearrangement to find an answer.
- **Students can now begin Exercise 9M from the Student Book.**

| A 1–10, 12–18 | Calculator n/a | CM n/a | MR 19 | PS 11 | EV n/a |
|---|---|---|---|---|---|

## Part 3

- Molly is three years older than Paul. Tina is twice as old as Molly. Molly, Paul and Tina have a combined age of 41. How old is each person?
- Make equations:
  - Molly: $m$
  - Paul: $p = m - 3$
  - Tina: $t = 2m$
  - $m + p + t = 41$
- Substitute for $p$ and $t$ to get an equation in $m$. Solve it to find $m$.
  - $m + m - 3 + 2m = 41$
  - $4m - 3 = 41$
  - $4m = 44$
  - $m = 11$
- Molly is 11 years old. Paul is 8 years old. Tina is 22 years old.

# Chapter 10 Ratio, proportion and rates of change: Ratio, speed and proportion

**Overview**

| | |
|---|---|
| **10.1** Ratio | **10.3** Direct proportion problems |
| **10.2** Speed, distance and time | **10.4** Best buys |

**Prior learning**

Know multiplication tables up to 12 × 12.
Know how to simplify fractions.
Know how to find a fraction of a quantity.
Know how to multiply and divide, with and without a calculator.

**Learning objectives**

**Ensure that students can: understand what a ratio is; divide an amount in a given ratio; calculate speed; solve problems involving direct proportion; compare prices of products.**

In the examination, students will be expected to:
* simplify a ratio
* express a ratio as a fraction
* divide amounts into given ratios
* complete calculations from a given ratio and partial information
* recognise the relationship between speed, distance and time
* calculate average speed from distance and time
* calculate distance travelled from the speed and the time taken
* calculate the time taken on a journey from the speed and the distance
* recognise and solve problems that involve direct proportion
* find the cost per unit mass
* find the mass per unit cost
* use the above to find which product is better value.

**Extension**

Direct **more able** students to the more challenging MR and PS questions in the exercises throughout this chapter.

**Curriculum references**

| Section | GCSE specification |
|---|---|
| 10.1 | R4–7 |
| 10.2 | R11 |
| 10.3 | R10 |
| 10.4 | R11,12 |

## Route mapping

| Exercise | Accessible | Intermediate | Challenging | AO1 | AO2 MR CM | AO3 PS EV | Key questions |
|---|---|---|---|---|---|---|---|
| 10A | 1–5 | 6–8 | 9–12 | 1–8 | 9, 10 | 11, 12 | 1, 2, 5 |
| 10B | 1–4 | 5–7 | 8–10 | 1–5, 6a–c, 7 | 6d, 8 | 9, 10 | 1, 2, 5, 7 |
| 10C | 1–4 | 5–7 | 8–13 | 1–5 | 6, 7 | 8–13 | 3, 5 |
| 10D | 1–5 | 6–13 | 14–16 | 1–5, 6a, 7, 8, 11–13 | 6b, c, 9, 10, 15 | 14, 16 | 1–3, 5, 9 |
| 10E | 1–5 | 6, 7 | 8–10 | 1–6, 7a | 7b, 8a | 8b, 9, 10 | 1–3, 6, 7 |
| 10F | 1–4 | 5, 6, 9 | 7, 8, 10–13 | 1–4 | 5, 7–9 | 6, 10–13 | 1, 2, 4 |

*Key questions are those that demonstrate mastery of the concept, or which require a step-up in understanding or application. Key questions could be used to identify the questions that students must tackle, to support differentiation, or to identify the questions that should be teacher-marked rather than student-marked.*

## About this chapter

**Making connections**: This chapter starts with the core parts of ratio and proportion before covering more complex topics such as speed–distance–time calculations and direct proportion. Students will use the skills they learn in this chapter in areas of Science (compound measures) and Geography (ratio and proportion).

**Relevance**: We use fractions, decimals, percentage, ratio and proportion in everyday life to help us calculate quantities or to compare two or more pieces of information.

**Working mathematically**: Students will find multipliers to increase or decrease by different percentages. They will also find multipliers to calculate original values after percentage increases or decreases.

**Assessment**: In each section of this chapter, ensure that students have a good grasp of the key questions in each exercise before moving on. (Refer to the 'Route mapping' table.) Encourage students to read and think about the 'Ready to progress?' statements on page 252 of the Student Book. Check students' understanding at the end of the chapter, formatively, using peer assessment. Students could do a mini test in the form of the 'Review questions' on pages 252–253 of the Student Book. Follow up the test with an individual target-getting session, based on any areas for development that a student may have.

## Worked exemplars from the Student Book (page 250) – suggestions for use

- Present students with the same question but different numbers. They should use the exemplar to mirror the working, in full or just refer to the notes.
- Copy and cut the exemplars into cards. Students should match the working with the notes.
- Alternatively, copy and cut the working into cards but split the label/description from the working.

## Answers to the Student Book questions are available on the CD-ROM provided.

## Section 10.1 Ratio

### Learning objectives

- Simplify a ratio
- Express a ratio as a fraction
- Divide amounts into given ratios
- Complete calculations from a given ratio and partial information

### Resources and homework

- Student Book 10.1: pages 231–238
- Practice Book 10.1

### Making mathematical connections

- Sharing in a ratio
- Simplifying fractions
- Proportion

### Making cross-curricular connections

- **Geography** – ratio within populations
- **Food technology** – working with ratio of ingredients in a recipe
- **Relevance** – using ratio in daily tasks

### Prior learning

- Students should know their multiplication tables up to 10 × 10, how to cancel fractions, how to find a fraction of a quantity and how to multiply and divide, with and without a calculator.

### Working mathematically

- Ratio can cause problems for some students, so encourage them to write down or verbalise their methods in order to embed their learning.
- Structure tasks so students can work out the methods for themselves, either by increasing the difficulty incrementally, or through one straightforward and one complex example.

### Common misconceptions and remediation

- A common error is to forget to express all the quantities in the same units. Keep reminding students to sort out the units first.
- When expressing a ratio, e.g. 3 : 5, as portions of a whole quantity, students may simply write it as $\frac{3}{5}$. Keep asking students for the number of parts in the ratio. (8)

### Probing questions

- The ratio of boys to girls in a class is 4 : 1. Could there be exactly 35 children in the class? Why? Could there be seven girls? Why?

### Literacy focus

- Key terms: cancel, simplest form, common unit
- Make sure students are clear about what a ratio is. Encourage them to write a practical problem using ratio.

### Part 1

- Give students practice in converting between metric units by using quick-fire questions.
- Ensure that all the units in Exercise 10A are covered: pounds and pence, hours and minutes, hours and days, days and weeks, centimetres and millimetres, kilograms and grams, millimetres and metres. Write down the conversions for **less able** students.
- Ask more stretching conversions for **more able** students, e.g. litres and centilitres, tonnes and kilograms.

- Write pairs of fractions on the board with the numerator or denominator from one fraction missing. Ask students to provide the missing number to make the fractions equivalent.
- Challenge **more able** students with improper fractions using large numbers, e.g.

$$\frac{120}{40} = \frac{?}{5} \text{ or } \frac{720}{9} = \frac{?}{3} = \frac{?}{1}$$

# Part 2

### Common units; Ratios as fractions

- Explain that a ratio is a way to compare the sizes of two or more quantities and that to use ratios all quantities should be the same units, e.g. compare centimetres to centimetres.
- A ratio can be expressed as a fraction of a quantity. The denominator of the fraction is obtained by adding the numbers in the ratio.
- Explain that if the units of the quantities are different, then one must be converted before the ratio can be formed and simplified. This is because a ratio does not have units.
- Ask students how many times bigger 1 kilometre is than 1 metre. (1000)
- Write 1 metre to 1 kilometre = 1 m : 1 km = 1 : 1000
- Write 1 : 2, 2 : 4, 3 : 6 on the board and explain that these are all equivalent.
- Now write 4 : 12 on the board and ask for some equivalent ratios. (1 : 3, 2 : 6, and so on.)
- Now work through the text and examples 1 and 2 in the Student Book with the class; these examples combine the work on units with the work on ratios.
- **Students can now do Exercise 10A from the Student Book.**

| R&P 1–8 | Calculator n/a | CM n/a | MR 9, 10 | PS 11, 12 | EV n/a |
|---|---|---|---|---|---|

### Dividing amounts in a given ratio

- Ask students to tear a sheet of A4 paper into 16 pieces: tear the sheet in half (= 2); put the two pieces together and tear (= 4); put the four pieces together and tear (= 8); put the eight pieces together and tear (= 16).
- Write the ratio 1 : 3 on the board. Ask students to place the 16 pieces in two piles with three in the second pile for each one in the first pile. Say that they have shared the 16 pieces in the ratio 1 : 3. Ask what fraction of the 16 pieces are in the first pile ($\frac{1}{4}$); second pile ($\frac{3}{4}$).

  Reinforce this by stating that $\frac{1}{4}$ of 16 pieces = four pieces and $\frac{3}{4}$ of 16 pieces = 12 pieces.
- Work through the text and methods 1 and 2 in examples 3 and 4 in the Student Book.
- **Students can now do Exercise 10B from the Student Book.**

| R&P 1–5, 6a, b, c, 7 | Calculator 4, 6–9 | CM 6d | MR 8 | PS 9, 10 | EV n/a |
|---|---|---|---|---|---|

### Calculating with ratios when only part of the information is known

- Explain that sometimes, instead of giving the value of the whole amount, students will be given the value of one part of a ratio. For example: I share some money with my brother in the ratio 2 : 3, I get £2. How much does my brother get? (£3)
- Say that for Exercise 10B, the same question would have been: Divide £5 in the ratio 2 : 3.
- Give **more able** students more examples, e.g. mass of car and lorry are in the ratio 1 : 20; mass of lorry is 40 tonnes. What is the mass of the car? (Divide 42 tonnes in the ratio 1 : 20.)
- Now work through the text and Method 1 in Example 5 and Method 2 in Example 6.
- **Students can now do Exercise 10C from the Student Book.**

| R&P 1–5 | Calculator 1, 3, 5 | CM 6 | MR 7 | PS 8, 9, 11–13 | EV 10 |
|---|---|---|---|---|---|

# Part 3

- For each section, check students' understanding by going over the CM, MR, PS and EV questions in exercises 10A–10C.

# Section 10.2 Speed, distance and time

## Learning objectives

- Recognise the relationship between speed, distance and time
- Calculate average speed from distance and time
- Calculate distance travelled from the speed and the time taken
  Calculate the time taken on a journey from the speed and the distance

## Making mathematical connections

- Equations, expressions, identities and functions
- Rearranging formulae
- Solving equations

## Resources and homework

- Student Book 10.2: pages 238–241
- Practice Book 10.2

## Making cross-curricular connections

- **Science** – using compound measures
- **Computing** – using formulae in spreadsheets
- **Relevance** – relationships between speed, distance and time when travelling

## Prior learning

- Students need to know how to multiply and divide.
- Students should also be familiar with the common units for speed.

## Working mathematically

- This section teaches students how to calculate using the relationship between speed, distance and time.
- Students will discuss compound units, and the meanings of km/h and m/s.

## Common misconceptions and remediation

- Students often fail to realise that, e.g., 30 minutes is not 0.3 of an hour, 15 minutes is not 0.15 of an hour. Point out these common errors regularly.

## Probing questions

- What makes questions involving speed easy to solve? What makes them difficult to solve? Write some questions that are easy to solve and some that are difficult to solve.
- Explain why travelling a distance of 60 kilometres in 45 minutes is an average of 80 km/h.

## Literacy focus

- Key terms: distance, speed, time
- Ask students to write a step-by-step guide on how to use the DST triangle diagram.

## Part 1

- Give students some simple quick-fire speed questions. Students could display answers on mini-white boards. For example:
  - Speed 30 mph, how far in 30 minutes? (15 miles)
  - Speed 60 mph, how far in 2 hours? (120 miles)
  - Speed 20 mph, how far in 1 hour 30 minutes? (30 miles)
  - Distance 40 miles, time 1 hour, what is the average speed? (40 mph)
  - Distance 60 miles, time 2 hours, what is the average speed? (30 mph)

- o Distance 10 miles, time 30 minutes, what is the average speed? (20 mph)
- o Speed 50 mph, distance 50 miles. How long? (1 hour)
- o Speed 60 mph, distance 30 miles. How long? (30 minutes)
- o Speed 30 mph, distance 90 miles. How long? (3 hours)

## Part 2

- Continuing from Part 1, remind students of a question and ask them how they worked out the answer, e.g. Speed 60 mph, how far in 2 hours? Ask: 'How did you get 120 miles?' Prompt them to give you a formula, e.g. 60 miles in one hour, so in two hours 60 × 2 = 120. (speed × time = distance)
- Repeat for each type of question.
  - o Distance 60 miles, time 2 hours. Ask: 'How did you get 30 mph?' Again prompt students to give you a formula, e.g. 60 miles in two hours, 60 ÷ 2 = 30 miles in one hour, so 30 mph. (distance ÷ time = speed)
  - o Speed 30 mph, distance 90 miles. How long did the trip take? (3 hours) Again prompt students to give you a formula, e.g. 30 mph is 30 miles per hour, so 30 miles in one hour, 90 ÷ 30 = 3, so 3 hours. (distance ÷ speed = time)
- Now draw the triangle to show the three formulae.

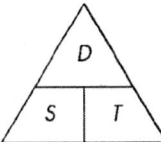

- Remind students how to convert hours and minutes into hours and vice versa, for example:
  - o 20 minutes = 20 ÷ 60 hour = $\frac{1}{3}$ hour
  - o 0.8 of an hour = 0.8 × 60 minutes = 48 minutes
- Work through Examples 7, 8 and 9 with the class.
- You will need to remind **less able** students to change hours and minutes to hours, so reinforce this point when discussing the Student Book text and Examples 7–9.
- **Students can now do Exercise 10D from the Student Book.**

| R&P 1–5, 6a, 7, 8, 11–13 | Calculator all | CM 6b, c, 9, 15 | MR 10 | PS 14 | EV 16 |

## Part 3

- Give students a question about a two-part journey, e.g. 100 miles at an average speed of 40 mph followed by 90 miles at an average speed of 60 mph.
- Go through the process of calculating the average speed of the whole journey. (190 miles in 4 hours = 47.5 mph)
- Discuss the checking methods outlined earlier to test whether the answers are sensible, e.g. point out that 100 miles at 40 mph followed by 100 miles at 60 mph would give an average of 50 mph. So the answer to the problem will be less than 50 mph.

# Section 10.3 Direct proportion problems

## Learning objectives
- Recognise and solve problems that involve direct proportion

## Resources and homework
- Student Book 10.3: pages 242–244
- Practice Book 10.3

## Making mathematical connections
- Inverse proportion
- Functions

## Making cross-curricular connections
- **Art** – proportion in paintings and drawings
- **Food technology** – adjusting ingredients in a recipe
- **Relevance** – using proportion in everyday life, e.g. mixing cement

## Prior learning
- Students should know how to multiply and divide without using a calculator.

## Working mathematically
- Students will think about how they know that given sets of numbers are in direct proportion.
- They will think about the tips they would give someone to help them solve problems involving direct proportion.
- Students will talk through the thinking that enabled them to solve problems.

## Common misconceptions and remediation
- Errors occur when the information in a question leads to an answer that is not sensible, e.g. when adapting a recipe, students may give an answer of 1.5 eggs (see Part 2). Point out that in practical situations answers must always be sensible.

## Probing questions
- Six apples cost £1.20. Explain how you would work out how much eight apples or 12 apples would cost.
- Three books cost £21. How would you work out the cost of four books?

## Literacy focus
- Key terms: direct proportion, unitary method, unit cost
- Ask students to explain how the key terms in this section help them to work out problems.

## Part 1
- Write the following on the board and ask students to give you an answer.
  $\boxed{6}$ cost $\boxed{36p}$. How much do $\boxed{5}$ cost?
- Students will have an intuitive idea of this and will answer 30p.
- Discuss the idea of finding the cost of one item and then scaling up to the required number.
- Repeat with other values such as: 8 cost 56p, how much will 6 cost?
- For **less able** students, use whole number answers.
- For **more able** students, use decimals, e.g. 7 cost £10.50, how much do 6 cost?

## Part 2

- Explain to students that the method they used in Part 1, of finding the cost of one item and then scaling, is called the 'unitary method'.
- Write this recipe on the board.
  **For 4 people**
  o 100 g butter
  o 300 g flour
  o 2 eggs
  o 1 cup of milk
- Ask students how they could change this for three people – don't worry about the eggs at this stage. (Divide by 4 and multiply by 3.)
- Now tell students that you only have 300 g butter and 600 g flour but plenty of eggs and milk and ask how many people you could serve and why. (eight, as there is only enough flour for eight people)
- Now go through the Student Book text and Examples 10, 11 and 12 with the class.
- Examples 10 and 12 cover both methods (using a table and the unitary method).
- Example 11 is a question about which shop sells cola more cheaply.
- **Students can now do Exercise 10E from the Student Book.**

| R&P 1–6, 7a | Calculator all | CM 7b | MR 8a | PS 9 | EV 8b, 10 |

## Part 3

- On the board, write a simple recipe for six people.
- Ask students how much of each ingredient would be needed for one person, two people, 12 people, and so on. Include an item, e.g. two eggs, which cannot be divided easily.
  Say to students that such a problem would not occur in an examination but could come up in real life.
- As a lead-in to the next section on best buys, ask students which of these are better value:
  o three chocolate bars for 90p
  o five chocolate bars for £1.50.
  (Answer: Neither, as both work out at 30p per bar.)
- Now discuss with students how they would compare values.

# Section 10.4 Best buys

## Learning objectives

- Find the cost per unit mass
- Find the mass per unit cost
- Use the above to find which product is better value

## Making mathematical connections

- Sharing in a ratio
- Simplifying fractions
- Proportion

## Resources and homework

- Student Book 10.4: pages 245–249
- Practice Book 10.4

## Making cross-curricular connections

- **Business Studies** – working out unit cost of items
- **Food technology** – working out the cost per unit of ingredients in a recipe
- **Relevance** – using ratio in daily tasks

## Prior learning

- Students need to know how to use a calculator to multiply and divide.

## Working mathematically

- Students will work out what numbers are key to solving problems. They will understand how the numbers help them to solve the problems.
- Students will estimate answers and be able to explain why they chose the estimated answer.

## Common misconceptions and remediation

- Students often make mistakes by not making the units the same for each item. Stress that they must always compare the same units.
- Students may not realise which is the best buy once they have completed the calculations. Careful thought and practice should help to minimise this problem.

## Probing questions

- Can you solve the problem in a different way?
- What do you look for when deciding on the most efficient way to solve a problem?

## Literacy focus

- Key terms: best buy, better value, mass, value for money
- Choose questions from some of the exercises that students have already done and ask which of the key terms are key to solving the particular problem. Also ask students to say how the words help students to solve the questions.

## Part 1

- Draw two jars of different sizes on the board. Label both jars 'jam'. Write 250 g and £0.55 on one and 600 g and £1.20 on the other. Ask students if they can tell which jar is the best value for money.
- Various methods could be explored, such as:
  - Find the cost of 50 g (11p and 10p).
  - Find a common multiple of 250 and 600 (3000), giving 12 × 55 = 660 and 5 × 120 = 600.
- Students may still be confused about which product is the best value.
- Emphasise the phrase 'More jam per penny'.
- Point out that this is a clue as to how to work out the problem as 'More jam per penny' can be worked out as jam ÷ money, with the word 'per' being replaced with ÷.

## Part 2

- Continuing with the example used in Part 1, make a list of possible answers for students to write down.
- Discuss each one and how to obtain it as it is written down.
- Explain that you have written them both in pence to make it easier to do the calculations.

|  | **250 g for 55p** | **600 g for 120p** |  |
|---|---|---|---|
| Dividing by 5 | 50 g for 11p | 50 g for 10p | Dividing by 12 |
| Dividing by 250 | 1 g for 0.22p | 1 g for 0.2p | Dividing by 600 |
| Multiplying by 12 | 3000 g for £6.60 | 3000 g for £6 | Multiplying by 5 |
| Dividing by 55 | Number of grams per penny = 250 ÷ 55 = 4.54 | Number of grams per penny = 600 ÷ 120 = 5 | Dividing by 120 |

- Now work through Examples 13, 14, 15 and 16 from the Student Book with the class.
- Explain that different students will prefer to use different methods to solve the problems, and that the more ideas with which they are comfortable, the easier they will find this topic.
- **Students can now do Exercise 10F from the Student Book.**

| R&P 1–4 | Calculator all | CM 7, 8 | MR 5, 9 | PS 6, 10–13 | EV n/a |
|---|---|---|---|---|---|

## Part 3

- Ask students if they think the larger quantities will be proportionally cheaper than the smaller quantities. Why might it not always be the best option to buy the biggest?
- Discuss the practicalities of buying large quantities to save money. For example, is it worth buying two loaves on a special offer when one will be thrown away if it does not get eaten?

# Chapter 11 Geometry and measures: Perimeter and area

## Overview

| | |
|---|---|
| **11.1** Rectangles | **11.5** Area of a trapezium |
| **11.2** Compound shapes | **11.6** Circles |
| **11.3** Area of a triangle | **11.7** The area of a circle |
| **11.4** Area of a parallelogram | **11.8** Answers in terms of $\pi$ |

### Prior learning
What 'area' means.
The common units of length and area.

### Learning objectives
**Ensure that students can: work out the perimeters and areas of rectangles, triangles, parallelograms, trapeziums and compound shapes; calculate the circumference and area of a circle and give their answers in terms of $\pi$.**

In the examination, students will be expected to:
- calculate the area and perimeter of a rectangle
- calculate the perimeter and area of a compound shape made from rectangles
- calculate the area of a triangle
- use the formula for the area of a triangle
- calculate the area of a parallelogram
- use the formula for the area of a parallelogram
- calculate the area of a trapezium
- use the formula for the area of a trapezium
- recognise terms used for circle work
- calculate the circumference of a circle
- calculate the area of a circle
- give answers for circle calculations in terms of $\pi$.

### Extension
Provide more complex problems involving composite shapes, as well as real-life problems, for students to solve.

### Curriculum references

| Section | GCSE specification |
|---|---|
| 11.1 | G16 |
| 11.2 | G16 |
| 11.3 | G16 |
| 11.4 | G16 |

| Section | GCSE specification |
|---|---|
| 11.5 | G16 |
| 11.6 | G17 |
| 11.7 | G17 |
| 11.8 | G17 |

## Route mapping

| Exercise | Accessible | Intermediate | Challenging | AO1 | AO2 MR CM | AO3 PS EV | Key questions |
|---|---|---|---|---|---|---|---|
| 11A | 1–5 | | | 1–3 | 4 | 5 | 2 |
| 11B | 1–4 | 5–10 | | 1, 5 | 3, 10 | 2, 4, 6–9 | 5 |
| 11C | | 1–8 | | 1, 5 | 2, 4, 7 | 3, 6, 8 | 4, 6 |
| 11D | | 1–7 | 8 | 1, 3, 4 | 5, 7 | 2, 6, 8 | 3, 4, 7 |
| 11E | | 1–4 | | 1 | 3 | 2, 4 | 1 |
| 11F | | 1–9 | | 1, 2, 4, 5 | 3, 9 | 6–8 | 1, 4, 5 |
| 11G | 1–4 | | | 1 | | 2–4 | 2 |
| 11H | | 1–15 | 16 | 1–3, 8–10 | 11–14, 16 | 4–7, 15 | 1, 3, 5 |
| 11I | | 1–12 | | 1–3, 6, 8, 9 | 5, 10, 12 | 4, 7, 11 | 1, 3, 6 |
| 11J | | 1–9 | | 1–4, 6 | 7, 9 | 5, 8 | 1, 2, 6 |

*Key questions are those that demonstrate mastery of the concept, or which require a step-up in understanding or application. Key questions could be used to identify the questions that students must tackle, to support differentiation, or to identify the questions that should be teacher-marked rather than student-marked.*

## About this chapter

**Making connections**: This chapter introduces regular mathematical shapes and how to find their perimeters and areas; it also shows students how to use these facts to solve problems.

**Relevance:** In many households, areas and perimeters need to be calculated in order to work out, e.g. how much wallpaper or carpeting to buy, or how much fencing is needed.

**Working mathematically**: Students will consider questions such as: 'How do you find out how many carpet tiles to buy to cover the floor space?' They will need to find the area of both shapes (the floor and the carpet tile). Students will use the formulae for circles and areas to find, e.g. the length a running track needs to be if the track is in the shape of a racecourse; where to mark the different starting points to make sure that each athlete runs the same distance.

**Assessment**: In each section of this chapter, ensure that students have a good grasp of the key questions in each exercise before moving on. (Refer to the 'Route mapping' table.) Encourage students to read and think about the 'Ready to progress?' statements on page 282 of the Student Book. Check students' understanding at the end of the chapter, formatively, using peer assessment. Students could do a mini test in the form of the 'Review questions' on pages 282–283 of the Student Book. Follow up the test with an individual target-getting session, based on any areas for development that a student may have.

## Worked exemplars from Student Book (page 281) – suggestions for use
- Present students with the same question but different numbers. They should use the exemplar to mirror the working, in full or just refer to the notes.
- Copy and cut the exemplars into cards. Students should match the working with the notes.
- Alternatively, copy and cut the working into cards but split the label/description from the working.

**Answers to the Student Book questions are on the CD-ROM provided.**

# Section 11.1 Rectangles

## Learning objectives

- Calculate the perimeter and area of a rectangle

## Resources and homework

- Student Book 11.1: pages 255–256
- Practice Book 11.1

## Making mathematical connections

- Units
- Substitution into formulae

## Making cross-curricular connections

- **Geography** – approximating land mass
- **Relevance** – finding land area

## Prior learning

- Students need to understand that 'area' is the amount of flat space that is covered by a 2D shape.

## Working mathematically

- Draw a rectangle on the board, labelled with measurements, and ask students: What is the perimeter? What is the area?

## Common misconceptions and remediation

- Students commonly make three mistakes when calculating the area of a rectangle:
  - They confuse perimeter with area.
  - They convert square centimetres into square millimetres by multiplying by 10.
  - They convert square metres into square centimetres by multiplying by 100.
- Write the formulae for perimeter and area on the board as a reminder.
- Before students attempt question 4 of Exercise 11A in the Student Book, carefully explain the principle behind converting units in area questions, reminding students of the principles, for example:
  - changing from square millimetres to square centimetres
  - knowing that $1 \text{ mm}^2 = 100 \text{ cm}^2$ ($10 \times 10$)
  - dividing the number of square millimetres by 100 to find the equivalent area in square centimetres.

## Probing questions

- Do you want to find perimeter or area?
- How do you calculate the perimeter of a rectangle?
- How do you calculate the area of a rectangle?

## Literacy focus

- Key terms: none
- To check that students understand the difference between perimeter and area, ask what perimeter a rectangle with an area of $12 \text{ cm}^2$ could have.

## Part 1

- Draw a 5 by 3 rectangle on the board. Ask: How can I find the area of this rectangle?
- Repeat for two more rectangles with different dimensions.
- Encourage **more able** students to use the key formula $A = lw$, making sure everyone understands that: $A$ = area, $l$ = length and $w$ = width.

## Part 2

- Draw a 5 by 4 rectangle on a square grid.
- Ask students to find its area by counting squares.
- Explain that the answer of 20 can also be found by multiplying 5 and 4.
- Work through Example 1 in the Student Book with the class to reinforce this method.
- Now draw a 6 by 10 rectangle (not on a grid) and ask students to give its area.
- Ensure that they understand that they must multiply the length by the width.
- Draw a rectangle with width and length labelled. Explain that: area = length × width. This can also be written as a formula: $A = l \times w$ or $A = lw$.
- When students are calculating the area of each rectangle, ensure that they write down the formula before substituting values for length and width.
- Now work through Example 2, which requires students to work out the perimeter of the rectangle.
- Give students a few more examples in which they need to find the perimeter of a rectangle.
- **Students can now do Exercise 11A from the Student Book.**

| G&M 1–3 | Calculator n/a | CM n/a | MR 4 | PS 5 | EV n/a |
|---------|----------------|--------|------|------|--------|

## Part 3

- Summarise the work done in this section by ensuring that students are aware of the rules, expressed either in words or as formulae:
  - $A = lw$
  - $L = \dfrac{A}{w}$
  - $W = \dfrac{A}{l}$

# Section 11.2 Compound shapes

## Learning objectives
- Calculate the perimeter and area of a compound shape made from rectangles

## Resources and homework
- Student Book 11.2: pages 257–260
- Practice Book 11.2

## Making mathematical connections
- Units
- Area of rectangles

## Making cross-curricular connections
- **Geography** – approximating land mass
- **Relevance** – calculating perimeter

## Prior learning
- Students need to be able to find the area of a rectangle, as covered in the previous lesson.

## Working mathematically
- Students will work out the area of compound shapes, e.g. comprising two rectangles.
- They will also discuss whether or not the perimeter of a compound shape is found by adding the two perimeters together. If not, then students should be able to explain why not.

## Common misconceptions and remediation
- Students often find it difficult to find the area of a compound shape. Remind students that a compound shape is always made up of simpler shapes and that finding the area is easier once they have split the shape into sections.
- Remind students that they should always draw a diagram that shows how they split the shape, and they must label all the lengths clearly.

## Probing questions
- Look at the shape in Example 3 of the Student Book with the class.
- Ask students if there is another way to split the shape into two rectangles.
- Will this give the same answer?
- What might help you to decide how to split the shape?

## Literacy focus
- Key term: compound shape
- The term 'compound shape' will arise in a few questions. Ask students to explain what a compound shape is, and to give you some examples.

## Part 1
- Draw the shape, as shown, on the whiteboard.
- Ask students: How might I find the area of this shape?
- Split the shape into two rectangles and find the area of each before adding them. Ask: Is there another way to find the area of this shape? Show that the same answer can be obtained by splitting the shape into two different rectangles.
- Emphasise to students that splitting a compound shape into rectangles, and clearly labelling those rectangles, will enable them to find the area of the shape.

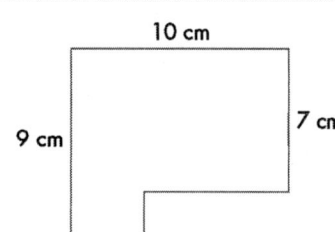

## Part 2

- Go over Example 3 with the class.
- Then ask students to read Example 4 and try to understand the method shown.
- Work through the example, talking students through the method as a class. Students must work out the area of the compound shape.
- To do this, they must split the shape into two rectangles A and B, as shown in the example. Work through the remaining calculations with the class to get an answer of 36 cm$^2$.
- **More able** students could draw their own compound shapes and then ask other students to find the areas.
- When students begin Exercise 11B, ensure that they copy the diagram for each question and show precisely how they are splitting up the compound shape. Make sure students label each rectangle clearly.
- Tell students that it is important for them to set out their work clearly, as in Example 4, so that they will still pick up marks for the method even if they get a dimension wrong.
- **Less able** students generally find working with compound shapes difficult. Allow these students to draw the first few examples in Exercise 11B on centimetre-squared paper to reinforce the concept discussed in the lesson. They could also work in pairs to complete questions 1 and 2.
- **Students can now do Exercise 11B from the Student Book.**

| G&M 1, 5 | Calculator n/a | CM 3 | MR 10 | PS 2, 6, 8, 9 | EV 4, 7 |
|---|---|---|---|---|---|

## Part 3

- Draw shape X, as shown, on the board.
- Ask students if they can see a way to calculate the area of the part that is shaded. They will probably suggest subtracting the smaller area from the larger area.
- Now draw shape Y on the board.
- Ask students if they can see a similar method of calculating the shaded area.
- Show how to set out the working.
  Area of the large rectangle = 5 × 10 = 50 cm$^2$
  Area of the small rectangle = 2 × 5 = 10 cm$^2$
  Area shaded = large area − small area = 50 − 10 = 40 cm$^2$

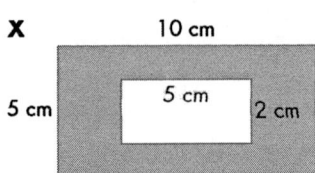

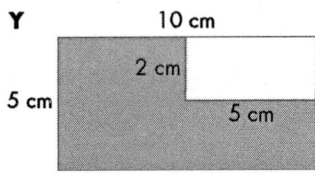

# Section 11.3 Area of a triangle

## Learning objectives
- Calculate the area of a triangle
- Use the formula for the area of a triangle

## Resources and homework
- Student Book 11.3: pages 260–264
- Practice Book 11.3

## Making mathematical connections
- Area of rectangles
  Fractions

## Making cross-curricular connections
- **Geography** – approximate land mass
- **Relevance** – area of walls to paint

## Prior learning
- Students should know how to calculate the area of a rectangle, as covered in Section 11.1.

## Working mathematically
- Students may initially draw a rectangle around the triangle, keeping the same base and having the same height to assist finding the area of the triangle.
- Students may draw a diagonal of the rectangle, shade in one of the triangles and find the area of this triangle.
- Point out these errors as they occur.

## Common misconceptions and remediation
- The most common error is to use a height that is not the perpendicular height. However, there is unlikely to be any ambiguity at this level as students will have no way of working out the perpendicular height if it is not given to them.
- Take every opportunity, though, to remind students that a perpendicular is always at right angles to its base, whichever side is taken as the base.

## Probing questions
- Can you always draw a rectangle round a triangle? In how many different ways?
- How do you halve an amount?

## Literacy focus
- Key term: perpendicular height
- Ensure that students know that they must use the base and the *perpendicular height*. Say that in Mathematics, 'height' generally means the perpendicular height.

## Part 1
- Draw three triangles on the board, one scalene, one isosceles and one equilateral.
- Ask students to describe each triangle, making sure they mention not only the shape but the correct names. Make sure they can classify the three types. Write the correct name below each triangle.
- Ask students: What do we mean by *perpendicular*? What do we mean by *height*?
- Ask some students to label the base and the perpendicular height for each triangle.
- Ask other students to re-label the triangles, using a different side as the base and drawing in the corresponding perpendicular height.

## Part 2

- For a **less able** class, allow two lessons for this topic.

### Area of a right-angled triangle

- Show students that a right-angled triangle is half of a rectangle. You could show this by cutting a rectangular piece of card into two right-angled triangles. To demonstrate the point more clearly, and if possible, give each student a sheet of A4 paper and ask them to cut it into two right-angled triangles themselves.
- Discuss the terms *base* and *height* for a right-angled triangle, using the diagrams in the Student Book to make the terms clear.
- Lead students to the idea that, in order to find the area of a right-angled triangle, they must multiply the base by the height and then divide by two. Put this into a formula for students: area of a triangle = ' base × height or $A = 'bh$.
- If the class is **less able**, just use the formula in words, to start with; they may not be able to follow an algebraic formula at this stage.
- Show students the word formula in action in Example 5. Use the example to explain that it is often easier to multiply the base by the height first and then divide this value by two.
- Students who are struggling to complete the exercise could work in small groups, or be partnered by a student who is more confident.
- **Students can now do Exercise 11C from the Student Book.**

| G&M 1, 5 | Calculator all | CM n/a | MR 2, 4, 7 | PS 3, 8 | EV 6 |

- It would be suitable to end the first lesson after students have completed Exercise 11C, leaving the remainder of this activity until the next lesson.

### Area of any triangle

- Once students have mastered finding the area of a right-angled triangle, they can move on to finding the area of any triangle.
- Work through Example 6 of the Student Book with the class.
- If necessary, remind students that the area of any triangle is given by the formula: area = ' × base × perpendicular height or $A = 'bh$. If the class is **less able**, continue to use the formula in words, until students can follow the algebraic formula. You could reinforce this work by demonstrating that a rectangle can be drawn around the triangle.
- Encourage **less able** students to draw the enclosing rectangle around the triangle, then to cut it out and show that the 'extra' parts can be combined to fit over the original triangle.
- Work through Example 7, using the fact that the shape can be split easily into a rectangle and a triangle. Encourage students to explore the ways in which compound shapes can be split, and to use the method that works best for them.
- **Students can now do Exercise 11D from the Student Book.**

| G&M 1, 3, 4 | Calculator all | CM 7 | MR 5 | PS 2, 6 | EV 8 |

## Part 3

- Ask students to draw as many triangles as they can that have an area of 24 cm$^2$, but with bases of different lengths.
- Ask **less able** students to find two different triangles that both have an area of 12 cm$^2$.

# Section 11.4 Area of a parallelogram

## Learning objectives

- Calculate the area of a parallelogram
- Use the formula for the area of a parallelogram

## Resources and homework

- Student Book 11.4: pages 265–266
- Practice Book 11.4

## Making mathematical connections

- Areas of rectangles and triangles

## Making cross-curricular connections

- **Geography** – approximating land mass
- **Relevance** – creating specific shapes

## Prior learning

- Students should know how to calculate the area of a rectangle, as covered in Section 11.1.
- They should also know how to calculate the area of a triangle, as covered in Section 11.3.

## Working mathematically

- Students will discuss parallelograms, and know how to divide this shape into smaller shapes of which they can find the areas.
- Students will know the formula for the area of a parallelogram and calculate the area.

## Common misconceptions and remediation

- When finding the area of a parallelogram, students may mistakenly halve the answer.
- They may use a height other than the perpendicular height if other measurements are given.
- Ensure that each student has the formula for finding the area of a parallelogram written clearly in their notes, with a diagram of the measurements that should be used.
- Encourage **less able** students to refer to their notes before attempting each question.

## Probing questions

- Ask students to demonstrate why the area of a parallelogram formula works.

## Literacy focus

- Key term: parallelogram
- Ensure that students are familiar with the word *parallelogram* and know the characteristics of a parallelogram, and can describe them to you.

## Part 1

- Ask students: What is a parallelogram? (a quadrilateral with two pairs of parallel sides)
- Ask: Does this mean that a rectangle is a parallelogram? Is a square a parallelogram? (Yes, in both cases)
- Ask students to point out parallelograms and rectangles in the classroom, explaining their decision each time.

## Part 2

- Draw a parallelogram on the board and show students how to split it into a rectangle and two right-angled triangles that can be put together to form a rectangle. You can show this easily on a whiteboard or by using a piece of card.
- Explain to the class that the area of a parallelogram can be found by multiplying the base by the height: $A = bh$

- The formula for the area of a parallelogram can be shown in two ways.
- Either: area of two congruent triangles = $2 \times \frac{1}{2} \times$ base $\times$ height = base $\times$ height
- Or:

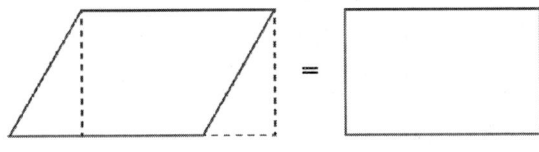

Area of parallelogram = area of a rectangle
= base $\times$ height

- Ensure that students give their final answers to a suitable degree of accuracy, usually three significant figures (3 sf).
- Ask students to read Example 8 in the Student Book. Check that they understand the example and especially that the perpendicular height is used in the calculation.
- Draw a parallelogram to explain the difference between a perpendicular height and a *slant height*.

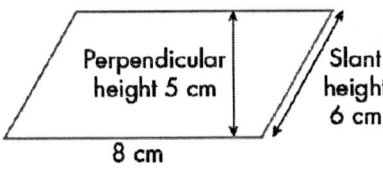

So area = $8 \times 5 = 40$ cm²

- This example should show students clearly why they must always identify the base and perpendicular height first, in questions on finding the area of a parallelogram.
- **Students can now do Exercise 11E from the Student Book.**

| G&M 1 | Calculator all | CM 3 | MR n/a | PS 4 | EV 2 |
|-------|----------------|------|--------|------|------|

## Part 3

- Ask students to draw three different parallelograms, each with an area of 12 cm².
- They should think about how they could find the base and perpendicular height, given the area. They need to find different ways of giving an area of 12 cm². This should reinforce the concept of perpendicular height.
- **Less able** students could think about parallelograms with bases that are factors of 12.
- You could ask **more able** students to find parallelograms with areas of 24 cm² or 36 cm².

# Section 11.5 Area of a trapezium

## Learning objectives
- Calculate the area of a trapezium
- Use the formula for the area of a trapezium

## Resources and homework
- Student Book 11.5: pages 266–268
- Practice Book 11.5

## Making mathematical connections
- Substitution into formula
- BIDMAS

## Making cross-curricular connections
- **Geography** – approximating land mass
- **Relevance** – area of roofing

## Prior learning
- Students should know how to calculate the areas of rectangles, triangles and parallelograms, as covered in Sections 11.1, 11.3 and 11.4.

## Working mathematically
- Students will know the properties of a trapezium.
- They will show how a trapezium can be split into two triangles to help them find the area of the whole shape.

## Common misconceptions and remediation
- The most common error is to calculate $(\frac{1}{2}a + b)$, which is generally down to lack of understanding in using a calculator. Avoid this by encouraging students to label their trapezium with letters, $a$, $b$ and $h$, before starting any calculations. They should set out their working appropriately, as shown in the worked examples.
- Students often try to split the trapezium into a rectangle and two right-angled triangles, thus having difficulty in finding the base of each triangle. Ensure that students fully understand the method required before they attempt Exercise 11F.
- As in the previous section for the area of a parallelogram, always emphasise in this context that height means perpendicular height and that they must add the two *parallel* sides.

## Probing questions
- What are the properties of a trapezium?
- How can you split a trapezium, to help you work out its total area?

## Literacy focus
- Key term: trapezium
- Ask students to describe and write down the definition of a trapezium. Make sure that they know that height refers to perpendicular height. A slant height is given in question 2 of Exercise 11F. Students will need to know the difference.

## Part 1
- Ask students: What is a trapezium? (A quadrilateral with just one pair of parallel sides)
- Ask: Does a rectangle count as a trapezium? What about a square? (No, in both cases, since they both have two pairs of parallel sides, although some mathematicians may define the trapezium differently.)

## Part 2

- The area of a trapezium is given by:
  A = half the sum of the parallel sides × height

  $A = \frac{1}{2}(a + b)h$

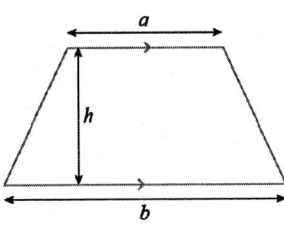

- This can be shown to be the case by splitting the trapezium into two triangles.

Area of triangle 1 = $\frac{1}{2}$ × base × height = $\frac{1}{2}ah$

Area of triangle 2 = $\frac{1}{2}$ × base × height = $\frac{1}{2}bh$

**Total area** = $\frac{1}{2}ah + \frac{1}{2}bh = \text{'}h(a + b) = \frac{1}{2}(a + b)h$

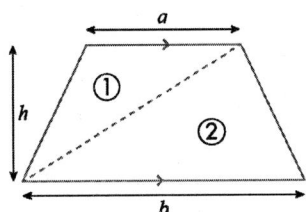

- Two identical trapeziums can be placed together (one upside down) to make a parallelogram.
  The area of the parallelogram is $(a + b)h$. So the area of one trapezium is half of this.

  This means that the area of a trapezium is $A = \frac{1}{2}(a + b)h$

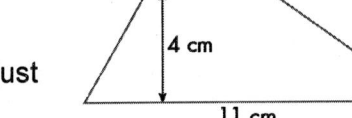

- Now take the class through an example, pointing out the best way to do the calculation.

  $A = \frac{1}{2}(a + b)h$      $a + b = 16$

           $16 × h = 16 × 4$
                   $= 64$
           $64 ÷ 2 = 32$
           So $A = 32$ cm$^2$

- Ask students to read Example 9 and match what they have just learnt to the calculation shown in the example.
- **Students can now do Exercise 11F from the Student Book.**

| G&M 1, 2, 4, 5 | Calculator all | CM n/a | MR 3, 9 | PS 7, 8 | EV 6 |
|---|---|---|---|---|---|

## Part 3

- Draw these shapes on the board.

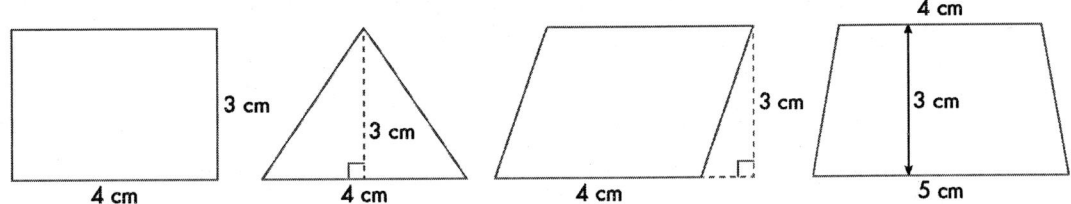

- Ask students: Which has the largest area?
  - Area of rectangle = 4 × 3 cm$^2$ = 12 cm$^2$
  - Area of triangle = $\frac{1}{2}$ × 4 × 3 cm$^2$ = 6 cm$^2$
  - Area of parallelogram = 4 × 3 cm$^2$ = 12 cm$^2$
  - Area of trapezium = $\frac{1}{2}$ × (4 + 5) × 3 cm$^2$ = 13.5 cm$^2$

## Section 11.6 Circles

### Learning objectives

- Recognise terms used for circle work
- Calculate the circumference of a circle

### Resources and homework

- Student Book 11.6: pages 269–274
- Practice Book 11.6

### Making mathematical connections

- Substitution into formula
  Using a calculator

### Making cross-curricular connections

- **Geography** – estimating land mass
- **Relevance** – uses in everyday life

## Prior learning

- Students should be able to round to a given number of decimal places (usually one or two) to give sensible answers.
- They should also be familiar with substituting values into a formula.

## Working mathematically

- Students will identify all the different parts of a circle by the first letter, and use the terms for working with circles.
- Students will also calculate the circumference of circles.

## Common misconceptions and remediation

- Students often confuse the radius ($r$) with the diameter ($d$), and consequently may calculate the circumference as $C \nabla \pi r$ or $C \nabla 2\pi d$. At a later stage, students may confuse the formula for circumference with that for area: $A \nabla \pi r^2$.
- Encourage students to make a simple poster, which you should display on the classroom wall, to help them to remember the key terms.

## Probing questions

- Tell me as many different words as you can that are linked to circles.
- What is another word for the perimeter of a circle?

## Literacy focus

- Key terms: $\pi$ (pi), arc, chord, circumference, diameter, radius, sector, segment, tangent
- Students need to be familiar with all these terms. Ask them to define each word without looking at any diagrams that might be on the classroom wall.

## Part 1

- Refer students to the first page of this chapter and read it with the class, so that they may appreciate the history of $\pi$ through the centuries.
- Use the activity of measuring around a cylinder (after Exercise 11G) to refresh students' knowledge of basic circle measures. This activity is particularly useful if students have not met the formula for the circumference of a circle before.
- The activity is best done in small groups so that students can help one another, particularly with the measuring. Cans of different sizes will give the best results and students are often surprised by the accuracy of their results.
- Students who are already familiar with the formula could start the lesson with a revision example.

# Part 2

### Circle terms

- Draw a circle on the board and introduce the formula $C = \pi d$. Point out to students that they can also write this as $C = 2\pi r$, since the diameter is twice the radius ($d = 2r$).
- If necessary, explain again that $\pi$ is a number that is used in mathematics (and in many other scientific applications) when dealing with circles. Stress that $\pi$ is not an exact number and can be written to millions of decimal places. In most cases $\pi$ can be approximated to 3.14 or 3.142 when dealing with everyday examples. On most calculators, the $\pi$ button gives $\pi$ as 3.141 592 654. You may need to show students where the button is on their calculators. When checking answers to see if they are sensible, $\pi$ can be taken to be 3.
- **Students can now do Exercise 11G from the Student Book.**

| G&M 1 | Calculator n/a | CM n/a | MR n/a | PS 3, 4 | EV 2 |
|---|---|---|---|---|---|

### Circumference of a circle

- Go through some examples to show students, particularly the **less able** students, how to set out a solution to a problem.
- Calculate the circumference of the place mat on the right.

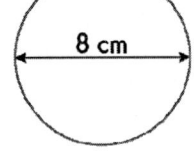

8 cm

$C = \pi d$

$\quad = \pi \times 8$

$\quad = 25.1$ cm (to 1 decimal place)

- Point out that answers of 25 cm or 25.13 cm are also acceptable. Remind students always to put the correct units with the answer.
- Work through examples 10 and 11 from the Student Book with the class.
- Encourage students to write down the formula each time they answer a question; this will help them to remember the formula.
- **Students can now do Exercise 11H from the Student Book.**
- In question 5, **less able** students could work out the circumferences of the smallest and largest tracks, omitting the questions in between. If these students complete question 7, they could omit question 12.

| G&M 1–3, 8–10 | Calculator all | CM 14 | MR 11–13, 16 | PS 4–7, 15 | EV n/a |
|---|---|---|---|---|---|

# Part 3

- Ask students to state the formula for the circumference of a circle.
- Describe some simple shapes and ask students to work out the circumference, mentally, using $\pi = 3$:
  - head, $r = 9$ cm (54 cm)
  - cup, $r = 4$ cm (24 cm)
  - football, $r = 12$ cm (72 cm)
  - oil drum, $r = 40$ cm (240 cm)
  - gas storage tank, $r = 10$ m (60 m)
  - pencil, $d = 8$ mm (24 mm).

## Learning objectives
- Calculate the area of a circle

## Resources and homework
- Student Book 11.7: pages 274–278
- Practice Book 11.7

## Making mathematical connections
- Area of a rectangle
- Circumference and sectors
  Substitution into formula

## Making cross-curricular connections
- **Technology** – calculating area
  **Relevance** – calculating area of circular items

## Prior learning
- Students should be able to round to a given number of decimal places, to give sensible answers. They also need to be able to find squares and take square roots, using calculators.

## Working mathematically
- Students will go through the rules of rounding to a given number of decimal places, e.g. 5.735 64 rounded to 1 dp, then 2 dp, then 3 dp, then 4 dp.

## Common misconceptions and remediation
- It is common for students to confuse the radius ($r$) and the diameter ($d$). Some students may work out $\pi r^2$ as $(\pi r)^2$. A simple poster, made by students and hung on the classroom wall, will help them to remember the formula.
- The area, $A$, of a circle is given by the formula $A = \pi r^2$, where $r$ is the radius and $\pi = 3.14$ or 3.142, or by using the calculator button.
- Students often forget to include the units with their answers, or they use units of length. Continually remind students of this as they work through the exercise in this section.

## Probing questions
- Tell me how you decide whether to round a number up or down.
- What is the difference between $r^2$ and $2r$?

## Literacy focus
- Key terms: none
- The words 'semicircle' and 'quadrant' crop up in Exercise 11I, so ensure that students know the meanings of these terms before starting the questions.

## Part 1
- Ask the class for the answers to $1^2$, $2^2$, $3^2$ and $15^2$, all calculated mentally.
- Then ask students to use a calculator to find $27.41^2$.
- Explain that students may take $\pi$ to be 3 for checking answers and 3.14 on basic calculators; they should use the $\pi$ button on a scientific calculator.

## Part 2

- Draw a circle on the board and divide it into as many sectors as is sensible.
- Show how, if you arrange these sectors together, it can make a shape that is approximately a rectangle.
- Show that the width of this rectangle is the radius, $r$, and the length will be half the circumference of the original circle, $' \times 2\pi r$, which is $\pi r$.
- Show how to multiply th4 width ($r$) by the base ($\pi r$) to give area = $\pi r^2$.
- Draw another circle on the board and use the formula for the area of a circle: $A = \pi r^2$.
- Explain to students that this can be written as $A = \pi \times r \times r$, but it is easier to use the ⟨x²⟩ button on a calculator.
- Show **more able** students this diagram to demonstrate that the area of the circle must be less than the area of the square that has an area of $4r^2$.
- Go through a couple of examples to show students, particularly **less able** students, of how to set out a solution to a problem.
  *Calculate the area of the CD shown on the right.*
  $A = \pi r^2$
    $= \pi \times 36$
    $= 113.1 \text{ cm}^2$ (to 1 decimal place)
- Remind students that the unit for the area is square centimetres (cm²).
- Work through Example 12 with students, for extra practice.
- Set more examples, as necessary.
  *Calculate the area of the circular pond on the right.*
  $d = 4.8$ m, so $r = 2.4$ m
  $A = \pi r^2$
    $= \pi \times 2.4^2$
    $= 18.1 \text{ m}^2$ (to 1 decimal place)
- Remind students that the unit for the area is square metres (m²). Work through Example 13, which is another problem in which the diameter is given. Use it as reinforcement.
- Encourage students to write down the formula each time they do a question, as this will help them to remember it.
- **Students can now do Exercise 11I from the Student Book.**

| G&M 1–3, 6, 8, 9 | Calculator all | CM 10 | MR 5, 12 | PS 4, 7 | EV 11 |
|---|---|---|---|---|---|

## Part 3

- Ask students to work out a few areas mentally, using $\pi = 3$; for example, for a pond, $r = 3$ m, for a window $d = 20$ cm.
- Emphasise that they must use the radius in the calculation, so if a diameter is given in the question they must divide it by two.
- Show students that a good way to learn the value of $\pi$ to 7 or 8 decimal places, is by counting the letters in the words of this sentence.

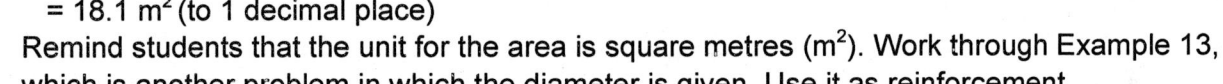

| How | • | I | wish | I | could | calculate | pi | quickly |
|---|---|---|---|---|---|---|---|---|
| 3 | • | 1 | 4 | 1 | 5 | 9 | 2 | 7 |

# Section 11.8 Answers in terms of $\pi$

## Learning objectives
- Give answers for circle calculations in terms of $\pi$

## Making mathematical connections
- Area of a circle
- Substitution into formulae

## Resources and homework
- Student Book 11.8: pages 278–280
- Practice Book 11.8

## Making cross-curricular connections
- **Geography** – calculating relative areas of land masses
- **Relevance** – comparison of areas where no actual figures are required, e.g. when looking at different land masses

## Prior learning
- Students should know and be able to use the formulae for the circumference and area of a circle.

## Working mathematically
- Students will discuss how to tell which of two circles has the greater area without actually calculating the area, when one has the radius given and the other has the diameter given.

## Common misconceptions and remediation
- Students may find it difficult to manipulate expressions involving $\pi$. Remind them that they should remember that it is a number.

## Probing questions
- How much bigger is a circle with radius of 2 cm than a circle of radius 1 cm?

## Literacy focus
- Key terms: none
- Ask students to explain the meanings of 'semicircle' and 'quadrant', as these terms are again used in the exercise in this section.

## Part 1
- Draw this circle on the board. Ask individual students to give the formula to find its circumference.
- On the board, write $C = \pi d$.
- Ask individual students to give different values for $\pi$ and to explain when to use their value.
- Ensure that the responses include:
  $\pi = 3$ (for checking answers)
  $\pi = 3.141\,592\,654$ (for scientific calculators).
- So to find the circumference of the circle:
- $C = \pi d$
  $= \pi \times 20$
  $= 20\pi$ cm
- Explain that the answer can be left in this format unless an actual numerical value is required. We say that the answer is given in terms of $\pi$ and this is an acceptable way of giving the answer.

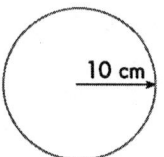

10 cm

- Point out that questions in the GCSE examinations often ask for answers to be given in this format, particularly on non-calculator papers.

## Part 2

- Carry on from Part 1 and show students how to find the area of a circle in terms of π.
- Using the same circle, write on the board:

$A = \pi r^2$
$= \pi \times 10^2$
$= 100\pi \text{ cm}^2$

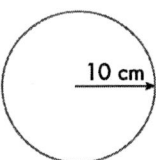

- Explain that this means that answers can be written down quickly; so it is often more convenient at the more advanced levels of mathematics and science.
- Ask students to copy Example 14 from the Student Book into their notes (as a summary of this work).
- Show **more able** students how to give answers in terms of π when finding the perimeters or the areas of shapes such as semicircles.
- Find the perimeter and area of this semicircle.
- The circumference of the whole circle is 6π.
- So the perimeter of the semicircle is 3π.
- Now add on the diameter to find the complete perimeter.
- The perimeter of the semicircle is therefore (3π + 6) cm.
- Make sure students remember to put in the units and the brackets.
- The area of the whole circle is π × $3^2$ = 9π.
- The area of the semicircle is therefore $\frac{9\pi}{2}$ cm$^2$.
- Point out to students that it is acceptable to leave the answer in this form and an answer of 4.5π cm$^2$ is equally as good.
- **Students can now do Exercise 11J from the Student Book.**

| G&M 1–4, 6 | Calculator n/a | CM | MR 7, 9 | PS 8 | EV 5 |
|---|---|---|---|---|---|

## Part 3

- Ask individual students to give the circumference and area in terms of π for different circles:
  - a circle with radius 12 cm (24π cm and 144π cm$^2$)
  - a circle with diameter 14 m (14π m and 49π m$^2$).

# Chapter 12 Geometry and measures: Transformations

## Overview

| | |
|---|---|
| **12.1** Rotational symmetry | **12.5** Enlargements |
| **12.2** Translation | **12.6** Using more than one transformation |
| **12.3** Reflections | **12.7** Vectors |
| **12.4** Rotations | |

### Prior learning

Know how to find the lines of symmetry of a 2D shape.
Know how to draw lines with the equations $x = \pm a$, $y = \pm b$, $y = x$ and $y = -x$.
Know how to measure lines and angles.

### Learning objectives

**Ensure that students can: work out the order of rotational symmetry for a 2D shape; translate, reflect, rotate and enlarge 2D shapes; understand what is meant by a transformation; add and subtract vectors.**

In the examination, students will be expected to:
- work out the order of rotational symmetry for a 2D shape
- recognise shapes with rotational symmetry
- translate a 2D shape
- reflect a 2D shape in a mirror line
- rotate a 2D shape about a point
- enlarge a 2D shape by a scale factor
- use more than one transformation
- represent vectors
- add and subtract vectors.

### Extension

Students could explore combinations of transformations and problem solving.

### Curriculum references

| Section | GCSE specification |
|---|---|
| 12.1 | G1 |
| 12.2 | G7, G24 |
| 12.3 | G7 |
| 12.4 | G7 |

| Section | GCSE specification |
|---|---|
| 12.5 | G7 |
| 12.6 | G7, G8 |
| 12.7 | G24, G25 |
| | |

## Route mapping

| Exercise | Accessible | Intermediate | Challenging | AO1 | AO2 MR CM | AO3 PS EV | Key questions |
|----------|-----------|--------------|-------------|-----|-----------|-----------|---------------|
| 12A | 1–7 | | | 1, 2 | 5 | 3, 4, 6, 7 | 1, 2, 6 |
| 12B | | 1–11 | | 1–5 | 7, 8, 11 | 6, 9, 10 | 3, 4 |
| 12C | 1–4 | 5–15 | | 1–4, 10–12 | 5–7, 9, 15 | 8, 13, 14 | 2, 4 |
| 12D | | 1–13 | | 1–3, 5a, 7, 8, 11, 12 | 4, 9, 13 | 5b, 6, 10 | 2, 4 |
| 12E | | 1–5 | 6, 7 | 1–4 | 5, 6 | 7 | 1, 2, 6 |
| 12F | | 1–8 | 9–11 | 1, 4, 7 | 2, 3, 5, 6, 8, 10 | 9, 11 | 3, 5 |
| 12G | | 1–6 | | 1–6 | | | 1, 4 |
| 12H | | | 1–10 | 1, 2, 5, 7 | 3, 4, 6, 8, 9 | 10 | 1, 2, 5 |

*Key questions are those that demonstrate mastery of the concept, or which require a step-up in understanding or application. Key questions could be used to identify the questions that students must tackle, to support differentiation, or to identify the questions that should be teacher-marked rather than student-marked.*

## About this chapter

**Making connections**: This chapter introduces the different types of transformations, their properties and relationship with symmetry.

**Relevance**: The emphasis is on looking at each transformation and applying them in theory as well as contextually. There are applications in design, architecture and manufacturing.

**Working mathematically**: There are transformations all around us in designs, from furniture to clothes to wallpaper, many using symmetry and transformations. Students will think about how they can use transformations to create new and interesting designs.

**Assessment**: In each section of this chapter, ensure that students have a good grasp of the key questions in each exercise before moving on. (Refer to the 'Route mapping' table.) Encourage students to read and think about the 'Ready to progress?' statements on page 311 of the Student Book. Check students' understanding at the end of the chapter, formatively, using peer assessment. Students could do a mini test in the form of the 'Review questions' on pages 311–313 of the Student Book. Follow up the test with an individual target-getting session, based on any areas for development that a student may have.

### Worked exemplars from the Student Book (page 309) – suggestions for use

- Present students with the same question but different numbers. They should use the exemplar to mirror the working, in full or just refer to the notes.
- Copy and cut the exemplars into cards. Students should match the working with the notes.
- Alternatively, copy and cut the working into cards but split the label/description from the working.

**Answers to the Student Book questions are available on the CD-ROM provided.**

### Learning objectives

- Work out the order of rotational symmetry for a 2D shape
- Recognise shapes with rotational symmetry

### Resources and homework

- Student Book 12.1: pages 285–286
- Practice Book 12.1

### Making mathematical connections

- Line symmetry
- Knowledge of plane figures

### Making cross-curricular connections

- **Technology** – designing
- **Relevance** – designing patterns

## Prior learning

- **Students need to know the names of the commonly used 2D shapes.**

## Working mathematically

- Draw a few regular shapes on the board or refer to posters on the wall and discuss the symmetries of these shapes.

## Common misconceptions and remediation

- **Not using tracing paper usually leads to inaccurate answers on the more complicated shapes. Students often say a shape has order 0 instead of order 1 for 'no' rotational symmetry. Students often confuse line symmetry and rotational symmetry.**
- **Less able students should always have access to mirrors and tracing paper. A line of symmetry can also be referred to as a mirror line, so remember to use a mirror for lines of symmetry. Remind students that tracing paper is allowed in examinations and encourage its use during lessons.**

## Probing questions

- Why can one not have a shape with rotational order of zero?
- Can you think of a shape with line symmetry but no rotational symmetry?

## Literacy focus

- Key terms: order of rotational symmetry, rotational symmetry
- Students need to become familiar with the difference between line and rotational symmetry.

## Part 1

- Draw a square with a dot in the top right-hand corner:
- In your head, turn it once clockwise and draw it:
- Do it again: , and again: , and again:
- How many different squares are there? (4)
- Do the same with a rectangle (2), an equilateral triangle (3) and a hexagon (6).
- What about a circle? (infinity) Or a right-angled triangle? (0)

# Part 2

- After doing Part 1, discuss with students how a square can be turned four different ways to fit exactly on top of itself.
- Explain that this is called rotational symmetry. A square can be fitted exactly over itself in four ways, so we say that a square has rotational symmetry of order 4.
- Use the board, or tracing paper, to demonstrate this to the class. Work through Example 1 in the Student Book with the class. Go through it step by step to ensure that students recognise that the method works for any shape with rotational symmetry.
- Ask the class to tell you the order of rotational symmetry for a rectangle and for a parallelogram. Again, demonstrate how to use tracing paper or the board to check.
- Ask students to copy the following diagrams, with the notes, into their books. Give **less able** students copies of the shapes.

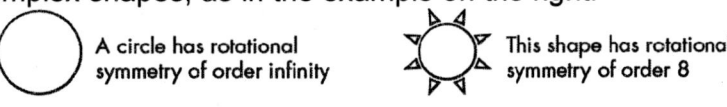

- Encourage students, particularly those who are **less able**, to use tracing paper to check the order of rotational symmetry for shapes.
- Now follow through the same procedure for an equilateral triangle and an isosceles triangle.
- An equilateral triangle has rotational symmetry of order 3.
- Explain that the isosceles triangle has no rotational symmetry. Since it fits exactly once on top of itself only once, we say that it has rotational symmetry of order 1.

    An equilateral triangle has rotational symmetry of order 3    An isosceles triangle has rotational symmetry of order 1

- **More able** students could discuss the number of lines of symmetry that a circle has, and then consider more complex shapes, as in the example on the right:

    A circle has rotational symmetry of order infinity    This shape has rotational symmetry of order 8

- **Students can now do Exercise 12A from the Student Book.**

| G&M 1, 2 | Calculator n/a | CM n/a | MR 5 | PS 3, 4 | EV 6, 7 |
|---|---|---|---|---|---|

# Part 3

- Ask students to name any capital letters with line symmetry.
- List them on the board. (A, B, C, D, E, H, I, M, O, Q, T, U, V, W, X, Y)
- Ask students to name any letters with rotational symmetry. (H, I, N, O, S, X, Z)
- Ask the class what is special about the words: BED? (line symmetry); NOON? (rotational symmetry). Can they think of any others?

# Section 12.2 Translation

## Learning objectives

- Translate a 2D shape.

## Resources and homework

- Student Book 12.2: pages 286–290
- Practice Book 12.2

## Making mathematical connections

- Coordinate geometry

## Making cross-curricular connections

- **Geography** – working out movement in travel
- **Relevance** – describing the travel movements of planes or boats

## Prior learning

- Students need to understand and be able to use coordinates in the first quadrant.

## Working mathematically

- How can you describe the movement from one place to another?

## Common misconceptions and remediation

- Students may use coordinate notation instead of vector notation, that is, $(x, y)$ instead of $\begin{pmatrix} x \\ y \end{pmatrix}$

- Students may use $\begin{pmatrix} x \\ y \end{pmatrix}$ but turn the vector into a fraction.

- The most common mistake is that students use the vector given as a coordinate pair and draw the shape from that point rather than using the vector to translate the shape.
- Pointing out these errors and repeatedly stressing the difference between coordinate notation and vector notation should help students to make fewer errors.

## Probing questions

- What is the difference between the translation of $\begin{pmatrix} 2 \\ 1 \end{pmatrix}$ and $\begin{pmatrix} 1 \\ 2 \end{pmatrix}$?

## Literacy focus

- Key terms: image, object, transformation, translation, vector
- Discuss the meaning of each key term and ask students to write them in their books.

## Part 1

- On the board, draw a set of coordinate axes, both labelled from 0 to 6.
- Plot a point and ask students for a set of coordinates, e.g. (3, 2).
- Plot another point and ask students for the coordinate, e.g. (5, 3).
- Ask students how to get from the first point to the second. They will probably say 2 across, 1 up. Suggest that they could simply express this as (2, 1).
- Now give a move of, e.g. (1, 3), from the first point and ask students where it moves to.
- Repeat with other moves, including some negative moves.
- Discuss the advantages (easy to understand) and disadvantages (students may confuse them with coordinates) of this notation.

## Part 2

- Refer students to Example 2 in the Student Book, and if possible, display it on the board.
- Ask students how to describe the transformation from triangle A to each of the others.
- Introduce the vector notation for a translation. Explain it clearly, to avoid confusion with coordinates.
- Emphasise that the top number represents a horizontal movement and the bottom number represents a vertical movement.
- Spend some time, particularly with **less able** students, ensuring that they understand the difference between vector and coordinate notation. Using the examples in Part 1 and Example 1, ask students for the vector notation.
- Now use Example 2 to introduce the idea of moving to the left and/or moving down.
- Explain that it is necessary to use negative numbers to differentiate these movements left or down from movements to the right or up.
- **Students can now do Exercise 12B from the Student Book.**

| G&M 1–5 | Calculator n/a | CM 7, 11 | MR 8 | PS 6, 9, 10 | EV n/a |
|---|---|---|---|---|---|

## Part 3

- Draw a 5 × 5 grid and draw a triangle ABC in the bottom left-hand corner.
- Draw a congruent triangle A'B'C' that has been translated 2 squares to the right and 3 up and ask for the vector describing the move of point A to A'. This should be $\begin{pmatrix} 2 \\ 3 \end{pmatrix}$.
- Then ask the same question about points B to B' and C to C'. In each case you should be given the answer $\begin{pmatrix} 2 \\ 3 \end{pmatrix}$.
- Discuss the fact that every point on the triangle moves in exactly the same way – by the vector $\begin{pmatrix} 2 \\ 3 \end{pmatrix}$.

# Section 12.3 Reflections

### Learning objectives

- Reflect a 2D shape in a mirror line

### Resources and homework

- Student Book 12.3: pages 290–294
- Practice Book 12.3

### Making mathematical connections

- Line symmetry
- Coordinate geometry

### Making cross-curricular connections

- **Technology** – designing
- **Relevance** – designing home furnishings, e.g. wallpaper or curtains

## Prior learning

- Students should be able to find the lines of symmetry of a 2D shape. Recap on students' knowledge as required.
- Students should also be able to draw the lines $y = x$ and $y = -x$, as well as lines such as $y = 3$ and $x = -2$.

## Working mathematically

- Students will represent an image as seen in a mirror.
- Students will think about: 'How far into the mirror is any reflection?'

## Common misconceptions and remediation

- Students often draw the image a different distance from the mirror line than the object is.

- They also draw 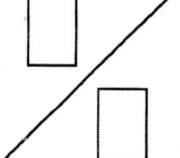 instead of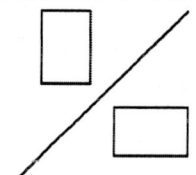

- Encourage students to check their reflections by folding along the mirror line.

## Probing questions

- Every shape will have a reflection in a mirror line, but how do we find out where the image of any point is?

## Literacy focus

- Key terms: mirror line, reflection
- Ask students to write the meanings of the key terms in their books. Ask them to do the same for 'image' from the previous lesson.

## Part 1

- On the board, draw a set of coordinate axes, both labelled from −5 to +5.
- Draw some horizontal and vertical lines and ask students for their equations.
- Make sure they understand that $x = a$ lines are vertical and $y = b$ lines are horizontal.
- Finish with $y = x$ and $y = -x$.

## Part 2

- Ask the class: Where do you see yourself in a mirror?
- If necessary, lead students to respond: Straight ahead.
- Use an actual mirror with **less able** students. Alternatively, ask them to imagine that the door is the mirror, then stand a student on one side and ask what they would see.
- Once students have understood that the image is straight ahead of the object, ask: How far into the mirror do you see yourself? (The same distance into the mirror as you are away from it.) Explain that as they move towards the mirror so does their image and as they walk away so does their image. Again, for **less able** students, an actual mirror would help to demonstrate this point.
- Look at Example 3 from the Student Book with the class. Talk through how the shape ABC is reflected in both axes. Explain that the method is to find the image of each vertex, and then join them. Label the image carefully so that it is clearly a reflection and not a translation.
- **Less able** students will need help when using reflections in the diagonal lines.
- Emphasise that corresponding points in the images and objects are always on a line at 90° to the mirror line and are the same distance from the mirror line.
- Encourage **more able** students to check their reflections by folding along the mirror line and seeing if the image fits exactly on the object. It may be easier if they work on separate sheets of paper until they have mastered the topic.
- **Students can now do Exercise 12C from the Student Book.**
  G&M 1–4, 10–12   Calculator all   CM 5–7, 15   MR 9        PS 8        EV 13, 14

## Part 3

- Ask students to copy this diagram on squared paper and to reflect the shape in each of the three mirror lines.

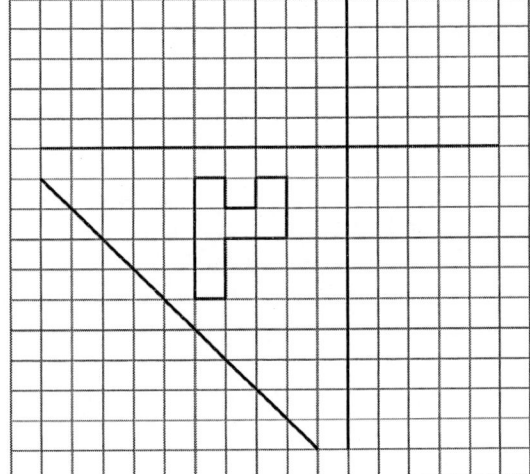

### Learning objectives

- Rotate a 2D shape about a point

### Resources and homework

- Student Book 12.4: pages 295–298
- Practice Book 12.4

### Making mathematical connections

- Angles around a point
- Coordinate geometry

### Making cross-curricular connections

- **Technology** – designing
- **Relevance** – designing for home and industry

## Prior learning

- Students should be able to find the order of rotational symmetry of a 2D shape. Recap students' knowledge as required.
- They should understand the terms 'clockwise' and 'anticlockwise'.

## Working mathematically

- Draw a solid flag on a flagpole on the board and ask pupils to discuss the route taken by each point as it falls to the ground.

## Common misconceptions and remediation

- Common mistakes are ignoring the centre of rotation if it is not situated on the shape, not using tracing paper and turning in the wrong direction. Pointing out these errors regularly to students should help them to avoid making them.

## Probing questions

- How can you find out where a point moves to as it rotates around the origin through 90° clockwise or anticlockwise?
- How can we use tracing paper to assist us to find where points move to under rotations?

## Literacy focus

- Key terms: angle of rotation, centre of rotation, rotation
- Ask students to explain the meanings of these words. Make sure that they are also familiar with the words 'clockwise' and 'anticlockwise'.

## Part 1

- Ask students to draw a T-shape.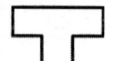

- Then ask them to draw another T-shape to add to the first to make a shape with rotational symmetry of order 2.
- Draw these three possibilities on the board.
- Ask: How many have a shape like one of these?
- Ask students what the difference is between the diagrams.
- Establish the concept of the centre of rotation. Mark the centre on each diagram.

## Part 2

- The use of tracing paper at the start of this topic is strongly recommended for all but the **most able** students.
- Ask students to draw a triangle, base 1 cm and height 2 cm, on squared paper with the vertices on the grid lines. They should then mark a centre of rotation as a point close to the triangle where gridlines cross. Ask them to trace the triangle and the centre of rotation. Then, keeping the centre of rotation aligned firmly with the sharp point of a pencil, they should rotate the tracing paper clockwise 90°.
- Explain to **less able** students that they can tell when they have rotated it through 90°, because a horizontal side of the original triangle will now be vertical.
- Once the tracing paper is in the new position students can mark the new positions of the vertices of the triangle on their paper by pressing the pencil firmly on each vertex on the tracing paper. They can then remove the tracing paper and draw the rotated shape.
- Encourage students to do this a few times until they are confident about rotating shapes. Once **more able** students have completed a few rotations using this method they should not need the tracing paper. However, tracing paper is allowed in examinations, so if they prefer they can continue using it.
- Work through Example 4 with the class and ask students to use their tracing paper to verify that the shape is rotated about the given centre of rotation.
- Mention to students that at this level they will only be asked to rotate a shape clockwise or anticlockwise through 90° or 180°. Establish that all students, especially the **less able**, know the difference between clockwise and anticlockwise.
- **Students can now do Exercise 12D from the Student Book.**

| G&M 1–3, 5a, 7, 8, 11, 12 | Calculator all | CM 9, 13 | MR 4 | PS 5b, 6 | EV 10 |
|---|---|---|---|---|---|

## Part 3

- Draw this diagram on the board:  | A | B |
- Ask students to describe all the transformations that take square A to square B. These could be a translation, a reflection or three different rotations.

# Section 12.5 Enlargements

## Learning objectives
- Enlarge a 2D shape by a scale factor

## Resources and homework
- Student Book 12.5: pages 299–301
- Practice Book 12.5

## Making mathematical connections
- Coordinate geometry
- Ratio
  Fractions

## Making cross-curricular connections
- **Geography** – drawing scale maps
- **Relevance** – working with scale drawings and models

## Prior learning
- Students need to know where the origin is on a set of axes.

## Working mathematically
- Draw a triangle on the board and ask students how you could draw it so that the sides are twice as big.
- Discuss the concept of a centre of enlargement, first in the middle of a shape and then move it around the inside, then outside, looking at the effect that each change has – and what does not change.

## Common misconceptions and remediation
- Students may not use the centre of enlargement that is given. They may also draw inaccurate construction lines from the centre of enlargement to the shape, and between shapes, or not draw them all. Working through several examples with students should help to reduce these errors.

## Probing questions
- What is the difference between the ray method of enlarging and using a coordinate grid?
- What differences does a different centre of enlargement make to an image?

## Literacy focus
- Key terms: centre of enlargement, enlargement
- Ask students to write the definitions of the key terms in their books. Also make sure that they know the term 'scale factor'.

## Part 1
- Draw a square of side length 1 cm, then another square of side length 2 cm, a few centimetres to the right of the first square.
  Draw the lines as shown; they should all meet at one point.
- Ask: What are the perimeters? (4 cm and 8 cm) Explain that the side lengths are doubled, so the perimeter of the second square is double that of the first square.
- Ask: What is the area of the first square?' (1 cm$^2$) The second? (4 cm$^2$)
  The side lengths are doubled, but the area is four times as big – why?
- Repeat with a square of side length 1 cm and a square of side length 3 cm.

## Part 2

- Explain that the point where all the lines meet is called the centre of enlargement; they will often need to enlarge a shape from a centre of enlargement. There are two methods of constructing an enlargement: one uses a square grid; the other is drawn on plain paper.
- Draw the enlargement on the board, as shown in the Student Book, to demonstrate how to enlarge triangle ABC from the given centre of enlargement. Find the image of each vertex by finding the vector from the centre to each vertex and multiplying this by 3, to find the vector of movement to the image.
- For **less able** students, rather than referring to vectors, use the terminology of, e.g. two along and one up; multiplied by 3 is six along and three up, for finding the new point C.
- Ask students to draw a triangle ABC (not too big) in the middle of their squared paper with vertices on grid lines, and to label a centre of enlargement at the left of the triangle, choosing a point of intersection of grid lines. Ask them to enlarge this triangle, scale factor 2, from that centre by the method described.
- Ask students to choose a centre of enlargement above the triangle and to repeat the process to produce a different enlarged triangle. **More able** students may extend this to include centres of enlargement to the right and underneath. The diagrams may overlap, making it hard to see the different triangles, so **less able** students may omit this.
- Discuss the images that students produce, and make sure they recognise that the diagrams will be congruent to each other.

### Ray method
- Use the diagram in the Student Book to describe the ray method, drawing lines from the centre to each vertex and beyond; then measuring three times the distance from the centre to find images of each vertex. The new vertices are then joined to give the enlarged shape.
- Now, on plain paper, ask students to draw a triangle (not too big) in the middle. Ask them to label a centre of enlargement close to the left of the shape and to find the enlargement, scale factor 2, from this centre. They should draw the rays and then measure double the distance from each vertex to its image, then finally join the new vertices. Again, repeat from a point above the triangle and discuss the congruent shapes.
- Illustrate two more enlargements, both on grids, but one should have the centre of enlargement at the origin and the other should have it at another point.

### Counting squares method
- Use the diagram in the Student Book to describe the counting squares method. Work through the text carefully so that all students understand the method of enlarging a shape.

### Fractional enlargement
- Again, use the diagram in the Student Book to describe fractional enlargement.
- Work through the text carefully so that all students understand this method.
- **Students can now do Exercise 12E from the Student Book.**

| G&M 1–4 | Calculator n/a | CM 6 | MR 5 | PS 7 | EV n/a |
|---------|----------------|------|------|------|--------|

## Part 3

- Write 'A' on a small square and 'B' on a larger square. Ask the following questions.
  - How do you get from square B to square A? What is the scale factor?
  - What is the centre of enlargement?
  - What is the ratio of the perimeters?
  - What is the ratio of the areas?

# Section 12.6 Using more than one transformation

## Learning objectives
- Use more than one transformation

## Resources and homework
- Student Book 12.6: pages 302–304
- Practice Book 12.6

## Making mathematical connections
- Translations
- Reflections
- Rotations
- Enlargements
  Coordinate geometry

## Making cross-curricular connections
- **Technology** – designing
- **Relevance** – designing fabrics and home furnishings and linen

## Prior learning
- Students need to be familiar with translations, reflections, rotations and enlargements, as learnt in the previous sections.

## Working mathematically
- Students will consider these questions: Will a reflection followed by a rotation be the same as a rotation followed by a reflection? Will this always be the case? How can we find out?

## Common misconceptions and remediation
- Students often miss out some of the information required to explain rotations and enlargements fully. Throughout the lesson, reinforce the information in the table here.
- Display a summary of all the transformations covered. Always have tracing paper available.

| Transformation | Information needed |
| --- | --- |
| Translation | Column vector |
| Reflection | Equation of mirror line |
| Rotation | Angle, direction, centre of rotation |
| Enlargement | Scale factor, centre of enlargement |

## Probing questions
- What will be the outcome of a reflection followed by the same reflection?
- What will be the outcome of a 90° rotation around a point followed by a 90° rotation around the same point?
- What transformations can bring a transformed image back to its starting point?

## Literacy focus
- Key terms: none
- Students should be familiar with all the words used in the previous lessons on transformations, so this is an opportunity to consolidate all those words.

## Part 1
- Display a coordinate grid, with the x- and y-axis labelled suitably. Add two squares: A with vertices at (–2, 0), (–2, 2), (2, 2) and (0, 2); B with vertices (0, 0), (0, 2), (2, 2) and (2, 0).
- Ask students if B is a transformation of A and, if so, if they can describe the transformation.
- Ask: 'Is it possible to describe it as a translation?' Similarly, can it be described as a reflection, a rotation or an enlargement?'

- Expect answers to include: translation by the vector $\begin{pmatrix} 2 \\ 0 \end{pmatrix}$; reflection in the line $x = 0$ or the $y$-axis; rotation of 90° clockwise about the origin, or 90° anticlockwise about (0, 2); no enlargement, as it has not been enlarged.

## Part 2

- Say that this section covers all the transformations they have met and combinations of them.
- Consider enlargements first, as they are the only transformations that change the size of the object and hence, are easily identified.
- Having ruled out enlargement, a translation is the next easiest to spot.
- Sometimes a shape may be transformed more than once, by a combination of transformations. In GCSE examinations only two combined transformations will be expected in a question. Work through two examples.
- **Example 1**: Display this diagram. Give **less able** students a copy or let them draw it themselves on squared paper.
- Ask students to describe fully the single transformation that maps triangle A onto triangle B: a rotation of 90° clockwise about the origin or (0, 0). Now ask students to describe fully the single transformation that maps triangle B onto triangle C: a reflection in the line $x = 0$ or the $y$-axis
- Explain that the combined transformation that maps triangle A onto triangle C is: a rotation of 90° clockwise about the origin, followed by a reflection in the line $x = 0$. Now ask students to give the single transformation that maps triangle C onto triangle A. Make sure they give a full description of the reflection: a reflection in the line $y = -x$.
- **Example 2**: Display this diagram. Give **less able** students a copy or let them draw it themselves on squared paper.
- Ask students to describe fully the single transformation that maps triangle A onto triangle B: a translation by the vector 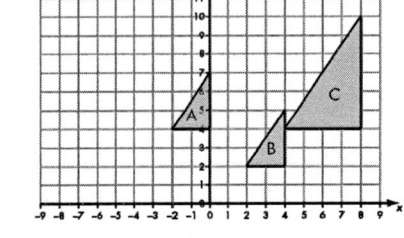 $\begin{pmatrix} 4 \\ -2 \end{pmatrix}$. Now ask students to describe fully the single transformation that maps triangle B onto triangle C: an enlargement by scale factor 2 from the origin or (0, 0).
- Explain that the combined transformation that maps triangle A onto triangle C is a translation by the vector $\begin{pmatrix} 4 \\ -2 \end{pmatrix}$ followed by an enlargement of scale factor 2 from the origin.
- Now ask students to give the single transformation that maps triangle C onto triangle A.
- Make sure they give a full description of the enlargement: an enlargement of scale factor $\frac{1}{2}$ from centre of enlargement (–8, 4)
- **Students can now do Exercise 12F from the Student Book.**

| G&M 1, 4, 7 | Calculator n/a | CM 3, 5, 6, 8, 10 | MR 2 | PS 9 | EV 11 |
|---|---|---|---|---|---|

## Part 3

- Ask pairs to design a poster to summarise all the transformations they have covered.
- Show this thought process diagram to help students and ask them to complete it.

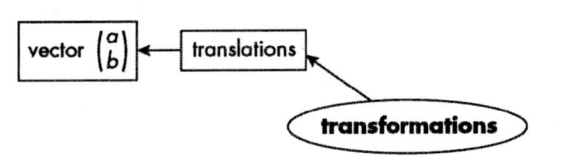

# Section 12.7 Vectors

## Learning objectives

- Represent vectors
- Add and subtract vectors

## Resources and homework

- Student Book 12.7: pages 304–308
- Practice Book 12.7

## Making mathematical connections

- Translations
- Coordinate geometry
- Algebra

## Making cross-curricular connections

- **Physics** – calculating forces
- **Relevance** – working with motion and a combination of forces, e.g. wind and engine power

## Prior learning

- Students should be able to use column vectors to describe translations.

## Working mathematically

- Students will combine two translations in a row, and then think about what combined transformation that would produce. They will consider whether a combination of two translations is always another translation.

## Common misconceptions and remediation

- Students often use wrong notation for vectors.
- Ensure that they are not using coordinates instead of column vectors.
- Encourage students to write a or $\underline{a}$ for a vector, explaining that $a$ is an algebraic variable that represents a number whereas a or $\underline{a}$ represents a vector representing movement.
- Similarly, $\overrightarrow{AB}$ is used to represent the movement from point A to point B.

## Probing questions

- What vector will reverse a translation?
- How does this help us to understand the vector **a** – **b**?

## Literacy focus

- Key terms: direction, magnitude, resultant vector, scalar
- It is important for students to understand the difference between 'scalar' and 'vector' – one has direction, the other does not.

## Part 1

- Draw these points on a square grid. Ask students to give the column vectors for:
  $\overrightarrow{AB}$, $\overrightarrow{BA}$, $\overrightarrow{CE}$, $\overrightarrow{EC}$, and so on.
  Using the same grid, explain that if one unit across = **a** and one unit up = **b**, we could express the above column vectors in terms of **a** and **b**, e.g.

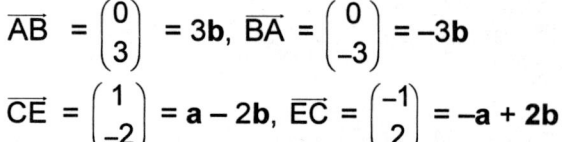 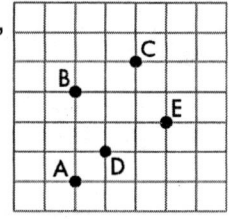

$$\overrightarrow{AB} = \begin{pmatrix} 0 \\ 3 \end{pmatrix} = 3\mathbf{b}, \quad \overrightarrow{BA} = \begin{pmatrix} 0 \\ -3 \end{pmatrix} = -3\mathbf{b}$$

$$\overrightarrow{CE} = \begin{pmatrix} 1 \\ -2 \end{pmatrix} = \mathbf{a} - 2\mathbf{b}, \quad \overrightarrow{EC} = \begin{pmatrix} -1 \\ 2 \end{pmatrix} = -\mathbf{a} + 2\mathbf{b}$$

## Part 2

- Make sure students are familiar with the representation and the notation used for vectors. They should be clear that a vector has both magnitude (length or distance) and direction.

Refer to the vector in the Student Book, which represents a translation that can be considered a journey or movement from A to B.

- On a diagram, the direction of the vector is shown by an arrow, which is usually in the middle of a line. This vector can be represented by **a** or <u>a</u> or $\overrightarrow{AB}$. The bold **a** is the printed notation in books and the underlined a, <u>a</u>, is the written notation in Student workbooks or on a whiteboard.
- The magnitude (size) of the vector is represented by the length of the line from A to B.
- Refer the class to Example 5 in the Student Book and explain that a vector can be multiplied by a number (a scalar quantity). For example, vector **2a** is twice as long as vector **a**, and acts in the same direction.
- **Students can now do Exercise 12G from the Student Book.**

| G&M 1–6 | Calculator n/a | CM n/a | MR n/a | PS n/a | EV n/a |
|---|---|---|---|---|---|

**Adding and subtracting of vectors**

- A vector can also be negative, e.g. vector –**c** has the same length (magnitude) as vector **c**, but acts in the opposite direction.

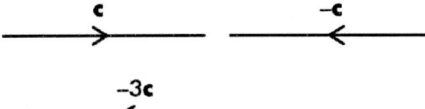

- The vector –**3c** can be drawn like this.

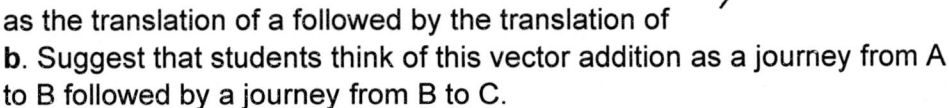

- Show the class how to add and subtract two vectors. For example, for two vectors **a** and **b**, **a** + **b** is defined as the translation of a followed by the translation of b. Suggest that students think of this vector addition as a journey from A to B followed by a journey from B to C.
  $\overrightarrow{AB} + \overrightarrow{BC} = \overrightarrow{AC}$.

  Similarly, for two vectors **a** and **b**, **a** – **b** is defined as the translation of a followed by the translation of –**b**.

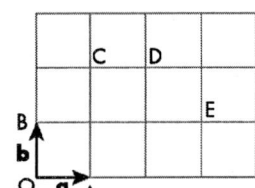

- Draw this grid on the board:
  OA = **a** and OB = **b**
  Show students how to find the vectors
  OC, BF,
  CE and DE, ensuring they use the correct notation.
  $\overrightarrow{OC}$ = **a** + 2**b**, $\overrightarrow{BF}$ = 4**a** + 2**b**, $\overrightarrow{CE}$ = 2**a** – **b**, $\overrightarrow{DE}$ = **a** - **b**

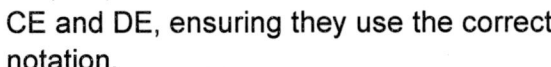
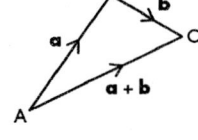
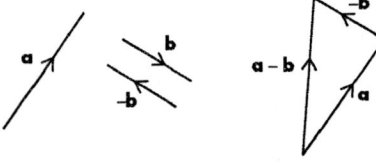

- **Students can now do Exercise 12H from the Student Book.**

| G&M 1, 2, 5, 7 | Calculator n/a | CM 6, 8, 9 | MR 3, 4 | PS 10 | EV n/a |
|---|---|---|---|---|---|

# Part 3

- On a grid on the whiteboard, draw a vector $\overrightarrow{AB}$. Ask someone to give you the column vector for $\overrightarrow{AB}$.
- Now add point C, drawing the vectors $\overrightarrow{AC}$ and $\overrightarrow{CB}$.
  Ask what $\overrightarrow{AC} + \overrightarrow{BC}$ equals, and why.
  Returning to the original vector diagram $\overrightarrow{AB}$, add new points $\overline{C}$, $\overline{D}$, $\overline{E}$, $\overline{F}$ and $\overline{G}$.
- Again, ask what is the sum of all the individual vectors: AC, CD, DE, EF, FG and GB.

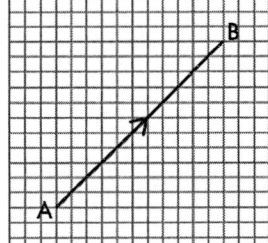
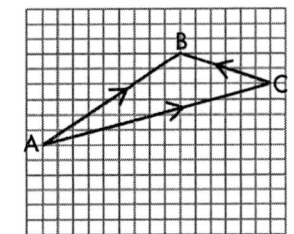
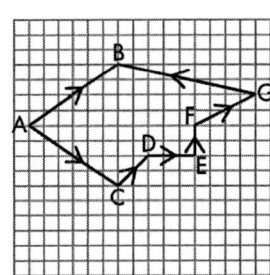

# Chapter 13 Probability: Probability and events

### Overview

| | |
|---|---|
| **13.1** Calculating probabilities | **13.4** Experimental probability |
| **13.2** Probability that an outcome will not happen | **13.5** Expectation |
| **13.3** Mutually exclusive and exhaustive outcomes | **13.6** Choices and outcomes |

---

**Prior learning**

Know how to cancel, add and subtract fractions.
Know that an event or trial has outcomes.
Know that outcomes cannot always be predicted and that the laws of chance apply to everyday events.
Know the meaning of the term 'bias'.

---

**Learning objectives**

**Ensure that students can: use the probability scale and the language of probability; work out the probability of an outcome of an event happening; work out the probability of an outcome of an event not happening; recognise mutually exclusive and exhaustive outcomes; work out experimental probabilities and relative frequencies from experiments; predict the likely number of successful outcomes, given the number of trials and the probability of any one outcome; use systematic strategies to list and count outcomes.**

In the examination, students will be expected to:
*   use the probability scale and the language of probability
*   calculate the probability of an outcome of an event
*   calculate the probability of an outcome not happening when you know the probability of that outcome happening
*   recognise mutually exclusive and exhaustive outcomes
*   calculate experimental probabilities and relative frequencies from experiments
*   recognise different methods for estimating probabilities
*   predict the likely number of successful outcomes, given the number of trials and the probability of any one outcome
*   apply systematic listing and counting strategies to identify all outcomes for a variety of problems.

---

**Extension**

Introducing probability in tables with missing values as $x$. Students must then use their knowledge that probabilities add up to 1. Introduce sample space when working out the experimental probabilities of two events.

---

## Curriculum references

| Section | GCSE specification |
|---------|-------------------|
| 13.1 | P2, 3, 4 |
| 13.2 | P2, 4 |
| 13.3 | P2, 4 |
| 13.4 | P1, 2, 4, 5 |
| 13.5 | P3, 4 |
| 13.6 | P4 |

## Route mapping

| Exercise | Accessible | Intermediate | Challenging | AO1 | AO2 MR CM | AO3 PS EV | Key questions |
|----------|-----------|--------------|-------------|-----|-----------|-----------|---------------|
| 13A | 1–9 | 10 | | 1–6 | 9 | 7, 8, 10 | 2, 8, 11 |
| 13B | 1–11 | | | 1–6, 9–11 | 7, 8 | | 4, 8, 10, 11 |
| 13C | 1–6 | 7–10 | | 1–6 | 7, 9, 10 | 8 | 1, 8, 9 |
| 13D | 1 | 2–9 | | 1–3 | 4–6, 9 | 7, 8 | 1, 2, 3 |
| 13E | | 1–12 | | 1–7, 9 | 8, 11 | 10, 12 | 3, 8, 9, 12 |
| 13F | | 1–7 | 8–15 | 1–8, 10–13, 15 | 9, 14 | | 1, 6, 7, 14 |

*Key questions are those that demonstrate mastery of the concept, or which require a step-up in understanding or application. Key questions could be used to identify the questions that students must tackle, to support differentiation, or to identify the questions that should be teacher-marked rather than student-marked.*

## About this chapter

**Making connections**: Students will need to be able to add, subtract and multiply fractions, decimals and percentages. Being able to recognise equivalents will be an advantage.

**Relevance**: Probability will help students to develop a logical and ordered approach in their workings.

**Working mathematically**: Students will need to be able to add, subtract and multiply fractions, decimals and percentages. Being able to recognise equivalents will be an advantage.

**Assessment**: In each section of this chapter, ensure that students have a good grasp of the key questions in each exercise before moving on. (Refer to the 'Route mapping' table.) Encourage students to read and think about the 'Ready to progress?' statements on page 337 of the Student Book. Check students' understanding at the end of the chapter, formatively, using peer assessment. Students could do a mini test in the form of the 'Review questions' on pages 337–339 of the Student Book. Follow up the test with an individual target-getting session, based on any areas for development that a student may have.

### Worked exemplars from the Student Book (page 335) – suggestions for use
- Present students with the same question but different numbers. They should use the exemplar to mirror the working, in full or just refer to the notes.
- Copy and cut the exemplars into cards. Students should match the working with the notes.
- Alternatively, copy and cut the working into cards but split the label/description from the working.

**Answers to the Student Book questions are available on the CD-ROM provided.**

# Section 13.1 Calculating probabilities

## Learning objectives

- Use the probability scale and the language of probability
- Calculate the probability of an outcome of an event

## Resources and homework

- Student Book 13.1: pages 315–318
- Practice Book 13.1

## Making mathematical connections

- Adding, subtracting and multiplying fractions, decimals and percentages

## Making cross-curricular connections

- **Science** – experimental probability
- **Relevance** – working logically

## Prior learning

- Students must know how to express one number as a fraction of another, how to simplify fractions and how to add fractions with the same denominator.

## Working mathematically

- Students will need to understand that 'even chance' and 'half' are the same and can be used to represent the probability of flipping a coin or similar.
- Students will need to be familiar with a pack of cards. Ask them what the total outcomes are (52) and ask them to describe the probability of getting an ace (4/52).
- Encourage students to verbalise reasons for their answers.

## Common misconceptions and remediation

- Students often express a probability incorrectly by writing an answer as 1 out of 5 or 1 : 5 instead of $\frac{1}{5}$.
- Correct this as soon as you see students making this error so that they realise their mistake.

## Probing questions

- Using a pack of cards, ask: What is the probability of a red card? What is the probability of a Jack? What is the probability of a Jack of Hearts? Why are a Jack and a Jack of Hearts different?

## Literacy focus

- Key terms: equally likely, event, outcome, probability, probability fraction, probability scale, random, trial
- Ask students to devise seven events, each with a different probability of impossible, very unlikely, unlikely, all the way to certain. Working in pairs, ask them to organise their events in the order of the way they happened.

## Part 1

- Prepare a bag containing a number of different-coloured balls, or similar.
- Ask students to select a ball without looking in the bag, check the colour and put it back.
- Ask one student to collect the data as it is generated.
- At different stages, ask for suggestions about what is in the bag. Ensure that students always give reasons for their suggestions.

## Part 2

- Take the balls out of the bag and discuss the activity and the results, now that students can see the contents.
- Explain the ways in which a probability can be expressed. For example, if there were six blue balls and four red balls then the chance of getting a blue is 6 out of 10.
- Write this on the board as a fraction and ask where each number has come from. The top number (numerator) is the number of blue balls and the bottom number (denominator) is the total number of balls.
- For **more able** students introduce the idea of cancelling this fraction to $\frac{3}{5}$, so the chance of getting a blue ball is $\frac{3}{5}$. Ask: What is the chance of getting a red ball? ($\frac{4}{10}$ or $\frac{2}{5}$)
- Introduce the idea that there are only two possibilities: students are bound to pick either a blue ball or a red ball. Picking one of these two colours is a certainty.
- The probability of picking blue or red is 1. Write this clearly on the board:
  for **less able** students, $\frac{6}{10} + \frac{4}{10} = 1$; for **more able** students, $\frac{3}{5} + \frac{2}{5} = 1$
- In summary, the probability of picking one of all the possible alternatives is 1.
- Next, introduce a dice. Ask: 'What is the probability of rolling this dice and getting a 5?' ($\frac{1}{6}$)
- Discuss the various answers from the class. Ask whether this is a good chance or not a good chance, using the correct vocabulary.
- Discuss the chance of getting each number on the dice. They all have the same probability of $\frac{1}{6}$ and the total of all these probabilities is $\frac{6}{6}$ or 1.
- Display a pack of cards. Ask: 'What is the chance of cutting the pack and getting an ace?' ($\frac{4}{52}$ or $\frac{1}{13}$) Each time, write the correct fraction on the board.
- If students use phrases such as 'one in four', explain that probabilities are not expressed in this way. In Mathematics, probabilities are always written as either a fraction or a decimal. If students mention percentages, remind them that percentages are fractions out of 100.
- For **more able** students, introduce the shorthand notation P(blue), which means the probability of getting blue. Explain this notation to **less able** students when going through the examples and a few questions in Exercise 13A, but **more able** students should use it.
- Refer to Example 1, which looks at getting a head when throwing a coin. This is impossible and has a probability of 0. Getting a 6 when rolling a dice is $\frac{1}{6}$, as only one of the six sides is a 6. The probability of getting Maths homework is a likely event, but difficult to put a fractional value to.
- Refer to Examples 2 and 3, which use the formula for the probability of an event. Encourage students to substitute into this before trying to simplify their fractions.
- **Students can now do Exercise 13A from the Student Book.**

| P 1–6 | Calculator n/a | CM n/a | MR 9 | PS 8, 10 | EV 7 |

## Part 3

- Use a target board with whole numbers on it and ask for probabilities of different outcomes of picking a number at random, e.g. P(prime number), P(less than 10) or P(multiple of 4).
- The outcomes choices will depend on the target board so add some impossible outcome.

# Section 13.2 Probability that an outcome will not happen

## Learning objectives
- Calculate the probability of an outcome not happening when you know the probability of that outcome happening

## Resources and homework
- Student Book 13.2: pages 318–320
- Practice Book 13.2

## Making mathematical connections
- Adding, subtracting and multiplying fractions, decimals and percentages
- Writing equivalents
- Cancelling fractions

## Making cross-curricular connections
- **Science** – experimental probability
- **Relevance** – working logically

## Prior learning
- **Students must know how to find the probability of an event.**
- Students need to know that probabilities add up to a whole.

## Working mathematically
- If the probability of an event happening is $a$, the probability of it not happening must be $1 - a$.

## Common misconceptions and remediation
- Students often do not take sufficient care in identifying mutual exclusivity of events, e.g. the events 'picking a prime number' and 'picking an even number' are not mutually exclusive.
- Students often do not take enough care in identifying the exhaustiveness of events, e.g. the events 'scoring less than 2' and 'scoring more than 2' when rolling dice are not exhaustive.
- In both cases, encourage students to list the outcomes for each event and then check for exclusivity or exhaustiveness to help to avoid possible errors.

## Probing questions
- If the probability of it raining is $\frac{1}{5}$ and the probability of it snowing is 25%, what is the probability of it not raining or snowing?

## Literacy focus
- Key terms: none
- Encourage students to verbalise their answers. For example, if the probability of the event happening is $\frac{1}{3}$, then the probability of the event not happening must be $1 - \frac{1}{3} = \frac{2}{3}$.
-

## Part 1
- Practise complements to 1, e.g. ask students to subtract $1 - \frac{4}{5}$.
- Ask students if they can see an easy way to work out these problems.

## Part 2
- Show students a die and ask: 'If I roll this die, what numbers could I get?' As they answer, write the numbers 1 to 6 in a list on the board.

- Ask: 'What is the probability of getting a 1?' Write the answer $\frac{1}{6}$ on the board. (Remind **less able** students of the work in the previous section.) Then ask about getting a 2, then a 3 and so on, putting the fraction $\frac{1}{6}$ next to the number in each case.

- Now ask: What is the probability of rolling a 1 or a 2 or a 3 or a 4 or a 5 or a 6? For **less able** students use the wording: *rolling a number bigger than 0*. The answer is 1, as it is certain. Remind students that a probability of 1 means that an outcome is certain to happen.

- Ask students what they get if they add up all the probabilities of all these numbers, i.e. $\frac{1}{6} + \frac{1}{6} + \frac{1}{6} + \frac{1}{6} + \frac{1}{6} + \frac{1}{6}$ leading to the answer 1.

- Now ask: What is the probability that I do *not* roll a six? This may bring various answers, with **less able** students just guessing. Ask for explanations.

- Eventually, lead students to recognise that to find the probability of not getting a six is simply 1 minus the chance of getting a six, i.e. $1 - \frac{1}{6} = \frac{5}{6}$. **Less able** students may need to count that there are five other numbers to choose from, also giving $\frac{5}{6}$.

- Now ask about the chance of not rolling a 4 and expecting an answer of $\frac{5}{6}$ again. Continue this for all six numbers of the dice until students have understood this concept.

- Show a pack of cards. Ask: What is the chance of cutting this pack and *not* getting the ace of hearts? This will lead to a discussion; again encourage students to justify their answers.

- Lead the class to seeing that the probability of getting the ace of hearts is $\frac{1}{52}$, so the chance of not getting the ace of hearts is $1 - \frac{1}{52} = \frac{51}{52}$.

- This subtraction of fractions may cause problems for **less able** students, so give plenty of practice to those who need it.

- Go through Example 4 with students. Place emphasis on the cards that are in a pack and how to find the probability of getting an ace, followed by not getting an ace.

- Continue with some more general questions, e.g. The chance of snow this Christmas is 0.4. What is the chance of no snow this Christmas? (0.6)

- Explain to **more able** students that they need to be very careful with questions such as: If the probability of it raining today is 0.5, what is the probability of it being sunny?

- This can lead to a good discussion with many students assuming the answer is 0.5, but just because it does not rain, doesn't mean it will be sunny. The probability of an outcome is only equal to 1 – the probability of another outcome if the two outcomes cover all possibilities.

- This is a challenging concept for many students, so do not rush it.

- Allow discussion of students' answers as attempting to justify their incorrect thinking often helps them to understand their errors.

- Example 5 combines two probabilities. Show that being late is the same as 1 minus the probability of being on time or being early.

- **Students can now do Exercise 13B from the Student Book.**

| P 1–6, 9–11 | Calculator n/a | CM 8 | MR 7 | PS n/a | EV n/a |
|---|---|---|---|---|---|

## Part 3

- Use a target board with whole numbers on it. Ask a variety of 'not' probability questions, e.g. P(not a multiple of 3), P(not less than 8) and P(not more than 1 digit).

## Section 13.3 Mutually exclusive and exhaustive outcomes

### Learning objectives
- Recognise mutually exclusive and exhaustive outcomes

### Resources and homework
- Student Book 13.3: pages 321–323
- Practice Book 13.3

### Making mathematical connections
- Adding, subtracting and multiplying fractions, decimals and percentages

### Making cross-curricular connections
- **Science** – experimental probability
- **Relevance** – working logically

### Prior learning
- Students will need to know that the probability of an event is outcome divided by total number of outcomes.
- Students will need to know that if the probability of an event is *a*, then the probability of an event not happening is 1 – *a*.

### Working mathematically
- Students need to add probabilities together to find mutually exclusive outcomes.
- They must also subtract probabilities from 1 to find the probability of an event not happening.

### Common misconceptions and remediation
- Students often do not take enough care in identifying mutual exclusivity of events, e.g. the events 'picking a prime number' and 'picking an even number' are not mutually exclusive.
- Students also do not take sufficient care in identifying the exhaustiveness of events. For example, the events 'scoring less than 2' and 'scoring more than 2' when rolling a dice are not exhaustive.
- In both cases, encourage students to list the outcomes for each event and then check for exclusivity or exhaustiveness to help to avoid possible errors.

### Probing questions
- What is meant by mutually exclusive outcomes?
- Can you think of three examples?

### Literacy focus
- Key terms: exhaustive, mutually exclusive
- In pairs, discuss how to make a mutually exclusive probability game using two from a coin, dice or spinner.
- Encourage students to add the key terms with definitions to their mathematical dictionaries.

### Part 1
- In a packet of chocolate sweets of various colours, five are red, five are blue, ten are orange, two are brown and three are pink. Ask students to find the probability of each colour.
- So $P(\text{red}) = \dfrac{5}{25} = \dfrac{1}{5}$. Ask students what the probability of red and blue is. Show students how we add the probabilities together for mutually exclusive events.

## Part 2

- Example 6 in the Student Book describes a bag that contains 12 red balls, eight green balls, five blue balls and 15 black balls. A ball is drawn at random.
- To find the probability that the ball is red students will need to work out how many red balls there are and divide by the total number of balls.
- To find the probability of black balls is the same method as for the red balls.
- To find the probability of red or black students need to work out the individual probabilities (as in parts a and b of the example) and add them together.
- To find the probability of 'not green' students need to find the probability of it being green and take this away from 1 as in the previous section's work.
- In Example 7, Trevor throws an ordinary six-sided dice.
- To find the probability that he throws an even number students need to work out how many numbers are even on a dice and divide this by how many sides there are on a dice.
- Using an odd number, you can subtract the probability of an even number from 1.
- **Students can now do Exercise 13C from the Student Book.**

| P 1–6 | Calculator n/a | CM n/a | MR 7, 9, 10 | PS 8 | EV n/a |

## Part 3

- A five-sided spinner labelled 1, 2, 3, 4 and 5 is spun.
- Ask students how they can ensure that it is unbiased.
- Once students have established that all the segments must be the same size, ask them to write questions based around the spinner such as, 'find the probability of spinning a prime number'.
- Ask students for a question each; then discuss these with the class.

# Section 13.4 Experimental probability

## Learning objectives

- Calculate experimental probabilities and relative frequencies from experiments
- Recognise different methods for estimating probabilities

## Resources and homework

- Student Book 13.4: pages 323–328
- Practice Book 13.4

## Making mathematical connections

- Theoretical probability
- Adding, subtracting and multiplying fractions, decimals and percentages

## Making cross-curricular connections

- **Science** – making an experiment more accurate
- **Relevance** – logical thinking

## Prior learning

- Students should already know how to calculate a probability in simple cases using equally likely outcomes.
- Students must know how to express one number as a fraction of another.

## Working mathematically

- Students need to calculate relative frequencies from experiments.
- Students will set up and record data from probability experiments.

## Common misconceptions and remediation

- Students often have difficulty in identifying the relevant information from data presented in tabular form. Make it clear to them that they need to use 'number of correct results' and 'number of trials' in all cases but they need to be able to interpret the table correctly to find these values.
- In some tables the values will be cumulative frequencies of the required outcome and in others they will be the frequencies of all the results.
- Ask students a few questions on aspects of the information given in any of the tables in Section 9.2, to help them feel more confident about using them.

## Probing questions

- If you rolled a fair dice and flipped a fair coin, what would be the probability of rolling an even number and flipping a head?

## Literacy focus

- Key terms: experimental data, experimental probability, relative frequency, theoretical probability
- Ask students to explain why, if they rolled a dice 600 times, you would expect it to land on a six 100 times.

## Part 1

- Prepare a bag or box containing a number of different-coloured balls, or similar.
- Ask students to select a ball without looking in the bag, note its colour and put it back.
- Ask one student to collect the data as it is generated.
- At different stages, e.g. after four selections and again after 10, ask for suggestions about what is in the bag.
- Ensure that students give reasons for their suggestions.

## Part 2

- Ask: 'What is the probability of tossing a coin and getting a head?' ($\frac{1}{2}$ or 0.5) Most students will know the answer. Say that this is the theoretical probability, but ask: Does it actually work out in practice?

| Number of throws | Number of heads | Probability |
|---|---|---|
| 30 | 18 | $\frac{18}{30} = 0.6$ |

- Ask students to toss a coin for heads or tails. Ask how many students tossed a head and make a note of this on the board in a table like the one shown.
- Show students how to find the probability and explain that it will be necessary to change fractions to decimals for comparison as more coins are thrown. Remind **less able** students how to do this, dividing the numerator by the denominator and, if necessary, simply writing down the first four or five decimal places.
- Ask the class to toss their coins again, count again how many heads and complete the next entry in the table.

| Number of throws | Number of heads | Probability |
|---|---|---|
| 30 | 18 | $\frac{18}{30} = 0.6$ |
| 30 + 30 = 60 | 18 + 14 = 32 | $\frac{32}{60} = 0.5333$ |

- Continue to build up the table in this way. Lead students to notice that the probability gets closer and closer to 0.5. Ensure that **more able** students understand that using the decimal notation is nearly always the best way to compare fractions.
- Explain that this is *experimental probability*, also called *relative frequency*. Often this is the only way to find a probability, such as that of dropping a slice of bread on the floor and it ending up butter side down! Students should also realise that the more trials are made, the more accurate the results should be.
- Explain the use of historical data to find probabilities of events where experiments are impossible such as the probability of an asteroid hitting Earth, or a volcano erupting.
- Refer to Example 8 in the Student Book, which uses the speeds of 160 cars to demonstrate relative frequency. Again emphasise that probability is the outcome divided by the total number of outcomes.

### Finding probabilities
- Example 9 ensures that students have a secure understanding of methods for finding probabilities.
- Discuss with the class what is meant by 'equally likely outcomes', 'conduct a survey or collect data' and how to 'look at historical data'. This example asks students to decide which method would be best suited for finding probabilities of various scenarios.
- **Students can now do Exercise 13D from the Student Book.**

| P 1–3 | Calculator all | CM 6 | MR 4, 5, 9 | PS 7 | EV 8 |
|---|---|---|---|---|---|

## Part 3

- Ask students to pick a number from zero to nine, inclusive, and write it down.
- Ask how many zeros, ones, twos, and so on … they would expect to get. They should understand that, for a class of 30, for example, there should be about three of each.
- Now collate the results. Are they as expected?
- It is unlikely, as seven tends to be chosen more than any other number.
- Discuss why the actual results did not meet expected results, or why they did.

### Learning objectives

- Predict the likely number of successful outcomes, given the number of trials and the probability of any one outcome

### Resources and homework

- Student Book 13.4: pages 329–331
- Practice Book 13.4

### Making mathematical connections

- Adding, subtracting and multiplying fraction, decimals and percentages

### Making cross-curricular connections

- **Science** – accuracy of experiments
- **Relevance** – logical thinking

## Prior learning

- Students should already know how to calculate a probability in simple cases using equally likely outcomes.
- Students must know how to calculate a fraction of a quantity.

## Working mathematically

- Students will need to add, subtract and multiply fractions, decimals and percentages to calculate the expectation of an event.

## Common misconceptions and remediation

- Mistakes are likely to be one of two kinds:
  - working out the required probability incorrectly,
  - working out the fraction of the number of trials incorrectly.
- Regular revision of the methods needed should help to minimise these errors.

## Probing questions

- If the probability of rolling a square number on a dice is one-third, how many times would you expect a square number if you rolled the dice 60 times?

## Literacy focus

- Key term: expectation
- What is meant by 'expectation'? If the probability of a head on a fair coin is 0.5, why would you expect 10 heads if the coin is flipped 20 times?

## Part 1

- Recap, or ask a student to explain, how to find a fraction of a quantity.
- Display the number 240 and ask students to choose a fraction of this number to find. It may be more appropriate to limit the choice of fractions to be used, e.g. halves, thirds, quarters, fifths, sixths, eighths, tenths, twelfths.

## Part 2

- Ask: If you roll a dice 600 times, how many times would you expect to have rolled the number 5? Discuss this with students and lead them to see that 600 breaks down into 100 for each number, so expect 100 fives.
- Ask: If you cut a pack of cards 100 times, how many times would you expect to have turned up the ace of diamonds? This is not so easy as there are 52 cards in a pack and not 50. Lead the class to see that the expected value would be close to 2 since, if the pack is cut 104 times, they might expect to turn up each number twice.
- Explain to **more able** students that although they are talking about the expected number, they will in practice not see this exact number very often but one close to it. The expected numbers are always an estimate.
- Explain that for the dice-rolling question, to obtain the answer they must multiply the theoretical probability by the number of rolls, i.e. $\frac{1}{6} \times 600 = 100$. For the cards-cutting question, they must multiply the probability 16 of cutting the ace of diamonds, $\frac{1}{52}$, by 100, which, using a calculator, gives 1.923, so they should expect to get the card 1.9 times, which rounds to 2.
- Ensure that students understand that expectation is the probability multiplied by the number of times the experiment is run.
- Work through Example 10 in the Student Book with the class. This example shows how to find the probability for different-coloured balls you would expect to get in an experiment.
- Example 11 shows how to use probability to work out the expected number of Japanese cars in Britain.
- **Students can now do Exercise 13E from the Student Book.**

| P 1–7, 9 | Calculator all | CM 11 | MR 8 | PS 10, 12 | EV n/a |
|----------|----------------|-------|------|-----------|--------|

## Part 3

- Display a sample space diagram of total scores from the roll of two dice.
- Ask students how many times they would expect to get different scores from 360 rolls of the dice. (Examples could be 4, 12, 5, less than 4 and so on.)
- Ask students which score they would expect to get most often.
- Ask students to think about why you picked 360 rolls.

# Section 13.6 Choices and outcomes

## Learning objectives
- Apply systematic listing and counting strategies to identify all outcomes for a variety of problems

## Resources and homework
- Student Book 13.3: pages 331–334
- Practice Book 13.3

## Making mathematical connections
- Multiplication
- Adding and subtracting fractions

## Making cross-curricular connections
- **Science** – accuracy of experiments
- **Relevance** – logical thinking

## Prior learning
- Students will need to be familiar with sample space diagrams and finding probabilities of events.

## Working mathematically
- Students will learn what the factorial function is and what this means in terms of probability and the number of outcomes.
- Students will explore what happens if you replace or do not replace counters or similar in experiments. This will help students to understand when to use the factorial function.

## Common misconceptions and remediation
- Students will often overlook a replacement in a question and go straight to use a factorial function to find the number of outcomes. Point out these errors as they occur.

## Probing questions
- If there are eight runners in a race, how many ways can they finish the race?

## Literacy focus
- Key terms: factorial, systematic counting
- Ask students to design a menu for a café. How many combinations, or groupings, of starters, mains and desserts can they make using their menu? Ask them to explain why.

## Part 1
- Steve has five coins in his pocket. He has a 2p, 10p, 20p, 50p and £2 coin.
- How many ways can he arrange these five coins?
- The first coin can be arranged in five different ways, the second coin can be arranged in the four remaining places, the third coin can be arranged in the three remaining places, the fourth coin in the two remaining places and finally, the fifth coin in the final remaining place.
- Show students that this is a very long-winded way of doing this.
- Then show them the ! function on the calculator and that 5! Is the same as $5 \times 4 \times 3 \times 2 \times 1$.

## Part 2

- Example 12 in the Student Book introduces the factorial function on the calculator. 5! is a much faster and more efficient way of doing 5 × 4 × 3 × 2 × 1.
- Explain to students how both 1! and 0! are both 1.
- Refer to Example 13 in the Student Book, which uses a sample space diagram to show all the possible ways of selecting various scarves and hats at random. This way is very visual and easy to find a combined probability of selecting the same colour hat and scarf.
- Example 14 shows students how they have to be mindful with replacement.
- Three numbers can be chosen from four numbers. The numbers can be used more than once. This means the first number can be selected from 4, as can the second and the third. This becomes 4 × 4 × 4 = 64 ways to select three numbers from 4. The second part of the questions asks for how many combinations of three-digit numbers without repeats can you make between 200 and 400. As the first digit must be 2 or 3, this leave three choices for the second number and two choices for the third, or 3 × 2 = 6. This is the same for a number starting with 2 or 3, so 6 + 6 = 12 choices in total.
- **Students can now do Exercise 13F from the Student Book.**

| P 1–8, 10–13, 15 | Calculator n/a | CM n/a | MR 9, 14 | PS n/a | EV n/a |
|---|---|---|---|---|---|

## Part 3

- A committee including three boys and four girls is to be formed from a group of 10 boys and 12 girls. How many different committees can be formed from the group?
- Ask students to find out how many ways three boys can be selected from 10 and how many ways four girls can be selected from 12. 10 × 9 × 8 = 720 boys and 12 × 11 × 10 = 1320 girls. Altogether there are 59 400 ways.

# Chapter 14 Geometry and measures: Volumes and surface areas of prisms

## Overview

| | |
|---|---|
| **14.1** 3D shapes | **14.3** Volume and surface area of a prism |
| **14.2** Volume and surface area of a cuboid | **14.4** Volume and surface area of cylinders |

### Prior learning

Know the formula for the circumference of a circle (circumference $C = \pi \times$ diameter or $C = \pi d$).

Know the formula for the area of a circle (area = $\pi \times$ radius$^2$ or $A = \pi r^2$).

Know the formula for the volume of a cuboid (volume = length × width × height or $V = lwh$).

Know the common metric units to measure area, volume and capacity shown below.

| Area | Volume | Volume to capacity |
|---|---|---|
| 100 mm$^2$ = 1 cm$^2$ | 1000 mm$^3$ = 1 cm$^3$ | 1000 cm$^3$ = 1 litre |
| 10 000 cm$^2$ = 1 m$^2$ | 1 000 000 cm$^3$ = 1 m$^3$ | 1 m$^3$ = 1000 litres |

### Learning objectives

**Ensure that students can: calculate the volume of a composite shape made from cuboids; calculate the volume and surface area of a prism; calculate the volume and surface area of a cylinder.**

In the examination, students will be expected to:
- use the correct terms when working with 3D shapes
- calculate the surface area and volume of a cuboid
- calculate the volume and surface area of a prism
- calculate the volume and surface area of a cylinder.

### Extension

Students could work out the volume and surface area of a sphere and hemisphere. Students could also look at volume and surface area of a frustum.

### Curriculum references

| Section | GCSE specification |
|---|---|
| 14.1 | N13, G16 |
| 14.2 | G16 |
| 14.3 | G16, 17 |
| 14.4 | G16, 17 |

## Route mapping

| Exercise | Accessible | Intermediate | Challenging | AO1 | AO2 MR CM | AO3 PS EV | Key questions |
|---|---|---|---|---|---|---|---|
| 14A | 1–6 | | | | 1–3, 6 | 4, 5 | 1, 3 |
| 14B | 1–5 | 6–12 | | 1–4, 6, 9, 10 | 7, 11 | 5, 8, 12 | 1, 2, 4, 9, 12 |
| 14C | | 1–6 | 7, 8 | 1, 2, 6 | 3, 5 | 4, 7, 8 | 1, 2, 7, 8 |
| 14D | | 1–10 | 11–13 | 1, 2, 5 | 3, 6, 7, 10 | 4, 8, 9, 11–13 | 1, 6, 10, 11 |

*Key questions are those that demonstrate mastery of the concept, or which require a step-up in understanding or application. Key questions could be used to identify the questions that students must tackle, to support differentiation, or to identify the questions that should be teacher-marked rather than student-marked.*

## About this chapter

**Making connections**: Students need to know the various properties of triangles, quadrilaterals and regular polygons. They should be able to find the area of a compound shape. Students should also know the metric equivalents.

**Relevance**: Students should be able to find the area of a square, a rectangle, a triangle and a compound shape and use this knowledge to find the volume of a prism. Using metric equivalents, students will be able to find areas and volumes and convert between units. Students will be able to use properties of shapes.

**Working mathematically**: Students will be able to find area and volume with different units. Students will be able to find the volume of a prism with a complex cross-section.

**Assessment**: In each section of this chapter, ensure that students have a good grasp of the key questions in each exercise before moving on. (Refer to the 'Route mapping' table.) Encourage students to read and think about the 'Ready to progress?' statementss on page 354 of the Student Book. Check students' understanding at the end of the chapter, formatively, using peer assessment. Students could do a mini test in the form of the 'Review questions' on pages 354–355 of the Student Book. Follow up the test with an individual target-getting session, based on any areas for development that a student may have.

## Worked exemplars from the Student Book (page 353) – suggestions for use

- Present students with the same question but different numbers. They should use the exemplar to mirror the working, in full or just refer to the notes.
- Copy and cut the exemplars into cards. Students should match the working with the notes.
- Or, copy and cut the working into cards but split the label/description from the working.

**Answers to the Student Book questions are available on the CD-ROM provided.**

# Section 14.1 3D shapes

## Learning objectives

- Use the correct terms when working with 3D shapes

## Resources and homework

- Student Book 14.1: pages 341–344
- Practice Book 14.1

## Making mathematical connections

- Areas of squares, rectangles and triangles
- Properties of shapes

## Making cross-curricular connections

- **Business** – packaging of items
- **Science** – finding volumes
- **Sport** – working out the space within an arena
- **Relevance** – logical thinking

## Prior learning

- Students should know how to work out the area of 2D shapes.
- Students should understand what a face, an edge and a vertex is.
- Students should understand the concept of volume.

## Working mathematically

- Students will need to work methodically to identify faces, edges and vertices.
- Students will need to find the area of a cross-section to find the volume of a prism.
- Students will need to work methodically to find the volume of a complex shape that is made up of cubes.
- Students should be able to convert between metric equivalents.

## Common misconceptions and remediation

- Students may not recognise the difference between a face, an edge and a vertex.
- Another problem is lack of accuracy. Use 3D shapes where possible.
- Students may have problems with visualising whether cubes are behind or inside a shape.

## Probing questions

- What is the difference between a pyramid and a prism?

## Literacy focus

- Key terms: edge, face, vertex (vertices), volume
- In pairs, define a face, an edge and a vertex and describe what is meant by 'volume'.

## Part 1

- Where possible, use multilink cubes or isometric paper.
- Ask students to work in pairs to make a $1 \times 1 \times 1$ cube, a $2 \times 2 \times 2$ cube, a $3 \times 3 \times 3$ cube, and so on.
- Ask students what they notice. Relate side length to volume.
- Ask students to devise a table to show how many cubes have three faces showing, two faces showing, one face showing, and then no faces showing.
- Can they design a rule that links any of these?

# Part 2

- Place a lot of emphasis on what a face, an edge and a vertex are.
- Explain that volume is the amount of space that a shape takes up.
- Work through Example 1 in the Student Book, which requires students to work out the volume of the shape.
- **Less able** students would benefit from using multilink cubes.
- Explain that by finding the area of the cross-section they can find the volume of the shape.
- They can either break the shape into manageable rectangles, or work out the full face.
- **Students can now do Exercise 14A from the Student Book.**

| G&M n/a | Calculator n/a | CM 3, 6 | MR 1, 2 | PS 4, 5 | EV n/a |
|---------|----------------|---------|---------|---------|--------|

# Part 3

- Tell students the following:
  - We have five cubes and we are going to put them together face-to-face.
  - We will paint the faces that we can see.
- Then ask these questions:
  - What arrangement of cubes will require the most paint and what arrangement will require the least paint?
  - What happens if you use more cubes, for example, 6, 7, 8 or more?
  - Can you find out the smallest number of faces to be painted and the largest number of faces to be painted in each case?
  - Can you predict the arrangement that will need as few faces to be painted as possible, and the arrangement that will need as many faces to be painted as possible?

## Section 14.2 Volume and surface area of a cuboid

### Learning objectives

Calculate the surface area and volume of a cuboid

### Resources and homework

- Student Book 14.2: pages 345–347
- Practice Book 14.2

### Making mathematical connections

- Area of a square and rectangle
- Volume

### Making cross-curricular connections

- **Science** – finding surface area to volume ratio
- **Relevance** – logical thinking

### Prior learning

- Students need to understand the concept of volume and know the standard conversions for length: 1 cm = 10 mm, 1 m = 100 cm.
- They also need to be able to calculate the area of a rectangle.

### Working mathematically

- Students need to find the volume of a shape by using the $V = lwh$ or finding the area of the cross-section and multiplying this by the height. Students need to work methodically to find the surface area of a shape, carefully not omitting any of the faces.

### Common misconceptions and remediation

- Students sometimes forget to ensure that they are working with consistent units. Difficulties also arise when algebraic formulae need to be rearranged, e.g. when students are required to find the length of a cuboid, given the width and height. Although more able students should be able to rearrange a formula such as $V = lwh$, less able students may struggle. Use multilink cubes with weaker students to help them visualise this.

### Probing questions

- How many centimetre cubes are in a metre cube?
- Ask students to look at a compound shape. Ask: How will you find the volume?

### Literacy focus

- Key terms: capacity, surface area
- What is the connection between volume and capacity?

### Part 1

- On the board, write the numbers 2, 3 and 5. Ask students to multiply them together, in the order in which they appear: 2 × 3 × 5 (to get 30). Then ask if they get the same answer if they multiply the same numbers in a different order, e.g. 5 × 2 × 3. A short discussion should lead to the conclusion that it makes no difference. Show **less able** students that these answers, and perhaps 3 × 5 × 2, are all the same.
- Now ask the class to multiply 2 × 17 × 5 (answer 170). Discuss with students how they did this. Lead students to realise that it is easiest to multiply 2 and 5 first, to get 10, then multiply 10 by 17 to get 170. This is a very useful fact that can save a lot of time and effort.

# Part 2

- Either draw a 2 × 3 × 4 cuboid on the board or, better still, use multicubes to show the shape. Ask students what the volume is. (24 cm$^3$)
- Draw another cuboid on the board, say 2 × 4 × 5. Ask: What is the volume? (40 cm$^3$)
- Ask students how they are calculating the volumes. Draw out that they are multiplying all the numbers together. Show that this works because one layer is the length × the width, then the number of layers is the height. Lead students to see that they can calculate the volume of a cuboid as: width × length × height.
- Work through Example 2 in the Student Book with the class, emphasising the rule for the volume of an object, and asking students to explain how to find the surface area, which involves calculating length × breadth for three pairs of faces. Ask students to explain why the formula for the total surface area needs two of each of the three different parts. Ask them how they would calculate with the 3.5 to get an answer without using a calculator. Help students to see that 4 × 3.5 = 14 is easier to work out than 24 × 3.5.
- Work through Example 3 in the Student Book, which brings together capacity and volume. Explain to students that first they must work out the volume. Remind them that 1000 cm$^3$ is the same as 1 litre, so by dividing by 1000 they will find the number of litres.
- **Less able** students will benefit from being given the explanation of the surface area calculation by means of multicubes, so that they can see why there are three pairs of faces, and follow the reasoning.
- Explain to **more able** students that 1000 cm$^3$ = 1 litre, and work with them to deduce how many litres there are in a cubic metre.
- 1 m$^3$ = 100 × 100 × 100 cm$^3$ = 1 000 000 cm$^3$ (one million).
  - So there will be 1 000 000 ÷ 1000 = 1000 litres.
  - Bring this to the attention of the less able students when they need it in question 2.
- **Students can now do Exercise 14B from the Student Book.**

| G&M 1–4, 6, 9, 10 | Calculator all | CM n/a | MR 7, 11 | PS 5, 12 | EV 8 |
|---|---|---|---|---|---|

# Part 3

- Pose this problem:
  - There are two cuboids.
  - One has the dimensions 4 cm × 5 cm × 9 cm.
  - The second has dimensions of 3 cm × 6 cm × 10 cm.
  - They both have an equal volume.
- Ask students: Which cuboid has the larger surface area?

## Section 14.3 Volume and surface area of a prism

### Learning objectives

Calculate the volume and surface area of a prism

### Resources and homework

- Student Book 14.3: pages 348–350
- Practice Book 14.3

### Making mathematical connections

- Area of a square and rectangle
- Volume

### Making cross-curricular connections

- **Science** – finding surface area to volume ratio
- **Relevance** – logical thinking

## Prior learning

- Students need to be able to calculate the areas of rectangles, triangles, trapezia and compound shapes.

## Working mathematically

- Students need to find the volume of a shape by using the $V = lwh$ for rectangular prisms or finding the area of the cross-section and multiplying this by the height for other prisms.
- Students need to work methodically to find the surface area of a shape, carefully not omitting any of the faces.

## Common misconceptions and remediation

- Students may sometimes mistake the length of the prism for a length occurring in the cross-section. Encouraging students to draw clear diagrams and solve the problem in stages should avoid this.

## Probing questions

- Why are the units for surface area in units$^2$ and the units for volume in units$^3$?

## Literacy focus

- Key terms: cross-section, prism
- Ask students to write a step-by-step instruction guide to work out the volume and surface area of a triangular prism.

## Part 1

- On the board, draw a rectangle, a triangle and a trapezium.
- Ask if anyone can remember how to find the area of each shape.
- Check that students know that the area of a rectangle is 'base × height'; the area of a triangle is 'half the base × height'; the area of a trapezium is 'half of $a + b$ × height'.
- To check and consolidate the use of the formulae, draw a few more shapes on the board, with dimensions marked. Ask students to find the area of each shape.

## Part 2

- Have some solid prisms available to show the class. Ask students the names of the shapes. Continue until students identify one shape as a prism. Write this on the board.
- Ask if anyone can define a prism. Remind them that there are many different types of prisms. Ask them to name a triangular prism. Look for an understanding that a prism has the same cross-section all the way along its length. Show students this aspect on the solid

shapes that are available. A prism has a constant or uniform cross-section wherever it is cut, perpendicular to its length.

- If you have some, show students some pyramid shapes to demonstrate the difference between a prism and a pyramid. It is essential to spend time with **less able** students so that they become familiar with these solid shapes and can actually see their cross-sections, in order to appreciate what a constant or uniform cross-section is.

## Volume

- Talk about how to find the volume of a prism. Start with a cuboid. Identify one face as its cross-section, and ask how to find the volume. Students should recall that they need to find the area of one layer – the base area – then multiply this by the height. Point out that the 'layer' is the same as a cross-section.
- Introduce the formula: volume of prism = area of cross-section × length. Tell students that although they do not need to remember this formula, as it is given in the GCSE examination, it will help them if they can learn it.
- Go through Example 4 in the Student Book with the class, showing them that to find the volume they need to work out the area of the triangular constant cross-section and multiply this by the length. $V$ = Cross-sectional area × length.

## Surface area

- Work through Example 5, where the total surface area includes every face of the shape, including its base, which students may not be able to see.
- Throughout this lesson, remind students about the units, and about the importance of using the correct, relevant units in solutions to problems involving volume and area.
- **Less able** students will most likely need help with recognising the constant cross-section in many of the shapes given. Ask them to think about which is the flat shape that does not change all the way through the solid shape. This is the constant cross-section.
- Make sure students know that the exception is a cuboid, where they can choose any face as the cross-section.
- **Students can now do Exercise 14C from the Student Book.**

| G&M 1, 2, 6 | Calculator all | CM 3 | MR 5 | PS 4, 7 | EV 8 |

# Part 3

- Ask students: What prisms do we see in everyday life?
- The answers should provoke some discussion. Obvious answers include: food packets, tissue boxes, a pane of glass, a packet of Swiss chocolate.
- Discuss any wrong answers that students may offer, explaining why they are not right.
- **More able** students might also identify cylinders as prisms.

## Learning objectives

Calculate the volume and surface area of a cylinder

## Resources and homework

- Student Book 14.4: pages 350–352
- Practice Book 14.4

## Making mathematical connections

- Area of a square and rectangle
- Area of a circle
- Circumference of a circle
- Volume

## Making cross-curricular connections

- **Science** – finding surface area to volume ratio
- **Relevance** – logical thinking

## Prior learning

- Students should know how to find the volume of a prism, as covered in Section 14.3, and they should be able to calculate the area of a circle, as covered in Section 11.7.
- A note on calculations involving circles: Chapter 11 of this book (Student Book and Teacher pack) covers everything you need on circles for this lesson. The most important part to refer to is Section 11.7 (The area of a circle).

## Working mathematically

- Students need to use the formula $V$ = cross-section × length.
- The cross-section is circular so students should be familiar with $\pi r^2$.
- Students should be familiar with surface area.
- The two ends are circles, hence $2(\pi r^2)$ and the curved face has a length the same as that for the volume, but its width is the same as the circumference of a circle, hence $\pi d$.

## Common misconceptions and remediation

- Less able students can be confused between $\pi r^2$ and $(\pi r)^2$. They may find it helpful to use a 'simpler' version of the formula in the form $V = \pi \times r \times r \times h$, until their confidence improves.

## Probing questions

- Why is the width of the curved surface of a cylinder the same as the circumference of the circular end?

## Literacy focus

- Key term: cylinder
- Ask students to visualise a can of something like, e.g. beans or spaghetti. Ask them to explain to the shop manager how to find the area of the label that goes around the can.

## Part 1

- Give students some practice with multiplying by 3 mentally. For example: say 7, look for the answer 21; say 12, look for the answer 36; say 32, look for the answer 96.
- Continue multiplying mentally for about two minutes, asking students who do not offer answers, to bring them into the activity.

## Part 2

- Draw a circle and ask students how to find the area. Draw out the answer of: $A = \pi r^2$. Remind students that they must learn this, as the formula is not given in the examination.
- Ask if anyone remembers what $\pi$ stands for. Look for the approximate figure of 3.1, 3.14 or 3.142. Write these on the board as a reminder. Ask the class where else they will see $\pi$. Apart from maybe $C = \pi d$, they should remember that it is on their calculators.
- Ask: What is the area of a circle with radius 4 cm? Tell the class that they can use their calculators if they wish, or give an approximate value.
- Write down the answers as students say them. Each time, ask: How did you get that answer? Responses could include: 48 cm$^2$ taking $\pi$ as 3; 49.6 cm$^2$ taking $\pi$ as 3.1; 50.24 cm$^2$ taking $\pi$ as 3.14; 50.272 cm$^2$ taking $\pi$ as 3.142; 50.265 482 46 using $\pi$ in the calculator.
- Ask: What value do all these answers round to? (50 cm$^2$)
- At this point, for **less able** students, ignore any rounding rules unless asked. Emphasise that the answer is an approximation. For **more able** students, introduce the idea of rounding to one more significant figure than in the given data. This also justifies an answer of 50 cm$^2$.

### Volume

- Show the class a cylinder and ask what shape it is. Some students may say it is a cylinder. Encourage them to recognise that it is also a prism. Establish that it is a prism because it has a constant or uniform cross-section, which is a circle.
- Now ask to find the volume of the cylinder. Stress that it is a prism and draw out the rule again: volume of a prism = area of uniform cross-section × length ($V = CSA$ × length).
- So for a cylinder, this will be: volume = area of circle × length (or height), or $V = \pi r^2 h$.
- Write this on the board and say that students should learn it as an aid to memory. The rule for the volume of a prism is given in the examination.
- Work through Example 6 with the class, emphasising that they can do all the work on a calculator, in one go, and then round the answer. Remind **more able** students that sometimes they will be asked to leave their answer in terms of $\pi$; here, that would be 300$\pi$.
- A simple rule for rounding is to round to one more dp or one more sf than in the given data. For **less able** students, keep this to one more dp, as it is easier to remember.

### Surface area

- Example 7 in the Student Book has a mixture of metric units, so remind students to change them to a common unit first. Total surface area = $2\pi rh + 2\pi r^2 = 2 \times \pi \times 15 \times 250 + 2 \times \pi$.
- Show students how to do this on a calculator in two steps and then using brackets, in one step. Draw a diagram to help **less able** students.
- **Students can now do Exercise 14D from the Student Book.**

| G&M 1, 2, 5 | Calculator all | CM 6, 7 | MR 3, 10 | PS 4, 9, 11–13 | EV 8 |

## Part 3

- Give students a length that is both the radius and the height of a cylinder. Ask them to calculate the volume, giving the correct units. Start with 2 cm. The expected answer is 8$\pi$ or approximately 24 cm$^3$. Now give them 3 cm. The expected answer is 27$\pi$ or approximately 81 or 85 cm$^3$. Now 10 cm. The expected answer is 1000$\pi$ or approximately 3140 cm$^3$.
- Now tell students that you are going to give them a length, which is both the diameter and the height. Ask them to calculate the volume, giving the correct units. Start with 4 cm. The expected answer is 16$\pi$ or approximately 48–50 cm$^3$. Then 6 cm. The expected answer is 54$\pi$ or approximately 162–170 cm$^3$.
- Encourage a mix of answers, from those using $\pi$ as 3 to those using a calculator.

# Chapter 15 Algebra: Linear equations

## Overview

| | |
|---|---|
| **15.1** Solving linear equations | **15.3** Solving equations with the variable on both sides |
| **15.2** Solving equations with brackets | |

### Prior learning

Know the basic language of algebra.
Know how to expand brackets and collect like terms.
Know that addition and subtraction are opposite (inverse) operations.
Know that multiplication and division are opposite (inverse) operations.

### Learning objectives

**Ensure that students can: solve linear equations with the variable on one side; solve linear equations involving brackets; solve linear equations with fractions; solve linear equations with the variable on both sides; set up linear equations from real-life problems.**

In the examination, students will be expected to:
- solve linear equations such as $3x - 1 = 11$ where the variable only appears on one side
- use inverse operations and inverse flow diagrams
- solve equations by balancing
- solve equations in which the variable (the letter) appears in the numerator of a fraction
- solve equations with brackets
- solve equations where the variable appears on both sides of the equals sign.

### Extension

Some students will take to the elements of this chapter quicker than others. The probing questions in Section 15.3 will provide very good practice, and opportunity, for students to come up with complex (and probably amusing) scenarios from which equations can be formed, and then solved.

### Curriculum references

| Section | GCSE specification |
|---|---|
| 15.1 | A17 |
| 15.2 | A17 |
| 15.3 | A17 |

## Route mapping

| Exercise | Accessible | Intermediate | Challenging | AO1 | AO2 MR CM | AO3 PS EV | Key questions |
|---|---|---|---|---|---|---|---|
| 15A | 1–3 | | | 1, 3 | 2 | | 3 |
| 15B | 1 | 2, 3 | | 1 | 3 | 2 | 1 |
| 15C | 1, 2 | 3, 4 | | 1 | 3 | 2, 4 | 4 |
| 15D | | 1–7 | | 1, 3 | 4 | 2, 5–7 | 3 |
| 15E | | 1–5 | 6 | 1 | 2, 5 | 3, 4, 6 | 5 |
| 15F | | 1–6 | 7, 8 | 1, 3 | 4, 7 | 2, 5, 6, 8 | 3, 8 |

*Key questions are those that demonstrate mastery of the concept, or which require a step-up in understanding or application. Key questions could be used to identify the questions that students must tackle, to support differentiation, or to identify the questions that should be teacher-marked rather than student-marked.*

## About this chapter

**Making connections**: This chapter looks at solving linear equations, whether the variable is on one or two sides, and whether brackets and fractional elements are included. This has connections with algebra Chapter 9, in that students now need to use the skills they mastered there to help them evaluate an equation.

**Relevance**: The skills students will learn in this chapter will become required prior learning for other topics such as working with ratio, percentages, plotting graphs and other algebra areas such as simultaneous equations.

**Working mathematically**: How easily can students expand brackets, balance an equation or apply an inverse rule? These skills are used in many areas of Mathematics and Science. Students need to be able to show all the stages of their working to demonstrate that they understand how to work toward a solution, not forgetting that these intermediate stages are awarded marks.

**Assessment**: In each section of this chapter, ensure that students have a good grasp of the key questions in each exercise before moving on. (Refer to the 'Route mapping' table.) Encourage students to read and think about the 'Ready to progress?' statements on page 370 of the Student Book. Check students' understanding at the end of the chapter, formatively, using peer assessment. Students could do a mini test in the form of the 'Review questions' on pages 370–371 of the Student Book. Follow up the test with an individual target-getting session, based on any areas for development that a student may have.

## Worked exemplars from the Student Book (page 368) – suggestions for use
*   Present students with the same question but different numbers. They should use the exemplar to mirror the working, in full or just refer to the notes.
*   Copy and cut the exemplars into cards. Students should match the working with the notes.
*   Alternatively, copy and cut the working into cards but split the label/description from the working.

## Answers to the Student Book questions are available on the CD-ROM provided.

# Section 15.1 Solving linear equations

## Learning objectives

- Solve linear equations such as $3x - 1 = 11$ where the variable only appears on one side
- Use inverse operations and inverse flow diagrams
- Solve equations by balancing
- Solve equations in which the variable (the letter) appears in the numerator of a fraction

## Resources and homework

- Student Book 15.1: pages 357–363
- Practice Book 15.1

## Making mathematical connections

- Forming equations
- Rearranging equations

## Making cross-curricular connections

- **Science; Business Studies** – solving problems
- **Relevance** – the ability to form and solve a simple equation to use in everyday situations

## Prior learning

- Students should be familiar with the basic language of algebra, know how to collect like terms, understand that addition is the opposite (inverse) operation to subtraction (and vice versa), and that multiplication is the opposite (inverse) operation to division (and vice versa).
- Students should also be familiar with inverse operations, and setting up equations using flow diagrams and inverse flow diagrams.

## Working mathematically

- It is important that students show all steps in their working – even if they think that the step is obvious. There are two reasons for this: they will find it easier to identify where a mistake may have occurred; there are method marks available for showing the working out steps.

## Common misconceptions and remediation

- Students often use the same operation for the inverse operation, forgetting to change the sign when they rearrange the equation. Constant emphasis on the balancing aspect of solving an equation will remedy this.
- Students also make errors with minus signs, especially when fractions are involved. Working with an equation such as $\frac{x}{2} = 4$ will often be solved as $x = 2$. Checking answers in the original equation is the only way students can eliminate these errors.

## Probing questions

- Set up questions with fractions on both sides of the equation, e.g. $\frac{2x + 3}{2} = \frac{22}{4}$ $(x = 4)$

## Literacy focus

- Key terms: balancing, inverse flow diagrams, solution
- Ask students to choose any of parts a to f in question 1 of Exercise 15D, and write annotations alongside each step of the solution to explain what they are doing.

## Part 1

- Ask ten quick-fire questions that will require students to use BIDMAS/BODMAS.
- Ask each student to think of a number, double it and add 3. Let some students give their result and ask others to say what the original number was. Do this for five or six results.
- Now ask students to say how they worked out the original number. **More able** students should realise that they first subtracted 3 from the result and then divided by 2. This will encourage the idea of working in reverse – finding the inverse of the problem.

## Part 2

- Recall Part 1 'think of a number, double it and add 3'. Write it as an equation: $2x + 3$ = result.
- Say that $x$ is the **variable** and takes whatever value students choose. To find the value of $x$, they need to solve the equation. Go through the text in the Student Book with the class.
- Say that 'solve the equation' instructs them to find the value of the letter that makes it true.
- Demonstrate with, e.g., $2x + 3 = 17$, for which the starting number, $x$, is 7.

**Inverse operations**
- Ask students to recall the inverse operation to add (subtract), subtract (add), multiply (divide), divide (multiply) in order to ready them for the next two exercises.
- Work through Example 1, which shows how the idea of inversing the operation is applied.
- **Students can now do Exercise 15A from the Student Book.**

| A 1, 3 | Calculator n/a | CM n/a | MR 2 | PS n/a | EV n/a |
|---|---|---|---|---|---|

**Inverse flow diagrams**
- Using inverse flow diagrams may be particularly good for students who are visual learners, as it clearly illustrates the idea of using the inverse of an operation.
- Work though Example 2 and then work on question 1a, b, and c of Exercise 15B together, drawing the diagrams, so that students get a clear idea of the method.
- **Students can now do Exercise 15B from the Student Book.**

| A 1 | Calculator n/a | CM n/a | MR 3 | PS 2 | EV n/a |
|---|---|---|---|---|---|

**Balancing**
- This method combines the previous ideas into a solution that can be written as stages of working. The idea of recalling the inverse operation is present. Students may find this tedious but it is worth doing, to get them into good habits. When students write out the solution in full, they can see the relationship between the operations and the inverse operations much more easily.
- Stress that showing the balancing element is important when working out; they must show it.
- Example 3 in the Student Book clearly illustrates this, so use it as a guide for students' work.
- **Students can now do Exercise 15C from the Student Book.**

| A 1 | Calculator n/a | CM n/a | MR 3 | PS 2 | EV 4 |
|---|---|---|---|---|---|

**Fractional equations**
- Examples 4 and 5 illustrate an important stage of working that many students do not think about carefully, thus making a serious error. Explain it clearly, showing a method error that produces an answer that does not check. Use Example 4: students may add (instead of subtract) 1 to the right-hand side to get 6; then multiply by 3, giving an answer of 18 for $x$. Then put this back into the question to check that it works – if not, they have made an error.
- **Students can now do Exercise 15D from the Student Book.**

| A 1, 3 | Calculator n/a | CM n/a | MR 4 | PS 2, 6, 7 | EV 5 |
|---|---|---|---|---|---|

## Part 3

Using an equation such as $3x - 4 = 5$, discuss the advantages and disadvantages of each method demonstrated. Encourage students to settle on one method and use this (although balancing is the most useful, as will be seen later when the variable appears on both sides).

# Section 15.2 Solving equations with brackets

## Learning objectives
- Solve equations with brackets

## Resources and homework
- Student Book 15.2: pages 364–365
- Practice Book 15.2

## Making mathematical connections
- Expanding brackets
- Rearranging equations
- Factorising

## Making cross-curricular connections
- **Science; Business Studies** – solving problems
- **Relevance** – the ability to form and solve a simple equation to use in everyday situations

## Prior learning
- Students should know how to expand expressions that include brackets (Section 9.3).

## Working mathematically
- Students should have mastered the content of the previous section since this section now adds the element of brackets to the equation that is to be solved. Remind students again how important it is to show all steps in their working – even if the step seems obvious.

## Common misconceptions and remediation
- Students often go wrong by multiplying only the first part of the expression inside the brackets by the term outside.
- Before they begin Exercise 15E, remind students that they must multiply everything inside the brackets by what is outside the brackets.

## Probing questions
- Working in pairs, say to students: 'Create a question similar to question 6 in Exercise 15E or Example 7. Your partner should work out the answer.'

## Literacy focus
- Key terms: None in this section
- Students take a question and write an annotation for each step of the working out.
- **Less able** students could use question 5; **more able** students could use question 6.

## Part 1
- Write on the board:
  31 + 32 + 33 = 96
  96 ÷ 3 = 32
- Repeat with three other consecutive numbers.
- Ask, 'Is the sum of three consecutive numbers always divisible by 3?'
- Let students try to prove this using algebra.
- Ask them to try to prove that the sum of five consecutive numbers is always divisible by 5.

## Part 2

- Ask the class to think of a number, add 3 to it and then multiply the result by 5. Ask some students to give their results and ask other students if they can say what the original number was. Do this for five or six results.
- Now ask students to explain how they worked out the original numbers.
- Try to establish that they first divided the result by 5 and then subtracted 3.
- Now show the original problem as an equation: $5(x + 3) = $ result.
- **Less able** students may wish to see this as a flow diagram.
- Demonstrate this with, e.g., $5(x + 3) = 50$ for which the starting number, $x$, is 7.
- It is advisable to spend some time on Examples 6 and 7 in the Student Book with the class because these examples are not fully illustrated with the balancing technique that was used in the previous section.
- It would be useful to rework Examples 6 and 7 showing the balancing that is taking place at each stage of the working..
- **Students can now do Exercise 15E from the Student Book.**

| A 1 | Calculator all | CM 5 | MR 2 | PS 3, 4, 6 | EV n/a |

## Part 3

- It would now be useful to draw students' memories back to factorisation (Section 9.4) and remind them that another pair of inverse procedures is that of factorising and expanding.
- Having spent Exercise 15E expanding brackets, now practise factorisation with the class. For example:

$4x + 8 = 4(...)$

$x^2 + 3x = x(...)$

$6x + 14 = ...$

- Do some more examples with just a single number or a single letter as the common factor.

# Section 15.3 Solving equations with the variable on both sides

## Learning objectives

- Solve equations where the variable appears on both sides of the equals sign

## Resources and homework

- Student Book 15.3: pages 365–367
- Practice Book 15.3

## Making mathematical connections

- Expanding brackets
- Rearranging equations
- Collecting like terms

## Making cross-curricular connections

- **Science; Business Studies** – solving problems
- **Relevance** – the ability to form and solve a simple equation to use in everyday situations

## Prior learning

- Students should know how to expand an expression that includes brackets. Students should also recall how to rearrange equations (Section 9.7).

## Working mathematically

- Students should have mastered the content of the previous two sections since this one adds an additional complication of placing the unknown variable on both sides of the equation that is to be solved. It is important that students show all steps in their working – even if they think that the step is obvious.

## Common misconceptions and remediation

- Students often get the wrong answer by not changing the signs when rearranging equations. They do not always grasp that the sign relates to the number that follows it. Encourage students to be logical and rearrange before simplifying; not try to do both at the same time.

## Probing questions

- Working in pairs, ask students to create a problem such as question 8 of Exercise 15F.
- Say that they should work the question in reverse (the inverse of solving a problem is to create it). Think of a value that will be $x$, work out some expressions that will make a balanced equation. Think up and write a scenario that fits the equation.
- Set up some questions that have fractions on both sides of the equation.

  For example: $\dfrac{2(3x - 4)}{4} = \dfrac{3(2x - 1)}{6}$ ($x = 3$).

## Literacy focus

- Key terms: None in this section
- Ask students to write a fully annotated solution to question 2 in Exercise 15F (or similar), explaining fully at each stage what they are doing.

## Part 1

- Put the following algebra pyramids on the board and ask students to solve them by adding the expressions in the bricks on the bottom row to get the middle row and then combining those to get the expression for the top row. The number sitting above the pyramid's top row is equal to the expression in the top row. Solve to find the value of $x$.

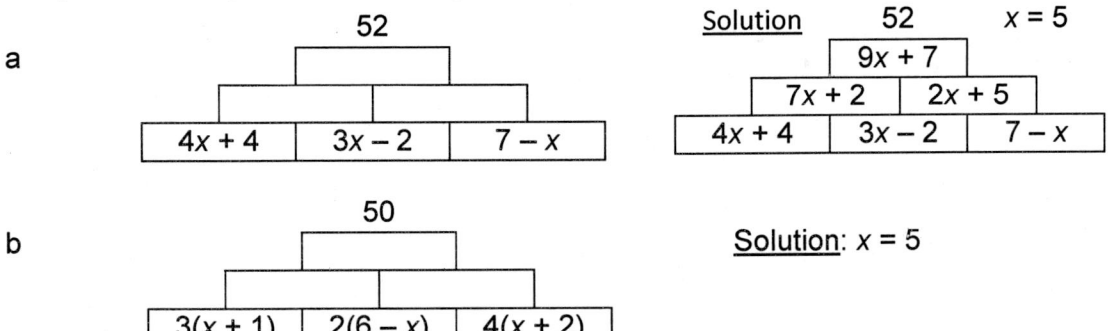

a

| 52 |
| |
| $4x + 4$ | $3x - 2$ | $7 - x$ |

Solution    52    $x = 5$

| 52 |
| $9x + 7$ |
| $7x + 2$ | $2x + 5$ |
| $4x + 4$ | $3x - 2$ | $7 - x$ |

b

| 50 |
| |
| $3(x + 1)$ | $2(6 - x)$ | $4(x + 2)$ |

Solution: $x = 5$

- Make up other algebra pyramids for students.
- You could also suggest that students make their own algebra pyramids.

## Part 2

- Tell students you are thinking of a number. You multiply it by 2 then add 5.
- The final result is 8 more than the original number you thought of.
- Ask students if they know what the number you started with was.
- This will not be as easy to solve as previous similar questions, as there is no easy method of using inverse operations. If no student comes up with the correct answer of 3, then tell them the answer and work through the problem, i.e. $2 \times 3 + 5 = 3 + 8$.
- Now set this up as an equation: $2x + 5 = x + 8$. Ask students why this is different from previous problems. Students should see that the variable is on both sides.
- Work through the method of solution:

  Subtract $x$ from both sides.    $2x - x + 5 = x - x + 8$
  $$x + 5 = 8$$

  Subtract 5 from both sides.    $x + 5 - 5 = 8 - 5$
  $$x = 3$$

- Work carefully through Examples 8, 9 and 10 in the Student Book with the class. Ensure that students are comfortable with expanding the brackets and rearranging the equation to get the variable on one side of the equals sign, and the constant terms on the other. Emphasise that the variable terms need to be collected on one side (normally the left-hand side, but this is not always the case, as shown in Example 10), and the numbers on the other side. Also remind students of BIDMAS/BODMAS and the need to expand before rearranging or collecting like terms.
- **Students can now do Exercise 15F from the Student Book.**

| A 1, 3 | Calculator n/a | CM 4 | MR 7 | PS 2, 5, 6, 8 | EV n/a |

## Part 3

- Give students a 'think of a number' problem, e.g. 'I am thinking of a number. I treble it and add 3. The result is 9 more than the number I originally thought of.' (3)
- Whether students solve it mentally or not, set up the equation $3x + 3 = x + 9$ and solve it.
- Repeat with similar examples.
- If some students have created questions from the probing questions part above, show them to the class and ask students to solve them.

# Chapter 16 Ratio and proportion and rates of change: Percentages and compound measures

## Overview

| | |
|---|---|
| **16.1** Equivalent percentages, fractions and decimals | **16.4** Expressing one quantity as a percentage of another |
| **16.2** Calculating a percentage of a quantity | **16.5** Compound measures |
| **16.3** Increasing and decreasing quantities by a percentage | |

### Prior learning

Know multiplication tables up to 12 × 12.
Know how to simplify fractions.
Know how to multiply and divide, with and without a calculator.
Know how to substitute values into expressions.

### Learning objectives

**Ensure that students can: convert between fractions, decimals and percentages; use a percentage multiplier; work out a percentage increase and decrease; work out one quantity as a percentage of another; calculate compound measures (rates of pay, density, pressure).**

In the examination, students will be expected to:
- convert percentages to fractions and decimals and vice versa
- calculate a percentage of a quantity
- increase and decrease quantities by a percentage
- express one quantity as a percentage of another
- work out percentage change
- recognise and solve problems involving the compound measures of rates of pay, density and pressure.

### Extension

Give **more able** students some calculations to work out, using different units in compound measures such as changing speeds in mph to km/h.

### Curriculum references

| Section | GCSE specification |
|---------|--------------------|
| 16.1 | N10 |
| 16.2 | N12, R9 |
| 16.3 | R9 |
| 16.4 | R9 |
| 16.5 | N13, R11 |

## Route mapping

| Exercise | Accessible | Intermediate | Challenging | AO1 | AO2 MR CM | AO3 PS EV | Key questions |
|---|---|---|---|---|---|---|---|
| 16A | 1–16 | | | 1–6, 8, 9, 13–15 | 7, 10, 12 | 11, 16 | 13–15 |
| 16B | | 1–15 | 16 | 1–3, 5–8, 11–15 | 4, 16 | 9, 10 | 3, 9, 16 |
| 16C | 1–5 | 6–9 | 10–13 | 1–5, 8a, 9, 12 | 6, 7, 10, 11, 13 | 8b, c | 3, 4, 8, 13 |
| 16D | 1–5 | 6–9 | 10–13 | 1–8 | 9–11 | 12, 13 | 1, 9, 12, 13 |
| 16E | 1–3 | 4–7 | 8–10 | 1–3, 5–7 | 4 | 8–10 | 1, 4, 8 |
| 16F | | 1–8, 16–20 | 9–15, 21–23 | 1–8, 10, 12a, c, 14, 20 | 9, 12b, 13, 15–18, 21, 23 | 11, 19, 22 | 1, 2, 12, 13, 16, 17 |

*Key questions are those that demonstrate mastery of the concept, or which require a step-up in understanding or application. Key questions could be used to identify the questions that students must tackle, to support differentiation, or to identify the questions that should be teacher-marked rather than student-marked.*

## About this chapter

**Making connections**: Students will need to be able to calculate fractions, decimals and percentages of amounts. They also need to be able to find equivalents and more compound measures.

**Relevance**: The connection between fractions, decimals and percentages emphasises the use of logic and thinking in steps. There are applications in engineering, architecture, manufacturing, project management and many more areas, with STEM careers being a strong focus.

**Working mathematically**: Students will find fractions, decimals and percentages of amounts and equivalents. They will also work out percentage increases and decreases. In addition, students will rearrange equations, using inverse operations to find densities and pressures.

**Assessment**: In each section of this chapter, ensure that students have a good grasp of the key questions in each exercise before moving on. (Refer to the 'Route mapping' table.) Encourage students to read and think about the 'Ready to progress?' statements on page 392 of the Student Book. Check students' understanding at the end of the chapter, formatively, using peer assessment. Students could do a mini test in the form of the 'Review questions' on pages 392–393 of the Student Book. Follow up the test with an individual target-getting session, based on any areas for development that a student may have.

### Worked exemplars from the Student Book (page 391) – suggestions for use
*   Present students with the same question but different numbers. They should use the exemplar to mirror the working, in full or just refer to the notes.
*   Copy and cut the exemplars into cards. Students should match the working with the notes.
*   Alterntatively, copy and cut the working into cards but split the label/description from the working.

### Answers to the Student Book questions are available on the CD-ROM provided.

## Section 16.1 Equivalent percentages, fractions and decimals

### Learning objectives

- Convert percentages to fractions and decimals and vice versa

### Resources and homework

- Student Book 16.1: pages 373–377
- Practice Book 16.1

### Making mathematical connections

- Equivalent fractions
- Percentages and decimals

### Making cross-curricular connections

- **Science** – finding amounts
- **Relevance** – working logically

### Prior learning

- Students should know how to cancel fractions and how to calculate with fractions.
- Students must be able to multiply and divide decimals by 100.
- Students should know some commonly used equivalent fractions, decimals and percentages.

### Working mathematically

- Students will convert between fractions, decimals and percentages.
- They will find equivalents and work out a percentage of an amount.

### Common misconceptions and remediation

- Most mistakes that students make are when they deal with fractions, e.g. writing $\frac{1}{3}$ as 30% or as 0.3. Encourage students to learn the common equivalent fractions, decimal and percentages.

### Probing questions

- You scored 34 out of 60 in a test. How do you convert this to a percentage?

### Literacy focus

- Key terms: equivalent, percentage, per cent
- Ask students to describe how to convert between fractions, decimals and percentages.

### Part 1

- Give students a copy of Resource 16.1 on equivalent fractions, decimals and percentages. Ask them to fill in the equivalent fractions, decimals and percentages that they know. Suggest to students that they could keep the sheet as a useful revision tool.
- Students could add extra rows to the sheet, completing other equivalent fractions, decimals and percentages. You can use this to assess students' prior knowledge.

### Part 2

- Following on from Part 1, ask students to give you their answers to Resource 16.1. Write the answers (plus those for the extra rows) on the board under the three column headings: 'Fractions', 'Decimals' and 'Percentages'.
- Suggest ways to group the answers, e.g. $\frac{1}{10}, \frac{2}{10}$, ... to form one group, and 25%, 50%, 75%, 100% to form a different group.

- Check that students understand that 'per cent' means 'out of 100', so, e.g., 52% = $\frac{52}{100}$ = 0.52, 100% = $\frac{100}{100}$ = 1 and that they realise, e.g., that 80% = 0.8 but 8% = 0.08.
- Converting from decimals: Explain to students that to convert from a decimal they are working backwards from making a fraction into a decimal, this time making it into a fraction first and then into a percentage. Use some examples that were used previously, e.g. 0.52. Ask for the fraction out of 100: ($\frac{52}{100}$) and then ask for the percentage (52%).
- Do not talk about multiplying by 100, as this implies something that is 100 times bigger. Multiplying by 100% is multiplying by 1, which means that the value is still equivalent.
- Converting from fractions: Start by looking at fractions with denominators that are factors of 100, e.g. $\frac{3}{10}, \frac{1}{25}, \frac{7}{50}$.
- Ask students to give the fractions out of 100 and then give the decimal and percentage equivalents. ($\frac{3}{100}$, 0.3, 30%, $\frac{4}{100}$, 0.04, 4%, $\frac{14}{100}$, 0.14, 14%)
- Now explain that not all fractions can be converted this way, e.g. $\frac{5}{12}, \frac{1}{7}$.
- Remind students that $\frac{5}{12}$ means 5 ÷ 12; $\frac{1}{7}$ means 1 ÷ 7 and that they can change these to decimals using a calculator or a division method such as long division.
- Demonstrate $\frac{5}{12}$ and $\frac{1}{7}$ using a calculator:

$\frac{5}{12}$ = 5 ÷ 12 = 0.41666... = 41.7%        $\frac{1}{7}$ = 1 ÷ 7 = 0.142857... = 14.3.

  Tell students that it is sensible to give percentages to one decimal place.
- With the class, work through the text and table in the Student Book.
- Then work through Example 1, which focuses on converting to a decimal.
- Work through Example 2, which focuses on converting to a percentage.
- Work through Example 3, which focuses on converting to a fraction in its simplest form. (Remind students how to do this.)
- **Students can now do Exercise 16A from the Student Book.**

| R&P 1–6, 8, 9, 13–15 | Calculator 13 | CM 12 | MR 7, 10 | PS 11, 16 | EV n/a |
|---|---|---|---|---|---|

## Part 3

- Say a fraction and ask a student to give the equivalent percentage.
- Ask another student to give the decimal.
- Repeat several times, sometimes starting with a decimal and sometimes with a percentage.
- Start with fractions that are easy to convert and gradually increase the difficulty.
- Point out any mistakes and explain any errors.

## Learning objectives

- Calculate a percentage of a quantity

## Resources and homework

- Student Book 16.2: pages 377–380
- Practice Book 16.2

## Making mathematical connections

- Percentage and decimal equivalents
- Decimal multiplication

## Making cross-curricular connections

- **Business; Accounting** – working with profit and loss
- **Relevance** – solving money problems

## Prior learning

- Students need to understand that 'per cent' means 'out of 100' and 'of' means '×'.

## Working mathematically

- Students will find a percentage of a quantity.
- Students will find the percentage as a decimal multiplier.

## Common misconceptions and remediation

- A common error that students make is to write, e.g., 8% as 0.8. Single-digit percentages should be used frequently in starter activities to reinforce the correct answer. (0.08)

## Probing questions

- How do you work out a percentage of an amount with and without a calculator?

## Literacy focus

- Key term: quantity
- What is the difference between 0.8 and 0.08 when they are multipliers? Similarly, show 1% and 10%, 2% and 20%, and so on. Ask students to explain the difference.

## Part 1

- Give students some simple quick-fire questions; they could display their answers on mini-whiteboards; e.g. 50% of 40 (20), 10% of 30 (3), 25% of 8 (2), 30% of 100 (30), 75% of 80 (60), 5% of 100 (5).
- Before moving on to other percentages, ensure that **less able** students fully understand how to find 50%, 25%, 75% and 10% of amounts.
- Develop this by asking linked questions, e.g. 50% of 30 (15), 25% of 30 (7.5); 10% of 60 (6), 5% of 60 (3), 15% of 60 (9); 10% of 20 (2), 20% of 20 (4), 30% of 20 (6), 70% of 20 (14).
- Ask **more able** students to find 1% of 30 (0.3) and then 51% of 30 (15.3).
- Ask for other percentages such as 11% of 60 (6.6), 21% of 20 (4.2), 19% of 20 (3.8).

# Part 2

## Using a build-up method

- Using the examples in Part 1, ask students how they worked out each answer. (50% is half, 25% is one-quarter, 10% is one-tenth, 5% is half of 10%, and so on)
- Work through Examples 4 and 5 in the Student Book with the class. Example 5 partitions a percentage into easier chunks.

## Using a percentage multiplier

- Write 13% of 45 on the board.
- Ask students to convert the percentage to a decimal and the 'of' to a multiplication symbol. (0.13 × 45)
- Now ask a student to work this out on a calculator (5.85).
- Refer students to Example 6 in the Student Book. Remind them that per cent is per hundred and to divide the percentage by 100 to find the decimal multiplier.
- Students will now need calculators. Give questions for students to do on their calculator, e.g. 34% of 70 (23.8), 87% of 95 (82.65).
- **Students can now do Exercise 16B from the Student Book.**

| R&P 1–3, 5–8, 11–15 | Calculator all | CM 16 | MR 4 | PS 9, 10 | EV n/a |

# Part 3

- Go around the class asking for the equivalent percentage multiplier for various percentages, e.g. 45% = 0.45, 62% = 0.62. Include some that often cause difficulty, e.g. 3% = 0.03 but is often given as 0.3.
- Now give the multiplier and ask for the percentage.
- Move on to multipliers greater than 1, e.g. 1.25 (125%). Explain that this represents a 25% increase and is covered in the next section.

# Section 16.3 Increasing and decreasing quantities by a percentage

## Learning objectives

- Increase and decrease quantities by a percentage

## Resources and homework

- Student Book 16.3: pages 380–382
- Practice Book 16.3

## Making mathematical connections

- Percentage and decimal equivalents.
- Decimal multiplication.

## Making cross-curricular connections

- **Business; Accounting** – working with profit and loss
- **Relevance** – solving money problems

## Prior learning

- Students need to know how to use a percentage multiplier and how to work out a percentage of a quantity.

## Working mathematically

- Students will find a percentage of a quantity.
- They will find the percentage as a decimal multiplier.
- Students will add on a percentage for an increase or subtract for a decrease.
- Students will increase and decrease quantities in one step using a multiplier.

## Common misconceptions and remediation

- When students are asked to increase or decrease a quantity by a percentage; they often simply work out the percentage. For example, when set the problem of increasing 30 by 5%, they work out 5% of 30 but forget to add it on to get the required answer. Encourage students to read questions more than once, to check that they have answered it correctly.

## Probing questions

- What is meant by a percentage increase and a percentage decrease?

## Literacy focus

- Key terms: None in this section
- Ask students to describe a real-life example of a percentage increase and decrease. Try to lead students to describing, e.g., mortgages, loans and bank accounts.

## Part 1

- Revise the use of percentage multipliers by asking students questions such as: 'What is two per cent as a multiplier?' (0.02) Include some more difficult questions such as: 'What is 0.8% as a multiplier?' (0.008) 'What is 3.4% as a multiplier?' (0.034)
- Ask students questions about working out a percentage of a quantity to check prior knowledge, e.g. ask how they would work out 13% of 40.
- Lead to questions involving increasing by a percentage, e.g. ask how they would increase an amount by 13%. Students will usually say: 'Work out 13% and add it on'.
- Repeat for other values.
- Now move on to decreasing by a percentage. Ask students, for example, how they would work out 6% of 70. Then ask them how they would decrease 70 by 6%.

## Part 2

- Following on from Part 1, display this table of multipliers.

| 1.05 | 0.05 | 0.95 | 1.5 | 0.5 |
|------|------|------|------|------|
| 0.85 | 0.15 | 1.15 | 0.25 | 1.25 |
| 0.75 | 0.55 | 0.45 | 1.55 | 1.45 |

- Ask students questions about the multipliers, starting with simple percentages, e.g. 'What percentage is equivalent to the multiplier 0.05?' (5%), 0.45? (45%), 0.5? (50%) and so on.
- Now ask what percentage is equivalent to the multiplier 1.25 (125%).
- Check if students remember that this represents a 25% increase when used as a multiplier.
- Repeat for 1.5 (50% increase), 1.15 (15% increase), 1.05 (5% increase), 1.55 (55% increase).
- Refer students to Example 7, pointing out that they can use the adding on or subtracting methods but that it is also good to understand the multiplier method. Now refer students to Example 8. Spend time explaining that an increase means that you want to keep 100% and add on the percentage. This may help the concept of the multiplier being 1 point something.
- Now ask students to identify the multiplier from the table that represents a 5% decrease (0.95). Repeat for other decreases, e.g. 0.85 (15% decrease), 0.75 (25% decrease).
- Example 9 in the Student Book shows how to work out the percentage and then decrease the original value by this amount.
- Example 10 uses the multiplier method. Explain that you have 100% but need to deduct the percentage from this and keep the rest. This will help the concept of the multiplier being zero point something.
- **Students can now do Exercise 16C from the Student Book.**

| R&P 1–5, 8a, 9, 12 | Calculator all | CM 6, 7, 10, 11, 13 | MR n/a | PS n/a | EV 8b, c |
|---|---|---|---|---|---|

## Part 3

- Tell students that they have £100.
- Ask half the class to increase the £100 by 10% and then decrease the answer by 10%. (£99)
- Ask the other half to decrease the £100 by 10% and then increase the answer by 10%. (£99)
- Then ask all students to show their answers on a mini-whiteboard at the same time.
- Establish that the result is always £99 but ask students why it is not £100. (The decrease is from a larger amount each time.)

### Learning objectives
- Express one quantity as a percentage of another
- Work out percentage change

### Resources and homework
- Student Book 16.4: pages 382–385
- Practice Book 16.4

### Making mathematical connections
- Percentage and decimal equivalents.
- Decimal multiplication.

### Making cross-curricular connections
- **Business; Accounting** – working with profit and loss
- **Relevance** – solving money problems

### Prior learning
- Students need to know how to use a percentage multiplier.

### Working mathematically
- Students will use fractions of amounts to find the value as a percentage.
- Students will find percentage change.

### Common misconceptions and remediation
- Students frequently forget to make sure that the units are the same. Encourage students to look at the units carefully for ever question.

### Probing questions
- If you scored 34 out of 60 in a test last year, and 54 out of 60 in the same test this year, what is the percentage change in your results?

### Literacy focus
- Key terms: percentage change, percentage decrease, percentage increase, percentage loss, percentage profit
- Ask students when they would need to work out one quantity as a percentage of another in real life. Discuss test scores with them and how, in the examinations, Foundation is 25% Number, but Higher is only 15% Number.

### Part 1
- Review the previous lesson by asking mental maths questions involving increasing or decreasing quantities by a percentage. For example:
- Increase £50 by 10% (£55)          Increase 100 cm by 2% (102 cm)
- Decrease 40 kg by 25% (30 kg)      Decrease 70 g by 50% (35 g)
- Write this table on the board for use in Part 2 of this section.

| Original amount | Percentage change | New amount |
|---|---|---|
| £50 | +10% | £55 |
| 40 kg | −25% | 30 kg |
| 100 cm | +2% | 102 cm |
| 70 g | −50% | 35 g |

- Repeat for other values. Increase the level of difficulty for **more able** students.

## Part 2

- Explain that this continues from Part 1 where, given the information in the first two columns of the table, they found the answers for the third column.
- Now, given the first and third columns or the first column and the value of the change, they can work out the percentage change.
- Explain that if the change is an increase, it is a percentage increase.
- Ask students to name each of these changes.
  - Change is a decrease (percentage decrease).
  - Change is a loss (percentage loss).
  - Change is a profit (percentage profit).
- Now ask students to look at the table and see if they can see how to get from £50 and £55 to 10%. **Less able** students may need the extra column showing the change.

| Original amount | Percentage change | Change | New amount |
|---|---|---|---|
| £50 | +10% | + £5 | £55 |
| 40 kg | −25% | − 10 kg | 30 kg |
| 100 cm | +2% | + 2 cm | 102 cm |
| 70 g | −50% | − 35 g | 35 g |

- Ask students how to get from £5 and £50 to 10%. (£5 is 10% of £50) Repeat for the other rows.
- Now explain that to express a quantity as a percentage of another, you write the first quantity as a fraction of the second quantity and then convert to a percentage.
- Work through Examples 11 and 12 with the class. Explain that these are the same as working out a percentage change; the change in Example 11 is £6; the change in example 12 is 75 cm.
- Write the formula on the board: Percentage change = $\dfrac{\text{change}}{\text{original amount}} \times 100\%$
- Show students that the formula works for each row in the table.
- For example, for £50 to £55 (Change = £5): percentage change = $\dfrac{5}{50} \times 10\%$
- Work through Example 13 in the Student Book where percentage change is again used to work out the profit or change.
- Example 14 requires students to work out the decimal multiplier, and again using the change, they can work out the percentage.
- **Students can now do Exercise 16D from the Student Book.**

| R&P 1–8 | Calculator all | CM 9–11 | MR n/a | PS 12 | EV 13 |
|---|---|---|---|---|---|

## Part 3

- Check students' understanding of the different types of problems by going through Exercise 16D again and identifying the questions about: percentage increase, percentage decrease, one quantity as a percentage of another.

# Section 16.5 Compound measures

## Learning objectives

- Recognise and solve problems involving the compound measures of rates of pay, density and pressure

## Resources and homework

- Student Book 16.5: pages 385–390
- Practice Book 16.5

## Making mathematical connections

- Equivalent fractions
- Rearranging equations and substitution

## Making cross-curricular connections

- **Science** – using formulae
- **Relevance** – developing logical thinking

## Prior learning

- Students should have come across speed, distance and time and know that compound measures use three variables connected in a triangle.

## Working mathematically

- Students will link the three variables in rates of pay, density and pressure within a triangle.
- **More able** students will transpose these formulae themselves and will not need to use the triangles.

## Common misconceptions and remediation

- Students often mix up or confuse what appears where in the triangle. Encourage students to learn a formula before writing it in a triangle.

## Probing questions

- What is meant by pressure?

## Literacy focus

- Key terms: compound measure, density, pressure
- Describe to an employee how you work out their rate of pay.

## Part 1

- Mass = density × volume
- Density = mass ÷ volume
- Volume = mass ÷ density
- Ask students to come up with a way to link all of these variables together.
- Encourage students to think about the DST triangle and how this might be used to help them work out a triangle for this question.

# Part 2

## Rates of pay

- Pay = hours worked × hourly rate.
- Describe to students how they can work out each of the three variables using a compound measure triangle.
- Work through Example 15, which uses the rate of pay triangle. Once students have worked out the total (or gross) earnings, students need to work methodically to find the deductions.
- Explain to students how they can find the take-home pay.
- **Students can now do Exercise 16E from the Student Book.**

| R&P 1–3, 5–7 | Calculator all | CM 4 | MR n/a | PS 8–10 | EV n/a |
|---|---|---|---|---|---|

## Density

- Density = mass ÷ volume.
- Use a compound measure triangle and show students how they put all the variables into this. Describe how to work out each of the three variables using the triangle.
- Work through Examples 16 and 17, which use the density triangle to work out density and then mass. Discuss with students again how to input the variables they know to work out the variable they want.

## Pressure

- Pressure = $\dfrac{\text{force}}{\text{area}}$ .
- Use a compound measure triangle and show students how they put all the variables into this. Describe how to work out each of the three variables using the triangle.
- Example 18 uses the pressure compound measure triangle. Show students with this example how important it is to spot the units. Students will often overlook that area is given in one unit but the question requires their answer to be in another unit such as $cm^2$ or $m^2$.
- **Students can now do Exercise 16F from the Student Book.**

| R 1–8, 10, 12a, c, 14, 20 | Calculator all | CM 9, 12b, 23 | MR 13, 15–18, 21 | PS 11, 19, 22 | EV n/a |
|---|---|---|---|---|---|

# Part 3

- Ask students the questions that follow.
- Using the knowledge gained from compound measures, make a compound measure triangle for this question and describe why it works.
    - The area of Trinidad and Tobago is 1980 square miles.
    - The estimated population density in June 2014 was 618 people per square mile.
    - Work out the population of Trinidad and Tobago.
      (Population density = population ÷ area
      Population = population density × area
      Area = Population ÷ population density)

# Chapter 17 Ratio and proportion and rates of change: Percentages and variation

## Overview

| | |
|---|---|
| **17.1** Compound interest and repeated percentage change | **17.3** Direct proportion |
| **17.2** Reverse percentage (working out the original value) | **17.4** Inverse proportion |

**Prior learning**

Know multiplication tables up to 12 × 12.
Know how to simplify fractions.
Know how to multiply and divide, with and without a calculator.
Know how to substitute values into expressions.
Know how to solve simple algebraic equations.

**Learning objectives**

**Ensure that students can: calculate compound interest and repeated percentage change; calculate a reverse percentage; solve problems where two variables are in direct proportion; solve problems where two variables are in inverse proportion; recognise graphs that show direct and inverse proportion; work out problems about growth and decay; work out problems about original values.**

In the examination, students will be expected to:
- calculate simple interest
- calculate compound interest
- solve problems involving repeated percentage change
- calculate the original amount, given the final amount, after a known percentage increase or decrease
- solve problems in which two variables have a directly proportional relationship (direct variation)
- work out the constant of proportionality
- recognise graphs that show direct variation
- solve problems in which two variables have an inversely proportional relationship (inverse variation)
- recognise the constant of proportionality.

**Extension**

Challenge **more able** students with reverse percentage change and more complex direct proportion and inverse proportion problems.

## Curriculum references

| Section | GCSE specification |
|---|---|
| 17.1 | R9, 16 |
| 17.2 | R9, 16 |
| 17.3 | R7, 10, 13, 14 |
| 17.4 | R7, 10, 13, 14 |

**Route mapping**

| Exercise | Accessible | Intermediate | Challenging | AO1 | AO2 MR CM | AO3 PS EV | Key questions |
|---|---|---|---|---|---|---|---|
| 17A | 1–5 | 6–10 | | 1–8a, 9a | 8b, 9b, 10 | | 1, 8, 10 |
| 17B | 1 | 2–10 | | 1–10a | 10b | | 1, 2, 8, 10 |
| 17C | | 1, 2 | 3–10 | 1, 2a, b, 3a, b, 4, 5, 6 | 2c, 4, 7 | 3c, 8–10 | 1, 4, 7, 8, 9 |
| 17D | | | 1–10 | 1–4, 6 | 5, 7, 8 | 9, 10 | 1, 4, 7, 10 |

*Key questions are those that demonstrate mastery of the concept, or which require a step-up in understanding or application. Key questions could be used to identify the questions that students must tackle, to support differentiation, or to identify the questions that should be teacher-marked rather than student-marked.*

## About this chapter

**Making connections**: Students will calculate percentages of amounts, work with ratio and the unitary ratio. They will read from and interpret graphs, especially conversion graphs. The material in this chapter brings together algebraic manipulation, solving equations and rearranging formulae.

**Relevance**: There is an emphasis on the use of logic and thinking in steps. There are applications in engineering, architecture, manufacturing, project management and many other areas, with STEM careers being a strong focus.

**Working mathematically**: Students will work on problems about finding repeated percentage increases and compound increases of an amount. They will rearrange equations using inverse operations and finding the value of the constant of proportionality, $k$.

**Assessment**: In each section of this chapter, ensure that students have a good grasp of the key questions in each exercise before moving on. (Refer to the 'Route mapping' table.) Encourage students to read and think about the 'Ready to progress?' statements on page 408 of the Student Book. Check students' understanding at the end of the chapter, formatively, using peer assessment. Students could do a mini test in the form of the 'Review questions' on pages 408–409 of the Student Book. Follow up the test with an individual target-getting session, based on any areas for development that a student may have.

## Worked exemplars from the Student Book (page 407) – suggestions for use
- Present students with the same question but different numbers. They should use the exemplar to mirror the working, in full or just refer to the notes.
- Copy and cut the exemplars into cards. Students should match the working with the notes.
- Alternatively, copy and cut the working into cards but split the label/description from the working.

**Answers to the Student Book questions are available on the CD-ROM provided.**

# Section 17.1 Compound interest and repeated percentage change

## Learning objectives
- Calculate simple interest
- Calculate compound interest
- Solve problems involving repeated percentage change

## Resources and homework
- Student Book 17.1: pages 395–397
- Practice Book 17.1

## Making mathematical connections
- Percentage and decimal equivalents.
- Decimal multiplication.

## Making cross-curricular connections
- **Business; Accounting** – working with profit and loss
- **Relevance** – solving money problems

## Prior learning
- Students need to know how to find a percentage of an amount and how to write a percentage increase or decrease as a decimal multiplier.

## Working mathematically
- Students need to understand the difference between simple and compound interest. In order to do both they will need to be able to calculate a percentage of an amount.
- Compound interest requires students to use a decimal multiplier to do the repeated percentage.
- Students must find a single decimal multiplier so that they can use the efficient method for calculating compound interest.

## Common misconceptions and remediation
- When finding the decimal multiplier for a new quantity after a percentage decrease, students often forget to subtract the percentage from 100. Remind students that they are looking for what is left after a reduction.

## Probing questions
- What is the difference between simple interest and compound interest?
- As a single decimal multiplier, what would an increase of 4% per year be after three years for simple interest and compound interest?

## Literacy focus
- Key terms: annual rate, compound interest, principal, simple interest
- Ask students to explain which bank investment would be best in terms of financial gain (encourage students to show their workings):
  - £100 in a 3% simple interest account for two years
  - £100 in a 3% compound interest account for two years.

## Part 1

- Work out the decimal multiplier for:
  - o increases of 30%, 12%
  - o decreases of 6.4%, 1.5%.
- Encourage students to write their numbers as a percentage first and then as a decimal, e.g.:
  - o 100 + 30 = 130% = 1.3
  - o 100 + 12 = 112% = 1.12
  - o 100 − 6.4 = 93.6% = 0.936
  - o 100 − 1.5 = 98.5% = 0.985.

## Part 2

- Discuss the difference between simple interest and compound interest with students.
- Example 1 in the Student Book shows a comparison of a simple interest and a compound interest bank account.
- Demonstrate to students that a simple interest bank account pays the same interest each year; a compound interest account pays interest yearly (annually) on the amount that is in the account, so one actually gets interest on the interest from previous years.
- Very often with these types of questions, students are asked to compare two types of accounts. Ensure that students are able to write down an explanation for their workings.

**Using your calculator**

- Refer the class to this heading in the Student Book.
- Students will notice that compound interest calculations are very long, so it is easy to make an error due to having to repeat the calculations.
- Encourage students to use the formula $A = P(1 + \frac{r}{100})^n$ to be able to find compound interest in one calculation.
- **Students can now do Exercise 17A from the Student Book.**

| R 1–7, 8a, 9a | Calculator all | CM n/a | MR 8b, 9b, 10 | PS n/a | EV n/a |
|---|---|---|---|---|---|

## Part 3

- A scientist grows bacteria in a Petri dish. At the start there are 1000 bacteria.
- The bacteria double in number every 20 minutes.
- How many bacteria will be present after four hours? (Answer: 4 hours = 240 minutes; 240 ÷ 20 = 12 × 1000 = 12 000)

### Learning objectives

- Calculate the original amount, given the final amount, after a known percentage increase or decrease

### Resources and homework

- Student Book 17.2: pages 397–399
- Practice Book 17.2

### Making mathematical connections

- Percentage and decimal equivalents.
- Decimal multiplication

### Making cross-curricular connections

- **Business; Accounting** – working with profit and loss
- **Relevance** – solving money problems

## Prior learning

- Students need to know how to find a percentage of an amount and how to write a percentage increase or decrease as a decimal multiplier.

## Working mathematically

- A single decimal multiplier will be needed to find the original price.
- Students will need to be able to rearrange formulae to find the original cost of an item.

## Common misconceptions and remediation

- When finding percentage decrease as a decimal students often forget to subtract the percentage from 100. Remind students they are looking for what is left after a reduction.

## Probing questions

- The sale price after a 15% discount is £42.50. What was the original price?

## Literacy focus

- Key terms: None in this section
- Encourage students, particularly in sale price examples, to discuss what percentage of the original value the item is now worth, before they work out the actual value.

## Part 1

- Practise complements of 100 with the class, e.g. ask students to work out 100 – 49, 100 – 32, 100 – 93.
- Ask students if they can see an easy way to work out these problems.

## Part 2

**The unitary method**

- Refer to the three steps in the Student Book, as follows (write them on the board):
  Step 1: Set the final percentage equal to the final value.
  Step 2: Use this to calculate the value of 1% of the original value.
  Step 3: Multiply by 100 to work out 100% (the original value).
- Work through Examples 2 and 3, which consolidate the unitary method.
- Point out to students that they need to divide amount by the percentage to find 1%, before finding the 100% or original value.

**The multiplier method**

- Refer to the two steps in the Student Book, as follows (write them on the board):
  Step 1: Write down the multiplier.
  Step 2: Divide the final value by the multiplier to give the original value.
- Now work through Example 4, which shows how a reduction of 12% can be found using the unitary and multiplier method.
- Using complements of 100%, students need to understand that 88% of the value remains; 88% as a decimal is 0.88; by dividing the value by 0.88 they will get the original value.
- Remind students that the original value will be a bigger value.
- **Students can now do Exercise 17B from the Student Book.**
  R 1–10a          Calculator all          CM 10b          MR n/a          PS n/a          EV n/a

# Part 3

- Give students three household items of which the prices have been reduced, e.g.:
  o Washing machine A is now £200 after a 5% reduction.
  o Washing machine B is now £180 after an 8% reduction.
  o Washing machine C is now £210 after a reduction of 2.5%.
- Work out which washing machine was the most expensive before the price reductions.
- Which washing machine has the biggest decrease in price?

## Learning objectives

- Solve problems in which two variables have a directly proportional relationship (direct variation)
- Recognise the constant of proportionality
- Recognise graphs that show direct variation.

## Resources and homework

- Student Book 17.3: pages 399–403
- Practice Book 17.3

## Making mathematical connections

- Equivalent fractions
- Rearranging equations and substitution

## Making cross-curricular connections

- **Science** – using formulae
- **Relevance** – developing logical thinking

## Prior learning

- Students will find that knowing squares, square roots, cubes and cube roots of integers speeds up working out the answers to many of the questions.
- They should be able to substitute values into algebraic expressions and solve simple algebraic equations.

## Working mathematically

- Encourage students to articulate their methods for numerical fractions and then to apply these to algebraic fractions.
- Structure tasks so that students can work out the methods for themselves, either by increasing the difficulty incrementally or through one straightforward and one complex example.

## Common misconceptions and remediation

- Some students find the constant of proportionality $k$ and then stop, without completing the question. Encourage them to check that they have answered the question completely.
- Students sometimes assume that all relationships are linear. They should highlight or underline words such as square, cube, square root and cube root, to ensure that they use them in their equations.

## Probing questions

- In a spring, the tension ($T$ newtons) is directly proportional to its extension ($x$ cm).
- When the tension is 150 newtons, the extension is 6 cm.
  - How would you find a formula for $T$ in terms of $x$?
  - How would you calculate the tension in newtons when the extension is 15 cm?

## Literacy focus

- Key terms: constant of proportionality, direct proportion, direct variation
- Tell students that they need to be explicit about the language of equivalence and avoid 'cross-multiplication'. Ask students to explain why a constant is needed.

## Part 1

- Give students an oral test on squares, square roots, cubes and cube roots. (GCSE requirements are to know the square numbers of 1–15, and the cube numbers of 1–5 and

10.) Include the corresponding square roots and cube roots, with which students should also be familiar.
- Draw a table showing square numbers and ask students to give you the corresponding square roots.
- Repeat for cubes.

## Part 2

- Display this table and ask students for the connections between $y$ and $x$. ($y = 2x$). Try to get across that $y$ is two lots of $x$, or if you halve $y$ you get $x$. Students need to spot that the pattern is linear.

| $x$ | 1 | 2 | 3 | 4 | 5 |
|-----|---|---|---|---|----|
| $y$ | 2 | 4 | 6 | 8 | 10 |

- Ask for the value of $y$ when $x = 150$ (300). Explain that as $x$ increases, $y$ increases, and as the graph of $y = 2x$ passes through the origin, they are directly proportional.
- Show students how to obtain the equation if they cannot spot it.
- Write: '$y$ is directly proportional to (or varies directly as) $x$, so using symbols this is $y \propto x$'.
- Point out that this means that $y$ is a constant multiple of $x$, so $y = kx$, where $k$ is called the constant of proportionality. Now explain that as they know some values for $x$ and $y$ they can find $k$. For example, using $x = 1$ and $y = 2$ gives $2 = k \times 1$, so $k = 2$ and $y = 2x$.
- Example 5 requires students to work out how many hours the sun shines. Then they need to multiply this by 5 (each hour of sun light generates 5 kW of electrical energy). Tell students that they need to be careful with units in the second part and change the total payment in pounds and pence to pence only. Then they need to divide by 4.4p to find the total hours of sunshine.
- Work through Example 6, which uses a unitary method to find the cost of one hour before finding the cost of 5 hours. The cost of one hour is then used to find how many hours it will take if the repair cost is £240, by dividing by the repair cost for one hour.
- Example 7 uses an equation for two variables, which are in direct proportion. Show students how to substitute into the formula to find the missing variable. In part b, students need to rearrange the equation. Remind students to use inverse operations. Part c requires students to work out the value of $T$ at 12 and again at 30, and then subtract the values.
- Example 8 allows students to think about what 80 is. Encourage discussion on the constant of proportionality. Once they have this, parts b and c are about substituting values into the formula as in the previous example. Part d is multistep and students will need to find the cost of three cups of tea; then seven cups of tea and subtract the products to find the difference. At this point, show students how they could have used a graph to reach the same endpoint.
- Example 9 uses a graph to demonstrate variables in direct proportion. Students will need to work out the constant of proportionality themselves by dividing $y$ by $x$. Once they know the constant, they can substitute their values into the equation.
- **Students can now do Exercise 17C from the Student Book.**

| R 1, 2a, b, 3a, b, 4–6 | Calculator 3c, 4–7 | CM n/a | MR 2c, 4, 7 | PS 3c, 9, 10 | EV 8 |
|---|---|---|---|---|---|

## Part 3

- Prepare students for the next section on inverse variation by asking them to think of variables where, as one increases the other decreases, e.g. number of people building a wall and time taken.

# Section 17.4 Inverse proportion

## Learning objectives

- Solve problems in which two variables have an inversely proportional relationship (inverse variation)
- Recognise the constant of proportionality

## Resources and homework

- Student Book 17.4: pages 404–406
- Practice Book 17.4

## Making mathematical connections

- Rearranging simple formulae
- Solving equations
- Using reciprocal

## Making cross-curricular connections

- **Science** – using formulae
- **Computing** – applying logic
- **Relevance** – programming languages; business use of flow diagrams

## Prior learning

- As in the previous lesson, students will find that knowing squares and square roots, cubes and cube roots of integers speeds up working out the answers to many of the questions.
- They should also be able to substitute values into algebraic expressions and solve simple algebraic equations.

## Working mathematically

- Encourage students to be able to move forwards and backwards when rearranging an equation and to be able to articulate how they are balancing at each step.
- Give students numbers and fractions and ask for their reciprocals.
- Extend students by asking them to create formulae from a proportionality statement that include more complicated elements – powers, roots.

## Common misconceptions and remediation

- Students ignore the word 'inversely' and treat it as direct proportion, or they incorrectly rearrange the equation, after substituting, to find the value of the required variable. Point out these errors as students make them and provide extra examples for practice.
- As in the previous lesson, students often ignore words such as: square, cube, square root, cube root. It will help if they highlight or underline these words and 'inverse' or 'indirect'.

## Probing questions

- What is meant by 'direct proportion'?
- What is meant by 'inverse proportion'?
- How do you write an equation from a statement of proportionality?

## Literacy focus

- Key terms: inverse proportion, inverse variation
- Ask students to describe the steps from the statement of proportionality, to the equation, to finding the constant to substituting values in.

## Part 1

- Pose the following problems:
  o Tom (or pick a student) hired a taxi to take him ice-skating. It cost him £30.
  o If Tom and a friend went, how much would it cost each of them?
  o If Tom and two friends went, how much would it cost each of them?
  o If Tom and three friends went, how much would it cost each of them?

In other words, the more people who use the taxi, the less it costs each of them – this is inverse proportion. Put the information in a table.

| People in taxi | 1 | 2 | 3 | 4 | 5 |
|---|---|---|---|---|---|
| Cost per person | £30 | £15 | £10 | £7.50 | £6 |

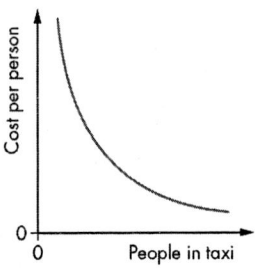

- Sketch the graph on the right to show inverse proportion.
- Explain that this is a reciprocal graph.

## Part 2

- Explain that the only difference between direct and inverse proportion is that inverse proportion uses reciprocals. Make a table to illustrate this. Ask students to complete it for square roots and cube roots.
- Show students how to set up the equation to find the constant from the statement of proportionality. Once students have found the constant, show them how to substitute values into the equation.
- Show students a relationship between $y$ and $x$ that is inversely proportional. Discuss setting up the equation from the statement of proportionality and how to find the constant.

| Direct proportion | | Inverse proportion | |
|---|---|---|---|
| $y \alpha x$ | $y = kx$ | $y \alpha \dfrac{1}{x}$ | $y \alpha \dfrac{k}{x}$ |
| $y \alpha x^2$ | $y = kx^2$ | $y \alpha \dfrac{1}{x^2}$ | $y \alpha \dfrac{k}{x^2}$ |
| $y \alpha x^3$ | $y = kx^3$ | $y \alpha \dfrac{1}{x^3}$ | $y \alpha \dfrac{k}{x^3}$ |

$y \infty \dfrac{1}{x} \therefore y = \dfrac{k}{x}$. Substitute in values of $y$ and $x$ to find the constant.

- For Example 10, lead students through the thought process. If four men take three days to build a wall, how long will it take one man? Show students that we multiply the values together to get the value for one man. Talk students through the assumptions.
- Example 11 uses the compound measure of speed. It is important that students understand how to convert a fraction of an hour into minutes and can confidently convert between minutes and hours. Use the DST triangle if weaker students are struggling to manipulate the formula.
- You will need to show students how to substitute into the equations.
  **Recognising graphs that show inverse proportion**
- In Example 12, students find the constant by multiplying together the values from the graph. Once students have the constant they simply need to substitute in their values.
- **Students can now do Exercise 17D from the Student Book.**

| R 1–4, 6 | Calculator 1, 5, 7, 10 | CM n/a | MR 5, 7, 8 | PS 9, 10 | EV n/a |
|---|---|---|---|---|---|

## Part 3

- Students may not understand why inverse proportion graphs all have similar shapes when the functions are different. Ask students to plot the graphs for each of the following functions on the same grids in order to demonstrate the differences. Use a scale 0 to 6 for both axes.

$y = \dfrac{6}{x}$

| $x$ | 1 | 2 | 3 | 4 | 5 | 6 |
|---|---|---|---|---|---|---|
| $y$ | 6 | 3 | 2 | 0.5 | 1.1 | 1 |

$y = \dfrac{6}{\sqrt{x}}$

| $x$ | 1 | 2 | 3 | 4 | 5 | 6 |
|---|---|---|---|---|---|---|
| $y$ | 6 | 4.2 | 3.5 | 3 | 2.7 | 2.4 |

$y = \dfrac{6}{x^2}$

| $x$ | 1 | 2 | 3 | 4 | 5 | 6 |
|---|---|---|---|---|---|---|
| $y$ | 6 | 1.5 | 0.7 | 0.4 | 0.2 | 0.2 |

# Chapter 18 Statistics: Representation and interpretation

## Overview

| | |
|---|---|
| **18.1** Sampling | **18.3** Scatter diagrams |
| **18.2** Pie charts | **18.4** Grouped data and averages |

| Prior learning |
|---|
| Know how to draw and interpret pictograms, bar charts and line graphs.<br>Know how to extract information from tables and diagrams.<br>Know how to draw and measure angles.<br>Know how to plot coordinates.<br>Know how to work out the mode, the median, the mean and the range. |

| Learning objectives |
|---|
| **Ensure that students can: test a hypothesis; collect data to obtain an unbiased sample; draw and interpret pie charts; identify the modal group and estimate the mean from grouped data; draw scatter diagrams and lines of best fit; interpret scatter diagrams and the different types of correlation.**<br><br>In the examination, students will be expected to:<br>•  obtain a random sample from a population<br>•  collect unbiased and reliable data for a sample<br>•  draw and interpret pie charts<br>•  draw, interpret and use scatter diagrams<br>•  draw and use a line of best fit<br>•  identify the modal group<br>•  calculate an estimate of the mean from a grouped table. |

| Extension |
|---|
| Have students collect data from their class about student shoe size and height. Using this data, students could produce: pie charts for each data set, a scatter graph, estimated mean for each data set. The charts must be fully labelled. |

## Curriculum references

| Section | GCSE specification |
|---|---|
| 18.1 | S1 |
| 18.2 | S2 |
| 18.3 | S6 |
| 18.4 | S4 |

## Route mapping

| Exercise | Accessible | Intermediate | Challenging | AO1 | AO2 MR CM | AO3 PS EV | Key questions |
|----------|-----------|--------------|-------------|-----|-----------|-----------|---------------|
| 18A | | 1–7 | | 1 | 2–6 | 7 | 1, 2, 6 |
| 18B | 1–4 | 5–8 | | 1, 2 | 3–6 | 7, 8 | 2, 4, 8 |
| 18C | | 1–8 | | 1–4 | 5, 6, 8 | 7 | 1, 3, 6 |
| 18D | | 1–9 | | 1, 2, 5, 7 | 3, 4, 6, 9 | 8 | 1, 3, 8 |

*Key questions are those that demonstrate mastery of the concept, or which require a step-up in understanding or application. Key questions could be used to identify the questions that students must tackle, to support differentiation, or to identify the questions that should be teacher-marked rather than student-marked.*

## About this chapter

**Making connections**: This chapter extends the understanding and interpretation of the process of collecting and analysing data. Starting with how the source of data is decided on, the process of creating charts, which was begun in Chapter 3, is continued.

**Relevance**: There are many application areas for this analysis, ranging across the Humanities, Science, Engineering, Business Studies and Social Studies. The key skills here are of interpreting data as well as creating informative, visual summaries.

**Working mathematically**: Students should recall the work done in Chapter 3 on statistical measures, particularly estimating the mean and the median. Students should be able to decide on a course of action that will enable a hypothesis to be tested and conclusions made. Students should be able to work with frequency tables to produce pie charts and scatter diagrams. From any of these graphical presentations of data students should be able to make interpretive statements and comparisons.

**Assessment**: In each section of this chapter, ensure that students have a good grasp of the key questions in each exercise before moving on. (Refer to the 'Route mapping' table.) Encourage students to read and think about the 'Ready to progress?' statements on page 430 of the Student Book. Check students' understanding at the end of the chapter, formatively, using peer assessment. Students could do a mini test in the form of the 'Review questions' on pages 430–431 of the Student Book. Follow up the test with an individual target-getting session, based on any areas for development that a student may have.

### Worked exemplars from the Student Book (page 427) – suggestions for use
- Present students with the same question but different numbers. They should use the exemplar to mirror the working, in full or just refer to the notes.
- Copy and cut the exemplars into cards. Students should match the working with the notes.
- Alternatively, copy and cut the working into cards but split the label/description from the working.

**Answers to the Student Book questions are available on the CD-ROM provided.**

# Section 18.1 Sampling

## Learning objectives

- Obtain a random sample from a population
  Collect unbiased and reliable data for a sample

## Resources and homework

- Student Book 18.1: pages 411–414
- Practice Book 18.1

## Making mathematical connections

- Percentages
- Two-way tables
- Ratio

## Making cross-curricular connections

- **Geography; Science; Business Studies** – developing the skills for investigative statistical analysis in a wide variety of subjects
- **Relevance** – many applications in the sciences, humanities and business

## Prior learning

- Students should be comfortable with data presented as a two-way table.
- Students should also have a reasonable understanding of what a questionnaire or survey actually is, especially when the conversation through this section turns to bias.

## Working mathematically

- Encourage students to see the cross-curricular nature of this topic and its application in other aspects of their studies such as in Geography, Physical Education or English.
- A statistician's tasks encompass identifying the population and sample size for data collection as well as summarising and analysing the data collected to convey meaningful information.

## Common misconceptions and remediation

- Students sometimes confuse 'population' with, literally, the whole population of their home country, rather than the whole set of the subjects of the investigation, e.g. eels in the North Sea, players of a particular online game.
- Sometimes students are confused about what 'secondary' data is – clearly illustrate that this is data that has already been collected (and summarised) by someone else.

## Probing questions

- Ask students to explore the concept of 'bias', both in the wording of questions in a questionnaire, and when selecting the sample of a population.

## Literacy focus

- Key terms: bias, hypothesis, population, primary data, random sample, sample size, secondary data, survey, unbiased
- Ask students to define each key term. Also ask students to articulate the stages needed to carry out a successful investigation, thus drawing suitable and meaningful conclusions.

## Part 1

- Tell students that now you will do a quick survey on their television-watching habits.
- Choose five students randomly and ask silly questions about programmes on television.
- After asking the questions, ask the open question: What was wrong with my sample? Students may argue that it was not completely random, but you can argue otherwise!

- Ask the class how to choose a more appropriate sample. Must the sample be exactly half boys and half girls? In a single-sex class, question the five oldest students? Age and gender often influences viewing habits, especially if the sample contains a certain age range.

# Part 2

### Data collection
- Say that collecting data is the most important aspect of statistics. It is time consuming (and can be expensive), so students should take steps to ensure that they collect useful data.
- Discuss this hypothesis: 'Boys get more pocket money than girls'.
- Say that you want to test this; ask a student to say how much pocket money he or she receives. Then ask: 's the hypothesis true? Ask: Can I improve the investigation of this hypothesis? (yes) How? (by asking more students)
- Collect data from the rest of the class and ask students to calculate the average pocket money for girls and boys. Collate and display the results.
- Discuss whether or not the hypothesis is true.
- Again, ask: Can we improve on the investigation of this hypothesis?
- Prompt students if necessary, to get suggestions such as by asking: people of different ages; from different classes, schools or geographical areas.
- Work through the text in the Student Book, which describes the process for testing hypotheses. Explain how the process begins with a given problem, often a hypothesis.
- The next step is to make a plan about how to test the hypothesis.
- Next, gather the data and analyse it to see if it proves the hypothesis.
- Ask students how to describe how they could test the hypothesis: *Teachers are quicker at mental arithmetic than students*. Remind students that they do not need to collect the data, only consider how the hypothesis could be tested.
- Work through Example 1, highlighting the four parts that correspond to the hypothesis-testing diagram. Question students about this scenario, pointing out the key terms introduced so far and how they apply to this example.

### Random samples; Sample size
- Read through the text under both of these headings in the Student Book with the class and discuss how or why random sampling could present a problem (bias). Discuss why some measure of proportionality is required to keep the sample representative of the population.
- Work through Example 2 with the class.
- Test students' understanding by asking them to describe how they could choose a representative sample for each of the following scenarios.
  - You work for a national music magazine that wants to find out the country's favourite band. You attend a local music concert and hand out a questionnaire.
  - A local forestry group wants to find the mean size of conkers.
  - A biologist wants to find out the size and frequency of house spiders.
- **Students can now do Exercise 18A from the Student Book.**

| S 1 | Calculator n/a | CM 2, 3 | MR 4–6 | PS 7 | EV n/a |
|-----|----------------|---------|--------|------|--------|

# Part 3
- Test students' understanding of the key terms and concepts in this section through the use of scenarios for testing hypotheses or choosing representative samples.

# Section 18.2 Pie charts

| Learning objectives | Resources and homework |
|---|---|
| • Draw and interpret pie charts | • Student Book 18.2: pages 414–418<br>• Practice Book 18.2 |

| Making mathematical connections | Making cross-curricular connections |
|---|---|
| • Ratio<br>• Fractions<br>• Circles<br>• Percentages | • **Geography; History; Science, Business Studies** – comparing categories of data<br>• **Relevance** – interpretation of pie charts to illustrate data collected in many situations and contexts |

## Prior learning

• Students must know how to express one number as a fraction of another, how to calculate a fraction of a quantity, and how to draw and measure angles.

## Working mathematically

• Pie charts can be drawn to show values or percentages but they are constructed in the same way. If you have access to spreadsheet software it would be useful to show the completed pie chart so that **less able** students have a guide of what theirs should look like.
• It is often advisable to start drawing the smallest sectors first – see comment in Part 2.

## Common misconceptions and remediation

• When drawing a pie chart, students' biggest mistake is to measure each angle from the same starting point. Demonstrate the correct method of drawing pie charts, with particular emphasis on starting the measurement of each angle at the end of the previous sector.
• Students sometimes forget that the sectors are drawn in proportion to one another.
• When comparing two pie charts they need to concentrate on this fact and not confuse this with the sectors representing quantities (see Example 5 of the Student Book).

## Probing questions

• Ask students to look at the pie chart in question 7 of Exercise 18B. If it is known that the 'Don't know' sector represents 200 passengers, can students work out how many passengers are represented in the other sectors, and therefore how many passengers took part in the survey? (200 = 40°, so total passengers = 360° ÷ 40 = 9 × 200 = 1800 people)

## Literacy focus

• Key term: pie chart
• Ask students to write a set of instructions explaining how to draw a pie chart.

## Part 1

• Ask students a series of 'fractions of a quantity' questions with easily worked out answers, e.g. $\frac{45}{180} \times 200$ (50)... include some with a denominator of 360.
• Ask students to find all the factor pairs of 360. They will need these when working on Exercise 18B, so it may be worthwhile to ask students to write them down in their notes.

## Part 2

- Use Example 3 in the Student Book to illustrate a pie chart.
- Explain that it is a circular diagram (shaped like a pie), split into slices or sectors.
- Each sector represents a category of the data, and its size represents the frequency.
- Stress that each sector should be labelled clearly and the pie chart should also have a title.
- Explain that, in general, students will need to do some calculations when they draw pie charts themselves. Work through Example 4 to illustrate this.
- Point out the table of results and explain that the circle will be split into sectors.
- The size of each sector indicates the frequency of the data it represents.
- Ask: What fraction of the people surveyed used a train? **Less able** students will need help to see that this is $\frac{24}{120}$. Write how to reach this fraction. First, ask how many people are involved (120). Then ask how many used the train (24). This is 24 out of 120, or $\frac{24}{120}$. Write this fraction on the board; go through each category to give practice in finding the fractions.
- Say: We know that $\frac{24}{120}$ of the population uses the train; how do we show it on the chart?
- **Less able** students may not see how this fraction links to the circle. Lead the class to understand that they need to find this fraction of 360° (the angle at the centre of the circle), which will give the angle of the sector. **More able** students may see that 120 divides into 360 three times, so one person will be represented by 3° and they can just multiply the frequency by 3° each time to get the angle of the sector.
- Ask: How do we find $\frac{24}{120}$ of 360°? Look for understanding that they have to multiply 360 by this fraction. If students recognise it as 'divide 360 by 120 and then multiply by 24', great.
- Ensure that students have calculators, and that they know how to do this calculation.
- Go through each calculation to ensure that all students see how to find the angles.
- Discuss how to draw this pie chart using a protractor for the sector angles.
- **Less able** students would benefit from practice with drawing angles before they try to draw pie charts. Say that when drawing pie charts it is good practice to draw the smallest angles first so that any cumulative errors will be made on the largest angle. Ask **more able** students to suggest why. If necessary, explain that it is because the fractional error is small on the large angle, but the same-sized error on a small angle could be half that angle.
- Example 5 highlights a very important concept that often confuses students – the fact that pie charts show proportions; not quantity or actual numbers. Make sure students realise this. Say that it is vital that they remember this when trying to compare one pie chart with another.
- **Students can now do Exercise 18B from the Student Book.**

| S 1, 2 | Calculator n/a | CM n/a | MR 3–6 | PS 7, 8 | EV n/a |

## Part 3

- Draw a pie chart on the board with sectors of 120°, 90°, 45° (the other angle is 105°).
- Label the sectors, e.g. 'red', 'blue', 'white' and 'yellow'. Give the pie chart a suitable title and say that the whole pie chart represents 400 people. Ask how many each sector represents.
- Lead students to note that 90° is one-quarter of 360°, so the 90° sector represents 100 people. Repeat for the 120° and 45° sectors. Ignore the 105° sector unless students ask.
- Now say that the pie chart represents a different set of people; the 120° sector = 80 people. Ask: How many do the 90° and 45° sectors represent? (Ignore the 105° sector.)
- For **more able** students, change the numbers: 120° sector = 300 people. Ask how many the other sectors represent. Work out what 30° represents; then 90°, and halve this to get to 45°.

## Section 18.3 Scatter diagrams

### Learning objectives
- Draw, interpret and use scatter diagrams
  Draw and use a line of best fit

### Resources and homework
- Student Book 18.3: pages 418–423
- Practice Book 18.3

### Making mathematical connections
- Plotting a variable in two axes

### Making cross-curricular connections
- **Science; Geography; Physical Education** – working with mass, speed, population density, air quality, points scored, league position
- **Relevance** – uses in many situations when trying to find a connection between two sets of variables

### Prior learning
- Students must be able to plot points, using coordinates, and use appropriate scales on axes and interpret intermediate positions on them.

### Working mathematically
- Remind students that they will not usually see a near-perfect line created by their plots; it is vital to draw a line of best fit carefully. Any value that they read from the graph via the line of best fit is approximate, not an exact, expected value, and shows correlation, not causation.

### Common misconceptions and remediation
- The greatest difficulty that students have is drawing the line of best fit appropriately. Students often try to join all the plotted points, as in a line graph. They also try to make the line of best fit pass through the origin. Ensure that students have adequate practice to overcome this. Students could plot a point representing the mean of each variable, which will give a point that the line of best fit will pass through.

### Probing questions
- Ask students to make a presentation on data sets that show no correlation and the fact that correlation does not show causation. Use the data sets, 'IQ and hair length', and 'amount of rainfall and umbrella sales', to form the presentation.

### Literacy focus
- Key terms: correlation, extrapolation, interpolation, line of best fit, negative correlation, no correlation, positive correlation, scatter diagram
- Ask students to draw sketches and write descriptions with examples of positive, negative and no correlation relationships.

### Part 1
- Draw a coordinate grid. Call out coordinates of points; students should plot them on the grid.
- Show students sections of number lines marked in different scales and ask for intermediate values. First, indicate random points and ask students to identify them, then call out values and ask students to indicate where they are on the lines.
- Draw a coordinate grid and add a straight-line graph to it. Give students the value of one variable on the line and ask them to state the corresponding value of the other variable.

## Part 2

- Ask: If you get good marks in your Maths exam, will you get good marks in your English exam? This should lead to some useful discussion about trends and bucking the trend.
- Look at the scatter diagram in the Student Book, which shows Mathematics and English test results. Say that the points have been plotted from data and the pattern shows clearly that, for this group of students, there is a clear link between a good English mark and a good Mathematics mark – the higher the English mark, the higher the Mathematics mark.

### Correlation

- Introduce the word 'correlation', which students need to know. The first scatter diagram shows 'positive correlation' – as one variable increases in value, so does the other.
- This is not always the case. Discuss the three diagrams in the Student Book, which show positive, negative and no correlation. Ensure that students understand the clear difference between positive and negative correlation. Point out that 'no correlation' indicates that there is no clear link between the two sets of data, which is often useful to know.
- With **more able** students, extend this discussion to include 'strong positive' and 'weak positive' correlation, then 'strong negative' and 'weak negative' correlation.
- Patterns showing a slight correlation can be described as weak; those showing a very clear link are strong. Sketch some examples on the board.
- Use Example 6 to remind students that the question, 'What *type* of correlation?' needs an answer of positive, negative or no correlation, but the question, '*Describe* the correlation', requires a sentence: 'As people get older they eat less ice cream.'

### Line of best fit

- Talk about lines of best fit. Discuss the line of best fit drawn over the Mathematics/English marks scatter graph in the Student Book and ask the class to describe the lines.
- Identify that a line of best fit is just a straight line that shows the trend. It does not need to go through all the points, or even through any of them, but must simply be as close to them all as possible. There should be as many points on one side of the line as on the other.
- Talk to **more able** students about 'outliers', which are points that clearly buck the trend. It is usual for outliers to be present and, as long as there are only one or two in the data set, they can be ignored. Explain to **more able** students that a line of best fit can be a curve but, again, must just be one smooth curve, not an attempt to join all the points together.
- Ask: What English mark might you expect from Kim, who gained 70 marks in the Mathematics test? Follow the line from 70 on the Mathematics axis to the line of best fit, then back along to the English axis to find the mark of about 68.
- Ensure that the **more able** students see this as an approximation.
- **Students can now do Exercise 18C from the Student Book.**

| S 1–4 | Calculator n/a | CM 5, 6, 8 | MR n/a | PS 7 | EV n/a |

## Part 3

- Ask: What correlation is there between the distance you live from school and your marks in your last Maths test? Students should recognise that there is no correlation.
- Ask students for any correlations they can think of relating to themselves, e.g. distance of home from school and time taken to get to school (positive); height and shoe size (positive). Now ask about any correlations relating to cars.

# Section 18.4 Grouped data and averages

## Learning objectives
- Identify the modal group
- Calculate an estimate of the mean from a grouped table

## Resources and homework
- Student Book 18.4: pages 423–426
- Practice Book 18.4

## Making mathematical connections
- Averages
- Frequency tables

## Making cross-curricular connections
- **Science; Geography; Business Studies** – working with data, e.g. temperature, population, salaries
- **Relevance** – working out 'average' value in many contexts, where the data to be analysed is grouped

## Prior learning
- Students should know how to identify the mode, and work out the median, mean and range of a set of data. They should also be familiar with frequency tables and inequality symbols.

## Working mathematically
- Students will often be reluctant to add to tables of data given in a question.
- Encourage students to add new columns to tables, e.g. to record midpoints, to record *fm*.

## Common misconceptions and remediation
- Students often misunderstand the instruction 'find an estimate for the mean', which they understand as being 'guess the mean'. Stress that estimating involves doing a calculation.
- Students often make mistakes finding the midpoints of the groups. Encourage them to use the method of adding the endpoints and then dividing by 2.

## Probing questions
- Ask students to look at question 8 in Exercise 18D. Later Helen checked the data and realised that the numbers recorded in the table are actually correct.
- Why did you at first guess that that the frequencies for groups 10–19 and 20–29 should have been swapped?
- Should the frequencies naturally produce a kind of 'bell' shape? Why? or Why not?

## Literacy focus
- Key terms: continuous data, discrete data, estimated mean, grouped data, mid-class value, modal group
- Ask students to write definitions of these key terms in their 'mathematical dictionaries'.

## Part 1
- Give students some inequalities and ask them to suggest numbers that are included in them. Make sure that some of the inequalities are inclusive and that some of the suggestions are the extreme values.
- Use inequalities such as $5 \le x < 10$ and $10 < x \le 20$. Discuss what they mean.

## Part 2

- Put on the board some data similar to, but not the same as, Example 12, e.g.:

| Pocket money, $p$ (£) | $2 < p \leq 4$ | $3 < p \leq 4$ | $4 < p \leq 5$ |
|---|---|---|---|
| No. of students | 3 | 10 | 12 |

- Remind **less able** students what the inequality symbols mean, especially the difference between the symbols, and ask why they are used. Students must understand that the class boundaries need to be clearly defined so that each person can only be in one class.
- Ask the class for the modal group (£4–£5). If necessary, remind them that this is the range of values with the highest frequency.
- Ask for the median. It relates to the $\frac{26}{2}$ = 13th student, in order and is in the £3–£4 group, but the exact amount is not known. Explain to **more able** students that it is possible to estimate this amount by estimating how far into this class interval it is.
- Ask what two pieces of information are needed to calculate the mean (total amount of pocket money and total number of students). Ask students if they can find the total amount of pocket money. (No, because they do not know exactly how much each student got.) Stress that exact figures are not known, but that each figure lies in a certain range. This means that only an estimate for the mean can be calculated – a 'calculated estimate', not a guess.
- Explain that as they do not know exact values they can assume each student got the midpoint value of the group they are in. Some may have got more and some less. Take some time explaining this, as it is important that students understand why the midpoint is used. Using the £2–£3 group of three students, ask for three suggestions of possible amounts and work out their mean. Repeat this with another three suggestions and then compare these with the mean, if all three got £2.50.
- Draw a new vertical table, adding new columns – first the midpoint column. Ask students for the midpoints of the groups. **Less able** students may need help in finding the midpoints.

| Pocket money, $p$ (£) | Frequency, $f$ | Midpoint value, $m$ |
|---|---|---|
| $2 < p \leq 3$ | 3 | 2.50 |
| $3 < p \leq 4$ | 10 | 3.50 |
| $4 < p \leq 5$ | 12 | 4.50 |

- Explain that they can add the endpoints of the group and divide by 2.
- Ask how to estimate the total amount of pocket money for all students. (Multiply the frequency by the midpoint value.) Emphasise that this is an estimate, not a guess.
- Add the final column heading: $f \times m$, and with students' help, complete the column. Then ask what they need to do next. (Find the total of $f \times m$ and find the total of the frequency.)
- Ask students to work out these totals. (96.5 and 25)
- Students can now work out the estimated mean. (96.5 ÷ 25 = 3.86)
- Ask what 3.86 means. As it is money, it represents £3.86. Explain that this value does not need rounding but that as it is an estimate. They could give the mean as £3.90 – a rounded figure. Go through Example 7 to reinforce the method, explaining each step carefully.
- Explain the difference between discrete and continuous data. Discrete data consists only of separate numbers – number of students, shoe sizes, goals scored – whereas continuous data can take any value within a certain range – height, weight, time, capacity.
- **Students can now do Exercise 18D from the Student Book.**

| S 1, 2, 5, 7 | Calculator n/a | CM 6, 9 | MR 3, 4 | PS 8 | EV n/a |
|---|---|---|---|---|---|

## Part 3

- Give students some pairs of numbers and ask them for the midpoint of each pair.

# Chapter 19 Geometry and measures: Constructions and loci

## Overview

| | |
|---|---|
| **19.1** Constructing triangles | **19.3** Defining a locus |
| **19.2** Bisectors | **19.4** Loci problems |

**Prior learning**

Know how to measure lines and angles.
Know how to use scale drawings.

**Learning objectives**

**Ensure that students can: construct a triangle from given data; bisect a line and an angle; construct angles of 60° and 90°; define a locus; solve locus problems.**

In the examination, students will be expected to:
- construct accurate drawings of triangles, using a pair of compasses, a protractor and a straight edge
- construct the bisectors of lines and angles
- construct angles of 60° and 90°
- draw a locus for a given rule
- solve practical problems using loci.

**Extension**

Students can construct quadrilaterals and pentagons accurately. 30° and 45° angles can also be constructed.

## Curriculum references

| Section | GCSE specification |
|---|---|
| 19.1 | G1, 2 |
| 19.2 | G1, 2 |
| 19.3 | G1, 2 |
| 19.4 | G1, 2 |

## Route mapping

| Exercise | Accessible | Intermediate | Challenging | AO1 | AO2 MR CM | AO3 PS EV | Key questions |
|----------|-----------|-------------|-------------|-----|-----------|-----------|---------------|
| 19A | | 1–8 | | 1, 2 | 4, 8 | 3, 5–7 | 1, 3, 4, 7 |
| 19B | | 1–14 | | 2–5, 7–9, 12–14 | 11 | 1, 6, 10 | 1, 5, 10, 11 |
| 19C | | 1–10 | | 1, 2, 4, 6 | 5, 9 | 3, 7, 8, 10 | 2, 3, 9, 10 |
| 19D | | 1–17 | 18, 19 | 1–5, 7–13 | 16, 17 | 6, 14, 15, 18, 19 | 1, 4–6 |

*Key questions are those that demonstrate mastery of the concept, or which require a step-up in understanding or application. Key questions could be used to identify the questions that students must tackle, to support differentiation, or to identify the questions that should be teacher-marked rather than student-marked.*

## About this chapter

**Making connections**: Students need to know the various properties of triangles and quadrilaterals and the properties of regular polygons. Students should be able to use a protractor and a pair of compasses.

**Relevance**: The material in this chapter will enable students to define the locus of a point using a pair of compasses and straight edge to show construction lines. Using construction lines, students will be able to define regions within diagrams. Students will also be able to use properties of shapes in their constructions.

**Working mathematically**: Students will use a protractor, a pair of compasses and a straight edge to construct various 2D shapes using their properties. Students will also construct a perpendicular bisector and angle bisector to define the locus of a point.

**Assessment**: In each section of this chapter, ensure that students have a good grasp of the key questions in each exercise before moving on. (Refer to the 'Route mapping' table.) Encourage students to read and think about the 'Ready to progress?' statements on page 450 of the Student Book. Check students' understanding at the end of the chapter, formatively, using peer assessment. Students could do a mini test in the form of the 'Review questions' on pages 450–451 of the Student Book. Follow up the test with an individual target-getting session, based on any areas for development that a student may have.

### Worked exemplars from the Student Book (page 447) – suggestions for use
* Present students with the same question but different numbers. They should use the exemplar to mirror the working, in full or just refer to the notes.
* Copy and cut the exemplars into cards. Students should match the working with the notes.
* Alternatively, copy and cut the working into cards but split the label/description from the working.

**Answers to the Student Book questions are available on the CD-ROM provided.**

# Section 19.1 Constructing triangles

## Learning objectives

- Construct accurate drawings of triangles, using a pair of compasses, a protractor and a straight edge

## Resources and homework

- Student Book 19.1: pages 433–436
- Practice Book 19.1

## Making mathematical connections

- Accurately measure angles
- Properties of triangles and quadrilaterals

## Making cross-curricular connections

- **Physical Education** – defining regions
- **Relevance** – thinking logically

## Prior learning

- Students should be able to draw and measure straight lines, use a protractor to draw and measure angles accurately, open a pair of compasses and set them to a given radius, and draw arcs from a fixed point.

## Working mathematically

- Students will need to work methodically to construct SAS and ASA triangles.
- Students will need to measure lines and use a protractor and a pair of compasses to construct quadrilaterals.

## Common misconceptions and remediation

- Most errors in this type of construction are due to poor accuracy in drawing triangles. Tell the class that using good equipment and working carefully can help them to avoid losing marks in what are usually quite easy GCSE questions.
- Remind students to leave their construction lines on their diagrams.

## Probing questions

- What is the difference between constructing an ASA and SAS triangle?

## Literacy focus

- Key terms: construct, included angle
- Write a list of instructions for all the different constructions you make.

## Part 1

- Students will almost certainly have done this activity before, but it is a useful exercise in using compasses.
- Ask students to draw a circle of any radius, to fit the page.
- Now, keeping the compasses set to the same radius, they should place the point anywhere on the circumference and draw an arc to cut the circle in two places. They repeat, but now using as centres the points where the arcs cut the circle. They do this until they have drawn six arcs. If they have drawn the arcs accurately, they will produce a flower pattern with sharp pointed petals.

## Part 2

- Have plenty of plain paper available, as students will use a lot in these lessons. Ensure that they each have a pair of compasses fitted with a sharp pencil, a ruler, a protractor and another sharp pencil for drawing.
- Go through Example 1 in the Student Book with the class – to construct a triangle with three sides known. Then ask students to construct a few more triangles, giving them the three sides each time. Emphasise to **less able** students that they should always start by drawing the longest side as the base.
- Ask students to measure the largest angle (opposite the longest side), so that they can compare their accuracy and practise using a protractor.
- When students are confident about constructing triangles, given all three sides, go through Example 2 in which they are given two sides and the included angle. Again, they should draw the longest side first; then use the protractor to measure the angle and draw in a faint line. Remind **less able** students where to place the protractor to draw the given angle. Finally, they should use compasses to mark the length of the second given line, to find the third corner of the triangle. Ask students to measure the length of the new line to check their accuracy. Give them more triangles to draw, given two sides and the included angle.
- Now go through Example 3, constructing a triangle in which two angles and a side are known. Again, ask them to measure the length of the two other sides as a means to check accuracy. Remind students that, since they know the angle sum of a triangle (180°), they can always work out the third angle. Set them a few more examples of drawing triangles, given two angles and one side.
- Discuss with **more able** students why they would not necessarily be able to draw the triangle if they just knew two sides and one non-included angle. Give them an example, such as AC = 8 cm, BC = 5 cm, ∠BAC = 35°, and let them draw it to recognise the ambiguity for themselves.

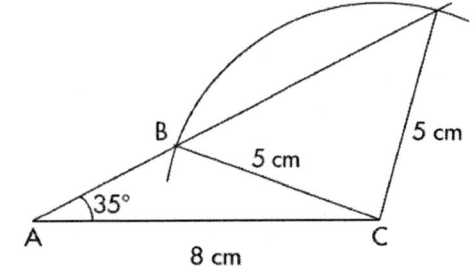

- **Students can now do Exercise 19A from the Student Book.**

| G&M 1, 2 | Calculator all | CM 8 | MR 4 | PS 3, 5–7 | EV n/a |

## Part 3

- Ask students to draw a line 5 cm long. To do this, they should draw a straight line, and then open their compasses so that the point is on zero on a ruler and the pencil point is on 5 cm. They should mark a point near the end of the line they have drawn, then mark the 5-cm length with an arc.
- Now ask students to draw arcs above the line, centred on each end of the 5-cm line they have marked. Then they should join each point on the line to the point where the arcs cross.
- Ask students what type of triangle they have drawn. Let them measure all the angles to check. (An equilateral triangle, 60°.)

## Learning objectives

- Construct the bisectors of lines and angles
- Construct angles of 60° and 90°

## Resources and homework

- Student Book 19.2: pages 436–439
- Practice Book 19.2

## Making mathematical connections

- Measure angles accurately
- Properties of triangles and quadrilaterals

## Making cross-curricular connections

- **Physical Education** – defining regions
- **Relevance** – thinking logically

## Prior learning

- Students should be able to use a pair of compasses correctly.

## Working mathematically

- Students will need to work methodically to bisect a line and an angle.
- Students will need to measure lines and use a protractor and a pair of compasses to construct angles and perpendiculars from a point.

## Common misconceptions and remediation

- Students may just measure lengths rather than construct them. You could tell students that many examiners would say 'arcs mean marks'.

## Probing questions

- What is meant by 'bisect'?
- What is a perpendicular bisector?
- What is an angle bisector?

## Literacy focus

- Key terms: angle bisector, perpendicular bisector
- Ask students to work in pairs. One partner should describe a perpendicular bisector (or angle bisector) without using the words. The other partner must guess what is being described.

## Part 1

- Ask students what they think 'bisect' means. Ask them to suggest other words that start 'bi-', such as *bicycle*, *bifocal*. Explain that 'bi' means two, so 'bisect' means cut in two.
- Ask students what they think 'perpendicular' means. Remind them that it means 'at right angles to'. Ask them for examples of lines in the room that are perpendicular to each other.

## Part 2

- Ensure that each student has a pair of compasses fitted with a sharp pencil, a straight edge and another sharp pencil for drawing. Also ensure that there is plenty of plain paper.
- With the class, go through how to construct a line bisector, reminding students that the arcs drawn are construction lines and so should be faint, but still visible. Get students to draw a few straight lines and then bisect them all.

**To construct an angle bisector**

- Talk about an angle bisector and go through how to construct this. They will need to draw quite a few angles of their own just to practise this skill, and they could use a protractor to check their accuracy.
- Then go through constructing an angle of 60°. **More able** students could try constructing an angle of 30° at this point, by constructing an angle of 60° and then bisecting it.

**To construct a perpendicular from a point to a line**

- Now show all students how to construct a perpendicular line from a point on a line and practise this with a few perpendiculars from various lines on their plain paper.
- **Less able** students may omit drawing a perpendicular from a point to the line at this stage, but **more able** students should attempt it.

**To construct the perpendicular bisector of a line**

- Place emphasis on setting the compasses more than halfway so that the arcs cross.
- Discuss with students how to construct an angle bisector. Place emphasis on not changing the radius of the compasses once starting this bisector.

**To construct an angle of 60°**

- Discuss with students how to construct a 60° angle. Again place emphasis on not changing the radius of the compasses.

**To construct a perpendicular from a point on a line (an angle of 90°)**

- Discuss with students how to construct a perpendicular from a point on a line (an angle of 90°) and how to construct a perpendicular from a point to a line.
- Ensure that students know they need to keep their construction lines on their drawings to gain full credit for these questions.
- **Students can now do Exercise 19B from the Student Book.**

| G&M 2–5, 7–9, 12–14 | Calculator all | CM 11 | MR n/a | PS 10 | EV 1, 6 |
|---|---|---|---|---|---|

# Part 3

- You will need a board pen with a piece of string (at least 50 cm long) tied to it.
- Ask one volunteer to bisect a 120° angle with the pen and the string.
- Ask a second volunteer to bisect one of the resulting 60° angles.
- Ask a third volunteer to bisect one of the 30° angles.
- Ask a fourth volunteer to check the size of the 15° angle with a board protractor.
- Draw a horizontal line, 40 or 50 cm in length, on the board.
- Give another volunteer the pen and the string and ask them to bisect the line.
- Ask the last volunteer to bisect one of the two halves.

# Section 19.3 Defining a locus

## Learning objectives
- Draw a locus for a given rule

## Resources and homework
- Student Book 19.3: pages 440–441
- Practice Book 19.3

## Making mathematical connections
- Measure angles accurately
- Properties of triangles and quadrilaterals

## Making cross-curricular connections
- **Relevance** – thinking logically

## Prior learning
- Students should be able to use a pair of compasses to draw a circle.
- They should know that the direct distance from the centre to any point on the circumference is always the same, the radius of the circle.

## Working mathematically
- Students will need to work methodically to bisect a line and an angle
- Students will need to measure lines and use a protractor and a pair of compasses to construct angles and perpendiculars from a point.

## Common misconceptions and remediation
- Students may not recognise the difference between the distance 'from a point' and the distance 'from a line'.
- Another problem is lack of accuracy. Students may have problems with scale; they need to take care to ensure they use the correct scale.
- Advise students that they also need to take care to interpret 'closer to' and 'further away' correctly.

## Probing questions
- What is meant by a 'region' within the diagram?

## Literacy focus
- Key terms: equidistant, loci (locus)
- Describe what is meant by equidistant.

## Part 1
- Pick a point in the classroom (or go outside if space is limited). Ask a student to move, always staying two metres from the point. Discuss the shape of the path traced out.
- Now choose two points. Ask a student to move, always staying the same distance from the two points. Discuss the shape of the path traced out.
- Now choose three points, call them A, B and C. Ask a student to move, staying the same distance from the lines AB and AC. Discuss the shape of the path that they have traced out.

## Part 2

- Provide plain paper and ensure that all students have rulers. Ask them to put a dot on the paper, about 10 cm down from the top and in from the left-hand side. Label this point C.
- Now ask students to mark four more dots on the paper, all 4 cm away from the point C, and label each of these four points P. Check quickly that students have the correct idea.
- **Less able** students may be confused, putting the points 4 cm away from each other.
- Now ask them to mark another four points, each 4 cm away from point C, still labelling them all P; then ask them to mark another four points.
- Unless a student has already commented, ask them what is so special about this set of points P that they are all marking. They should answer that they are making a circle around point C. Confirm this and explain that this circle is the path or *locus* (plural *loci*) of point P. The locus of point P, 4 cm from point C, is a circle, centre C, of radius 4 cm.
- Ask them to mark another point, D, on their paper and to find the locus of point P that is always 3 cm away from point D. Students should now be trying to draw a circle, radius 3 cm, around point D. Discuss what they have drawn and tell them they should all have drawn a circle, centred on point D, with radius 3 cm.
- Now ask them to draw a straight line, 4 cm long, somewhere in the space on their paper. Ask them to mark four points 3 cm away from this line, labelling each one P. Watch carefully what **less able** students do, as they may not realise that they need to be measuring the perpendicular distance from the line as 3 cm. It may take some time and discussion for students to understand this. Do not rush the point, as it is vital that they understand why the distance must be perpendicular.
- Now ask students to mark another four points P, then another four points. Then talk about what shape they are making. This will lead to useful discussion. Encourage students to describe where their points are. Some will only have marked points on one side of the line, whereas they can be on either side; at each end of the line, the points form a semicircle. Take time over this discussion as there are lots of issues, even for **more able** students to grasp. Say that the locus could be described as a racecourse shape.
- Ask students to draw another line, 3 cm long, and to draw the locus of a point P that is always 2 cm away from this line. Again, a racecourse shape should be drawn.
- Work through Example 4, which recaps that a locus of a fixed point produces a circle.
- Work through Example 5, which recaps that a locus between two fixed points produces a straight line that is equidistant from the two points.
- Work through examples 6 and 7, which provide practical examples.
- Remind students that the locus will be equidistant from the fixed points.
- **Students can now do Exercise 19C from the Student Book.**

| G&M 1, 2, 4, 6 | Calculator n/a | CM 9 | MR 5 | PS 3, 7, 8 | EV 10 |

## Part 3

- Ask students to imagine a bird tied by a tether that is 1 metre long to a point on a perch. What is the locus of the possible area of the bird's flight? (A sphere.)
- Now ask students to imagine the same bird tied to a perch that is 3 metres long by a tether of 1 metre in length. This time the tether is on a ring that can slide along the perch.
- What is the locus of the possible area the bird can fly this time? (A sausage shape with hemispherical ends.)

# Section 19.4 Loci problems

## Learning objectives
- Solve practical problems using loci

## Resources and homework
- Student Book 19.4: pages 442–446
- Practice Book 19.4

## Making mathematical connections
- Measure angles accurately
- Properties of triangles and quadrilaterals
- Finding the locus of a point

## Making cross-curricular connections
- **Relevance** – thinking logically

## Prior learning
- Students should be able to use a pair of compasses to draw a circle.
- They should know that the direct distance from the centre to any point on the circumference is always the same, the radius of the circle.

## Working mathematically
- Students will need to work methodically to bisect a line and an angle.
- Students will need to measure lines and use a protractor and a pair of compasses to construct angles and perpendiculars from a point.

## Common misconceptions and remediation
- As in the previous section, students may not recognise the difference between the distance 'from a point' and the distance 'from a line'.
- Another problem is lack of accuracy. Students may have problems with scale; they need to take care to ensure they use the correct scale.
- Advise students that they also need to take care to interpret 'closer to' and 'further away' correctly.

## Probing questions
- If a boat is travelling at night between two cliffs with a lighthouse on each, what path should the boat take to ensure it does not go into the cliffs either side?

## Literacy focus
- Key terms: none
- Describe the path of a locus from a fixed single point.
- Describe the path of a locus from a straight line.

## Part 1
- Provide plain paper and ask students to put three small crosses on their paper to represent local towns, e.g. Barnsley, Rotherham and Doncaster. Make sure that they choose three places that are not all in a line.
- Accuracy at this stage is not too important. Ask students to label the points, then to find all the points that are the same distance between, say Barnsley and Rotherham. This will be the perpendicular bisector of the line drawn between Barnsley and Rotherham. Then ask students to find all the points that are the same distance from Rotherham and Doncaster.
- Discuss the lines they have drawn and talk about what is special about the point of intersection of both lines. Draw out that this point is *equidistant* from all three towns.

## Part 2

- Ensure that every student has a pair of compasses with a sharp pencil in it, as well as another sharp pencil and a ruler.
- Talk through Example 8 to demonstrate a practical locus problem. Ensure that students understand what the problem is in the first place, before going to the solution.
- **Less able** students should do this work themselves, on their own plain paper, in order to be able to comprehend fully what it is they are doing. They can trace the points that are equidistant between the two towns and those that are a radius of 20 km from a fixed point.
- Talk through Example 9, which is a different type of locus problem using two intersecting circles. Again, **less able** students will learn more if they draw this solution for themselves. Ensure that students draw the circles and keep them on their diagram.
- Go through Example 10 only with the **more able** students, as the idea of having three metres of rope from one corner but only one metre of rope left for the opposite corner may confuse them.
- **Less able** students may be able to cope if they draw the diagram using a logical approach.
- **Students can now do Exercise 19D from the Student Book.**

| G&M 1–5, 7–13 | Calculator n/a | CM 16, 17 | MR n/a | PS 6, 14, 15, 18, 19 | EV n/a |

## Part 3

- Ask: What is the locus of a point that is one metre away from the walls, ceiling and floor of this classroom?
- This should provoke discussion and comment.
- Say to the class: There are two regions to consider, one inside the room, which will give a locus of a smaller cuboid shape; the other is outside the room (over and under), which will give an interesting shape of a cuboid with rounded corners. Talk about the shape of these corners. (They will be quarter spheres.)

# Chapter 20 Geometry and measures: Curved shapes and pyramids

## Overview

| | |
|---|---|
| **20.1** Sectors | **20.3** Cones |
| **20.2** Pyramids | **20.4** Spheres |

**Prior learning**

Know the formula for the area of a rectangle (area = length × width *or A = lw*)
Know the formula for the area of a triangle (area = ' × base × height *or A = ' bh*)
Know the formula for the area of a circle (area = π × radius$^2$ *or A = πr$^2$*)
Know the formula for the circumference of a circle (circumference = π × diameter *or C = πd*)
Know the formula for the volume of a prism (volume = area of cross section × length).

**Learning objectives**

**Ensure that students can: calculate the length of an arc; calculate the area and angle of a sector; calculate the volume and surface area of a pyramid; calculate the volume and surface area of a cone and a sphere.**

In the examination, students will be expected to:
- calculate the length of an arc
- calculate the area and angle of a sector
- calculate the volume and surface area of a pyramid
- calculate the volume and surface area of a cone
- calculate the volume and surface area of a sphere.

**Extension**

Students will need to be able to solve problems involving the shapes, for example, displacement. Students could work out the volume and surface area of a frustum.

### Curriculum references

| Section | GCSE specification |
|---|---|
| 20.1 | G18 |
| 20.2 | G17 |
| 20.3 | G17 |
| 20.4 | G17 |

## Route mapping

| Exercise | Accessible | Intermediate | Challenging | AO1 | AO2 MR CM | AO3 PS EV | Key questions |
|----------|-----------|--------------|-------------|-----|-----------|-----------|---------------|
| 20A | | | 1–9 | 1–4, 6 | 5, 8 | 7, 9 | 1–3, 7, 9 |
| 20B | | | 1–7 | 1, 3 | 2, 5, 6 | 4, 7 | 1, 2, 5, 7 |
| 20C | | | 1–5 | 1 | 2, 5 | 3, 4 | 1, 3, 4 |
| 20D | | | 1–4 | 1–3 | 4 | | 1, 4 |
| 20E | | | 1–5 | 1, 4 | 3 | 2, 5 | 4, 5 |
| 20F | | | 1–6 | 1–3 | 5 | 4, 6 | 2, 3, 5, 6 |

*Key questions are those that demonstrate mastery of the concept, or which require a step-up in understanding or application. Key questions could be used to identify the questions that students must tackle, to support differentiation, or to identify the questions that should be teacher-marked rather than student-marked.*

## About this chapter

**Making connections**: Students should be confident with finding the area and perimeter of shapes and should be able to substitute and rearrange formula. Students will be confident in using the formula for the area and circumference of a circle and finding the volume of a cylinder and a prism.

**Relevance**: Students should be able to work out the circumference of a circle and use this formula to work out the length of an arc. Students should be able to work out the area of a circle and use this to find the area of a sector. Students should be able to make repeated additions to find the surface area of a pyramid, cone and sphere. Students should be able to substitute into a formula to work out the volume of a sphere and cone.

**Working mathematically**: Students will identify the correct formulae to use to find the volume and surface area of a 3D shape. They will use the area of a circle or circumference of a circle formula to find the area of a sector or length of an arc. Using these skills will help students to find lengths, areas and volumes of different shapes.

**Assessment**: In each section of this chapter, ensure that students have a good grasp of the key questions in each exercise before moving on. (Refer to the 'Route mapping' table.) Encourage students to read and think about the 'Ready to progress?' statements on page 466 of the Student Book. Check students' understanding at the end of the chapter, formatively, using peer assessment. Students could do a mini test in the form of the 'Review questions' on pages 466–467 of the Student Book. Follow up the test with an individual target-getting session, based on any areas for development that a student may have.

### Worked exemplars from the Student Book (page 464) – suggestions for use

- Present students with the same question but different numbers. They should use the exemplar to mirror the working, in full or just refer to the notes.
- Copy and cut the exemplars into cards. Students should match the working with the notes.
- Alternatively, copy and cut the working into cards but split the label/description from the working.

**Answers to the Student Book questions are available on the CD-ROM provided.**

# Section 20.1 Sectors

## Learning objectives
- Calculate the length of an arc
- Calculate the area and angle of a sector

## Resources and homework
- Student Book 20.1: pages 453–455
- Practice Book 20.1

## Making mathematical connections
- Finding the circumference of a circle
- Finding the area of a circle
- Find a fraction of an amount

## Making cross-curricular connections
- **Physical Education** – working with or calculating lengths and areas of track
- **Relevance** – working logically

## Prior learning
- Students should know how to find the area and circumference of a circle.
- Students should also be able to find a fraction of an amount.

## Working mathematically
- Using the formula for the area of a circle and the circumference of a circle, students will find a fraction of this amount by substituting in given values into the formula.

## Common misconceptions and remediation
- Students often use the diameter instead of the radius in area calculations.
- Students also forget to square the radius, but instead multiply by 2 when finding the area.
- Students multiply the diameter by 2 instead of the radius in circumference calculations.
- Pointing out these errors as they occur will help to make students aware of them.

## Probing questions
- What is special about the angles in a circle?

## Literacy focus
- Key term: subtend
- Ask students to describe how to find the area and circumference of a circle.
- Ask students to describe how to find the circumference and area of a semi-circle.

## Part 1
- Draw three circles on the board; two with a diameter and one with a radius.
- Ask students to work out the area and circumference of each circle.
- Discuss what is meant by leaving your answers in terms of π.
- Using the same circles, cut them in half to make semicircles.
- Ask students to work out the area and perimeter of each semicircle.
- Area should be straightforward, as its half of a full circle.
- Perimeter will require more thought, as the curved length is half the circumference but students will need to add on the diameter to enclose the shape.

# Part 2

- Area of a sector = $\dfrac{x}{360°} \times \pi r^2$

- Length of arc = $\dfrac{x}{360°} \times \pi d$

- Discuss with students that all they are doing is working out a fraction of a full circle.

### Length of an arc and area of a sector

- Examples 1 and 2 in the Student Book show how to substitute into the formula to work out sector area and arc lengths.
- Remind students how to rearrange an equation to find the angle, as they are given the arc length and radius.
- **Students can now do Exercise 20A from the Student Book.**

| G&M 1–4, 6, 8 | Calculator all | CM n/a | MR 5 | PS 9 | EV 7 |
|---|---|---|---|---|---|

# Part 3

- A craftsperson would like to make a table with a width of 70 cm and a straight edge of 100 cm.
- At the top of the table is a semicircle with a diameter of 70 cm.
- What is the area of the table?
- Ask students to work logically though this problem, first working out the area of the rectangle and then adding the area of the semicircle (8924 cm²).

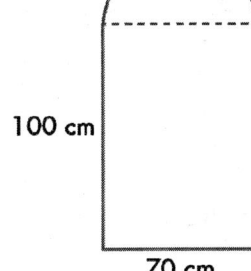

100 cm

70 cm

# Section 20.2 Pyramids

## Learning objectives
- Calculate the volume and surface area of a pyramid

## Resources and homework
- Student Book 20.2: pages 455–459
- Practice Book 20.2

## Making mathematical connections
- Finding the area of a triangle
- Finding the area of a square

## Making cross-curricular connections
- **Science** – calculating surface area to volume ratio
- **Relevance** – working logically

## Prior learning
- Students should be able to work out the area of a triangle and square.
- Students should be able to substitute into formulae.

## Working mathematically
- Students will substitute into the formula $\frac{1}{3}$ × area of base × vertical height to find the volume of a pyramid.
- Students will also substitute into the formula for area of triangles and squares and work methodically to add these together to find the surface area of a pyramid.

## Common misconceptions and remediation
- When finding the area of triangle students often forget to halve their answer. Encourage students to write down their formula and show where they have substituted.
- When working out the surface area of a pyramid, some students may forget to add on the base. Encourage these students to draw the faces, or even the net, so that they include all the faces.

## Probing questions
- How many faces does a square-based pyramid have?
- How do you work out the area of a triangle?
- How do you work out the area of a square?

## Literacy focus
- Key terms: apex, pyramid, slant height, vertical height
- Give students, in pairs or groups, a net of a pyramid and ask them to construct the pyramid. Then they should describe to each other all the key features of a square-based pyramid.

## Part 1
- Draw a mixture of five cubes and cuboids on the board.
- Give students the formula: volume = length × width × height
- Ask students to work out the volume of each 3D shape.
- Tell students that all they need to do is to substitute their values into the formula.
- Draw one further cube, with the length 3 cm, width 4 cm and volume 120 cm.
- Ask students how they would work out the height of the cuboid.

## Part 2

### Volume

- Volume = $\frac{1}{3}$ × area of base × perpendicular height.
- Remind students that they need to use their values in the volume formula.
- Work through Examples 3 and 4 in the Student Book with the class. Say that these examples show that students need to work out the area of the base and multiply the height by this.
- Encourage students to use the perpendicular height and not the slant height.
- **Students can now do Exercise 20B from the Student Book.**

| G&M 1, 3 | Calculator all | CM n/a | MR 2, 5, 6 | PS 4, 7 | EV n/a |

### Surface area

- Work through Example 5, which shows a square-based pyramid.
- To work out the surface area, students need to find the area of the base and the area of the triangles. A square-based pyramid has one square base and four triangles.
- Encourage students to write their working clearly or draw diagrams.
  **Students can now do Exercise 20C from the Student Book.**

| G&M 1 | Calculator all | CM 2, 5 | MR n/a | PS 3 | EV 4 |

## Part 3

- Tell students that they have a square-based pyramid with four equilateral triangles, all with the same side lengths.
- Tell them that the surface is 48 cm$^3$.
- Ask students to work out the side length (4 cm).

## Section 20.3 Cones

### Learning objectives
- Calculate the volume and surface area of a cone

### Resources and homework
- Student Book 20.3: pages 460–462
- Practice Book 20.3

### Making mathematical connections
- Volume and surface area of a pyramid
- Areas of sectors
- Lengths of arcs

### Making cross-curricular connections
- **Physical Education** – calculating length and area of tracks
- **Relevance** – working logically

### Prior learning
- Students should know how to calculate areas and circumferences of circles.
- Students need to be able to find the area of a sector.
- Students should be able to work out the length of an arc.
- They should be able to work out the volume and surface area of a pyramid.

### Working mathematically
- Students should be able to substitute into the formula for:

$$\text{volume} = \frac{1}{3} \times \text{area of base} \times \text{vertical height.}$$

- Similarly, they should be able to substitute into the formula for the curved surface area of a cone $A = \pi r l + \pi r^2$ where $l$ is the slant height.

### Common misconceptions and remediation
- Students often input the numbers incorrectly into the formula. Encourage students to write down the value of each letter first, and then write out the formula and substitute into it.

### Probing questions
- What would the curved surface of a cone look like if it were flat?

### Literacy focus
- Key terms: none
- Design a question based around the volume of a cone in real life.

### Part 1
- Tell students that they will design a party hat.
- Ask them what the template would look like.
- Once they have realised it is a sector of a circle, discuss how to work out the curved surface of a cone.
- Discuss the similarities of the curved surface of a cone and the area of a sector.
- Ask students what would happen if the party hat was to have a solid base.
- What would happen to the formula? (Students should realise this is $\pi r^2$)

# Part 2

- Students need to follow the instructions in the Student Book to work out the formula for the volume of a cone. Offer help as needed.
- **Students can now do Exercise 20D from the Student Book.**

| G&M 1–3 | Calculator n/a | CM 4 | MR n/a | PS n/a | EV n/a |
|---|---|---|---|---|---|

## Volume and surface area

- Discuss the following formula with students and ask them what each letter stands for.
  - $V = \dfrac{1}{3}\pi r^2 h$
  - $A = \pi r l + \pi r^2$
- Work through Example 6 in the Student Book with the class.
- This example substitutes the variables straight into the formula but the answers are left exact, in terms of $\pi$.
- Remind students how to this.
- **Students can now do Exercise 20E from the Student Book.**

| G&M 1, 4 | Calculator n/a | CM n/a | MR 3 | PS 2 | EV 5 |
|---|---|---|---|---|---|

# Part 3

- How much paper would be needed to cover a cornet-shaped ice-cream exactly (no gaps and no overlap) if it is 15 cm long, 17 cm slant height and a radius of 4 cm?
- Encourage students to draw a diagram to visualise the problem ($346 \text{ cm}^2$).

## Section 20.4 Spheres

### Learning objectives
- Calculate the volume and surface area of a sphere

### Resources and homework
- Student Book 20.4: page 463
- Practice Book 20.4

### Making mathematical connections
- Volume and surface area of a pyramid
- Volume and surface area of a cone

### Making cross-curricular connections
- **Physical Education** – calculating volume and surface area of sports equipment
- **Relevance** – working logically

## Prior learning
- Students should be able to substitute into formulae to work out the volume and surface area of a pyramid and cone.

## Working mathematically
- Students should be able to use the formulae for volume and surface area of a sphere to work out values using given variables.

## Common misconceptions and remediation
- When doing volume calculations students often get the 4/3 at the start incorrect. It may help students if you ask them to think that they are multiplying the numerator by 4 and dividing the answer by 3.

## Probing questions
- How do you work out the volume and surface area of a sphere? How is this similar to the volume and surface area of a cone?

## Literacy focus
- Key term: sphere
- Ask students to think about a piece of string tethered at one end. If the string is 5 cm long, describe the locus of its points.

## Part 1
- Show students a selection of footballs, tennis balls and table tennis balls.
- Ask them to work out how much material it takes to make each one and the amount of space each one takes up.
- Some students will notice that they need to find the radius.
- Although this is difficult to find, ask them to find the maximum length (diameter) and halve this to find the radius.

  Give them the formula: $V = \dfrac{4}{3}\pi r^3$

  Surface area is $A = 4\pi r^2$
- Ask students to work out the volume and surface area of each of the balls.

# Part 2

$$V = \frac{4}{3}\pi r^3$$

Surface area is $A = 4\pi r^2$

Remind students how to substitute into formula.

- Work through Example 7 with the class, which shows students how to substitute into the formulae to find the area and the volume of a sphere.
- **Students can now do Exercise 20F from the Student Book.**

| G&M 1–3 | Calculator all | CM n/a | MR 5 | PS 4, 6 | EV n/a |
|---------|----------------|--------|------|---------|--------|

# Part 3

Write down an equation and solve it to find the value of $x$ in each case.

a)   Volume = 600 cm³                    b)   Volume = 270 cm³

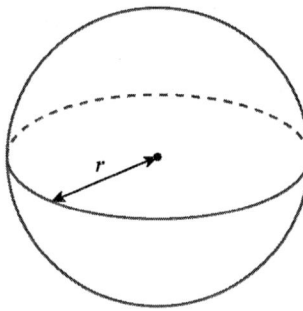
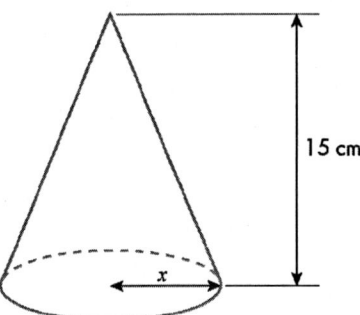

Answers:
a) 5.23
b) 4.15

# Chapter 21 Algebra: Number and sequences

## Overview

| | |
|---|---|
| **21.1** Patterns in number | **21.4** Special sequences |
| **21.2** Number sequences | **21.5** General rules from given patterns |
| **21.3** Finding the *n*th term of a linear sequence | |

| Prior learning |
|---|
| Know how to substitute numbers into an algebraic expression.<br>Know how to state a rule for a simple linear sequence in words.<br>Know how to factorise simple linear expressions. |

**Learning objectives**

**Ensure that students can: recognise rules for sequences; express a rule for a sequence, in words and algebraically; generate the terms of a linear sequence, given a formula for the *n*th term; find the *n*th term of a linear sequence; recognise some common sequences of numbers.**

In the examination, students will be expected to:
*   recognise patterns in number sequences
*   recognise how number sequences are built up
*   generate sequences, given the *n*th term
*   find the *n*th term of a linear sequence
*   recognise and continue some special number sequences
*   find the *n*th term from practical problems involving sequences.

**Extension**

**More able** students could find the *n*th term of a quadratic sequence. They could also find the rule for a geometric progression.

## Curriculum references

| Section | GCSE specification |
|---|---|
| 21.1 | A23 |
| 21.2 | A23–25 |
| 21.3 | A23–25 |
| 21.4 | A23–25 |
| 21.5 | A23–25 |

## Route mapping

| Exercise | Accessible | Intermediate | Challenging | AO1 | AO2 MR CM | AO3 PS EV | Key questions |
|---|---|---|---|---|---|---|---|
| 21A | 1–3 | 4 | 5–7 | 1–4 | 5, 7 | 6 | 4-7 |
| 21B | 1–3 | 4, 5 | 6–12 | 1–7 | 10–12 | 8, 9 | 1, 6–8 |
| 21C | | 1–6 | 7–12 | 1–7 | 9, 10a–c, 11 | 8, 10d, 12 | 1, 2, 4, 10 |
| 21D | 1, 2 | 3–6 | 7–17 | 1, 7–10, 14, 17a–c | 2–6, 11–13, 17d | 15, 16 | 3, 4, 11, 15 |
| 21E | | 1–10 | 11–16 | 1–7, 8a, 11a, b, 16 | 8b, 13, 14 | 9, 10, 11c, 12, 15 | 1, 4, 10, 11 |

*Key questions are those that demonstrate mastery of the concept, or which require a step-up in understanding or application. Key questions could be used to identify the questions that students must tackle, to support differentiation, or to identify the questions that should be teacher-marked rather than student-marked.*

## About this chapter

**Making connections**: The chapter brings together substitution into expressions, factorisation of simple expressions and stating the term-to-term rule for a sequence of numbers. For much of the chapter, the next step is Higher content with quadratics.

**Relevance**: Students will be able to find the general rule for a linear sequence. They will be able to work out if a term fits into a sequence and justify why. Students will also be able to draw and extend practical sequences.

**Working mathematically**: Students will work out the general rule, or *n*th term of a linear sequence, and a sequence in a practical context.

**Assessment**: In each section of this chapter, ensure that students have a good grasp of the key questions in each exercise before moving on. (Refer to the 'Route mapping' table.) Encourage students to read and think about the 'Ready to progress?' statements on page 490 of the Student Book. Check students' understanding at the end of the chapter, formatively, using peer assessment. Students could do a mini test in the form of the 'Review questions' on pages 490–491 of the Student Book. Follow up the test with an individual target-getting session, based on any areas for development that a student may have.

## Worked exemplars from the Student Book (page 489) – suggestions for use

- Present students with the same question but different numbers. They should use the exemplar to mirror the working, in full or just refer to the notes.
- Copy and cut the exemplars into cards. Students should match the working with the notes.
- Alternatively, copy and cut the working into cards but split the label/description from the working.

**Answers to the Student Book questions are available on the CD-ROM provided.**

# Section 21.1 Patterns in number

## Learning objectives
- Recognise patterns in number sequences

## Resources and homework
- Student Book 21.1: pages 469–470
- Practice Book 21.1

## Making mathematical connections
- Recognise square numbers and square roots
- Odd and even numbers
- Multiplication and multiples

## Making cross-curricular connections
- **Science** – spotting patterns and making predictions
- **Relevance** – working logically

## Prior learning
- Students should be familiar with the basic sequences such as even and odd numbers, and multiples of numbers up to 10.

## Working mathematically
- Students need to be able to work logically and recognise and identify patterns in number sequences.

## Common misconceptions and remediation
- Students may miscount digits or miscalculate with BIDMAS/BODMAS. Reminding them of the BIDMAS/BODMAS rules at the start may help to circumvent this.

## Probing questions
- What is the 100th odd number?
- What method did you use to find this out?

## Literacy focus
- Key terms: pattern, sequence
- Ask students to describe what an odd number is, and what an even number is.
- Ask students to explain what a multiple is, and how they would find a multiple.

## Part 1
- Play 'Make me say 25'.
- Tell students that you are thinking of a rule of the form $an \pm b$ and students must find out what the rule is.
- Say that they should try to find a number that gives the response of 25.
- As students suggest a value of $n$, give them the resulting value from applying the rule.
- For example, for the rule $2x - 1$, a suggested value of 5 gives a response of 9.
- Continue in this way, looking for a student to suggest 13, so the response for this rule would be 25.
- Discuss the rule, then play 'Make me say ...' again, changing the number (and the rule).

## Part 2

- Allow students to use calculators for this lesson.
- Write 0 × 9 + 1 on the board and ask students to work out the answer: 0 × 9 + 1 = 1.
- Repeat with 1 × 9 + 2 = 11, 12 × 9 + 3 = 111.
- Write these in a column, as:

  0 × 9 + 1 = 1
  1 × 9 + 2 = 11
  12 × 9 + 3 = 111

- Ask students to give the next two left-hand parts of this pattern without working them out (123 × 9 + 4, 1234 × 9 + 5).
- Ask students to predict the answers and then let them work them out to check (1111, 11111).
- Keep the pattern going until it breaks down (12 345 678 × 9 + 9 = 111 111 111).
- Both **more able** and **less able** students can generally find these patterns.
- Repeat this with the other patterns at the start of the section in the Student Book.
- The last possible calculations of the patterns are:
  - 9 × 3 × 37 = 999
  - 123 456 789 × 8 + 9
  - 66 667 × 66 667 = 4 444 488 889 (although this continues, the calculator display may go to standard form). It may be worth showing **more able** students that we can write very big numbers in standard form, and how to interpret the calculator display.
- Encourage students to look for symmetries and repeating patterns in numbers.
- **Students can now do Exercise 21A from the Student Book.**

| A 1–4 | Calculator n/a | CM 7 | MR 5 | PS n/a | EV 6 |
|-------|----------------|------|------|--------|------|

## Part 3

- Play 'Make me say …' again, but this time use rules of the form $n \div a + b$.
- Do not inform students of the change, but ask only for even numbers if, e.g. $a = 2$ and multiples of 3 if $a = 3$, and so on.

# Section 21.2 Number sequences

## Learning objectives

- Recognise how number sequences are built up
- Generate sequences, given the $n$th term

## Resources and homework

- Student Book 21.2: pages 471–474
- Practice Book 21.2

## Making mathematical connections

- Recognising odd and even numbers
- Multiplication and multiples
- Substitution into expressions
- Using BIDMAS/BODMAS

## Making cross-curricular connections

- **Science** – spotting patterns and making predictions
- **Relevance** – working logically

## Prior learning

- Students should know how to recognise number patterns.

## Working mathematically

- Students should be able to spot the pattern in the numbers and extend a sequence – the term-to-term rule.
- Students should be able to substitute into the position-to-term rule to extend a number sequence.

## Common misconceptions and remediation

- Students find sequences accessible and usually do well. Errors are mainly related to their method, so stress the need to take care while working.

## Probing questions

- What is a term?
- What is a position?
- What is the difference between the term-to-term rule and the position-to-term rule?

## Literacy focus

- Key terms: consecutive, $n$th term, difference, term-to-term, position-to-term
- Describe how to extend the odd and even number sequence.
- How would you find the 50th term in a sequence?

## Part 1

- Explain that a number sequence is an ordered set of numbers with a rule that allows you to find every number in the sequence. Each number is a *term* and it has its own place in the order.
- The first step in finding the general rule for a sequence is to find the link between the terms. This is the *term-to-term rule*. Often, the easiest way to find this link is to look at the differences between consecutive terms.
- Write the numbers 2 and 4 on the board and ask students what the next two numbers in the pattern could be. The most likely answer is 6 and 8. Write this on the board. Ask students how the pattern is built up (+ 2).
- Now write 2, 4, 8, 16, … on the board and ask students how this is built up (× 2).
- Then write 2, 4, 7, 11, … on the board and ask how this is built up (+ 2, + 3, + 4, …).

- Repeat with the starting numbers 1, 5, … and ask students for different series starting 1, 5, …. and so on.
- Ask students to describe how each series is building up.

## Part 2

### Terms and rules; Term-to-term sequences
- Ask students to suggest some sequences and to describe how they are built up.
- First of all, ask for sequences that increase by a fixed amount, such as + 3. Then ask for series that decrease by a fixed amount, such as − 4.
- Ask for series that increase by a different amount each time, e.g. + 1, + 2, + 3 or + 2, + 4, …
- Then ask for sequences that involve multiplication by the same number each time, such as × 2. These get large very quickly, so keep the starting numbers simple or allow calculators.
- Now ask for sequences that involve division by the same number each time, e.g. ÷ 10.
- As these soon start producing terms that are decimals, often recurring, it is a good idea to keep to, e.g. ÷ 2, ÷ 5 or ÷ 10.
- The majority of students can usually see how these patterns build up mentally.

### Differences
- Use Example 1 in the Student Book to demonstrate using differences. This may confuse **less able** students, so take it slowly and move on, if necessary. However, the concept of differencing is important when dealing with quadratic sequences.
- Quadratic sequences are not within the Foundation specification, but if **more able** students are likely to go on to do the Higher paper, then working through Example 1 may be helpful.
- Make sure students are familiar with the key terms and that the way the series builds up is called the term-to-term rule (the word 'term' in this context simply means any number in a sequence or a series).

### Position-to-term sequences
- Example 2 shows students how to substitute the position number into the position-to-term rule to work out the term. Use the key terms to place emphasis on their meaning here. **Less able** students would benefit from seeing the rule as a function machine and the position as the input and the term the output.
- Example 3 also uses the $n$th term to find the first five terms.
- Remind students that to find the first five terms, they need to input 1, 2, 3, 4 and 5.
- **Students can now do Exercise 21B from the Student Book.**

| A 1–7 | Calculator n/a | CM 10–12 | MR n/a | PS 8, 9 | EV n/a |

## Part 3
- Write some non-mathematical sequences on the board and ask for the next term. For example:
  31, 28, 31, 30, 31, 30, …, 31 (days in a month)
  O, T, T, F, F, …, T (starting letters of the numbers, one, two, three, … to ten)
  1, 2, 5, 10, 20, 50 (British coins below £1)
- Ask students to find some non-mathematical or unusual sequences for Section 21.4.

# Section 21.3 Finding the *n*th term of a linear sequence

## Learning objectives
- Find the *n*th term of a linear sequence

## Resources and homework
- Student Book 21.3: pages 475–478
- Practice Book 21.3

## Making mathematical connections
- Finding the difference
- Multiples
- Substitution into expressions

## Making cross-curricular connections
- **Science** – spotting patterns and making predictions
- **Relevance** – working logically

## Prior learning
- Students should know how to recognise number patterns and how to find the differences between consecutive terms.

## Working mathematically
- Students should be able to find the difference between terms of an arithmetic sequence. They should be able to identify this as the coefficient $A$ of $n$ in the formula $An \pm b$. Students should then be able to work out the *n*th term by subtracting $A$ from the first term to get b.

## Common misconceptions and remediation
- When finding the 10th term, students often just double the value of the 5th term. Emphasise the correct method. Students often forget to write $7n$ and just write + 7.

## Probing questions
- What is meant by consecutive terms within a sequence?

## Literacy focus
- Key terms: arithmetic sequence, linear sequence
- Show students the sequence 3, 5, 7, 9, … . Ask them to describe all the features of this sequence and to extend it.

## Part 1
- Give students a start number and an answer, e.g. 3 and 16.
- Ask them to give a rule of the form 'multiply by a number then add or subtract a number' to get from 3 to 16, e.g. × 3 + 7.
- Write this as a linear expression in *n*, e.g. $3n + 7$.
- Ask students for similar rules and ask them to write them as linear expressions.
- This should give rules such as $5n + 1$, $2n + 10$, $4n + 4$. $6n - 2$, $7n - 5$.

## Part 2

- Discuss the rules written down for the sequences students have met so far.
- Establish that they contain a term in the variable $n$ and a constant term.
- They do not use squares or higher powers. Explain that they are using linear expressions.
- Ask students to suggest similar linear expressions in $n$.
- When students suggest linear expressions such as $3n + 2$, ask the class to substitute $n = 1, 2, 3, \ldots$ into this expression and write the results in a list: 5, 8, 11, 14, 17, ... .
- Ask students if they can see any connections with previous work. They should see that the expression generates a series with a constant difference between pairs of adjacent terms.
- This constant difference is the coefficient of $n$, and this type of series is a linear sequence.
- In such an expression, $n$ is a variable, and its value determines the value of the $n$th term in the sequence. When $n = 4$, this determines the value of the 4th term, and so on.
- Repeat with another linear expression.
- Work through Examples 4 and 5 in the Student Book with the class. These are further examples of linear expressions.
- Show students that the difference becomes the coefficient $A$, in the formula $An \pm b$. To find $b$, students need to subtract $A$ from the first term.
- Taking any of the sequences used at the beginning of the lesson, write the linear expression and the sequence on the board and ask students if they can see any connections.
- The difference and the coefficient of $n$ is the most obvious.
- Students may also spot that the first term of the sequence is the difference plus or minus the constant term.
- Work through this section, which reinforces finding the $n$th term of a linear sequence and the work covered at the beginning of the lesson, and work through Example 6.
- Example 6 reinforces working out the $n$th term of the sequence but also allows students to substitute in values into their expression to find the 50th term in a sequence.
- The last part of Example 6 asks students to find the first value that is above 1000.
- Talk this through with students and remind them that it is just like solving an inequality.
- **Students can now do Exercise 21C from the Student Book.**

| A 1–7 | Calculator n/a | CM 9, 10a–c, 11 | MR n/a | PS 10d, 12 | EV 8 |

## Part 3

- Write the sequence 2, 4, 8, 16, ... on the board.
- Ask students how this is built up.
- Ask them to find the $n$th term.
- It will help to write it as 2, 2 × 2, 2 × 2 × 2, ...
- The $n$th term should be recognisable as $2^n$.
- In a similar way, do this for the $n$th term of the sequence 10, 100, 1000, 10 000, ...

# Section 21.4 Special sequences

## Learning objectives
- Recognise and continue some special number sequences

## Resources and homework
- Student Book 21.4: pages 478–482
- Practice Book 21.4

## Making mathematical connections
- Finding the difference
- Multiples
- Substitution into expressions
- Square numbers
- BIDMAS/BODMAS

## Making cross-curricular connections
- **Science** – spotting patterns and making predictions
- **Relevance** – working logically

## Prior learning
- Students should be able to recognise number patterns and should be familiar with powers.

## Working mathematically
- Students need to use BIDMAS/BODMAS correctly when substituting into formulae to find the terms of the sequence.

## Common misconceptions and remediation
- Some students may not realise that sequences such as the Fibonacci series and square numbers are not built up using addition of a constant factor. Make sure that students are aware of these special sequences.

## Probing questions
- What is the difference between an arithmetic sequence, geometric sequence, Fibonacci sequence and prime number sequence?
- What are the key features of each?

## Literacy focus
- Key terms: geometric sequence, powers of 2, powers of 10, quadratic sequence
- Ask students to compare a geometric sequence and arithmetic sequence.
- Try to extract from them that the arithmetic sequence has a common difference but a geometric sequence does not.

## Part 1
- Recall the non-mathematical and power sequences from Part 3 in the previous two sections.
- Ask students if they found any other unusual or non-mathematical sequences.
- If so, write these on the board and discuss what they are.
- If not, other non-mathematical sequences may include:
  - 3, 3, 5, 4, 4, 3, ... 3 (number of letters in numbers 1–10 as words)
  - 15, 26, 40, 16, 37, ... 58 (sums of squares of digits in previous term, e.g. $1^2 + 5^2 = 26$; $2^2 + 6^2 = 40$)
- Students may have found some other unusual sequences such as the Fibonacci sequence or powers series.
- Remind students about 2, 4, 8, 16, ... and 10, 100, 1000, ... .

# Part 2

- Go through the sequences listed in the Student Book. Make sure students understand the $n$th terms for the odd and even number sequences.
- Students are not required to find the $n$th terms of quadratic sequences at Foundation level, but they may need to substitute numbers into non-linear expressions for $n$th terms.
- The $n$th terms of the square numbers and the triangle numbers should be tested as this is an essential part of functional skills. Ask students to test the square number rule for $n = 15$ and then show that the 15th square number is 225.
- Ask students to extend the triangle number sequence for the first 10 terms.
- Then test the rule for $n = 10$. Both answers should be 55.
- Students will not be required to give the $n$th terms of power series at Foundation level. However, they should be able to recognise a sequence that is, e.g. 'doubling every time'.
- Test the rules for value of $n = 10$, $2^{10} = 1024$ and $10^{10} = 10\,000\,000\,000$.
- Remind students about prime numbers. There is no pattern to these, but it is very important that students know that 2 is the only even prime number.

## Geometric sequences
- This is a progression of numbers with a constant ratio between each number and the one before (e.g. 1, 3, 9, 27, 81).

## Fibonacci sequences
- The Fibonacci sequence is a series of numbers where a number is found by adding up the two numbers before it.

## Prime numbers
- A prime number is a whole number that is greater than 1, whose only two whole-number factors are 1 and itself.
- With the class, work through Example 7, which uses substitution to find out if sequences are odd, even or both. Then work through Examples 8 and 9, which find terms within a sequence by substituting in values. Remind students about BIDMAS/BODMAS.
- **Students can now do Exercise 21D from the Student Book.**

| A 1, 7–10, 14, 17a–c | Calculator 7, 12, 14 | CM 3–6, 11, 12, 17d | MR 2, 13 | PS 15, 16 | EV n/a |
|---|---|---|---|---|---|

# Part 3

- Put a copy of the current month's calendar on the screen or board, e.g.

| September 2010 | | | | | | |
|---|---|---|---|---|---|---|
| Mon | Tue | Wed | Thu | Fri | Sat | Sun |
| 30 | 31 | 1 | 2 | 3 | 4 | 5 |
| 6 | 7 | 8 | 9 | 10 | 11 | 12 |
| 13 | 14 | 15 | 16 | 17 | 18 | 19 |
| 20 | 21 | 22 | 23 | 24 | 25 | 26 |
| 27 | 28 | 29 | 30 | 1 | 2 | 3 |

- Highlight a row, column or diagonal and ask students to give the $n$th term. For example: 2nd row is $n + 5$, 3rd column is $7n - 6$.
  Diagonal 1, 9, 17, 25; $8n - 7$
  Diagonal 4, 10, 16, 22, 28; $6n - 2$
- Ask students what days the square numbers, triangle numbers, prime numbers and powers of 2 fall on.

## Learning objectives

*   Find the *n*th term from practical problems involving sequences

## Resources and homework

*   Student Book 21.5: pages 483–488
*   Practice Book 21.5

## Making mathematical connections

*   Finding the difference
*   Multiples
*   Substitution into expressions
*   Square numbers
*   BIDMAS/BODMAS

## Making cross-curricular connections

*   **Science** – spotting patterns and making predictions
*   **Relevance** – working logically

## Prior learning

*   Students will need to know how to find the *n*th term of a linear sequence.

## Working mathematically

*   Using the given patterns, encourage students to complete a table for the pattern to see how the pattern is growing and from that work out the general rules.

## Common misconceptions and remediation

*   When working on patterns shown in diagrams, students may just count the number of elements (sticks, matches) in the first pattern and multiply, to find the number in several repeats. Make sure that students realise that some of the elements are part of the second and subsequent stages of the patterns.

## Probing questions

*   Give students a sequence, e.g. 4, 7, 10, 13…
*   Ask them to come up with a practical sequence that could fit the sequence.
*   Ask students what the 40th term would be.

## Literacy focus

*   Key terms: None in this section
*   Describe in words how a practical sequence is increasing. This should help students to move away from counting objects twice.

## Part 1

*   Show students the diagram of squares from Resource 21.1. Ask the class:
    o 'How many lines are needed to make the pattern with four squares?' (13)
    o 'What about five squares?' (16)
    o 'What about *n* squares?' (3*n* + 1)

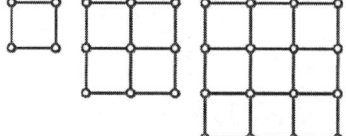

- Repeat with triangles: $4n - 1$

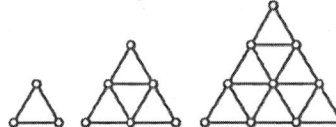

## Part 2

- Work through Example 9 in the Student Book with the class.
- Emphasise the idea of putting the number of elements in each pattern in a table.
- Extend the table for a few columns (or rows). Test a generalisation to make sure that the rule works. Students generally like problems in which they can see diagrams that show a pattern building up, but ensure that students do not spend all their time drawing the patterns.
- Encourage students to be logical in their approach to solving the problems.
- They should start with the simplest case and move on in an ordered and logical way.
- They should make tables, look for patterns and then find the rules.
- They must check that their rules work for all cases.
- **More able** students are likely to spot how the patterns are built up quite quickly, and may choose to experiment with sequences of their own; e.g. suggest that they try a variation on Sierpinski's triangle, seeing if it works with a different shape.
- These skills are vital for investigational pieces of work. Students should be able to solve problems in AO3 sections of the examination.
- **Students can now do Exercise 21E from the Student Book.**

| A 1–7, 8a, 11a, b, 16 | Calculator 9 | CM n/a | MR 8b, 13, 14 | PS 9, 10, 11c, 12 | EV 15 |
|---|---|---|---|---|---|

## Part 3

- Put the following diagrams on the board.

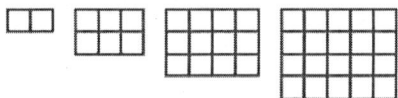

- Ask students how many squares will be in Pattern 5 (30). They may not spot this at first.
- Ask how they can work it out. (The pattern goes up + 4, + 6, + 8, + 10, …)
- Ask them to work out a rule for the $n$th term.
  - Look at the width of each block: 2, 3, 4, 5, …, $n + 1$
  - Look at the height of each block: 1, 2, 3, 4, … $n$

  The number of squares is $1 \times 2$, $2 \times 3$, $3 \times 4$, $4 \times 5$, $n \times (n + 1)$.

# Chapter 22 Geometry and measures: Right-angled triangles

## Overview

| | |
|---|---|
| **22.1** Pythagoras' theorem | **22.7** Calculating angles using trigonometry |
| **22.2** Calculating the length of a shorter side | **22.8** Trigonometry without a calculator |
| **22.3** Applying Pythagoras' theorem in real-life situations | **22.9** Solving problems using trigonometry |
| **22.4** Pythagoras' theorem and isosceles triangles | **22.10** Trigonometry and bearings |
| **22.5** Trigonometric ratios | **22.11** Trigonometry and isosceles triangles |
| **22.6** Calculating lengths using trigonometry | |

### Prior learning
Know how to calculate the square and square root of a number.
Know how to solve equations.

### Learning objectives
**Ensure that students can: use Pythagoras' theorem in right-angled triangles; solve problems using Pythagoras' theorem; use trigonometric ratios in right-angled triangles; use trigonometry to solve problems.**

In the examination, students will be expected to:
- discover Pythagoras' theorem
- calculate the length of the hypotenuse in a right-angled triangle
- calculate the length of a shorter side in a right-angled triangle
- solve problems using Pythagoras' theorem
- use Pythagoras' theorem in isosceles triangles
- define, understand and use the three trigonometric ratios
- use trigonometric ratios to calculate a length in a right-angled triangle
- use the trigonometric ratios to calculate an angle
- work out and remember trigonometric values for angles of 30°, 45°, 60° and 90°
- solve practical problems using trigonometry
- solve problems using an angle of elevation or an angle of depression
- solve bearing problems using trigonometry
- use trigonometry to solve problems involving isosceles triangles.

### Extension

Students could use repeated Pythagoras and trigonometry to find lengths and angles of shapes made up of right-angled triangles.

### Curriculum references

| Section | GCSE specification | Section | GCSE specification |
|---|---|---|---|
| 22.1 | G6, 20 | 22.7 | G20, 21 |
| 22.2 | G6, 20 | 22.8 | G20, 21 |
| 22.3 | G6, 20 | 22.9 | G20, 21 |
| 22.4 | G6, 20 | 22.10 | G20, 21 |
| 22.5 | R12, G20, 21 | 22.11 | G15, 20, 21 |
| 22.6 | G20, 21 | | |

## Route mapping

| Exercise | Accessible | Intermediate | Challenging | AO1 | AO2 MR CM | AO3 PS EV | Key questions |
|---|---|---|---|---|---|---|---|
| 22A | | 1–5 | | 5 | 1–4 | | 1, 5 |
| 22B | | 1–7 | | 1, 6 | 3, 5, 7 | 2, 4 | 1, 5, 7 |
| 22C | | 1–6 | 7 | 1–3 | 6, 7 | 4, 5 | 2, 5, 7 |
| 22D | | 1–13 | | 2 | 9, 11 | 1, 3–8, 10, 12, 13 | 1, 2, 6, 9, 13 |
| 22E | | | 1–12 | 1, 2, 9 | 4, 5, 7, 8 | 3, 6, 10–12 | 1, 3, 4, 8 |
| 22F | 1, 2 | 3 | | 1a–ci, 2, 3 | 1cii | | 1–3 |
| 22G | 1–4 | 5–7 | | 1–4, 6 | 7 | 5 | 1, 2, 5, 6 |
| 22H | | | 1–11 | 1, 2, 5, 6, 8, 9 | 3, 4, 10 | 7, 11 | 1, 2, 9, 10 |
| 22I | | | 1–4 | 1 | 3, 4 | 2 | 1–4 |
| 22J | | | 1–9 | 1–6, 9 | | 7, 8 | 1–3, 9 |
| 22K | | | 1–6 | 3 | 1, 2, 5, 6 | 4 | 1, 3, 5 |
| 22L | | | 1–11 | 1, 3, 4, 7 | 8, 10 | 2, 5, 6, 9, 11 | 5, 6, 8 |
| 22M | | | 1–9 | 1–3, 5–7 | 4, 8 | 9 | 1, 2, 4, 8, 9 |
| 22N | | | 1–8 | 1, 2, 4, 5, 7 | 3 | 6, 8 | 1, 2, 8 |
| 22O | | | 1–4 | 1, 2 | | 3, 4 | 1–3 |

*Key questions are those that demonstrate mastery of the concept, or which require a step-up in understanding or application. Key questions could be used to identify the questions that students must tackle, to support differentiation, or to identify the questions that should be teacher-marked rather than student-marked.*

## About this chapter

**Making connections**: Students should be able to find the square and square root of a number. Students should be able to multiply numbers and plot coordinates.

**Relevance**: Students should realise that there are relationships between angles and lengths in right-angled triangles.

**Working mathematically**: Students will become competent at using a calculator. They will know when to use Pythagoras' theorem and when to use trigonometry. Students will work out missing lengths and angles of right-angled triangles. Students will also problem-solve to find missing angles and lengths.

**Assessment**: In each section of this chapter, ensure that students have a good grasp of the key questions in each exercise before moving on. (Refer to the 'Route mapping' table.) Encourage students to read and think about the 'Ready to progress?' statements on page 526 of the Student Book. Check students' understanding at the end of the chapter, formatively, using peer assessment. Students could do a mini test in the form of the 'Review questions' on pages 526–527 of the Student Book. Follow up the test with an individual target-getting session, based on any areas for development that a student may have.

## Worked exemplars from Student Book (page 524) – suggestions for use

* Present students with the same question but different numbers. They should use the exemplar to mirror the working, in full or just refer to the notes.
* Copy and cut the exemplars into cards. Students should match the working with the notes.
* Alternatively, copy and cut the working into cards but split the label/description from the working.

**Answers to the Student Book questions are available on the CD-ROM provided.**

# Section 22.1 Pythagoras' theorem

## Learning objectives

- Discover Pythagoras' theorem
- Calculate the length of the hypotenuse in a right-angled triangle

## Resources and homework

- Student Book 22.1: pages 493–496
- Practice Book 22.1

## Making mathematical connections

- Finding squares and square roots

## Making cross-curricular connections

- **Architecture; Physics** – designing and building
- **Relevance** – thinking logically

## Prior learning

- Students must know how to find the square and square root of a number.
- It will help students if they are familiar with square numbers.
- Students should know how to round numbers correctly and they should have an appreciation of a suitable level of accuracy, given the context of the problem involved.

## Working mathematically

- Students will work methodically to square the small sides and add them together.
- By taking the square root of the sum of the squares, students will find the hypotenuse.

## Common misconceptions and remediation

- Students often forget to take the square root to find the final answer. They can avoid making this error by paying attention to the layout of solutions.
- The other error is that students often try to apply the theorem in unsuitable situations, e.g. when the triangle in question is not known to be a right-angled triangle.

## Probing questions

- What is the hypotenuse?

## Literacy focus

- Key terms: hypotenuse, Pythagoras' theorem
- Describe $a^2 + b^2 = c^2$ in words.

## Part 1

- Display a target board of whole numbers and ask students to find any square numbers on it.
- Ask for any known square numbers that are missing from the board.
- Try to elicit the first 12 square numbers, with some other commonly known numbers such as: 400, 625 and 1 000 000.
- Ask students to give you a definition of square numbers.
- Ask for squares of some simple decimal numbers such as: 0.5 and 0.1.

## Part 2

- Lead the class through an activity called 'Squares on triangles': On centimetre-squared paper, ask students to draw a 3-, 4-, 5-cm triangle and draw the squares on the 3-cm and 4-cm sides. Ask them to add the two squares, that is, $9 + 16 = 25$ cm$^2$. Ask students to draw the square on the 5-cm side. They should notice that the square also adds up to 25 cm$^2$. If you have counters available, **less able** pupils would benefit from making the two squares with counters and then physically moving them to make the 5-cm side square.
- Allow students to verify for themselves that, in a right-angled triangle, the sum of the squares on the two smaller sides is equal to the square on the hypotenuse.
- It would help students if they could see how this works, rather than you simply telling them.
- Remember that **less able** students may be inaccurate in their drawing and measuring, so their figures may be slightly out. Encourage them to see that the relationship they are looking for is very close to the figures they have, so they should try to be as accurate as possible.

### Rediscovering Pythagoras' theorem

- Discuss Pythagoras' theorem and some of the history around it.
- Make sure students realise that Pythagoras' theorem only works for right-angled triangles.
- Tell students that Pythagoras' theorem can also be used to check if a triangle is right-angled or not. Extend this idea for **more able** students by leading them to discover that if the sum of the squares on the two smaller sides is less than the square on the hypotenuse, then the triangle is obtuse-angled.
- Ensure that every student knows how to identify the hypotenuse of a right-angled triangle – it is the side opposite the right angle, or the longest side. Explain that identifying this is good practice, and helps them to see what they are doing. It is also vital that in the examinations students show that they are using the right method, even if they make an arithmetical error.
- **Students can now do Exercise 22A from the Student Book.**

| G&M 5 | Calculator n/a | CM n/a | MR 1–4 | PS n/a | EV n/a |
|-------|----------------|--------|--------|--------|--------|

### Calculating the length of the hypotenuse

- Talk students through Example 1. Stress that they need to be careful with their working, to ensure that it makes sense and is set out neatly.
- Remind students that they must remember to show every stage in their calculations in order to gain full credit for their answers.
- Go through the suitable degree of accuracy again. **Less able** students should round to one more decimal place (dp) than given in the data; **more able** students should round to one more significant figure (sf) than in the data.
- Work through Example 2, which shows how to find the distance between two coordinates. Students should find the change in the $x$-coordinate and the change in the $y$-coordinate in order to find the length of the shorter sides. Once students know the lengths they can find the hypotenuse.
- **Students can now do Exercise 22B from the Student Book.**

| G&M 1, 6 | Calculator all | CM 5 | MR 3, 7 | PS 2, 4 | EV n/a |
|----------|----------------|------|---------|---------|--------|

## Part 3

- Ask students for a Pythagorean triple: 3, 4, 5 is the most common and 5, 12, 13 is another well-known Pythagorean triple.
- Encourage students to see that multiples of these are also triples, e.g. 6, 8, 10.
- Draw a list up on the board of these triples as students say them. Ask someone to verify them, using a calculator as you go along.

## Learning objectives

- Calculate the length of a shorter side in a right-angled triangle

## Resources and homework

- Student Book 22.2: pages 497–499
- Practice Book 22.2

## Making mathematical connections

- Finding squares and square roots
- Finding the hypotenuse

## Making cross-curricular connections

- **Sport** – measuring distances on pitches
- **Relevance** – thinking logically

## Prior learning

- Students must know how to find the square and square root of a number. It will also help if students are familiar with square numbers.
- Students must know how to round numbers correctly and should have an appreciation of a suitable level of accuracy, given the context of the problem involved.
- For this section, students must be familiar with using Pythagoras' theorem to find the length of the hypotenuse of a right-angled triangle, as studied in Section 22.1.

## Working mathematically

- Students will square numbers accurately, and find square roots accurately to find solutions.

## Common misconceptions and remediation

- Students often muddle the two methods seen in sections; this is usually due to a lack of care when identifying the hypotenuse. The common mistakes highlighted in the previous section also apply in this section.

## Probing questions

- What is special about the length of the hypotenuse?

## Literacy focus

- Key terms: none
- Ask students if they can think of a simple way to remember Pythagoras' theorem. Students could come up with, e.g. square it, add it, and root it for the hypotenuse.

## Part 1

- Give students the number 100 as a target and, using a target board or a list of numbers, ask what needs to be added to each to give the target number. Repeat for other target numbers such as 64, 81 and 25.
- Ask what the target numbers have in common. Students will hopefully say that they are all square numbers. Now repeat, using targets such as $7^2$ or $12^2$.
- Ask what type of calculation has to be done to find the required numbers, aiming to draw out 'subtraction' from students.

# Part 2

- Ask the class if they can remember Pythagoras' theorem.
- Write this again on the board with a suitable diagram.
- Ensure that someone has also said, 'only used for right-angled triangles.'
- Show students how $a^2 + b^2 = c^2$ can be rearranged to give $a^2 = c^2 - b^2$.
- Justify this carefully with **less able** students. Ask **more able** students to justify it themselves.

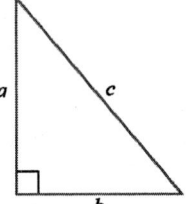

- To do this, they should use the Pythagorean triple, 3, 4, 5:
  $3^2 + 4^2 = 5^2 (9 + 16 = 25)$
  so $9 = 25 - 16$ and hence $3^2 = 5^2 - 4^2$
- Emphasise that Pythagoras' theorem is used to find the missing length of a right-angled triangle, given two other lengths. Always square first and either add or subtract; then find the square root.
- Ask: What is the difference between finding the hypotenuse and finding a small side? Elicit from students that to find the hypotenuse, the largest side, they need to add the squares, while, to find a smaller side, they need to subtract one square from the other.
- Work through Example 3 in the Student Book with the class, ensuring that students realise the importance of setting out their working clearly, to show what they are doing while reaching the final answer.
- Use Example 4 to demonstrate to students that the triangle can be oriented in any position, but that the hypotenuse is always opposite the right angle.
- Go through the rounding procedure again, reminding **less able** students to round to one more dp, and to one more sf for **more able** students. Here, as is very often the case, the result of 10.2 cm is the same. Ensure that students give the answer a unit.
- **Students can now do Exercise 22C from the Student Book.**

| G&M 1–3 | Calculator all | CM 6, 7 | MR n/a | PS 4, 5 | EV n/a |
|---------|----------------|---------|--------|---------|--------|

# Part 3

- On the board, draw three lengths, e.g. 10 cm, 14 cm and 17 cm. Ask students if they think these could be the sides of a right-angled triangle.
- The answer is 'no', but students should justify this: $10^2 + 14^2 \neq 17^2$.
- Repeat for other sets of lengths, including some that do give right-angled triangles.
- Any multiple of 3, 4, 5 will work, as will any multiple of 5, 12 and 13.
- Challenge students to find other triples.

## Section 22.3 Applying Pythagoras' theorem in real-life situations

### Learning objectives
- Solve problems using Pythagoras' theorem

### Resources and homework
- Student Book 22.3: pages 500–501
- Practice Book 22.3

### Making mathematical connections
- Finding squares and square roots
- Finding the hypotenuse

### Making cross-curricular connections
- **Sport** – finding distances on pitches
- **Relevance** – thinking logically

### Prior learning
- Students must know how to use Pythagoras' theorem to find either the hypotenuse or a shorter side.
- This section provides a wide variety of real-life situations in which Pythagoras' theorem can be used to solve problems. The extra skills that students require include:
  - the use of compass directions
  - the use of coordinates
  - finding the area of a rectangle.

### Working mathematically
- Encourage students to sketch the scenario that is given to them. From this, they can work methodically to find either the hypotenuse or the shorter sides.

### Common misconceptions and remediation
- Students often have difficulty identifying the appropriate information from the contextualised problem so they can apply Pythagoras' theorem. In particular, identifying the position of the right angle can cause difficulties for students.

### Probing questions
- A ladder is 20 m long but the foot of the ladder has to be at least 1.5 m away from the wall. Will the ladder reach a window that is 18 m from the ground?

### Literacy focus
- Key terms: none
- Ask students to define, in their own words, the conditions needed for a triangle to be a right-angled triangle.

### Part 1
- Give students a number and ask them to estimate its square root.
- Start with 30. Look for an approximate square root of 5.5; ask students to justify this, for example, 30 is between 25 and 36, so it is between $5^2$ and $6^2$.
- Then give them 52. Look for a square root just bigger than 7, such as 7.2; again, ask for justification.
- Continue like this, always asking for reasons for their answers.

## Part 2

- Ask students to point out places in the classroom or outside where they can see right angles.
- Ask where they may see right-angled triangles in real life, e.g. a ladder against a wall, guy ropes on a tent, supports for bridges.
- Show pictures, or sketches on the board, of sailing boats with sails or masts and stays, or any other examples in which students may see right-angled triangles.
- Draw a diagram illustrating someone walking directly north, then directly east before they turn directly towards their starting position. Ask: How far is the person from the starting position when they turn for home?
- The point where the direction changed from due north to due east illustrates a right angle.
- All these examples of right-angled triangles should help students to recognise that there are many everyday situations where they might find right-angled triangles, and hence be able to use Pythagoras' theorem to solve a problem.
- On the board, draw a sketch of a wall with a ladder leaning against it. Add the length of the ladder (hypotenuse) as 8 m and the distance of its base away from the wall as 1 m.
- Ask: How far up the wall does this ladder reach?
- Then ask: Can we use Pythagoras' theorem to help us answer this question?
- Students should respond that they can, but they need to justify this with: We can see that it is a right-angled triangle.
- Now ask: Are we finding the hypotenuse or a small side? Students should see that it is a small side.
- Ask: Do we square and add or do we square and subtract?' Students should answer: Square and subtract.
- Go through the complete solution to give the rounded answer of 7.9 m.
- Work through Example 5 on the board with the class. First, show students how to draw the scenario as a diagram. Carefully take the **less able** students through each part of the question, as well as the solution.
- **Students can now do Exercise 22D from the Student Book.**

| G&M 2 | Calculator all | CM 9, 11 | MR n/a | PS 1, 3–8, 10, 12 | EV 13 |

## Part 3

- Ask students to summarise the use of Pythagoras' theorem to find missing lengths in right-angled triangles.
- Ask them to state the similarities and the differences between finding the hypotenuse and one of the shorter sides.
- Finish by asking again for the well-known Pythagorean triples. Two that students should try to learn and recognise are 3, 4, 5 and 5, 12, 13.

## Section 22.4 Pythagoras' theorem and isosceles triangles

### Learning objectives
- Use Pythagoras' theorem in isosceles triangles

### Resources and homework
- Student Book 22.4: pages 502–504
- Practice Book 22.4

### Making mathematical connections
- Use Pythagoras' theorem in 2D
- Finding squares and square roots

### Making cross-curricular connections
- **Sport** – using lengths and areas
- **Science** – using formulae
- **Relevance** – developing logical thinking

### Prior learning
- Students should know how to use Pythagoras' theorem to find the sides of right-angled triangles. Students should be able to find the area of a triangle.

### Working mathematically
- Students will explain their methods and show each stage, step by step, in their calculation.
- On their diagrams, students will write the sides they know and the sides they want, to help them to identify which ratio to use.
- Students will write the formula they are using and show how they are substituting into it.
- Structure tasks so students can work out the methods for themselves, either by increasing the difficulty incrementally or through one straightforward and one complex example.

### Common misconceptions and remediation
- Premature rounding is always a problem, which can result in students losing marks in examinations. Make students aware that if they round off their answers while they are doing the working, then the final answer may well be incorrect and they could lose a mark.

### Probing questions
- What are the properties of an isosceles triangle?

### Literacy focus
- Key terms: none
- Ask students to describe the key features of all the triangles they know.

### Part 1
- Draw an isosceles triangle on the board. Ask students where the line of symmetry is.
- Do this for different orientations of the triangle.
- Ask students what is special about the base of the triangle and the line of symmetry.
- Once they have realised that it is perpendicular, ask students how they could work out its length. Ask why they need the length.
- Once students have the 'height' of the triangle and the 'base' of the triangle, show students that they can now find the area.

# Part 2

- Recap with students that to find the area of a triangle they need to know the base measurement and the perpendicular height.
- Refer to Example 6 in the Student Book. The isosceles triangle shows the slant heights and the base measurement, but we do not know the perpendicular height of the triangle.
- Show students that by adding in the line of symmetry, we get the perpendicular height.
- We can use Pythagoras' theorem to work out the height by squaring the slant height and subtracting the square of half the base. Use the diagram in the example to show this.
- Once students have subtracted the squares, remind them to find the square root, but to write down all of the figures shown on the calculator. Tell students again that that they need to avoid making rounding errors; to do so, they should not round answers until the final step.
- Students should use the full number for the height, multiply it by the base of the isosceles triangle and then halve their answer. Finally, students can round their answer.
- **Students can now do Exercise 22E from the Student Book.**

| G&M 1, 2, 9 | Calculator n/a | CM 7, 8 | MR 4, 5 | PS 3, 6, 10, 11 | EV 12 |
|---|---|---|---|---|---|

# Part 3

- A rhombus has sides of 14 cm.
- One of its diagonals is 11 cm long.
- Find the length of the other diagonal.
- Encourage students to draw a diagram and then use Pythagoras' theorem to find the height; then double it to find the length of the second diagonal. (25.7 cm)

## Section 22.5 Trigonometric ratios

### Learning objectives
- Define, understand and use the three trigonometric ratios

### Resources and homework
- Student Book 22.5: pages 504–510
- Practice Book 22.5

### Making mathematical connections
- Use Pythagoras' theorem in 2D

### Making cross-curricular connections
- **Sport** – using lengths and areas
- **Science** – using formulae
- **Relevance** – developing logical thinking

### Prior learning
- Students should know how to use Pythagoras' theorem to find the sides of right-angled triangles.

### Working mathematically
- Students will define, understand and use the three trigonometric ratios.
- Structure tasks so that students can work out the methods for themselves; either increase the difficulty incrementally, or through one straightforward and one complex example.

### Common misconceptions and remediation
- Premature rounding is always a problem and can lose students marks in examinations. Remind students that if they round off their answers in intermediate working, then the final answer may well be incorrect and they could lose a mark in an examination.
- Say to students that they should only write down the side they know and the side they want to find in trigonometry, to help them to decipher which ratio to use.

### Probing questions
- When should you use tan, cosine or sine? What is the biggest difference here?
- Ask students to talk you through their answers in a step-by-step fashion to improve their understanding of what to use when.

### Literacy focus
- Key terms: adjacent, cosine, opposite, sine, tangent, trigonometry, trigonometric functions, trigonometric ratios
- Ask students to write the definition of each key term in the mathematical dictionaries they started at the beginning of the year.
- Encourage students to be explicit about the language of the names of the sides, the formulae they are using and describing the stages in their workings.

### Part 1
- Explain that the lesson is about using trigonometry. Remind students about Pythagoras' theorem and the three trigonometric ratios for right-angled triangles.

$$\sin\theta = \frac{O}{H} \quad \cos\theta = \frac{A}{H} \quad \tan\theta = \frac{O}{A}$$

- Pythagoras' theorem $H^2 = O^2 + A^2$
- On the board, draw three more triangles with angles and ask students to work out the names of the sides.

## Part 2

- Remind students how to label the sides. Students will discover some interesting rations in Exercise 22F of this section.
- **Students can now do Exercise 22F from the Student Book.**

| G&M 1a, b, ci, 2, 3 | Calculator all | CM n/a | MR 1cii | PS n/a | EV n/a |
|---|---|---|---|---|---|

- Exercise 22F will have introduced students to the trigonometric ratios and what sides to use when using each ratio.
- Work through examples 7 and 8 in the Student Book, which looks at which trigonometric ratio of the angle which uses the marked lengths.
- **Students can now do Exercise 22G from the Student Book.**

| G&M 1–4, 6 | Calculator all | CM n/a | MR 7 | PS n/a | EV 5 |
|---|---|---|---|---|---|

### Trigonometry using your calculator

- Ensure that students all have their calculators in degree mode.
- Work through Example 9 in the Student Book with the class. This example provides students with practice at inputting values into their calculators and reading off the correct values.
- **Students can now do Exercise 22H from the Student Book.**

| G&M 1, 2, 5, 6, 8, 9 | Calculator all | CM n/a | MR 3, 4, 10 | PS 11 | EV 7 |
|---|---|---|---|---|---|

## Part 3

- The lesson is designed to consolidate students' knowledge. Go through some questions in class, so that as many students as possible understand the different types of approaches used to solve basic trigonometric problems.
- Ask students to list all the topics they have used in the lesson.

# Section 22.6 Calculating lengths using trigonometry

## Learning objectives

- Use trigonometric ratios to calculate a length in a right-angled triangle

## Making mathematical connections

- Use Pythagoras' theorem in 2D

## Resources and homework

- Student Book 22.6: pages 510–512
- Practice Book 22.6

## Making cross-curricular connections

- **Sport** – using lengths and areas
- **Science** – using formulae
- **Relevance** – developing logical thinking

## Prior learning

- Students should know how to use Pythagoras' theorem to find the sides of right-angled triangles.

## Working mathematically

- When working on calculations, students will explain their methods and show each stage, step by step:
  o Students will write the sides they know and the sides they want, to be able identify which ratio to use.
  o Students will write the formulae they use and will show how they substitute into it.
- Structure tasks so that students can work out the methods for themselves. Either increase the difficulty incrementally or through one straightforward and one complex example.

## Common misconceptions and remediation

- As has been mentioned in previous sections, premature rounding is a problem and can lose students marks in examinations. Keep reminding students not to round off their answers while they are working, as the final answer may then be incorrect and they could lose a mark in an examination. Students should only round off right at the end of their working.
- Remind students that they should only write down the side they know and the side they want in trigonometry, to help them to decipher which ratio to use.

## Probing questions

- When should you use tan, cosine or sine?
- What sides do you need to know for each of them?

## Literacy focus

- Key terms: none
- Say that 'SOHCAHTOA' is used to remember the trigonometric ratios. Challenge students to try and think of a way to remember this easily.

# Part 1

- Label the missing sides for each triangle.
- Which sides do you need when using each of the trigonometric ratios?

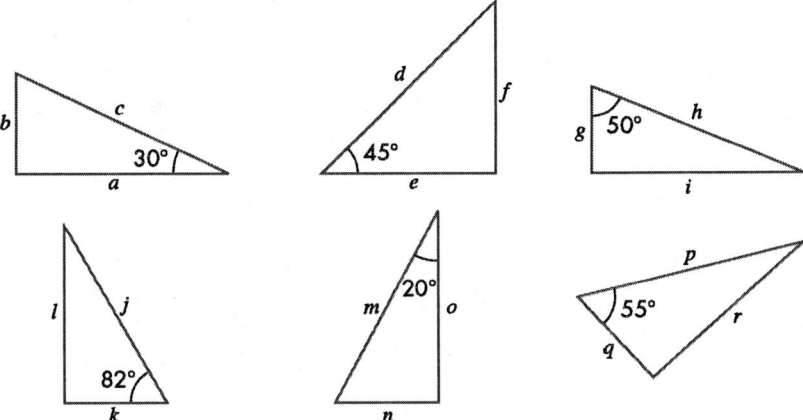

# Part 2

- Students are given the angle and a length and asked to work out a second missing length. Encourage them only to label the side they know and the side they want. Remind students that this will make it easier to identify the ratio they will use.
- Work through Example 10 in the Student Book, which shows a triangle with a known length and a missing length. Encourage students to label what they know and what they want.
- Say that as we have the adjacent and opposite we use tan and rearrange the formula to find the opposite side. Show students how to rearrange the formula.
- **Students can now do Exercise 22I from the Student Book.**

| G&M 1 | Calculator all | CM 4 | MR 3 | PS n/a | EV 2 |

# Part 3

- Ask students to work out the missing lengths of the following triangles.

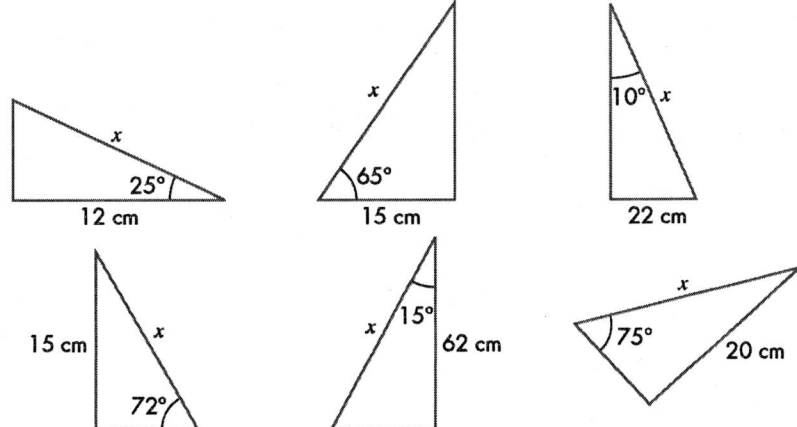

## Learning objectives

- Use the trigonometric ratios to calculate an angle

## Resources and homework

- Student Book 22.7: pages 512–514
- Practice Book 22.7

## Making mathematical connections

- Use Pythagoras' theorem in 2D
- Missing lengths using trigonometry

## Making cross-curricular connections

- **Sport** – using lengths and areas
- **Science** – using formulae
- **Relevance** – developing logical thinking

## Prior learning

- Students should know how to use Pythagoras' theorem to find the sides of right-angled triangles. Students should also be able to find the missing sides using trigonometry.

## Working mathematically

- As in the previous section, students will show each stage of their workings, step by step.
- Students will use the trigonometric ratios to calculate an angle.
- Structure tasks so students can work out the methods for themselves, either by increasing the difficulty incrementally or through one straightforward and one complex example.

## Common misconceptions and remediation

- Premature rounding is always a problem. Make students aware that if they round off their answers too soon during their working, then the final answer may well be incorrect and they could lose a mark in an examination.
- Tell students that in trigonometry, writing down only the side they know and the side they want, will help them to decipher which ratio to use.

## Probing questions

- Looking at your calculator, what functions are above the sin, cos and tan key?
- When might you use these functions?

## Literacy focus

- Key term: inverse
- Ask students to discuss the meaning of 'inverse'.
- Encourage students to be explicit about the language of the names of the sides, the formulae they are using and describing the stages in their workings.

## Part 1

- Draw a triangle.
- Start with: sin $x°$ = opposite/hypotenuse    sin $x°$ = $\frac{18.88}{30}$

- Calculate $\frac{18.88}{30}$ : sin $x°$ = 0.6293...
- What angle has sine equal to 0.6293...?
- The 'inverse sine' will tell us.
- Inverse sine: $x°$ = $\sin^{-1}(0.6293...)$
- Use a calculator to find $\sin^{-1}(0.6293...)$: $x°$ = 39.0° (1 dp)
- The angle '$x$' is 39.0°.
- With the class, discuss that to find the missing angle we use the inverse function on the calculator.
- Provide further examples to give students practice with using the inverse function.

## Part 2

- Students need to be able to find missing angles.
- To do this, they must use the inverse function.
- Some calculators may use brackets; ensure that all students try it out on their calculators to see which method their calculator requires them to use.
- Refer the class to Example 11 in the Student Book. This example ensures that students are confident in using the inverse function on their calculators. Make sure that all students know how to input the functions correctly.
- **Students can now do Exercise 22J from the Student Book.**

| G&M 1–6, 9 | Calculator all | CM n/a | MR n/a | PS n/a | EV 7, 8 |
|---|---|---|---|---|---|

## Part 3

- Give students this problem:
  - A ladder, 2 m long is leaning against a wall.
  - The angle between the ladder and the wall is 67°.
  - Work out to 2 sf, the distance between the foot of the ladder and wall. Show your working clearly.
- Show students how to draw a diagram and calculate the missing length.
- Then ask students to design a scenario where a missing angle must be found.

## Learning objectives

- Work out and remember trigonometric values for angles of 30°, 45°, 60° and 90°

## Resources and homework

- Student Book 22.8: pages 514–515
- Practice Book 22.8

## Making mathematical connections

- Use Pythagoras' theorem in 2D
- Missing lengths and angles using trigonometry

## Making cross-curricular connections

- **Sport** – using lengths and areas
- **Science** – using formulae
- **Relevance** – developing logical thinking

## Prior learning

- Students should know how to use Pythagoras' theorem to find the sides of right-angled triangles.
- Students should be able to find the missing sides using trigonometry.
- Students should also be able to find missing angles using trigonometry.

## Working mathematically

- Students will explain their methods and show each stage of their calculation, step by step.
- On their diagrams, students will write the sides they know and the sides they want, in order to help to identify which ratio to use.
- Students will also write the formula they are using and show how they are substituting into it.
- Structure tasks so students can work out the methods for themselves, either by increasing the difficulty incrementally or through one straightforward and one complex example.

## Common misconceptions and remediation

- Premature rounding can result in students losing marks in examinations. Remind students they should only round off their answers right at the end of their working.
- Say to students: Only write down the side you know and the side you want in trigonometry, to help to decipher which ratio to use.

## Probing questions

- What is special about the trigonometric values for 30, 45, 60 and 90°?

## Literacy focus

- Key terms: none
- Ask students to explain when to use each of the trigonometric ratios.

## Part 1

- Ask students to copy and complete the following table.

| Angle | Sin x | Cos x | Tan x |
|-------|-------|-------|-------|
| 0 | 0 | 0 | 0 |
| 30 | | | |
| 45 | | | |
| 60 | | | |
| 90 | | | |

- Play a memory game with your students. Give them one minute to study the correct version of the table and then, rapidly, ask them quick-fire questions.

## Part 2

- Remind students about Pythagoras' theorem.
- Once students have all three sides, though one side may be an exact value, students can put these into the relevant trigonometric ratio to get exact answers.
- **Students can now do Exercise 22K from the Student Book.**

| G&M 3 | Calculator n/a | CM 1, 2, 6 | MR 5 | PS n/a | EV 4 |
|-------|----------------|------------|------|--------|------|

## Part 3

- Referring back to Part 1, ask students some quick-fire questions about what exact value corresponds to which trigonometric function.
- Say that there will be more than one answer.
- Students could play a game against each other with these questions to see who can remember the most, or they could play a game against the clock.

# Section 22.9 Solving problems using trigonometry

## Learning objectives
- Solve practical problems using trigonometry
- Solve problems using an angle of elevation or an angle of depression

## Resources and homework
- Student Book 22.9: pages 516–519
- Practice Book 22.9

## Making mathematical connections
- Use Pythagoras' theorem in 2D
- Missing lengths and angles using trigonometry
- Exact values

## Making cross-curricular connections
- **Sport** – using lengths and areas
- **Science** – using formulae
- **Relevance** – developing logical thinking

## Prior learning
- Students should know how to use Pythagoras' theorem to find the sides of right-angled triangles. Students should be able to find the missing sides using trigonometry.
- Students should be able to find missing angles using trigonometry. Students should also know exact values.

## Working mathematically
- Again, students will explain their methods and show each stage of their calculations, step by step. Students will also write the formula they are using and show how they are substituting into it.
- Structure tasks so students can work out the methods for themselves, either by increasing the difficulty incrementally or through one straightforward and one complex example.

## Common misconceptions and remediation
- Students need to take care that they do not round prematurely, while still busy with a calculation. Remind them that they will lose marks in examinations if they do this. Say that they should do the rounding off right at the end.
- To avoid confusion, students should only write down the side they know and the side they want in trigonometry, to help them to decipher which ratio to use.

## Probing questions
- What is the difference between an angle of elevation and an angle of depression?

## Literacy focus
- Key terms: angle of depression, angle of elevation
- Describe how to find missing lengths and missing angles in right-angled triangles.

## Part 1
- An isosceles triangle has two sides of 8 m and a base angle of 55° What is its area?
- Encourage students to start by drawing a diagram.
- The area of a triangle is half the base × height. Students need to find the height (6.55 ...).
- Once students have found the height, they need to find the length of the base.
  (4.58 × 2 = 9.18 ...)
- Now students can find the area (30.055 ...)

- Discuss the fact that students should always break down problems into small and thus more manageable chunks.

## Part 2

- The questions in Exercise 22L require students to break down the problems into smaller chunks and then draw diagrams so that they can visualise the problems.
- Example 12 in the Student Book shows the importance of drawing a diagram first.
- Drawing a diagram allows students to label what they know and what they are looking for
- Once they have done this, they can decide which trigonometric ratio to use.
- **Students can now do Exercise 22L from the Student Book.**

| G&M 1, 3, 4, 7 | Calculator all | CM 8 | MR 10 | PS 2, 5, 9, 11 | EV 6 |
|---|---|---|---|---|---|

### Angles of elevation and depression

- From the horizontal, the angle of depression is the angle when you look down.
- The angle of elevation is when you look up.
- Example 13 in the Student Book again places emphasis on drawing a diagram to visualise the problem.
- As with previous examples, encourage students to label what they know and what they want, in order to decipher which trigonometric ratio to use.
- **Students can now do Exercise 22M from the Student Book.**

| G&M 1–3, 5–7 | Calculator all | CM 4, 8 | MR n/a | PS n/a | EV 9 |
|---|---|---|---|---|---|

## Part 3

- A boat is moored 50 m from the foot of a vertical cliff.
- The angle of depression of the boat from the top of the cliff is $52°$.
- Calculate the height of the cliff (39.06 …).
- The boat is released from its mooring and it drifts 350 m further away from the cliff.
- Calculate the angle of elevation of the top of the cliff from the boat. (5.577…)
- Encourage students to draw a diagram to visualise the problem, and then to solve it step by step.

# Section 22.10 Trigonometry and bearings

## Learning objectives
- Solve bearing problems using trigonometry

## Resources and homework
- Student Book 22.10: pages 520–521
- Practice Book 22.10

## Making mathematical connections
- Use Pythagoras' theorem in 2D
- Missing lengths and angles using trigonometry

## Making cross-curricular connections
- **Sport** – using lengths and areas
- **Science** – using formulae
- **Relevance** – developing logical thinking

## Prior learning
- Students should know how to use Pythagoras' theorem to find the sides of right-angled triangles. Students should be able to find the missing sides using trigonometry.
- Students should also be able to find missing angles using trigonometry.

## Working mathematically
- Students will explain their methods and show each stage of their calculation, step by step.
- Students should also write the formula they are using and show how they are substituting into it.
- Structure tasks so students can work out the methods for themselves, either by increasing the difficulty incrementally or through one straightforward and one complex example.

## Common misconceptions and remediation
- Premature rounding can result in students losing marks in examinations. Remind students they should only round off their answers right at the end of their working.
- Say to students: Only write down the side you know and the side you want in trigonometry, to help to decipher which ratio to use.

## Probing questions
- How do you measure a bearing?

## Literacy focus
- Key terms: none
- Ask students to describe their position within the classroom in relation to (teacher decides) one another using bearings. For example, Kath is on a bearing of 045° to Jenson and on a bearing of 270° to Steve.

## Part 1
- Go through with students how the wording of bearings questions can be complicated.
- A 'bearing of B from A', as used in the diagram on the right, means: Measure clockwise from point A.

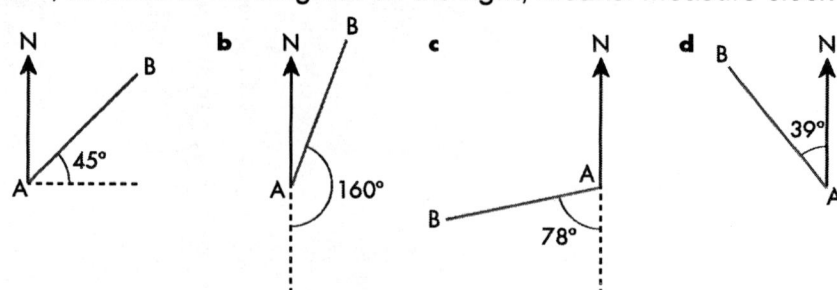

## Part 2

- Encourage students to draw a diagram and break down the problems into smaller manageable chunks.
- Work through Example 14 with the class.
- This example uses a diagram to break down the problem.
- Remind students about the compass points, so: 090° is east; 180° is south; and 270° is west. This should help students when they are drawing diagrams.
- **Students can now do Exercise 22N from the Student Book.**

| G&M 1, 2, 4, 5, 7 | Calculator all | CM 3 | MR n/a | PS 6 | EV 8 |
|---|---|---|---|---|---|

## Part 3

- A plane (P) flies on a bearing of 132° from an airport (A) for 300 km.
- How far south and east is it (B) from the airport, to 3 sf?
- Draw a sketch. First, start with a north line, N, and measure the bearing clockwise from the bottom of this line point (A).

AB = the distance south

BP = the distance east

- Using supplementary angles, we know that angle

∠BAP is 180° − 132° = 48°

Distance south = AB

$$\cos\theta = \frac{adj}{hyp}$$

$$\cos 48 = \frac{AB}{300}$$

AB $= 300 \times \cos 48$
$= 200.73 ...$
$= 201$ km (3 sf)

Distance east = BP

$$\sin\theta = \frac{opp}{hyp}$$

$$\sin 48 = \frac{BP}{hyp}$$

BP $= 300 \times \sin 48$
$= 222.94$
$= 223$ km (3 sf)

## Learning objectives

- Use trigonometry to solve problems involving isosceles triangles

## Resources and homework

- Student Book 22.11: pages 522–523
- Practice Book 22.11

## Making mathematical connections

- Use Pythagoras' theorem in 2D
- Missing lengths and angles using trigonometry

## Making cross-curricular connections

- **Sport** – using lengths and areas
- **Science** – using formulae
- **Relevance** – developing logical thinking

## Prior learning

- Students should know how to use Pythagoras' theorem to find the sides of right-angled triangles.
- Students should be able to find the missing sides using trigonometry.
- Students should also be able to find missing angles using trigonometry.

## Working mathematically

- Students will explain their methods and show each stage of their calculations. On their diagrams, students will write the sides they know and the sides they want, in order to help them to identify which ratio to use. Students will also write the formula they will use, and show how they will substitute into it.
- Structure tasks so students can work out the methods for themselves, either by increasing the difficulty incrementally or through one straightforward and one complex example.

## Common misconceptions and remediation

- Premature rounding can result in lost marks in examinations. Students need to be aware that if they round off their answers during their working, then the final answer may be incorrect.
- Only write down the side you know and the side you want in trigonometry to help decipher which ratio to use.

## Probing questions

- What are the special features of an isosceles triangle?

## Literacy focus

- Key terms: none
- Ask students: How can trigonometry and Pythagoras' theorem be used in an isosceles triangle?'(You could add that students should 'think about symmetry'.)

## Part 1

- Give students four or five isosceles triangles and ask them to draw the line of symmetry for each triangle.
- Ask students: If we know the base angles of an isosceles triangle and size of the slanted sides how could we use trigonometry to work out the height and base?
- Use diagrams to help students figure this out.

## Part 2

- Students need to work logically with isosceles triangles and use symmetry to split each triangle into two exact and equal right-angled triangles.
- Work through Example 15, uses a symmetry line to find the height of an isosceles triangle.
- Once the symmetry line is in place, it halves the triangle into two equal right-angled triangles.
- The missing lengths and angles can be found using trigonometry.
- The height and base can be used to find the area using the formula for the area of a triangle.
- **Students can now do Exercise 22O from the Student Book.**

| G&M 1, 2 | Calculator all | CM n/a | MR n/a | PS 3, 4 | EV n/a |

## Part 3

- Give students this problem:
  - o Lynda wants to measure the height of a tree.
  - o She walks exactly 100 ft from the base of the tree and looks up.
  - o The angle from the ground to the top of the tree is 33°. How tall is the tree? (64.94…ft)
- Jon is also 100 ft from the tree. His kite is stuck at the top of the tree.
- Before the wind dropped, what was the maximum height the kite could have been flying? (119.24…ft).

# Chapter 23 Geometry and measures: Congruency and similarity

## Overview

| 23.1 Congruent triangles | 23.2 Similarity |
|---|---|

### Prior learning
Know how to enlarge a shape by a given scale factor.
Know how to solve equations.

### Learning objectives

**Ensure that students can: show that two triangles are congruent; work out the scale factor of two similar shapes; work out lengths of sides in similar shapes.**

In the examination, students will be expected to:
- demonstrate that two triangles are congruent
- recognise similarity in any two shapes
- show that two shapes are similar
- work out the scale factor between similar shapes.

### Extension
Ask students to use the scale factor for length to work out area and volumes of similar shapes.

## Curriculum references

| Section | GCSE specification |
|---|---|
| 23.1 | R12, G6, 7, 19 |
| 23.2 | R12, G6, 7, 19 |

## Route mapping

| Exercise | Accessible | Intermediate | Challenging | AO1 | AO2 MR CM | AO3 PS EV | Key questions |
|---|---|---|---|---|---|---|---|
| 23A | | | 1–9 | 1, 3 | 2, 5, 6, 8 | 4, 7, 9 | 1, 2, 4, 5, 8 |
| 23B | | 1–5 | | | 1–5 | | 1, 2, 5 |
| 23C | | 1–6 | 7, 8 | 2, 5, 6 | 1, 3, 4, 8 | 7 | 2, 4, 6, 8 |
| 23D | | | 1–8 | 6 | 2, 7 | 1, 3–5, 8 | 1, 2, 6, 8 |

*Key questions are those that demonstrate mastery of the concept, or which require a step-up in understanding or application. Key questions could be used to identify the questions that students must tackle, to support differentiation, or to identify the questions that should be teacher-marked rather than student-marked.*

## About this chapter

**Making connections**: Students should be able to enlarge a shape by a given scale factor and understand that the scale factor increases the lengths of all of the sides. Students should be able to substitute into expressions.

**Relevance**: Students will use knowledge of enlargements to find scale factors and apply this to work out the missing lengths in similar triangles.

**Working mathematically**: Students will be able to decide if shapes are congruent or not, using simple rules and stating their reasons why they have given their answers. Students will be able to use scale factors to find missing lengths in similar triangles.

**Assessment**: In each section of this chapter, ensure that students have a good grasp of the key questions in each exercise before moving on. (Refer to the 'Route mapping' table.) Encourage students to read and think about the 'Ready to progress?' statements on page 543 of the Student Book. Check students' understanding at the end of the chapter, formatively, using peer assessment. Students could do a mini test in the form of the 'Review questions' on pages 543–545 of the Student Book. Follow up the test with an individual target-getting session, based on any areas for development that a student may have.

## Worked exemplars from the Student Book (page 542) – suggestions for use
* Present students with the same question but different numbers. They should use the exemplar to mirror the working, in full or just refer to the notes.
* Copy and cut the exemplars into cards. Students should match the working with the notes.
* Alternatively, copy and cut the working into cards but split the label/description from the working.

**Answers to the Student Book questions are available in the CD-ROM provided.**

# Section 23.1 Congruent triangles

## Learning objectives

- Demonstrate that two triangles are congruent.

## Resources and homework

- Student Book 23.1: pages 529–533
- Practice Book 23.1

## Making mathematical connections

- Transformations
- Angles
- Properties of shapes
- Constructions

## Making cross-curricular connections

- **Science, Art, Engineering** – working out heights, enlarging shapes, making patterns
- **Relevance** – working logically

## Prior learning

- No prior knowledge is needed.

## Working mathematically

- Students need to work methodically through various conditions to decipher whether or not shapes are congruent.

## Common misconceptions and remediation

- Students often do not recognise that identical shapes can be rotated and still be congruent. By using tracing paper as the method for finding congruent shapes, students should be able to avoid making this error.

## Probing questions

- What makes two triangles congruent?

## Literacy focus

- Key term: congruent
- Ask students to describe the conditions for shapes being congruent, drawing diagrams where necessary.

## Part 1

- Ask students, using squared paper, to draw a shape with four squares that touch, edge to edge, as shown. Five different shapes are possible.

- Go around the class and collect examples. It is likely that students will have the same shapes but in different orientations. Show the different examples.
- Make sure that students have an intuitive idea of congruency.

## Part 2

- Use students' collected shapes to talk about those that are actually the same but are simply turned around or back to front. Introduce the word 'congruent'.
- Ask students to look at the building materials that may be present in the classroom, e.g. tiles, bricks or wooden blocks on the floor.
- Discuss the fact that these are congruent and why these shapes have been used – so that they can all fit together properly, without gaps.

- Draw two circles of different sizes on the board and ask if these two shapes are congruent. Some of the **less able** students may think that they are congruent since all circles are the same shape. Reinforce the idea that they are not congruent because they are not both exactly the same size. Congruent shapes are exactly the same size and shape.
- Introduce the word 'similar' to **more able** students, explaining that shapes that are the same but different sizes, e.g. large and small circles, are called *similar* shapes.
- Encourage students to use tracing paper. Emphasise that the best way to check if two shapes are congruent is to trace one of the shapes and see if the tracing fits exactly over the other shape, putting it on top either way around.

**Conditions for congruent triangles**
- Discuss all four of the conditions for congruence from the Student Book with the class.
- Discuss with students how the notation works.
- Work through Examples 1 and 2, which show how to prove if two triangles are congruent.
- Students need to state which sides are identical and which angles are identical using the formal notation.
- **Students can now do Exercise 23A from the Student Book.**

| G&M 1, 3 | Calculator n/a | CM 5, 6 | MR 2, 8 | PS n/a | EV 4, 7, 9 |
|---|---|---|---|---|---|

# Part 3

- Revisit Part 1, this time drawing five squares on a sheet of paper.
- You could suggest that students begin by using their four-square shapes and deciding where they can add a square to each, remembering that there might be more than one possibility.
- After a certain amount of time, collect the different shapes that students have drawn and see which shapes are congruent.
- Twelve possible shapes can be made with five squares.

## Learning objectives

- Recognise similarity in any two shapes.
- Show that two shapes are similar.
- Work out the scale factor between similar shapes.

## Resources and homework

- Student Book 23.2: pages 533–541
- Practice Book 23.2

## Making mathematical connections

- Enlargements
- Scale factors
- Congruence

## Making cross-curricular connections

- **Science, Art, Engineering** – working with and comparing; constructing, e.g. heights, shapes, patterns
- **Relevance** – working logically

## Prior learning

- Students should be familiar with enlarging shapes and using scale factors.

## Working mathematically

- Students should be able to identify corresponding side lengths and angles. Students will work out scale factors by using corresponding side lengths and work out angle size.

## Common misconceptions and remediation

- Ensure that students are able to identify the corresponding side lengths, even if the shapes are in different orientation.

## Probing questions

- What is meant by 'a corresponding side length'?

## Literacy focus

- Key term: similar
- Draw two similar triangles on the board, ask students to describe the similar features and how to find the scale factor of the shapes.

## Part 1

- Draw a triangle and a quadrilateral on the board.
- Ask students to enlarge the shape by scale factors of 2, 3, 5, and 0.5.
- Ask students to tell you what the scale factor changes and what the scale factor does not change.

## Part 2

- Show students that similar shapes have the same corresponding angles but different side lengths.
- The shapes can be in the same orientation or a different orientation, but the corresponding side lengths must be the same.
- **Students can now do Exercise 23B from the Student Book.**

| G&M n/a | Calculator n/a | CM n/a | MR 1–5 | PS n/a | EV n/a |

- Work through Examples 3, 4 and 5, which require students to work out a scale factor.
- Once they have the scale factor they are able to use this to work out lengths of missing sides.
- **Students can now do Exercise 23C from the Student Book.**

| G&M 2, 5, 6 | Calculator all | CM 1, 3, 4, 8 | MR n/a | PS 7 | EV n/a |

- **Solving problems with similar triangles**
- Work through Examples 6 and 7, which show, with a diagram, that shapes are similar. Students need to work out a scale factor and from this work out the missing lengths.
- **Students can now do Exercise 23D from the Student Book.**

| G&M 6 | Calculator all | CM 2 | MR 7 | PS 1, 3–5 | EV 8 |

# Part 3

- Ask students to look at the following diagram.
- Ask them to work out the scale factor and then find (work out) missing length BC. (BC = 24)

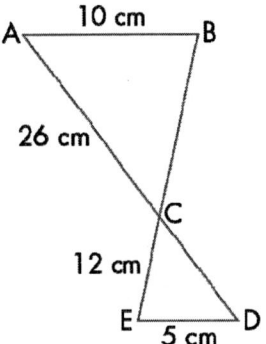

# Chapter 24 Probability: Combined events

## Overview

| | |
|---|---|
| **24.1** Combined events | **24.3** Probability and Venn diagrams |
| **24.2** Two-way tables | **24.4** Tree diagrams |

**Prior learning**

Know how to use theoretical or experimental models to work out the probabilities of outcomes of events.

**Learning objectives**

**Ensure that students can: work out the probabilities for two or more events; use two-way tables to solve probability problems; use Venn diagrams to solve probability problems; draw and use frequency tree diagrams; draw and use probability tree diagrams to solve probability problems.**

In the examination, students will be expected to:
- work out the probabilities when two or more events occur at the same time
- read two-way tables and use them to work out probabilities
- use Venn diagrams to solve probability questions
- understand frequency tree diagrams and probability tree diagrams
- use probability tree diagrams to work out the probabilities involved in combined events.

**Extension**

You could ask students to work out the probability of events when there is no replacement. Or, ask students to find the probability of at least one event happening.

## Curriculum references

| Section | GCSE specification |
|---|---|
| 24.1 | P6, 7 |
| 24.2 | P6 |
| 24.3 | P6, 8 |
| 24.4 | P1, 6, 8 |

## Route mapping

| Exercise | Accessible | Intermediate | Challenging | AO1 | AO2 MR CM | AO3 PS EV | Key questions |
|---|---|---|---|---|---|---|---|
| 24A | 1–9 | 10–12 | | 1–7, 10 | 9, 11 | 8, 12 | 4, 7, 11, 12 |
| 24B | 1–8 | | | 1–6 | 8 | 7 | 4, 7, 8 |
| 24C | 1, 2 | 3–11 | 12, 13 | 1–6 | 7, 11, 12 | 8–10, 13 | 1, 3, 6, 12 |
| 24D | | 1 | 2–10 | 1–6 | 9, 10 | 7, 8 | 1, 4, 6, 8, 10 |

*Key questions are those that demonstrate mastery of the concept, or which require a step-up in understanding or application. Key questions could be used to identify the questions that students must tackle, to support differentiation, or to identify the questions that should be teacher-marked rather than student-marked.*

## About this chapter

**Making connections**: Students will calculate theoretical and experimental probabilities of events. They will add, subtract and multiply fractions and calculate the expectation.

**Relevance**: Students will be able to calculate the probabilities of events and use this to calculate the probability of combining events. They will present their work using tree diagrams, two-way tables, sample space or Venn diagrams. Students will also understand which diagram is the most appropriate diagram to use in each circumstance.

**Working mathematically**: Students will learn how to present probability information by using the most efficient method. Students will add, subtract and multiply fractions, decimals and percentages to find probabilities. Students will also make use the fact that probabilities add up to 1.

**Assessment**: In each section of this chapter, ensure that students have a good grasp of the key questions in each exercise before moving on. (Refer to the 'Route mapping' table.) Encourage students to read and think about the 'Ready to progress?' statements on page 568 of the Student Book. Check students' understanding at the end of the chapter, formatively, using peer assessment. Students could do a mini test in the form of the 'Review questions' on pages 568–569 of the Student Book. Follow up the test with an individual target-getting session, based on any areas for development that a student may have.

### Worked exemplars from the Student Book (page 566) – suggestions for use
- Present students with the same question but different numbers. They should use the exemplar to mirror the working, in full or just refer to the notes.
- Copy and cut the exemplars into cards. Students should match the working with the notes.
- Alternatively, copy and cut the working into cards but split the label/description from the working.

**Answers to the Student Book questions are available on the CD-ROM provided.**

## Learning objectives

- Work out the probabilities when two or more events occur at the same time

## Resources and homework

- Student Book 24.1: pages 547–550
- Practice Book 24.1

## Making mathematical connections

- Adding and subtracting fractions
- Equivalent fractions
- Finding the probability of a single event

## Making cross-curricular connections

- **Science** – accuracy in experiments
- **Relevance** – logical thinking

## Prior learning

- Students should already know how to calculate a probability in simple cases using equally likely outcomes.

## Working mathematically

- Students should be able to find the probability of an event happening.
- Students should be able to make a sample space diagram to show the outcomes for two events visually.
- Using the sample space diagram students should be able to calculate combined probabilities.

## Common misconceptions and remediation

- The most common mistake with this type of problem is that students do not pay enough attention to the instructions. Make it clear to students that a sample space diagram can be used, either to record two separate categories in each direction (horizontal or vertical), or to combine outcomes, e.g. adding the outcomes or finding the difference between them, or anything else that may be required in the question. Students should decide what to record themselves, although a brief discussion should help them to decide what is needed.

## Probing questions

- If two fair dice are rolled and their numbers are added together, what is the probability of rolling a number less than 2?

## Literacy focus

- Key terms: probability space diagram, sample space diagram
- Say to students: If a five-sided spinner that has been labelled fairly from 1 to 5 is spun and a coin is flipped, what are all the possible outcomes? Explain your answer. What probability questions might you be asked?

## Part 1

- Provide each pair of students in the class with two dice. Set a time limit of two minutes.
- Ask each pair to roll the dice, add the scores for each roll and record each total score.
- While they are doing this, prepare a tally chart on the board.
- When all pairs have finished, collate all the results from the class.
- Ask for the relative frequencies, or experimental probabilities, for each score.

# Part 2

- Ask: Which total came up most often? Each group may have a different total, but the answer 7 is likely to occur most often.
- Now ask: Why did these numbers seem to occur more than others? (There are more ways to get some totals.) For example, the totals 12, 11, 3 and 2 are unlikely to have occurred very often, since they can only be achieved by double 6, 5 and 6, 2 and 1, double 1, respectively. The total number 6 may be achieved by 1 and 5, 2 and 4, double 3.
- Ask: How could you find the number of ways of getting each total?
- After a discussion, lead into describing a sample space diagram.
- Draw the sample space diagram for two dice on the board.
- Show students that there are six ways to get a total of 7, but only two ways to get a total of 11, so they should expect to get more 7s than 11s.
- Explain in detail to **less able** students that each entry represents one possible outcome, so the diagram on the board provides information about the total number of possibilities as well as the numbers that satisfy the required outcome.

### Throwing two dice

- Example 1 uses a sample space diagram to calculate combined probabilities.
- Tell students that to find the probability of a 3, we look how many times a three occurs on the sample space diagram and divide this by the number of outcomes there are in total.
- Add that, similarly, when we are asked to find the probability of a double, we look in the sample space diagram for the number of doubles that occur and divide this by the number of outcomes there are in total.

### Throwing two coins

- Example 2 refers to flipping two coins.
- Say that this is quite a straightforward example, so the possibilities are shown on the coins.
- To find the probability of two heads, we find how many times this happens and divide by the number of outcomes there are in total.
- To find a head and a tail, students must realise that this can happen in two ways H, T or T, H.

### Throwing a dice and a coin

- Example 3 shows a sample diagram where event A and event B are different, in this case, flipping a coin and rolling a dice.
- To find the probability of a head and an even number we use the sample space diagram and count how many of this outcome there are and divide by the total number of outcomes.
- To find the probability of a tail and a number that is greater than two, we use the sample space diagram to identify them. However, students should remember that it is asking for greater than two – not 2.
- **Students can now do Exercise 24A from the Student Book.**

| P 1–7, 10 | Calculator n/a | CM n/a | MR 9, 11 | PS 8, 12 | EV n/a |

# Part 3

- Ask students if there is any difference between their theoretical probabilities in question 1d of Exercise 24A and the experimental probabilities they obtained in Part 1.
- Should they expect any differences? Again, this should emphasise that the experimental results should eventually be similar to the theoretical results.
- **More able** students may well note that in practice they will hardly ever be the same.

## Section 24.2 Two-way tables

### Learning objectives
- Read two-way tables and use them to work out probabilities

### Resources and homework
- Student Book 24.2: pages 550–554
- Practice Book 24.2

### Making mathematical connections
- Find probabilities from experiments recorded in two-way tables
- Add and subtract fractions
- Probabilities add up to 1

### Making cross-curricular connections
- **Science** – accuracy of experiments
- **Sport** – recording results
- **Relevance** – logical thinking

## Prior learning
- Students must be able to retrieve information that is presented in tabular form.
- Students should know how to calculate a probability in simple cases, using equally likely outcomes.
- Students must be able to find the expected number of results from the total number of trials and the probability of the event in question.

## Working mathematically
- Students should be able to interpret the results from a table and calculate the total number of outcomes.
- Students should be able to interpret questions carefully.

## Common misconceptions and remediation
- Most mistakes will come from misunderstandings of how to read the data from a two-way table. As many examples as possible, with as much discussion as possible, will assist students' understanding of how to interpret these tables.

## Probing questions
- How do you find a total from a two-way table?

## Literacy focus
- Key term: two-way table
- Explain how to fill in the numbers in a two-way table. Once you have the overall total, how can you find the probability of each event?

## Part 1
- Construct a table with column headings 'Male' and 'Female', and row headings, e.g. of four popular artists or groups, or four football teams.
- Say that this is about students' favourite people. Collect the data from the class, and tally the results into the table.
- Ask the class to provide the probabilities of selecting different classes of people (e.g. a girl who supports Man United or a boy whose favourite sport is golf).
- Choose a relatively straightforward multiple of the number of students in the class and ask how many of this total would be expected to fall into each category in the table.

## Part 2

- Explain that the table used in Part 1 is a two-way table. These tables are often used to display information about groups. They can be used to calculate probabilities, and to estimate numbers in larger groups, based on the information shown for the smaller group.
- Go through Example 4 with the class. A two-way table is given but the 'Total' column has been omitted. First, show students how to find the totals. Say: To find the probability of a left-handed boy you have to read this value from the table and divide this value by the total of all the outcomes. To find the probability of a right-handed girl you will need to add up the number of right-handed girls there are and divide by the number of girls there are altogether.
- The questions in Exercise 24B are varied; this gives **less able** students valuable practice in the earlier questions and allows **more able** students to move swiftly to the more challenging questions.
- **Students can now do Exercise 24B from the Student Book.**

| P 1–6 | Calculator n/a | CM n/a | MR 8 | PS 7 | EV n/a |
|---|---|---|---|---|---|

## Part 3

- Revisit Part 1 but vary the numbers so that the totals are out of a multiple of 10, or some values are easy percentages of the column, row or table totals.
- Ask students to carry out quick surveys within the class using two-way tables to record the results, and to calculate the percentage of, e.g. 'girls that support a named football team' or 'boys that like a current popular band'.

## Learning objectives

- Use Venn diagrams to solve probability questions

## Resources and homework

- Student Book 24.3: pages 554–558
- Practice Book 24.3

## Making mathematical connections

- Finding probabilities of events happening
- Finding probabilities of events not happening
- Adding and subtracting fractions

## Making cross-curricular connections

- **Science** – conducting experiments
- **Relevance** – logical thinking

## Prior learning

- Students should already know how to calculate a probability in simple cases, using equally likely outcomes.
- Students must know how to add fractions with the same or with different denominators.

## Working mathematically

- Students will learn that formal notation for an event that is happening could be P($A$) and it not happening would be P($A'$).
- The outcomes are elements of a set, which is a collection of outcomes represented within {}.
- A Venn diagram shows a visual way to show how two events can occur and what it means when they overlap or intersect.

## Common misconceptions and remediation

- Students often make mistakes when adding probability fractions. Revise the rules for the addition of fractions.
- Students often learn how to add probabilities but do not understand when it is appropriate to do so and when it is not. Explaining their mistakes should help students to avoid the errors.

## Probing questions

- What is meant by an independent event?
- What is meant by mutually exclusive outcomes?

## Literacy focus

- Key terms: complement, element, intersection, set, union, universal set, Venn diagram
- With a blank Venn diagram, describe the set, elements, universal set, union and intersection using any scenario.

## Part 1

- Give students the probability of $A$, e.g. P($A$) = 0.2, P($A$) = $\frac{2}{5}$ and P($A$) = 32%.

- Ask students to find the complement of $A$ using formal notation, e.g. if:
  - P($A$) = 0.2 then P($A'$) = 0.8
  - P($A$) = $\frac{2}{5}$ then P($A'$) = $\frac{3}{5}$
  - P($A$) = 32% then P($A'$) = 68%.

## Part 2

- Remind students how to draw a Venn diagram.
- Discuss the diagrams in the Student Book. Show that a full circle represents the $P(A)$.
- The area of the rectangle surrounding the circle is $P(A')$.
- When there are two circles or two sets, one set could be $P(A)$ and the other $P(B)$.
- If the sets intersect the region is $P(A \cap B)$, or the probability of A and B.
- The whole area of the two circles and intersection is called the union and is represented by $P(A \cup B)$ or the probability of A or B.
- Work through Example 5, which discusses finding the complement of a probability. Remind students that probabilities add up to a whole.
- Work through Example 6, which asks students to work out the total number of students, and shows that by adding all the component parts they can find the total number of people.
- To find the probability of a member having blue eyes, students must find the total of the blue circles. Here, discuss that a blue-eyed student either has blonde hair or does not have blonde hair -- this will not affect the eye colour.
- The complement of A or $P(A') = 1 - P(A)$. To find $P(A \cap B)$ students will need to identify the intersection and divide this by the total number of members; the $P(A \cup B)$ will be the total of both circles added together. Fair hair and not blue eyes is the part of A set that does not intersect the blue-eyed set.
- **Students can now do Exercise 24C from the Student Book.**

| P 1–6 | Calculator n/a | CM 11, 12 | MR 7 | PS 8–10, 13 | EV n/a |
|-------|----------------|-----------|------|-------------|--------|

## Part 3

- Give students the following problem.
- In a class, there are:
  - eight students who play football and hockey
  - seven students who do not play football or hockey
  - 13 students who play hockey
  - 19 students who play football.
- How many students are there in the class?
- Set up a Venn diagram to solve the puzzle. (Students should find that there are 31 students in the class.)

# Section 24.4 Tree diagrams

### Learning objectives

- Understand frequency tree diagrams and probability tree diagrams
- Use probability tree diagrams to work out the probabilities involved in combined events

### Resources and homework

- Student Book 24.4: pages 559–565
- Practice Book 24.4

### Making mathematical connections

- Adding, subtracting and multiplying fraction
- Using complements

### Making cross-curricular connections

- **Science; Economics** – conducting surveys
- **Relevance** – logical thinking

## Prior learning

- Students should know how to find the probability of an event and be familiar with $1 - P$.

## Working mathematically

- Encourage students to be able to visualise the outcomes of an experiment such as rolling a six on a dice or not rolling a six.
- This activity lends itself to ordering the steps; finding the probability of one event and then another event.
- Extend students by asking them what to do if more than two events are being trialled.
- Show students that in this case a sample space diagram would not work, but a tree diagram would.

## Common misconceptions and remediation

- Students are often careless about reading instructions. Make it clear that a sample space diagram can be used either to record two separate results in each cell such as ($H$, 1) or the outcome of both results, e.g. adding them or finding the difference between them, or anything else that is required by the question.

## Probing questions

- If a question asks what the probability of rolling a six on a fair dice is, how would you calculate the probability of not rolling a six?

## Literacy focus

- Key terms: frequency tree diagram, probability tree diagram
- In pairs, give students three dice. Ask them to discuss possible outcomes, how they would record their results and what questions they could be asked.

## Part 1

- Ask students how they would find the probability of rolling two dice and getting a double (for each number from one to six).
- Discuss how they could record their results clearly and simply. (A sample space diagram gives the information.) Students may mention a two-way table.
- Ask students how they would find the probability of rolling two dice and not getting a double.
- At this point, remind students about sample space diagrams from Section 24.1, and demonstrate how they can use them.

## Part 2

- Refer back to Part 1 where students used a sample space diagram to display their results.
- Ask if they can think of other ways to display the results. Introduce the idea of a tree diagram. Show students that each set of branches represent the outcomes of an event and should add up to 1.
- When we move across a tree diagram we multiply. Ask them to find the probability of rolling a six and another six. They should notice that they get 36 as their denominator, the same as in the sample space diagram.
- Ask students how to write the probability that in trial one we get a six and in trial 2 we get a six. We should get $\frac{1}{6}$ and $\frac{1}{6}$.
- Ask students how to write the probability of not a six and not a six. We should get $\frac{5}{6}$ and $\frac{5}{6}$. Demonstrate how we can place this onto a tree diagram.
- Show students how to move across the tree on which we multiply.

### Frequency tree diagrams

- Work through Example 7, which shows that 400 people take a two-part test. In the first part of the test, the probability that someone passes is 0.8. In the second part of the test, the probability that someone passes is 0.6. Show the outcomes on a frequency tree.
- First part: P(pass) = 0.8, so 400 × 0.8 = 320 pass. So 80 people fail. Emphasise that a frequency tree looks for the number of people rather than the probability on the branches.
- In the second part, students must use the frequencies from the first part.
- Second part: P(pass) = 0.6, so if someone passes the first part, then 0.6 × 320 = 192 pass the second part and 128 fail the second part. Second part: P(pass) = 0.6, so if someone fails the first part, then 0.6 × 80 = 48 pass the second part and 32 fail the second part.

### Probability tree diagrams

- Work through Example 8, which looks at a given probability space diagram. Students need to find the total outcomes and then work out the probability of each event by finding it within the sample space diagram.
- Now work through Example 9, which uses the same scenario as Example 8. This time we use a tree diagram.
- Show students how to multiply when moving across the tree diagram and to add when moving down the tree diagram. Each branch must add up to 1.
- Discuss with students when you cannot use a sample space diagram.
- **Students can now do Exercise 24D from the Student Book.**

| P 1–6 | Calculator n/a | CM n/a | MR 9, 10 | PS 7, 8 | EV n/a |
|-------|----------------|--------|----------|---------|--------|

## Part 3

- If you roll an ordinary dice three times, what is the probability of getting one, two or three sixes?
- Using a tree diagram, ask students to work out:

P(three sixes) = $\frac{1}{216}$     P(exactly two sixes) = $\frac{15}{216}$

P(exactly one six) = $\frac{75}{216}$     P(no sixes) = $\frac{125}{216}$

So P(one, two, three sixes) = $\frac{(1+15+75)}{216} = \frac{91}{216}$

# Chapter 25 Number: Powers and standard form

## Overview

| 25.1 Powers (indices) | 25.3 Standard form |
|---|---|
| 25.2 Rules for multiplying and dividing powers | |

| Prior learning |
|---|
| Know how to multiply and divide by 10, 100, 1000, … |

### Learning objectives

**Ensure that students can: calculate with powers (indices); write numbers in standard form; calculate with standard form.**

In the examination, students will be expected to:
*   write a number as a power of another number
*   use powers (also known as indices)
*   multiply and divide by powers of 10
*   use rules for multiplying and dividing powers
*   multiply and divide numbers by powers of 10
*   write a number in standard form
*   calculate with numbers in standard form.

### Extension
Extend the probing question in Section 25.1 for **more able** students to answer this question: $2^{10} = 4^5 = 1024$, $3^6 = 9^3 = 729$. Why? Students should try to explain this using the rules in Section 25.2 that state: $2^{10} = (2^2)^5 = 4^5$.

### Curriculum references

| Section | GCSE specification |
|---|---|
| 25.1 | N6 |
| 25.2 | N6, A4 |
| 25.3 | N9 |

### Route mapping

| Exercise | Accessible | Intermediate | Challenging | AO1 | AO2 MR CM | AO3 PS EV | Key questions |
|---|---|---|---|---|---|---|---|
| 25A | 1–5 | | 6–14 | 1–5, 7, 9–11, 14 | 12, 13 | 6, 8 | 2, 13 |
| 25B | | 1–12 | 13–16 | 1–4, 10, 11, 13–15 | 5–7, 12 | 8, 9, 16 | 10, 11, 14 |
| 25C | | 1–9 | 10–13 | 1, 2, 6–12 | 3, 13 | 4, 5 | 1, 7, 11 |
| 25D | | 1–5 | 6–18 | 1, 2, 4–14, 16–18 | 15 | 3 | 6, 7, 13 |

*Key questions are those that demonstrate mastery of the concept, or which require a step-up in understanding or application. Key questions could be used to identify the questions that students must tackle, to support differentiation, or to identify the questions that should be teacher-marked rather than student-marked.*

## About this chapter

**Making connections**: The chapter brings together the concepts of indices and evaluating numbers with indices, multiplying and dividing indices, and working with powers of 10. When combined, these produce the powerful method of standard form. It is important to work through the exercises in this chapter in a linear progression, as each one builds on the work in the previous section.

**Relevance**: This topic has connection to any subject where either very large or very small numbers are in use, whether recording or calculating, for example, Physics, Chemistry, Biology, Engineering and Astronomy.

**Working mathematically**: How can students quickly and successfully carry out calculations on very large or very small numbers? Students will learn this and how they can compare them easily. They will break these into a number multiplied by a multiple of 10, and then change the multiple of 10 into a power of 10.

**Assessment**: In each section of this chapter, ensure that students have a good grasp of the key questions in each exercise before moving on. (Refer to the 'Route mapping' table.) Encourage students to read and think about the 'Ready to progress?' statements on page 585 of the Student Book. Check students' understanding at the end of the chapter, formatively, using peer assessment. Students could do a mini test in the form of the 'Review questions' on page 585 of the Student Book. Follow up the test with an individual target-getting session, based on any areas for development that a student may have.

### Worked exemplars from the Student Book (page 584) – suggestions for use
*   Present students with the same question but different numbers. They should use the exemplar to mirror the working, in full or just refer to the notes.
*   Copy and cut the exemplars into cards. Students should match the working with the notes.
*   Alternatively, copy and cut the working into cards but split the label/description from the working.

**Answers to the Student Book questions are available on the CD-ROM provided.**

# Section 25.1 Powers (indices)

### Learning objectives

- Write a number as a power of another number
- Use powers (also known as indices)
- Multiply and divide by powers of 10

### Resources and homework

- Student Book 25.1: pages 571–573
- Practice Book 25.1

### Making mathematical connections

- Multiplication of integers

### Making cross-curricular connections

- **Science** – evaluating expressions and solving problems
- **Relevance** – links to geometry (area and volume) and solving algebraic equations

## Prior learning

- Students will need to know the multiplication tables to 10 × 10.
- They will need to know square numbers to 15 × 15, with their corresponding square roots.

## Working mathematically

- Encourage students to write out power terms in full before working out the answer on a calculator, which will serve as a reminder that the calculation is repetitive multiplication.

## Common misconceptions and remediation

- Students often ignore powers of 1, e.g. by giving $2^5 \times 2$ as $2^5$ instead of $2^6$.
  Say that they can avoid this error if they write the power 1 into their copy of the question.
- Students assume that anything to the power of 0 gives an answer of 0. Include questions using this special power in exercises regularly.
- Students write, e.g., $4^5$ as $4 \times 5$. Writing out the terms as repetitive multiplication will help.

## Probing questions

- What powers of 2 and 4 create an answer of 1024 ($2^{10}$, $4^5$)? Do students see a relationship between the two answers? (base number squared, indices halved). This will not work if students think that the base number doubles.
- Is this true for the powers of 3 and 9 creating an answer of 729?

## Literacy focus

- Key terms: index (indices), power
- Ask students to write a set of instructions on how to use the power button on their calculator.

## Part 1

- Revise working with squares and square roots (sections 5.6, 5.7).
- Draw the puzzle on the right.
- Students need to find the number in the middle. To do this, they must:
  - multiply the number in each square by the number in the next square and write the answer in the circle in between
  - add the numbers in the circles and write the total in the diamond in the middle
  - estimate the square root of the number in the middle.

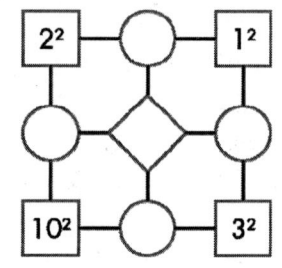

- Answer: $(2 \times 2) \times (1 \times 1) = 4$; $(1 \times 1) \times (3 \times 3) = 9$; $(3 \times 3) \times (10 \times 10) = 900$; $(10 \times 10) \times (2 \times 2) = 400$. Total $= 4 + 9 + 900 + 400 = 1313$, which has a square root of about 36 (36.235...).
- Explain that powers are a shorter way to write repeated multiplications.
- Now introduce cubes of numbers. Ask students the value of $10 \times 10 \times 10$ (1000).
- Ask students how they can write it using powers ($10^3$).
- Ensure that students read this as '10 cubed' or 'the cube of 10' or '10 to the power 3'.
- Repeat for the other cubes that students are expected to know: $1^3$, $2^3$, $3^3$, $4^3$, $5^3$.

# Part 2

- Explain that this section is about working out the values of powers of numbers.
- Go around the class asking students to start from 1 and keep doubling the previous answer. (1, 2, 4, 8, 16, 32, ...) See how far students can get before making an error.
- Ask students to imagine a chess or draughts board with 64 small squares. Ask them to imagine 1p on the first square, 2p on the second square, 4p on the next square and so on. Ask students to write down, without discussing it, how much money they think will be on the board when all 64 squares have been covered (over $£9 \times 10^{16}$). Students will probably underestimate the answer. This is a good example to explain how quickly powers grow.
- Explain that a power defines how many times to multiply a number by itself, but the language needs care. For example, $4^5$ means $4 \times 4 \times 4 \times 4 \times 4$ and is pronounced as *four to the power of five*. However, it is *not* four multiplied by itself five times, which would be $4^6$.
- When working with powers of 10, the power is the same as the number of zeros in the calculated answer, e.g. $10^3 = 1000$.
- Go through Example 1 with students, saying each: *two to the power of five*, and so on.
- Now ask students to input 7 into the calculator, press =, then press ×7 and repeatedly press the = button. This will display powers of 7: 7, 49, 343 and so on.
- For **less able** students, start with the number 2, to give the powers of 2. Link this with the work on doubling and the money on the chessboard.
- Show students how to use the $x^2$ button, the $x^3$ button and the power button on a calculator.

**Working out powers on your calculator**
- Go through Example 1 again, this time using the power button instead of repeated multiplication.

**Two special powers**
- Write the two rules in the Student Book on the board and ask students to write them in their notebooks. These rules need special reference as students tend to forget them.
- **Students can now do Exercise 25A from the Student Book.**

| N 1–5, 7, 9–11, 14 | Calculator 3, 4, 11, 13 | CM n/a | MR 12, 13 | PS 6 | EV 8 |
|---|---|---|---|---|---|

# Part 3

- Draw the puzzle shown on the right. The same rules apply as in Part 1. Ask students to find the middle number by finding the cube root of the total in the diamond. (Total = 35 035)
- Ask **more able** students to **estimate** its cube root.
- **Less able** students can use a calculator (approx. 32.72)
- The number 531 441 is a power of 3. It is also a power of 9 and 27.
- Ask students to write 531 441 as powers of 3, 9 and 27 ($3^{12}$, $9^6$, $27^4$).
- **Less able** students could find the powers of 2 and 4 that create an answer of 1024 ($2^{10}$, $4^5$).

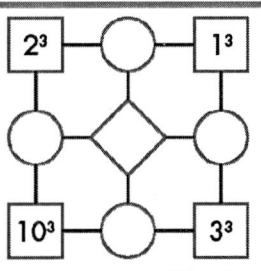

# Section 25.2 Rules for multiplying and dividing powers

### Learning objectives

- Use rules for multiplying and dividing powers
- Multiply and divide numbers by powers of 10

### Resources and homework

- Student Book 25.2: pages 573–579
- Practice Book 25.2

### Making mathematical connections

- Using powers (indices)
- Algebraic fractions
- Adding and subtracting positive and negative integers

### Making cross-curricular connections

- **Science** – evaluating expressions and solving problems
- **Relevance** – links to algebraic fractions

## Prior learning

- Students should know the multiplication tables to 10 × 10, the meaning of a number expressed to a power and be able to add and subtract positive and negative integers.

## Working mathematically

- Encourage students to write out the power terms in the calculation fully before working out the answer. Doing this will remind students of why the resulting power is generated.

## Common misconceptions and remediation

- Students often struggle to remember the term 'reciprocal'. Reciprocal appears in Section 14.3, so use the term regularly to establish familiarity.
- Some students assume that a negative power implies a negative answer, e.g. they think that $3^{-2}$ means $-3^2 = -9$, when in fact, it is $\frac{1}{3^2} = \frac{1}{9}$.

## Probing questions

- Ask students to use the ideas in this section to prove why the value of any number to the power of 0 is 1, and any number to the power of 1 is the same as the original number.

## Literacy focus

- Key terms: None in this section
- Ensure that students are familiar with term terms 'power', 'indices' and 'reciprocal'.

## Part 1

- Write out the powers of 2 as a table (shown on the right).
- Ask students to work out the following and write the full calculations on the board:

| $2^1$ | $2^2$ | $2^3$ | $2^4$ | $2^5$ |
|---|---|---|---|---|
| 2 | 4 | 8 | 16 | 32 |

  $2 \times 4 = 8$      $4 \times 8 = 32$      $2 \times 8 = 16$      $2 \times 16 = 32$.
- Ask students if they can see any connection between the calculations and the powers. If not, write the powers underneath the original calculations.

  $2 \times 4 = 8$      $4 \times 8 = 32$      $2 \times 8 = 16$      $2 \times 16 = 32$
  $2^1 \times 2^2 = 2^3$    $2^2 \times 2^3 = 2^5$    $2 \times 2^3 = 2^4$    $2 \times 2^4 = 2^5$

  Students may spot the connection in this form.
- Now do the same with powers of 2 for division, e.g. $32 \div 8 = 4$, which is $2^5 \div 2^3 = 2^2$
- Again, ask students to spot the rule or connection for this form.

## Part 2

### Positive indices

- Write on the board: $2^2 \times 2^3 = 2^5$  $3^2 \times 3^3 = 3^5$  $4^2 \times 4^3 = 4^5$
- Ask students for the answer to: $x^2 \times x^3$. ($x^5$)
- If necessary, refer to the full multiplication again: $x^2 \times x^3 = (x \times x) \times (x \times x \times x) = x^5$.
- Emphasise that this works only when the powers are of the same variable, so $m^2 \times n^3$ is simply $m^2 n^3$ and not $mn^5$.
- Write on the board: $4^5 \div 4^3 = 4^2$  $3^5 \div 3^3 = 3^2$  $2^5 \div 2^3 = 2^2$
- Ask students for the answer to: $x^5 \div x^3$. ($x^2$)
- Highlight the two rules of indices when multiplying and dividing (in the Student Book):
To multiply, add the indices. When dividing, the rule is to subtract.
- Again, stress that these rules only work when the numbers are expressed as powers of the same algebraic unknown. For **less able** students, give more examples such as:
$8^3 \times 8^4 = (8 \times 8 \times 8) \times (8 \times 8 \times 8 \times 8) = 8^7$  $8^4 \div 8^3 = (8 \times 8 \times 8 \times 8) \times (8 \times 8 \times 8) = 8^1 = 8$
- For **more able** students, include combined multiplication and division, e.g. $2^7 \times 2^3 \div 2^4$, to prepare for Part 3 (expressions are written as a fraction with a numerator and denominator).

### Negative indices

- Work through the Student Book examples with the class. Students should have no problem getting a result of $c^{-2}$, but they may feel uncomfortable with the idea of the reciprocal.
- Work through, e.g. $h^4 \div h^6 = h^{-2}$; show the full division and strike out/cancel four $h$s from the top with four from the bottom to leave two $h$s ($h^2$) on the bottom.

### Powers of powers

- Work through the Student Book text with the class. The only difficulty here is for students to remember that all indices need to be multiplied rather than added.
- The explanation of how $2a^2 \times 3a^4$ is worked out is an excellent format for students to copy.
- **Students can now do Exercise 25B from the Student Book.**

| N 1–4, 10, 11, 13–15 | Calculator n/a | CM 7 | MR 5, 6, 12 | PS 8, 9, 16 | EV n/a |
|---|---|---|---|---|---|

### Multiplying and dividing by powers of 10

- Note that when writing a number as a power of 10, the number of zeros is the number of the power, but when writing a number less than 1 as a power of 10 the number of zeros is 1 less than the negative power.

### Multiplication and division

- Work through Examples 2 and 3, noting the rules in the Student Book about moving the digits to the left and right, depending on whether the question is multiplication or division.

### Working with multiples of powers of 10

- The text under this heading illustrates a 'shortcut' mental method of working with large numbers that are multiples of powers of 10. Work through Examples 4 and 5 to clarify this.
- **Students can now do Exercise 25C from the Student Book.**

| N 1, 2, 6–12 | Calculator n/a | CM n/a | MR 3, 13 | PS 4, 5 | EV n/a |
|---|---|---|---|---|---|

## Part 3

- Talk about division expressed as: $\dfrac{2^3 \times 2^2}{2^4}$. Establish that the rules for multiplication and division can be combined in this problem.
- Talk about division expressed as: $3^2 \div 3^4$. Establish that answers can have negative indices.
- Students could set each other questions with more than two numbers or negative powers.

# Section 25.3 Standard form

## Learning objectives
- Write a number in standard form
- Calculate with numbers in standard form

## Resources and homework
- Student Book 25.3: pages 579–583
- Practice Book 25.3

## Making mathematical connections
- Multiplication of integers
- Powers (indices)
- Multiplying and dividing by powers of 10

## Making cross-curricular connections
- **Science** – evaluating expressions and solving problems
- **Relevance** – expression of very large or very small numbers

## Prior learning
- Students should be able to multiply and divide by 10, 100 and 1000.
- They should know powers of 10 such as: $10^5 = 10 \times 10 \times 10 \times 10 \times 10 = 100\ 000$.
- Students should also be able to convert numbers (e.g. 10 000) to a power of 10 ($10^4$).

## Working mathematically
- Encourage students to record all stages of working. This will help them see the progression of ideas that have been presented and remind them of the processing that is taking place.

## Common misconceptions and remediation
- When inputting numbers on a calculator, students often insert an extra [×][10], e.g. to key in $1.3 \times 10^6$ they key in [1][•][3][×][1][0][×10ʸ][6], giving an answer that is 10 times larger than required.
- Highlighting this error should help students to avoid making it.
- Students may also leave answers that are not in standard form, e.g. $23 \times 10^7$. Remind students to check that the first number is between 1 and 10.

## Probing questions
- How large or how small does a number have to be before it becomes more useful to write it in standard form?
- At what point does your calculator switch from showing numbers as ordinary numbers to showing numbers in standard form?

## Literacy focus
- Key terms: standard form, standard index form
- Ask students to create a small poster that explains how to enter a number in standard form into their calculator.

## Part 1
- Ask some quick-fire questions to familiarise students with multiplications by powers of 10.
  $5 \times 10$ (50), $5 \times 10 \times 10$ (500); $5 \times 10 \times 10 \times 10$ (5000)    $10^1$ (10); $10^2$ (100); $10^3$(1000)
  $5 \div 10$ (0.5); $5 \div 10 \div 10$ (0.05); $5 \div 10 \div 10 \div 10$ (0.005)    $10^{-1}$ (0.1); $10^{-2}$ (0.01); $10^{-3}$ (0.001)
- Now ask some quick-fire questions using decimals, e.g. 3.6 instead of 5.
- Repeat for numbers with two decimal places, e.g. 9.27.

# Part 2

- On the board, write the format of standard form numbers:
  $A \times 10^n$ where $1 \leq A < 10$, and $n$ is an integer.
- Look carefully at the examples in the text in the Student Book to identify these elements.
- Work through Examples 6 and 7 to demonstrate how to convert an ordinary number into standard form – and back.

## Standard form on a calculator

- Write 17 179 869 184 on the board and ask students to key this into their calculator and press ▨. The display should show: $1.717986918 \times 10^{10}$.
- Tell students that this number is displayed in standard form. (You will need to explain that the calculator has rounded the number because it can only display a certain number of digits. This means that the standard form number displayed could originally have been between 17 179 869 180 and 17 179 869 184).
- Ask students to find the ▨ key on their calculator and explain its use.
- Now students know where the ▨ key is, ask them to input ▨ ▨ ▨ ▨ ▨ ▨ giving an answer of 4 500 000.
- Repeat for other numbers.

## Standard form for numbers less than 1

- The only additional point to note is for students to make use of the unitary minus key (−), making the number negative, rather than wanting to *subtract*.

## Calculating with standard form

- Write $2 \times 10^7 \times 6 \times 10^3$ on the board and discuss ways of working it out. Work towards multiplying 2 and 6 and multiplying the powers of 10 leading to $12 \times 10^{10}$.
- Ask students if this is in standard form (no). Ask them to convert it to standard form ($1.2 \times 10^{11}$). Tell students they will need to be careful with this.
- Repeat for division, e.g. $4 \times 10^3 \div 8 \times 10^5 (5 \times 10^{-3})$. Discourage students from writing the numbers as ordinary numbers and then completing the calculation. Although this is a valid method, it can lead to errors with so many digits.
- Work through Examples 8, 9 and 10, highlighting again the need to check whether the final answer needs to be in standard form.

**Students can now do Exercise 25D from the Student Book.**

| N 1, 2, 4–14, 16–18 | Calculator 12–14 | CM 15 | MR n/a | PS 3 | EV n/a |
|---|---|---|---|---|---|

# Part 3

- Allow students to check their answers to non-calculator questions in Exercise 25D by using their calculators.
- Have some facts available, which students should convert to standard form, e.g.:
  - Lake Superior (in Canada and the USA) covers an area of about 82 400 $km^2$
  - The total area of water in the UK is about 3070 $km^2$
  - The moon has a diameter of almost 3500 km
  - The river Nile is about 6700 km long
  - A sheet of aluminium foil is 0.000 2 mm thick
  - A human blood cell has a diameter of about 0.000 007 m
  - The wavelength of green light is 0.000 000 5 m.

# Chapter 26 Algebra: Simultaneous equations and linear inequalities

## Overview

| | |
|---|---|
| **26.1** Elimination method for simultaneous equations | **26.4** Using simultaneous equations to solve problems |
| **26.2** Substitution method for simultaneous equations | **26.5** Linear inequalities |
| **26.3** Balancing coefficients to solve simultaneous equations | |

| Prior learning |
|---|
| Know the basic language of algebra.<br>Know how to collect together like terms.<br>Know how to solve basic linear equations.<br>Know how to substitute into formulae. |

| Learning objectives |
|---|
| **Ensure that students can: solve linear simultaneous equations algebraically; solve a linear inequality and represent the solution on a number line.**<br><br>In the examination, students will be expected to:<br>• solve simultaneous linear equations in two variables using the elimination method<br>• solve simultaneous linear equations in two variables using the substitution method<br>• solve simultaneous linear equations by balancing coefficients<br>• solve problems using simultaneous linear equations<br>• solve a simple linear inequality and represent it on a number line. |

| Extension |
|---|
| Ask students to consider simultaneous equations where it is necessary to balance coefficients in both equations. This is suggested as a probing question in Section 26.3, but encourage **more able** students to explore this type of question. |

## Curriculum references

| Section | GCSE specification |
|---|---|
| 26.1 | A19 |
| 26.2 | A19 |
| 26.3 | A19 |
| 26.4 | A21 |
| 26.5 | A3, A22 |

## Route mapping

| Exercise | Accessible | Intermediate | Challenging | AO1 | AO2 MR CM | AO3 PS EV | Key questions |
|----------|-----------|--------------|-------------|-----|-----------|-----------|---------------|
| 26A | | | 1–3 | 1–3 | | | 1 |
| 26B | | | 1–3 | 1–3 | | | 1 |
| 26C | | | 1–3 | 1–3 | | | 1 |
| 26D | | | 1–12 | 2 | 12 | 1, 3–11 | 2, 8, 12 |
| 26E | | 1–6 | 7–9 | 1, 7, 8 | 2, 3, 5, 6 | 4, 9 | 1, 4, 7 |
| 26F | | 1–5 | 6 | 1–3, 6 | | 4, 5 | 3, 6 |

*Key questions are those that demonstrate mastery of the concept, or which require a step-up in understanding or application. Key questions could be used to identify the questions that students must tackle, to support differentiation, or to identify the questions that should be teacher-marked rather than student-marked.*

## About this chapter

**Making connections**: The chapter expands the complexity of solving algebraic equations by taking skills that students have learnt (solving linear equations, rearranging equations, substitution into equations) and introducing the idea that two equations that share two unknown variables can be solved using a combination of the previously learnt skills. There is a strong link between linear graphs (Chapter 8) and inequalities.

**Relevance**: There is emphasis on the use of logic and thinking in steps; both are skills that are applicable in a whole range of subjects and careers.

**Working mathematically**: Students will think about whether any of the equations and inequalities in this chapter not solvable by graphical methods. They will also think about the advantages of solving equations algebraically rather than graphically, and then of solving graphically rather than algebraically.

**Assessment**: In each section of this chapter, ensure that students have a good grasp of the key questions in each exercise before moving on. (Refer to the 'Route mapping' table.) Encourage students to read and think about the 'Ready to progress?' statements on page 602 of the Student Book. Check students' understanding at the end of the chapter, formatively, using peer assessment. Students could do a mini test in the form of the 'Review questions' on pages 602–603 of the Student Book. Follow up the test with an individual target-getting session, based on any areas for development that a student may have.

## Worked exemplars from the Student Book (page 600) – suggestions for use
- Present students with the same question but different numbers. They should use the exemplar to mirror the working, in full or just refer to the notes.
- Copy and cut the exemplars into cards. Students should match the working with the notes.
- Alternatively, copy and cut the working into cards but split the label/description from the working.

## Answers to the Student Book questions are available on the CD-ROM provided.

## Learning objectives

- Solve simultaneous linear equations in two variables using the elimination method

## Resources and homework

- Student Book 26.1: pages 587–588
- Practice Book 26.1

## Making mathematical connections

- Rearranging simple formulae
- Solving equations

## Making cross-curricular connections

- **Science** – using formulae
- **Business** – optimising resources
- **Relevance** – linear programming, comparing scenarios such as best deals for mobile phone contracts, developing logical thinking

## Prior learning

- Students should be able to solve equations and rearrange simple formulae using the concept of 'balance'.

## Working mathematically

- This problem has a specific and logical order to the steps needed, as follows.
  - Combine equations.
  - Solve for one variable.
  - Substitute that variable.
  - Solve for the second variable.

## Common misconceptions and remediation

- Students may forget to label equations and explain steps, which can lead to confusion and errors. Remind students that they should always label equations and give a full explanation of the steps they take.

## Probing questions

- Get students to think about balancing coefficients in order to solve, for example, $3x + 2y = 16$ and $5x - 4y = 12$ ($x = 4$, $y = 2$). This is coming up in the work in Section 26.3; in the meantime, encourage students to think about how this could be achieved.

## Literacy focus

- Key term: eliminate
- Ask students to work in pairs to create a 'Hints and tips' box that outlines the 'rule' for deciding whether the two equations should be added or subtracted.

## Part 1

- Remind students that 'simultaneous' means at the same time or together and that two equations will be solved so that one solution is true for both equations.
- Read the text in the Student Book until just before steps 1 to 6.
- Write the equations $x - y = 3$ and $2x - y = 7$ on the board.
- Ask students to copy them into their notebooks and then come up with a range of solutions for each equation. Can they find a solution that satisfies both? ($x = 4$, $y = 1$)

## Part 2

- Refer the class to Example 1 and Example 2 in the Student Book. Make sure students can see (clearly) the six steps being applied and that they remember the importance of substituting both values into *both* of the *original* equations to check that they are correct.
- Emphasise the need to label equations and write down the operations performed on each one. Say that this will not only help them to keep track of their work, but it also helps examiners to follow students' work (and for students, sometimes, to gain extra marks).
- **Students can now do Exercise 26A from the Student Book.**

| A 1–3 | Calculator n/a | CM n/a | MR n/a | PS n/a | EV n/a |
|-------|----------------|--------|--------|--------|--------|

## Part 3

- Have ready ten additional questions with a comprehensive mix of each of the two variables with balanced coefficients with varying combinations of negative and positive values.
- Before they solve the questions, ask students to decide quickly whether they should add or subtract the equations. They must also justify their decisions.

## Section 26.2 Substitution method for simultaneous equations

### Learning objectives

- Solve simultaneous linear equations in two variables using the substitution method

### Resources and homework

- Student Book 26.2: pages 589–590
- Practice Book 26.2

### Making mathematical connections

- Rearranging simple formulae
- Solving equations
- Substitution

### Making cross-curricular connections

- **Science** – using formulae
- **Business** – optimising resources
- **Relevance** – linear programming, comparing scenarios such as best deals for mobile phone contracts, developing logical thinking

### Prior learning

- Students should be able to rearrange equations, substitute terms into an equation and solve equations.

### Working mathematically

- The substitution method has a specific and logical order.
  - Rearrange one equation.
  - Substitute that equation into the other.
  - Solve for one variable.
  - Substitute that variable.
  - Solve for the second variable.

### Common misconceptions and remediation

- Students often forget to multiply everything within the bracket when expanding, so refer back to Exercise 15E (Chapter 15, Section 15.2 – Solving equations with brackets) for review.
- Substitution sometimes goes wrong because the first stage of this method is replacing a single term with a new expression, and then there is substitution at the closing stages where a single term is replaced by a value.
- Make a clear distinction between these two parts of the process, highlighting the way in which the rearranged expression is substituted because this may be a new concept (compared with, e.g., Exercise 9B in Chapter 9, Section 9.2 – Substitution).

### Probing questions

- Ask students to look back at questions 3a and b in Exercise 26B, and to solve them by both elimination *and* substitution. Is one method easier than the other?
- Why do you say so?

### Literacy focus

- Key terms: None in this section. Students should know: substitution, rearrange.
- Ask students to consider whether it is possible to decide which method (elimination or substitution) should be used to provide the easiest method for working out the solution.

## Part 1

- Have several substitution questions ready, e.g. If $2x + 6y = 10$ and $x = 2y$ find the value of $x$ and $y$. ($x = 2$, $y = 1$). Distribute these questions to students.
- Students work in pairs. They think about how to solve the pair of equations and discuss how they will reach a solution.

## Part 2

- Example 3 is the only example of this method in the Student Book, so it might be a good idea to have at least two more examples to work through, as provided here:
  - $4x + 3y = 18$                      ($x = 3$, $y = 2$)
    $y = 5 - x$
  - $2x + 3y = 8$                       ($x = -2$, $y = 4$)
    $x = y - 8$
- Remind students that, as with elimination, it is important that they substitute both values into *both* of the *original* equations to check that they are correct.
- Emphasise the need to label equations and write down the operations performed on each. This not only helps students to keep track of their work, but it also helps examiners to follow students' work.
- **Students can now do Exercise 26B from the Student Book.**

| A 1–3 | Calculator n/a | CM n/a | MR n/a | PS n/a | EV n/a |
|-------|----------------|--------|--------|--------|--------|

## Part 3

- Provide students with ten additional questions with a comprehensive mix to work on, e.g. some questions should already have the second equation, in the form $y = \ldots$ or $x = \ldots$, others should not, e.g.as in question 3b of Exercise 26B.
- Ask students to make a quick decision about whether they should use elimination or substitution to solve the questions. They must justify each decision.

## Section 26.3 Balancing coefficients to solve simultaneous equations

### Learning objectives

- Solve simultaneous linear equations by balancing coefficients

### Resources and homework

- Student Book 26.3: pages 590–592
- Practice Book 26.3

### Making mathematical connections

- Rearranging simple formulae
- Solving equations

### Making cross-curricular connections

- **Science** – using formulae
- **Business** – optimising resources
- **Relevance** – linear programming, comparing scenarios such as best deals for mobile phone contracts, developing logical thinking

### Prior learning

- Students should be able to rearrange equations and be confident in using the elimination method as described in Section 26.1.

### Working mathematically

- The method in this section adds an important opening step that students should consider before beginning the elimination method.
- Students should bear in mind that there is no need to consider this method if substitution will be carried out. However, substitution often poses problems by creating fractional terms, and students should have already discovered that elimination is often the easiest method to use to find a solution.

### Common misconceptions and remediation

- Students often fail to multiply through the entire equation by their chosen factor. This leads to the equation failing to be equivalent to the original equation. Encourage students to check, repeatedly, that they have fully transformed the equation.
- Students may forget to label equations and explain steps, which can lead to confusion and errors. Remind students that they should always label equations and give a full explanation of the steps they take.

### Probing questions

- What do you do when it is not possible to multiply one equation by a factor, in order to balance a coefficient with the second equation? (Balancing coefficients in both equations)
- For example: $4x + 3y = 27$ and $5x + 2y = 25$ ($x = 3$, $y = 5$).

### Literacy focus

- Key terms: None in this section
- Ask students to create a flowchart to guide someone through the steps of solving a pair of simultaneous equations. The equation should also bring together the processes of balancing coefficients and elimination.

## Part 1

- Revise the process of elimination by going through a few questions in Exercise 26A.
- Introduce the concept of creating an equivalent equation by asking students to explain the differences or similarities between:

  a $y = 2x + 6$

  b $2y = 4x + 12$

  c $y = 4x + 12$

  d $y = x + 3$

  (Equation b is 2 × equation a.

  Equation c is not 2 × equation a, because the left-hand side has not been multiplied by 2.

  Equation d is not $\frac{1}{2}$ × equation a, because the left-hand side has not been divided by 2.)

## Part 2

- Carefully work through the text, ensuring that students have grasped the concept of creating an equivalent equation and that it does not matter which variable they choose as the one to be balanced.
- The steps from Section 26.1 are still being used but now there is an additional consideration – balancing the coefficients – which takes place before students use the method that they have already learnt.
- Example 4 is the only example of this method in this section, so, if necessary, also use this example:

  $4x + 2y = 24$        $(x = 5, y = 2)$

  $3x + 4y = 23$

- **Students can now do Exercise 26C from the Student Book.**

| A 1–3 | Calculator n/a | CM n/a | MR n/a | PS n/a | EV n/a |
|-------|----------------|--------|--------|--------|--------|

## Part 3

- Provide students with ten additional questions, which have a comprehensive mix of each of the two variables that have unbalanced coefficients with varying combinations of negative and positive values.
- Ask students to make a quick decision about what multiplying factors they will use to balance one of the variables, and then whether the equations should be added or subtracted. Tell students that they must justify each decision.

## Section 26.4 Using simultaneous equations to solve problems

### Learning objectives
- Solve problems using simultaneous equations

### Resources and homework
- Student Book 26.4: pages 592–595
- Practice Book 26.4

### Making mathematical connections
- Sequences
- Creating and solving equations

### Making cross-curricular connections
- **Business** – optimising resources
- **Relevance** – linear programming, developing logical thinking, applications to manufacturing and project management

### Prior learning
- Students should be confident in solving simultaneous equations, either by elimination (balancing coefficients where necessary) or substitution.
- Students should be able to create an equation from information that has been written as narrative.

### Working mathematically
- This section builds on the skills students learnt in the previous three sections and now adds another skill – creating a pair of simultaneous equations from a narrative scenario, and then solving them. This is a vital interpretive skill.

### Common misconceptions and remediation
- Students often create equations that are too simplistic by dropping values from the text into an equation without looking carefully for connections between the variables in the text.
- Encourage students to read the text carefully and write down the letters they want to use as variables – these do not have to be $x$ and $y$; it is more useful to use the initial letters of the nouns or objects being described.
- Students also tend to stop once the equations have been solved and do not refer back to the question to answer what is actually being asked. Emphasise the need to read the question carefully to check that the values are appropriate and that they have provided all the answers.

### Probing questions
- What is the minimum required number of pieces of information that can be placed in two simultaneous equations?

### Literacy focus
- Key terms: None in this section
- Ask students to choose a question from Exercise 26D, questions 5 to 9 and produce a full solution, as has been done in examples 5 and 6 in the Student Book.

## Part 1

- Ask the class to solve the following simultaneous equations:
  
  $5x + 2y = 26$         $3x + y = 15$         $(x = 4, y = 3)$
- If £$x$ is the cost of a cup of coffee, what might £$y$ represent? (Tea?)
- How much would an order of three cups of coffee and four cups of tea cost?
- Write the equation that represents this order.

## Part 2

- Explain that students will now take a practical problem and use it to set up a pair of simultaneous equations.
- Once they have done this step, they will then need to use the skills they have already covered to solve the equations.
- Give students the following problem: four gobstoppers and six chews cost 76p. How much does each cost?
- Clearly this has no unique solution, but students will probably suggest at least one valid answer such as 10p and 6p, or 7p and 8p.
- Add the following information: one gobstopper and eight chews cost 58p. How much does each cost? If students had suggested the previous answers, they will realise that 10p and 6p are the correct answers. (Answer: $10p + (6 \times 8p) = 10p + 48p = 58p$)
- Now set this up as a pair of equations, $4g + 6c = 76$, $g + 8c = 58$ and solve in the usual way. Make sure that students are confident about how the equations are created and what they represent.
- Work through Examples 5 and 6 in the Student Book, which illustrate the steps as learnt in the previous sections very well. However, make sure that students are clear about the setting up of the equations. Also ensure that students read the whole question to determine what the required answer is. Example 6 does not ask that the student simply work out the cost of each type of ticket – students are good at assuming what solution is required.
- **Less able** students may require help to set up the equations from the information provided.
- **Students can now do Exercise 26D from the Student Book.**

| A 2 | Calculator n/a | CM 12 | MR n/a | PS 1, 3–11 | EV n/a |
|-----|---------------|-------|--------|------------|--------|

## Part 3

- Working in pairs, one student should choose a question from Exercise 26C in the previous section and invent a scenario from which the two equations could have been created.
- The partner then solves the equations.

# Section 26.5 Linear inequalities

## Learning objectives

- Solve a simple linear inequality and represent it on a number line

## Resources and homework

- Student Book 26.5: pages 595–599
- Practice Book 26.5

## Making mathematical connections

- Solving linear equations

## Making cross-curricular connections

- **Computing** – efficient coding using 'repeat' or loops
- **Business** – optimising resources
- **Relevance** – applications to manufacturing and project management

## Prior learning

- Students should be able to solve linear equations, including those with the variable occurring on both sides of the equation.
- Students should also be able to place a number on a number line accurately.

## Working mathematically

- Ensure that students are confident with using the symbols: $<$, $\leq$, $>$, $\geq$ and are familiar with the concept of a number line to represent and identify values.

## Common misconceptions and remediation

- Students often solve linear inequalities as equations and do not put the inequality back in for the answer. Encourage students to keep the inequality in the solution at each step, because failure to recover the inequality in the final answer would result in zero marks, as the level of difficulty of the question will have been changed.
- It is important to stress that an inequality can have more than one solution. Encourage students to check that their answer fulfils the question.

## Probing questions

- What is wrong with this solution? $-5x > 12$, $x > -2.4$
- How might your working be adjusted so that it becomes correct? ($x < -2.4$)

## Literacy focus

- Key terms: inclusive inequality, inequality, strict inequality
- Ask students to describe a visual picture of how they remember that an open (empty) circle represents $<$ or $>$ and that a solid circle represents $\leq$ or $\geq$. (Answer: e.g. an empty circle does not hold the value; a solid circle contains the value.)

## Part 1

- Write on the board: $x < 5$. Ask students to say what it means. ($x$ is less than 5)
- Then ask: What is the biggest value of $x$ you can find that obeys the rule?
- Many will say 4, then 4.9. Until it is established that $x$ can be as large as 4.999..., keep on saying, 'No, there is a bigger number.' Students may be familiar with the recurring decimal notation; otherwise they will be content with 4.9 followed by an infinite number of 9s.
- Now ask students for the smallest value that obeys $x > 3$. This is more difficult, and the answer is 3.00000...0000001, where there is an infinite number of zeros.

- Write the following on the board: $x \leq 5$. Ask students to say what it means. ($x$ is less than or equal to 5)
- Ask: 'What is the biggest value of $x$ you can find that obeys the rule?' (The answer is 5.)
- Now ask students: 'What is the smallest value that obeys $x \geq 3$?' (The answer this time is 3.)

## Part 2

- Ask students to give the values of $x$ that are true for $x + 3 > 7$.
- Say: 'Clearly 5 will work, as will 4.5 – but what about 4? 4.1? 4.05, ...?'
  Establish that a value just bigger than 4 will work, so $x > 4$.
- Now show students how to solve this inequality:
$$x + 3 > 7$$
$$x + 3 - 3 > 7 - 3$$
$$x > 4$$
- Students should instantly recognise this as being the same basic method as solving an equation. Say that the methods are the same, but that the equals sign is replaced with an inequality sign.
- Work through the introductory text and Examples 7, 8 and 9 in the Student Book with the class.
- **Less able** students may find this topic difficult, but those who are able to solve equations should be able to access this. Provide students who do find this topic difficult with more practice of simple equations until they are confident they can do them.
- **Students can now do Exercise 26E from the Student Book**

| A 1, 7, 8 | Calculator n/a | CM 5 | MR 2, 3, 6 | PS 4, 9 | EV n/a |
|---|---|---|---|---|---|

**The number line**
- Go through the text in this section and work through Examples 10 and 11 which explain how to represent inequalities on a number line.
- Most students, even those who are **less able**, will find this accessible.
- **Students can now do Exercise 26F from the Student Book.**

| A 1–3, 6 | Calculator n/a | CM n/a | MR n/a | PS 4, 5 | EV n/a |
|---|---|---|---|---|---|

- **Less able** students should be able to do questions 1 and 2. Pre-printed number lines would help for question 2.

## Part 3

- Check students' understanding by drawing some number lines and then writing up some inequalities.
- Ask students to volunteer to draw these inequalities on the number lines.
- Vary the degree of complexity to suit the class.

# Chapter 27 Algebra: Non-linear graphs

## Overview

| | |
|---|---|
| **27.1** Distance–time graphs | **27.4** The significant points of a quadratic curve |
| **27.2** Plotting quadratic graphs | **27.5** Cubic and reciprocal graphs |
| **27.3** Solving quadratic equations by factorisation | |

### Prior learning

Know how to substitute into simple algebraic functions.
Know how to collect together like terms.
Know how to multiply together two algebraic expressions.
Know how to solve simple linear equations.
Know how to draw linear graphs.
Know how to plot a graph from a given table of values using all four quadrants.
Know how to find the equation of a graph.

### Learning objectives

**Ensure that students can: interpret a distance–time graph; draw and interpret graphs of the depths of a liquid as a container is filled; draw quadratic graphs; solve problems involving quadratic equations; solve quadratic equations by factorisation; solve quadratic equations graphically; recognise and find the significant points of a quadratic graph; recognise and draw cubic and reciprocal graphs.**

In the examination, students will be expected to:
* interpret distance–time graphs
* draw a graph of the depth of liquid as a container is filled
* draw and read values from quadratic graphs
* solve a quadratic equation by factorisation
* identify the significant points of a quadratic function graphically
* identify the roots of a quadratic function by solving a quadratic equation
* identify the turning point of a quadratic function
* recognise and plot cubic and reciprocal graphs.

### Extension

The next step would be for students to be able to transform graphs.

### Curriculum references

| Section | GCSE specification |
|---|---|
| 27.1 | A14 |
| 27.2 | A18 |
| 27.3 | A18 |

| Section | GCSE specification |
|---|---|
| 27.4 | A17, 19 |
| 27.5 | A17, 19 |
| | |

## Route mapping

| Exercise | Accessible | Intermediate | Challenging | AO1 | AO2 MR CM | AO3 PS EV | Key questions |
|----------|-----------|--------------|-------------|------|-----------|-----------|---------------|
| 27A | 1 | 2–8 | | 1–4 | 5, 6, 8 | 7 | 1, 2, 4, 6 |
| 27B | | 1, 2 | 3 | | 1–3 | | 1–3 |
| 27C | | 1–10 | | 1–7, 9 | 8, 10 | | 1, 6, 9 |
| 27D | | 1 | 2–8 | 1–4 | 5, 6 | 7, 8 | 1, 2, 4, 8 |
| 27E | | 1–3 | | 1–3 | | | 1–3 |
| 27F | | | 1–8 | 1–4, 6, 8 | 5, 7 | | 1, 5, 7, 8 |
| 27G | | | 1–5 | 1–3 | 4, 5 | | 4, 5 |

*Key questions are those that demonstrate mastery of the concept, or which require a step-up in understanding or application. Key questions could be used to identify the questions that students must tackle, to support differentiation, or to identify the questions that should be teacher-marked rather than student-marked.*

## About this chapter

**Making connections**: Students should be able to collect like terms, multiply expressions together, substitute into formulae, solve simple equations and plot a graph using a table of results.

**Relevance**: Students will learn about finding speed, velocity, distance or time. Students will also work out rates of change on a distance–time graph to find speed. In addition, students will find solutions graphically.

**Working mathematically**: Students will work out speed, distance or time, and plot and interpret distance–time graphs. They will solve quadratic equations, look at the main points of quadratic graphs, and cubic and reciprocal functions

**Assessment**: In each section of this chapter, ensure that students have a good grasp of the key questions in each exercise before moving on. (Refer to the 'Route mapping' table.) Encourage students to read and think about the 'Ready to progress?' statements on page 628 of the Student Book. Check students' understanding at the end of the chapter, formatively, using peer assessment. Students could do a mini test in the form of the 'Review questions' on pages 628–629 of the Student Book. Follow up the test with an individual target-getting session, based on any areas for development that a student may have.

**Worked exemplars from the Student Book (page 625) – suggestions for use**
- Present students with the same question but different numbers. They should use the exemplar to mirror the working, in full or just refer to the notes.
- Copy and cut the exemplars into cards. Students should match the working with the notes.
- Alternatively, copy and cut the working into cards but split the label/description from the working.

**Answers to the Student Book questions are available on the CD_ROM provided.**

# Section 27.1 Distance–time graphs

## Learning objectives

- Interpret distance–time graphs
- Draw a graph of the depth of liquid as a container is filled

## Resources and homework

- Student Book 27.1: pages 605–611
- Practice Book 27.1

## Making mathematical connections

- Substitution
- Interpreting graphs

## Making cross-curricular connections

- **Science** – using, e.g., compound measures, formulae, interpreting graphs
- **Relevance** – developing logical thinking

## Prior learning

- Students need to know that speed, distance and time are related by the formula: speed = distance ÷ time
- Students need to be confident in plotting points on coordinate axes, and they should be able to read scales on axes.

## Working mathematically

- Students will need to use the following information.
  - o Time is always plotted as the horizontal axis.
  - o The gradient of the line is the speed.
  - o Parts of journeys are always shown as straight lines, showing a steady average speed. However, in reality, speed varies due to traffic conditions.

## Common misconceptions and remediation

- Students often interpret minutes as decimals, e.g. entering 2 hours 30 minutes as 2.3 on a calculator instead of 2.5. If this problem persists, provide some common conversions on the board or on an information sheet.
- Students often misread scales and thus make mistakes. If necessary, remind them to pay special attention to this and give them extra practice in reading scales of different types.

## Probing questions

- What is half an hour as a decimal?
- What is one hour and 15 minutes as a decimal?
- How would you work out six minutes as a decimal?
- How would you work out what one-third of an hour is in minutes?

## Literacy focus

- Key terms: average speed, distance–time graph
- Ask students to draw their journey to school this morning, on a set of axes labelled 'distance' and 'time'.
- Ask some students to describe their journey and any key features.

## Part 1

- Ask students to convert the following times. From:
  - o minutes, to hours and minutes – 230 minutes (3 h 50 minutes), 165 minutes (2 h 45 minutes), 84 minutes (1 h 24 minutes)
  - o hours and minutes, to minutes – 1 h 55 minutes (115 minutes), 2 h 15 minutes (135 minutes), 3 h 16 minutes (196 minutes)

- o hours and minutes, to decimals – 1 h 30 minutes (1.5 h), 2 h 45 minutes (2.75 h), 3 h 20 minutes (3.3333… h)
  - o decimals in hours, to hours and minutes – 2.666… h (2 h 40 minutes), 3.25 h (3 h 15 minutes), 1.1 h (1 h 6 minutes)
- Make sure students are familiar with the decimal equivalents of, e.g., 15 or 30 minutes.

## Part 2

- Sketch a distance–time graph as shown on the right.
- Discuss the graph: it returns to 0 so it is an out-and-back graph.
- Discuss the slopes of the lines in this graph. Ask students which part shows the fastest part of the journey. Make sure they understand that the steeper the line, the higher the speed.

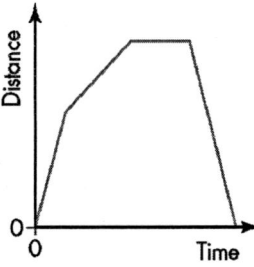

- Then ask which the second-fastest part of the graph is. This may cause confusion, as the return journey is the second fastest. Make it clear that the slope direction is not relevant.
- Ask students if they can recall the connection between speed, distance and time. Then draw the speed–distance–time triangle.
- Using a ratio is often easier to understand than using the formula.
- If you travel 15 km in one-third of an hour, multiply both sides by three to get 45 km in an hour.
- Example 1 displays a distance–time graph where students have to compare various parts. Encourage students to look at the time taken and distance travelled to make their conclusions. Use the DST triangle to help them work out speed.
- **Less able** students may have difficulty in working out average speed. Make sure they understand that it is the total distance travelled divided by the total time taken.
- When drawing a triangle to measure the gradient, use grid lines so that values are integers. Always divide change in the vertical direction (which is distance) by change in the horizontal direction (which is time). Lines that slope from top left to bottom right have a negative gradient, which on a distance–time graph means that the person or vehicle is returning.
- The gradient, whether positive or negative, is the speed. **More able** students may understand the concept of velocity. It is a vector, so has a value and a direction.
- **Students can now do Exercise 27A from the Student Book.**

| A 1–4 | Calculator n/a | CM 6 | MR 5, 8 | PS 7 | EV n/a |
|---|---|---|---|---|---|

### Filling containers

- Example 2 describes how a container depth increases with time. **Less able** students would benefit from seeing this done as a practical experiment. They need to imagine that a straight line shows straight vertical lines, as it is a constant rate. A curved line shows tapered sides.
- **Students can now do Exercise 27B from the Student Book.**

| A n/a | Calculator n/a | CM n/a | MR 1–3 | PS n/a | EV n/a |
|---|---|---|---|---|---|

## Part 3

- Ask quick-fire questions about calculating speed: How fast would you be travelling if you covered 60 miles in two hours? 3 kilometres in 30 minutes? 10 kilometres in 15 minutes? 210 miles in three hours? (Answers: 30 mph, 6 km/h, 40 km/h, 70 mph).

# Section 27.2 Plotting quadratic graphs

## Learning objectives
- Draw and read values from quadratic graphs

## Making mathematical connections
- Straight-line graphs
- Substitution

## Resources and homework
- Student Book 27.2: pages 612–616
- Practice Book 27.2

## Making cross-curricular connections
- **Science; Business Studies** – plotting graphs
- **Computing** – applying logic
- **Relevance** working with graphs

## Prior learning
- Students need to be familiar with drawing line graphs and substituting values into quadratic expressions.

## Working mathematically
- Students will substitute values into a quadratic formula to form a table of values. They will become confident with using positive and negative numbers in a quadratic formula. Students will be able to plot their values to form a smooth curve associated with a quadratic graph.

## Common misconceptions and remediation
- Some students may assume that the square of a negative number is itself negative.
- Students may fail to produce a continuous smooth curve. The most basic mistake here is to fail to use a sharp pencil.
- When a graph has its turning point at a point halfway between two plotted values, students often draw the bottom of the graph so that it is flat.

## Probing questions
- What sign does the answer have when you multiply a negative number by a negative number?

## Literacy focus
- Key terms: parabola, quadratic
- Ask students to explain the difference between a linear equation and a quadratic equation.

## Part 1
- Use quick-fire questions to check that students know the squares of numbers from 0 to 10.
- Repeat for negative numbers from −10 to 0.

## Part 2

- Explain that a quadratic equation is one that includes a term in $x^2$. The most basic quadratic equation is $y = x^2$. The graph of this equation is a smooth curve, called a parabola.
- All quadratic graphs are based on this equation and they all have the same basic shape.
- Make the following basic points about examination questions on quadratic graphs.
    - There will always be a range of values of $x$. The range of values may not be stipulated but students will need to be confident with substituting both positive and negative numbers into the quadratic function.
    - There is usually a table giving the $x$-values, with space for the corresponding $y$-values.
    - Intermediate rows in the table to help calculation of the values are not usually given.
    - Most values will already be filled in and there will only be two or three to calculate.
    - Coordinate axes are always provided.
- On the board, draw up a table of values and complete it for $y = x^2$. Students should copy the table into their notebooks.
- Demonstrate how to plot the points on a coordinate grid.
- **Less able** students may have difficulty with reading the scales. Check that students plot the points correctly.
- Demonstrate how to join the points with a smooth curve. Ask students to read through Example 3 in the Student Book, and the text that follows about drawing accurate graphs. Then let students draw their curves through the points they have plotted.
- Make sure that students know how to use the graph to find corresponding values.
- Starting from an $x$-value, move vertically to the curve, then horizontally to the $y$-value. Practise several times.
- Now start from a $y$-value and move across to the curve, then down to find the $x$-values.
- Stress that there will generally be two $x$-values for every one $y$-value, except at the turning point of the curve.
- Make sure that students label their graphs.
- **Students can now do Exercise 27C from the Student Book.**

| A 1–7, 9 | Calculator all | CM n/a | MR 8, 10 | PS n/a | EV n/a |
|---|---|---|---|---|---|

## Part 3

- Ask students to look at the tables they filled in in Exercise 27C.
- Ask if they can spot anything about the $y$-values. They should see that the $y$-values have symmetry about a point.
- Ask students to look at their graph and see if this can be related to the symmetry in the table of values. They should see that the $x$-value about which the table is symmetrical is also the line about which the graph is symmetrical.

### Learning objectives

- Solve a quadratic equation by factorisation

### Resources and homework

- Student Book 27.3: pages 616–617
- Practice Book 27.3

### Making mathematical connections

- Plotting a quadratic curve
- Factors

### Making cross-curricular connections

- **Science; Architecture** – working out proportional areas
- **Relevance** – experimental and business use

### Prior learning

- Students need to be familiar with substituting into an equation and interpreting from a graph. Students should also know how to plot a quadratic equation.

### Working mathematically

- Students will need to use factors of numbers. Students use their knowledge to factorise quadratics in order to find the solutions.

### Common misconceptions and remediation

- Some students may assume that the square of a negative number is itself negative.
- Students will probably benefit if you remind them about inverse operations.

### Probing questions

- What two numbers have a product of 12 but a sum of 7? (3, 4: $3 \times 4 = 12$; $3 + 4 = 7$)

### Literacy focus

- Key terms: None in this section
- What is the difference between a question that says 'factorise' and a question that says 'solve'?

### Part 1

- Ask students to factorise the following expressions.
  $3x + 15$ $[3(x + 5)]$
  $6x - 2$ $[2(3x - 1)]$
  $y^2 + 7y$ $[y(y + 7)]$
  $2x^2 + 8x$ $[2x(x + 4)]$
  $6a^2 - 9a$ $[3a(2a - 3)]$

## Part 2

- Recap how to factorise a quadratic expression. It may be worth revisiting Chapter 9. Remind students that the numbers in the brackets must make the product and the sum of the numbers in the expression.
- Go through factorising these quadratic equations on the board with students. Ask them to think of two numbers with a product of the number by itself and a sum of the $x$-coefficient. Writing out number pairs may help students.
  - $x^2 + 6x + 8 = 0$
  - $x^2 - 9x + 20 = 0$
  - $x^2 - 2x - 35 = 0$
  - $x^2 + x - 12 = 0$
- Once students have factorised each equation, ask them to solve by making each bracket 0. Remind them they should have two solutions for $x$.
  - $x = -2$ and $-4$
  - $x = 4$ and $5$
  - $x = -5$ and $7$
  - $x = -4$ and $3$
- Example 4 shows students that by making each bracket equal to 0, they can find each solution of $x$.
- **Students can now do Exercise 27D from the Student Book.**

| A 1–4 | Calculator n/a | CM 5, 6 | MR n/a | PS 7 | EV 8 |
|-------|----------------|---------|--------|------|------|

## Part 3

- A rectangle has an area of $x^2 + 3x - 4$
- What are the lengths of each side?
- Remind students that we have to factorise the expression $[(x - 1)(x + 4)]$.

# Section 27.4 The significant points of a quadratic curve

## Learning objectives

- Identify the significant points of a quadratic function graphically
- Identify the roots of a quadratic function by solving a quadratic equation
- Identify the turning point of a quadratic function

## Resources and homework

- Student Book 27.4: pages 618–621
- Practice Book 27.4

## Making mathematical connections

- Equations of straight lines
- Quadratic functions
- Graphs of straight lines and quadratic functions

## Making cross-curricular connections

- **Science** – interpreting graphs
- **Relevance** – logical thinking

## Prior learning

- Students should be familiar with the shape of a quadratic curve.
- Students should also be able to use the power button on their calculators.

## Working mathematically

- Students can use graphing software to explore quadratic functions and graphs.
- Students will describe key features of each type of graph using words such as 'turning point', 'minimum point' and 'maximum point'.

## Common misconceptions and remediation

- Miscalculating the square of a negative number is a common mistake here, but more practice and worked examples may help to reduce the frequency of this happening.
- Problems with arithmetic when substituting values into the function can occur, so practice will help reduce the frequency of this happening.

## Probing questions

- What is a turning point?
- What is a root?
- What is a $y$-intercept?

## Literacy focus

- Key terms: intercept, roots, turning point
- Describe how to solve a quadratic equation graphically.

## Part 1

- Draw a positive quadratic graph which crosses the $x$-axis twice on the board and ask students to put sticky notes on any interesting parts.
- They should label the two points where it crosses the $x$-axis, the single point where it crosses the $y$-axis and the highest or lowest point of the curve.
- Repeat with a negative quadratic graph so that students understand the important positions.

## Part 2

- Using Part 1 to discuss the names of the special features previously discussed, tell students that the highest point or the lowest point is called the turning point of a quadratic function.
- The place where it crosses the $y$-axis is the $y$-intercept.
- The two places where it crosses the $x$-axis are the roots.
- **Students can now do Exercise 27E from the Student Book.**

| A 1–3 | Calculator n/a | CM n/a | MR n/a | PS n/a | EV n/a |
|-------|----------------|--------|--------|--------|--------|

### The roots

- The roots are the same as the solution of a quadratic expression equal to zero.

### The *y*-intercept

- Is where it crosses the $y$-axis, where it has the coordinates $(0, c)$. This is the constant term.

### The turning point

- Quadratic functions have a turning point because they have a line of symmetry, which is in between the two roots. Tell students that they can find the $y$-value by reading from the graph or substituting the value of $x$ at the turning point into the original equation.
- Example 5 in the Student Book uses a quadratic curve. Using this example, show students how to find the $y$-intercept, roots and turning point.
- **Students can now do Exercise 27F from the Student Book.**

| A 1–4, 6, 8 | Calculator n/a | CM 5 | MR 7 | PS n/a | EV n/a |
|-------------|----------------|------|------|--------|--------|

## Part 3

- Use the following information to find the equation.
    - $(0, -6)$ is the $y$-intercept.
    - $(-3, 0)$ and $(2, 0)$ are the roots.
    - $(0.5, -6.25)$ is the turning point.
    - $(x^2 + x - 6 = 0)$

# Section 27.5 Cubic and reciprocal graphs

## Learning objectives
- Recognise and plot cubic and reciprocal graphs

## Resources and homework
- Student Book 27.5: pages 621–624
- Practice Book 27.5

## Making mathematical connections
- Equations of straight lines
- Quadratic functions
- Graphs of straight lines and quadratic functions

## Making cross-curricular connections
- **Science** – interpreting graphs
- **Relevance** – logical thinking

## Prior learning
- Students need good calculator skills to complete the table, especially in some graphs.
- Drawing these graphs requires the same skills as for drawing quadratic graphs – one smooth curve passing through all points plotted.
- Students should also be able to use the power button on their calculators.

## Working mathematically
- Students can use graphing software to explore cubic, reciprocal and exponential graphs.
- Students will describe key features of each type of graph.

## Common misconceptions and remediation
- Miscalculating powers is a common mistake. Provide practice and worked examples to help to reduce the frequency of the error.

## Probing questions
- What is the same and what is different about the graphs of quadratic and cubic functions?
- What would a reciprocal graph look like?

## Literacy focus
- Key term: cubic
- Ask students to write down the meanings of 'intercept' and 'minimum and maximum points'.
- As homework, or if there is spare time in class, encourage students to update their mathematical dictionaries with all the key terms and their meanings.

## Part 1
- Ask students to use their calculators to work out:
  - $2 \times (3^4 - 2^8) - 9$ (= −359)
  - $4^{0.5}$ (= 2)
  - $(3 + 8)^5$ (= 16 1051)
  - $3^{0.6}$ (= 1.933...)
- Provide more examples until you are sure that students can use the power button on their calculators.

## Part 2

### Cubic graphs

- Tell students that cubic graphs are drawn with the same techniques that are used for quadratic graphs and linear graphs.
- Work through Example 6 with the class, which reminds students to draw and complete a table of values and then draw the graph.
- Emphasise that when a negative number is cubed, the answer is still negative.
- Remind students that roots of the graph are found where it crosses the $x$-axis.
- Say that a quadratic can have up to two roots; a cubic up to three roots and so on.

### Reciprocal graphs

- Tell the class that a reciprocal function has the form $y = \dfrac{a}{x}$.
- Say that all reciprocal graphs have a similar shape and some have symmetrical properties.
- Remind students that the graph gets closer and closer to the axes, but never actually touches them.
- Encourage students to draw and complete a table of values before plotting the graph.
- **Students can now do Exercise 27G from the Student Book.**

| A 1–3 | Calculator all | CM 4 | MR 5 | PS n/a | EV n/a |
|-------|----------------|------|------|--------|--------|

## Part 3

- Ask students to link each of these types of equation to the highest power of $x$ that appears in the equation: cubic equation, linear equation, reciprocal equation, quadratic equation.
- Ask students to describe the main features of the graph of each type of equation.
- Match the graph to the equation:

$$y = 3x - 5 \qquad y = \dfrac{5}{x} \qquad y = 2x^3 \qquad y = x^2 - 2 \qquad y = 4 - x$$

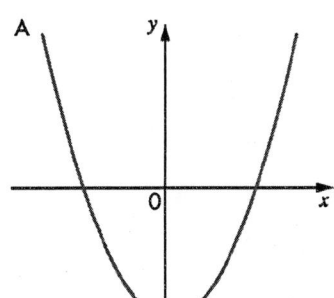

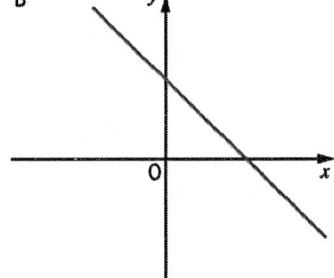

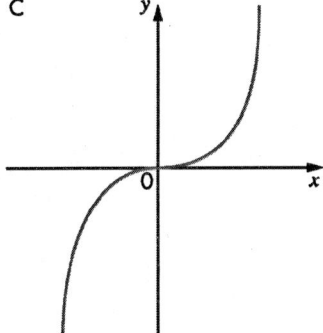

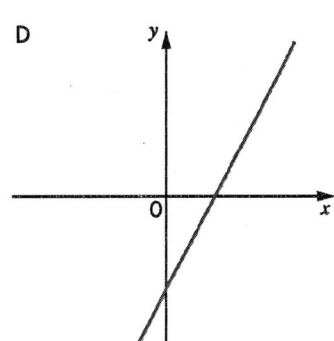

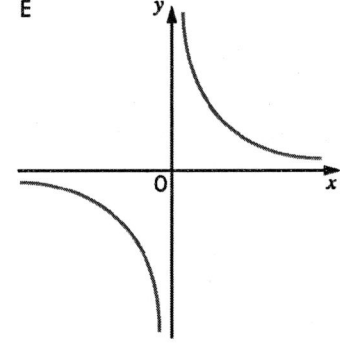